||||||| *The Syntactic Phenomena of English*

||||||

The
Syntactic
Phenomena
of English

Volume 1

James D. McCawley

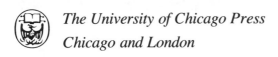

The University of Chicago Press
Chicago and London

JAMES D. MCCAWLEY is the Andrew MacLeish Distinguished
Service Professor in the Departments of Linguistics and East
Asian Languages and Civilizations at the University of
Chicago. He is the author of *Adverbs, Vowels, and Other
Objects of Wonder* (1979), *Everything That Linguists Have
Always Wanted to Know about Logic—But Were Ashamed to
Ask* (1980), and *Thirty Million Theories of Grammar* (1982),
all published by the University of Chicago Press.

The University of Chicago Press, Chicago 60637
The University of Chicago Press, Ltd., London

97 96 95 94 93 92 91 90 89 88   54321

Library of Congress Cataloging-in-Publication Data

McCawley, James D.
   The syntactic phenomena of English / James D. McCawley.
      p.   cm.
   Bibliography: p.
   Includes index.
   ISBN 0-226-55623-9 (v. 1).   ISBN 0-226-55625-5 (v. 2).   ISBN
0-226-55624-7 (pbk. : v. 1).   ISBN 0-226-55626-3 (pbk. : v. 2)
   1. English language—Syntax. 2. English language—Grammar,
Generative.   I. Title.
PE1361.M43   1988
425—dc19   88-14818
                                                    CIP

||||||| *Contents*

ⅠⅠⅠⅠⅠⅠ *Preface*

As with my logic textbook (McCawley 1981a), I have written this book because doing so was easier than not writing it. Until I reached the point of having enough of this book written that I could use the completed portions as the principal textbook in a syntax course, I was literally using a different textbook every year and vowing each year never to put up with the exasperations of that year's textbook a second time.

In most cases the syntax textbooks that I used were simply shoddy pieces of work,[1] in which the authors made no attempt to observe the standards of accuracy, of clarity, of solid argumentation, and of thoroughness that are usually enforced in linguistics journals. As I observed in my review (McCawley 1978) of one of the few syntax texts to rise above the dismal level that has prevailed, generally "the effort of writing a textbook affects transformational grammarians the same way that the full moon affected Lon Chaney." (In that review, I expressed relief that for once in reviewing a textbook of transformational grammar I could "concentrate on matters of substance and not spend most of my time cataloging bungling on the part of the author.") The few textbooks that displayed evidence of their authors' attempt to produce books that could be taken seriously either have shocking gaps in their coverage (as in the largely admirable book by Perlmutter and Soames [1979], whose 600-odd pages contain no discussion of either coordination or auxiliary verbs) or correspond to a very different style of syntax course from what I wanted to offer (as with the fine textbook by Matthews [1981], which is appropriate for a course that surveys ideas of syntactic structure but not for one devoted to surveying syntactic phenomena and applying a specific set of ideas in investigating those phenomena).

What I have written is a book that is useful for the sort of syntax course that I regularly participate in at the University of Chicago: a two-quarter sequence whose prerequisite is a reasonably demanding introductory linguistics sequence and which is devoted to detailed analysis of a large number of syntactic phenomena in English and to exposition of the ideas of syntactic theory that are valuable as aids to exploring and understanding syntactic phenomena. This course is taken by advanced undergraduates and first-year graduate students, most of whom are majoring in linguistics, but many of whom are from such fields as anthropology, psychology, and philosophy. I am fairly confident that the book will be useful to a considerably broader audience than the one I have used it on so far; for example, it should be of value to students in any of the diverse fields in which a detailed knowledge of the syntactic structures of English is an asset (English as a second language and artificial intelligence are two such fields that immediately come to mind), though I must await reports from instructors in those fields before I can declare my confidence to be justified.

The syntactic theory that I develop in this book is a highly revisionist version of transformational grammar that probably no one other than myself accepts in all its details and to which I refuse to give any name.[2] It has been my intention in developing this approach to syntax to exploit those ideas of more orthodox transformational grammar that I find of genuine value and to provide worthy alternatives to those parts of "standard" transformational frameworks that I regard as misguided or perverse. My approach shares with orthodox transformational grammar the gross outlines of its conception of syntactic structure and of the notion of "transformation" (the transformations of a language are a system of rules specifying how underlying and surface syntactic structure are related in that language), as well as the central ideas of many well-known analyses of particular syntactic constructions; however, there are many differences with regard to the goals of syntax and of linguistics, the relationship between syntax and other things both within and outside of linguistics, and in the more specific details of syntactic structure. These differences will be commented on as they become relevant to points taken up below.

Throughout most of the book I give top billing to the phenomena and second billing to the theory,[3] not because of any disdain for theory (much the contrary!) but because I think the greatest value of any theory is in the extent to which it makes phenomena accessible to an investigator: the extent to which it helps him to notice things that he would otherwise have overlooked, raises questions which otherwise would not have occurred to him, and suggests previously unfamiliar places in which to look for answers to those questions. I have accordingly striven after considerable thoroughness in the coverage of the syntactic phenomena of English but have been highly selective in the coverage of theoretical ideas. Well-known alternatives to the theoretical ideas discussed here are taken up principally to clarify issues in which those ideas figure and are discussed only in as much detail as is necessary to make those issues clear. I do, however, make a real attempt to deal in detail with those analyses of specific phenomena (analyses that I regard as mistaken as well as ones that I regard as substantially correct) that have become influential enough to have acquired the status of landmarks: analyses that much of the published literature presupposes familiarity with and which are alluded to in the terminology in which the syntactic constructions are commonly described. Since I regard it as important for students in introductory syntax courses to gain knowledge that will help them to understand the scholarly literature of the field, I have included critical expositions of particularly influential analyses[4] of the phenomena covered below, identifying both their virtues and their shortcomings.

While the course sequence that provided me with the stimulus to write this book lasts two quarters,[5] the book contains far more material than could be covered in a two-quarter sequence, probably even more than could be covered comfortably in a one-year sequence. (Eight chapters per quarter, or eleven or twelve chapters per semester, is an attainable goal if a fairly strenuous pace is maintained and not everything is covered in class.) I regard this surfeit of material as all to the good. First, it provides instructors with a fair amount of choice as to which chapters and sections they will cover. (While most of the chapters presuppose considerable material from the first ten chapters, it should be possible for the instructor to skip some of the subsequent chapters without losing important prerequisites for what he wants to cover.) Second, it will substantially decrease any danger of students mistakenly drawing the conclusion that the material covered in their syntax course constitutes the entire field of syntax, and it may help get across to them the idea that syntax is a vast area that holds enough puzzles and problems to fill many lifetimes of scholarly activity. It is hard to take a field seriously if one is led to believe that it is covered in full in a 200-page paperback. And third, it will provide students with a reason for retaining their copy of the book after the course is finished and using it subsequently as a reference work. As a connoisseur of well-crafted indexes (and a frequent complainer about the nearly useless indexes that reduce the value of many books), I have reasonable confidence that the index of this book will facilitate its use as a reference work on English syntax.

An important part of this book is the exercises that follow every chapter other than the first. In making up these exercises, I have attempted as much as possible to give students practice in doing real linguistics. Many of the exercises ask various parts of a question that a linguist must always ask himself: How general are the phenomena we are discussing? There are accordingly many exercises in which the student is asked to find additional examples of a particular phenomenon or to test whether the behavior that we have observed in one class of sentences is duplicated in some other class of sentences that was not taken up explicitly. This sort of exercise is generally not very difficult, but it has considerable value, since it gives the student experience in an activity that will be a major part of the effort that he will put into any original syntactic research that he may undertake. Another common exercise asks the student to give analyses of particular examples in accordance with the conclusions of the text. This is likewise a part of real linguistics: checking whether one's tentative conclusions about the language under study enable one to give a plausible account of the fine details of a broad selection of examples. Other exercises ask the student to identify whether particular examples are instances of phenomena that are studied in the text. Still others ask him to explore the implications of alternative ways that the phenomena might be described; in this sort of exercise, I have confined my attention to hypotheses that either have been seriously proposed or could very well have been,[6] so that the exercise will provide the student with an appreciation of a real issue rather than mere brownie points for finesse in manipulating symbols. A section at the end of the book entitled "Selected Wrong Answers to Exercises" identifies some errors that can easily be made in doing particular exercises and shows why they are errors; students may find it to their advantage to consult this section before handing in their assignments (and instructors will definitely find it to their advantage to consult it before correcting their students' assignments).

Two policies that some readers may find disconcerting should be mentioned here. First, while the greater part of this book is devoted to the description of specific English syntactic constructions in accurate and precise terms, using a particular version of transformational grammar, I reject the belief common among transformational grammarians that preciseness consists in the systematic use of a fixed "official" notational system. I regard the notational systems that have been popular in transformational grammar as embodying grossly inaccurate presuppositions about what factors play a role in syntactic phenomena and as forcing their users to pay attention to factors irrelevant to the phenomena at hand and to ignore factors that are of prime importance. Accordingly, "standard" transformational notations for syntactic rules will be largely ignored in this book, appearing only in isolated passages devoted to justification of my negative evaluation of them and in critical exposition of influential analyses in which some such notational system played a significant role. In fact I regard as mere wishful thinking the common belief among transformational grammarians that a notational system must exist in which the combinatoric possibilities for the symbols correspond exactly to "possible rules" of syntax.[7] I will thus not adopt any "official" notational system for the rules adopted in the chapters to follow but will generally just state in English what class of "inputs" each rule allows to correspond to what sort of "outputs," aiming at complete coverage of the factors that affect applicability of the rule and of the details of the ways in which the "output" differs from the "input."

Second, I reject as counterproductive, in language teaching and music teaching as well as in the teaching of academic subjects, the remarkably popular instructional practice of purposely avoiding exposure of one's students to any topic before they have had "the lesson on" that topic.[8] The chapters devoted to complements and to coordination will not be the first place in which the reader of this book will encounter examples like *John thinks that Lenin was gay* or *Most linguists either have pet cats or play the piano,* nor will they be the first places in which the reader will see (perhaps simplified) versions of the analyses of those constructions that are argued for in those chapters. Arguments in earlier chapters will in many cases be accompanied by promissory notes that are to be redeemed in later chapters for justifications of premises of those arguments. In the many cases in which important insights into phenomena discussed in earlier chapters can be obtained by examining interactions with phenomena discussed in later chapters, I will conduct the discussion of those interactions in terms of the analyses that are adopted later in the book, instead of wasting the reader's time with spurious "elementary" analyses of the phenomena in question. The common practice of relying on makeshift analyses that no professional linguist would take seriously, so as to attain the dubious goal of presenting material in "logical order,"[9] carries with it a real danger of turning out students who are proficient users of an obscure model of crutches but find when their crutches break that the sole producer of that model has gone out of business and their own legs have atrophied.

For valuable comments on earlier drafts of parts of this book, I wish to thank Duleim Al-Qahtani, Ruth Bar-Ilan, Robert Chametzky, Richard Hudson, Jeff Leer, Li Gucheng, Li Ligang, Salikoko Mufwene, Karen Peterson, Rudolf de Rijk, Jerrold Sadock, Eric Schiller, Rebecca Wheeler, and especially Guy Carden, Dee Ann Holisky, and Johanna Nichols. In addition I owe a great debt to the many students at the University of Chicago, and at summer courses at the University of Maryland, Georgetown University, and the University of Delhi, whose reactions to earlier drafts of many chapters and to classroom presentations of the material covered in them helped me greatly to clarify my ideas in my own mind and to put them into English that (I hope) will be intelligible to those who are not already well-informed about the questions that are taken up.

NOTES

1. I emphasize that this remark refers only to syntax textbooks and not to logic textbooks. My complaint with the logic textbooks that I used before writing my own was not with their accuracy as expositions of logic but with their appropri-

ateness for the sort of logic course that I was teaching, which gave top priority to the analysis of meaning in natural language and was relatively unconcerned with the mathematical metatheory of logic.

2. In McCawley 1981c, I give a number of reasons for adopting the apparently perverse policy of refusing to name my approach to syntax. Probably the most important of these is that any name is bound to give undue prominence to some one of the many issues that distinguish this approach from others (the way that the name "generative semantics" misleadingly suggested that the differences between generative semanticists and Chomskyan transformational grammarians had principally to do with the question of what part of a grammar they considered "generative"). Instructors who feel the need for a name for the kind of syntax done in this book are hereby authorized to make up their own name for it, just as long as the name chosen is not too misleading.

3. The title of this book was chosen to reflect this assignment of star and supporting roles. That policy was also reflected in the title that I originally gave the book: "More about English Syntax Than You Probably Want to Know," a title that hardly anyone but me seemed to like. (One of the few persons who said that he liked it was the representative of a competing publisher.) I encourage users of this book to refer to it informally by its original title and to complain if it does not measure up to that title, and I urge any Taiwanese publisher who rips the book off for a pirate edition to at least restore the original title.

4. The analyses alluded to here are what Kuhn (1970: 187) calls **exemplars:** a scientific community's prestigious problem solutions, typically taught to novices in the field as examples of good science. On the application of the notion "exemplar" to the recent history of linguistics, see McCawley 1985.

5. One quarter is 10 weeks of classes and one week of examinations; classes normally meet three hours a week.

6. Considering how frequently linguists have proposed thoroughly bizarre analyses, this is not a very stringent limitation.

7. See McCawley 1973c for a discussion of the nature of linguistic notation. I argue there that there is no reason to expect a notational system that exactly matches a class of possible phenomena even to be possible and note that assumptions governing the use of the notational system (e.g., assumptions about when expressions count as the same or as different) are equivalent to assumptions about the phenomena that are to be described with the notation and are responsible for any match that does exist between the phenomena and the notational system.

8. See Krashen 1980 for a frontal attack on that practice in language teaching.

9. There is no justification for the widespread belief that logic dictates a preferred order for taking up topics. Perhaps that misconception reflects confusion between the ordinary sense of the word *follow* and its technical sense in logic.

||||||| *Abbreviations and Special Symbols*

Abbreviations

A	Adjective
$\overline{\text{A}}$	Adjective phrase
AD	Anaphoric device
ad-S	Modifier of S
Adv	Adverb
$\overline{\text{Adv}}$	Adverb phrase, i.e., phrasal unit with Adv as head (do not confuse with "adverbial phrase")
ad-V	Modifier of V
ad-$\overline{\text{V}}$	Modifier of $\overline{\text{V}}$
AE	Anaphoric epithet
An	Animator
AN	Adjectival noun
AP	Adjective phrase (replaced by $\overline{\text{A}}$ from chapter 7 on)
AT	Attraction to tense
Au	Author
CNPC	Complex Noun Phrase Constraint
Comp	Complementizer
Comp-del	Complementizer Deletion
Comp-pl	Complementizer Placement
Conj	(Coordinating) Conjunction
CR	Conjunction Reduction
CSC	Coordinate Structure Constraint
CSt	Comparative stripping
Deg	Degree expression
Det	Determiner
Equi-NP-Del	Equi-NP-Deletion
IMP	(marker of imperative sentence type)
ISD	Imperative Subject Deletion
N	Noun
$\overline{\text{N}}$	Phrasal unit with N head (do not confuse with "NP")
NP	Noun Phrase

NPI	Negative polarity item
NR	Negative Raising
P	Preposition
$\bar{P}$	Prepositional phrase
PP	Prepositional phrase (replaced by $\bar{P}$ from chapter 7 on)
PPI	Positive polarity item
Pr	Principal
Ptcl	Particle
Q	(marker of interrogative sentence type)
Q-float	Quantifier-float
RCR	Relative clause reduction
RNR	Right Node Raising
RO	Raising to object
SpSC	Specified Subject Constraint
SSC	Sentential Subject Constraint
V	Verb
$\bar{V}$	Verb Phrase
VP	Verb Phrase (replaced by $\bar{V}$ from chapter 7 on)
X	(i) used as a variable category name, e.g., where X can stand for any part of speech, $\bar{X}$ will stand for the corresponding phrasal category; (ii) used in notation of early transformational grammar to mean "anything," e.g., "V X PP" would mean something that begins with a verb and ends with a prepositional phrase, irrespective of what intervenes between them)
0 (zero)	Lexical unit belonging to no part of speech
Ø	Phrasal unit whose head belongs to no part of speech

Special Symbols

i. SYMBOLS RELATING TO ACCEPTABILITY

**, *, *?, ??, ?	Unacceptability or awkwardness, decreasing in degree from ** to ?
%	Acceptability varies dialectically (also used for phrase boundary; see below)
0Ø	Position that is empty both syntactically and semantically. Used in conjunction with * to indicate that there must be an "understood" element in the given position for the example to be acceptable (see 319, 414 n.17)

ii. ABBREVIATORY SYMBOLS

/	Used in presenting a set of examples in which different things fill a given position (see 10n.3)
( )	Used in presenting a pair of examples that differ with regard to whether a particular position is filled (see 10n.3)
∧	Where alternative positions for an item are contrasted, carets are sometimes used to mark those positions; stigmata written under the caret indicate the acceptability of that item in that position (see 632, 659n.2)
[ ]	Indicates a syntactic constituent made up of the material inside the brackets; the left bracket is often subscripted to indicate the category of that constituent, e.g., $[_S[_{NP}$ many birds$][_{\bar{V}}$ eat insects$]]$
△	Indicates a syntactic constituent made up of the material that appears at the bottom of the triangle (thus, indicates that something is a constituent without specifying what its internal structure is; see 44n.2)

iii. MISCELLANEOUS SYMBOLS THAT APPEAR IN DIAGRAMS OF STRUCTURES AND IN DERIVATIONS

S_0, etc.	Numerical subscripts serve as an informal device for identifying nodes in a structure. The nodes usually are numbered with 0 at the top and numbers increasing as one goes down the tree (see 46n.15).
he_i, etc.	Numerical subscripts are also used to indicate purported reference; thus, items with the same subscript are to be interpreted as coreferential.
∅	Zero. Used (i) for morphemes that have no overt phonological form, such as the plural indefinite article in English, (ii) after an arrow, to indicate that the material before the arrow is deleted, and (iii) to indicate a position in which something has been deleted.
$Passive_1$, etc.	Numerical subscripts on a name of a transformation indicate the application of that transformation to the constituent corresponding to that subscript, here, the application of Passive to S_1 (see 153).
$\xrightarrow{Passive}$	An arrow connecting two structures indicates that in the given derivation the first structure is the input and the second structure the output for an application of the transformation whose name appears above the arrow. When

no transformation is indicated over the arrow, it is assumed that it is clear what the relevant transformation is.

iv. STRESS AND INTONATION

báseball	primary stress on the syllable indicated
whôle	secondary stress on the syllable indicated
thĕ	the indicated syllable is unstressed
/baseball	the indicated word bears a high rising pitch (see 498 n.1)
/baseball	the indicated word bears a low rising pitch
//baseball	the indicated word bears a pitch rising sharply from low to very high
\baseball	the indicated word bears a high falling pitch
ʌbaseball	the indicated word bears a rise-fall contour pitch
%	phrase boundary (see 275, 288 n.12)

v. SYMBOLS FROM FORMAL LOGIC

Ǝ	"Existential quantifier," roughly "there is . . ."
∀	"Universal quantifier," roughly "for every . . ."
λ	"Abstraction operator"; derives a property from a propositional formula, e.g., (λx) (x resembles Stalin) means "the property of resembling Stalin" (see 462 n.16).

||||||| *1. Introduction*

a. General Remarks

This book is primarily about the facts of syntax (mainly, indeed, those of English syntax), and only secondarily about linguistic theory. However, I feel that it demonstrates the value of linguistic theory more effectively than do textbooks in which theory is given top billing. Much of the value of theories, whether of language, of biological inheritance, or of the structure of matter, lies in their ability to tell an investigator what to look for, thereby enabling him to discover facts that would otherwise have escaped his notice or to see connections among facts that would otherwise have remained unrelated for him. Astronomers have been able to identify black holes only as a result of having theories of matter and of light that implied the possibility of such objects (that is, of objects with a density so great that their escape velocity exceeds the speed of light and which thus cannot emit light or radiation) and which indicated what the physical characteristics of such objects would be. A black hole is the sort of thing that an astronomer isn't going to find unless he has a very specific idea of what to look for. Indeed, without the necessary theories, the observations that have supported astronomers' claims to have discovered black holes would not provide any basis for saying that they had discovered **anything.**

In the chapters that follow, we will explore in detail a number of syntactic constructions, aided immeasurably by the theories of linguistic structure and of linguistic knowledge that will be developed in the course of the book. The facts taken up are in many cases things that would have gone unnoticed had there not been theories to direct our attention toward them. In other cases a theory shows well-known facts to have a significance that had previously not been recognized. For example, the fact that passive *be* cannot precede any other auxiliary verbs (you say *John has been arrested,* not **John is had arrested*)[1] will be seen below to be not merely an item of trivia about English but a reflection of general principles about the role of auxiliary verbs in syntactic structure and about how the rules relating underlying and surface syntactic structures may interact. These principles imply that while to learn English one must learn that the passive construction

1

is formed with the auxiliary verb *be,* one doesn't also have to learn where the *be* goes: given the way that language in general works, plus a couple of basic facts about English, there is only one place where it could go.

b. How "Syntax" Is Understood in This Book

The syntax of a language is the system of rules (principles? mechanisms? . . . ?—this early in the game, we don't have much of a basis for choosing among these words) that determine what combinations of words into larger units, especially into sentences, the language allows.[2] This includes rules (I'll arbitrarily adopt that word, warning the reader that nothing special should be read into the choice) determining possibilities of word order, thus accounting for the distinctions between normal and abnormal word orders noted in (1):[3]

(1) a.   I admire her.
     a'. *I her admire.
     b.   I will go to Boston soon/tomorrow.
     b'. I will soon/*tomorrow go to Boston.

determining what form a word may have in the various contexts in which it can be used, thus, accounting for the differences noted in (2):

(2) a.   Tom has/*have/*having a lot of money.
     b.   Tom's parents have/*has/*having a lot of money.
     c.   Anyone having/%has/*have a lot of money needs a tax shelter.
     d.   Tom has always had/*has/*having a lot of money.

determining whether expressions of various types may be present or may be absent in various complex expressions:

(3) a.   I put it there.
          *I put it.
          *I put there.
          What did you put (*it) there?
     b.   I saw (*at) John.
     b'. I looked at/*∅ John.

or determining any other aspect of combinability that we may later identify, for example, possibilities for pronouncing combinations as intonational wholes or with parts kept separate intonationally:

(4) a.   There will be an éarthquake, probably. (ˊ marks location of primary stress.)
     b.   *There will be an earthquake próbably.

In speaking of "combinations of words . . . the language allows," I do not mean to suggest that a simple binary distinction between "possible combination" and "impossible combination" can be drawn. **Stigmata** such as the * that appears at several places in (1)–(4) indicate "abnormality" or "deviance." They do not refer, though, just to a single undifferentiated kind of abnormality, nor to abnormality of a sentence regarded merely as a string of words. The position taken in this book is that a sentence is not simply a string of words but is an object having more structure than just the order in which its words occur. (What sort of structure this is will be clarified in the chapters that follow.) The reason that the *s in (1)–(4) might seem to attribute deviance to a string of words rather than to the more structured object alluded to here is that in these examples there is only one obvious way to impose a structure on the given string of words (e.g., the only obvious way to impose a structure on the string of words in (1a′) is to take *admire* as a verb, and *I* and *her* as its subject and object), and the structure that one thus obtains is deviant because then the direct object of a verb precedes it, which is excluded in English (though it is perfectly normal in such languages as Japanese and Hindi). However, it is not the string of words *I her admire* that violates the constraint in English against verbs following their objects, but rather the structure that we have imposed on that string of words. We could impose other structures on it and find other kinds of deviance; for example, if we were to interpret *her* as the possessive form of *she* and *admire* not as a present tense form of the verb but as a (deviant) agent noun corresponding to that verb (i.e., if we were to treat an occurrence of (1a′) as having a structure parallel to that of the normal sentence *I am her admirer*), we would obtain a structure that would still be deviant but for different reasons than before: absence of an appropriate suffix on the agent noun, and absence of the *be* that English requires when there is a predicate noun.

Actually, we cannot be completely sure that there is no structure we could impose on (1a′) that would render it normal. There are many cases in which the most obvious analysis to impose on a structure of words yields a deviant structure but some nonobvious analysis yields a structure that is not deviant. Consider the much-discussed example (5), taken from Bever (1970):

(5) The horse raced past the barn fell.

The most obvious way of imposing a structure on (5) is to take *raced* to be the past tense of the intransitive verb *race* and *the horse* to be the subject of that verb. That leaves no possibility for fitting *fell* into the structure in a nondeviant way; perhaps the best one could do would be to interpret *fell* as conjoined with *raced past the barn,* but English syntax then demands that *fell* be preceded by a coordinating conjunction (*and,* or perhaps *but*), and the structure would be deviant for the lack of such a conjunction. However, there is a nonobvious way in which a nondeviant structure could be assigned to (5). Suppose that *raced* were taken to be the **past participle** of the **transitive** verb *race* and *raced past the barn* to be a modifier of *horse.* Then (5) could be interpreted as a (nondeviant) reduced form of *The horse that was raced past the barn fell.*

The practice (though not the preaching) of linguists has generally been to employ stigmata to indicate deviance not of a string of words per se but of a structure obtained by imposing on the words either an "obvious" analysis or an analysis that the author indicates is the "relevant" one. In the remainder of this book I will dissociate myself from any preaching to the effect that strings of words are the objects of syntactic analysis (I will in fact not even use either the word "string" or the concept for which it stands in the remainder of the book) and adopt the general policy of applying notions of normalness and deviance to (partly explicitly, partly implicitly indicated) linguistic structures and not to strings of words.

I in addition explicitly recognize that a sentence may be normal or deviant not absolutely but only relative to possible (linguistic and/or extralinguistic) contexts for its use. For example, (6a) is a possible response to a question/offer such as (6b) but is not as far as I know otherwise possible as a sentence of English:

(6) a. Without, if you don't mind.
     b. Would you like that with ice?

That is, (6a) is an elliptical form of *I'd like it without ice if you don't mind* and is possible only in contexts that allow the ellipsis that it manifests, and when combined with a description of the nonelliptical form of (6a), a statement of the conditions under which that ellipsis is possible provides a characterization of the contexts in which (6a) is possible. In this case, a speaker of English can readily identify the example as elliptical and can guess the type of sentence of which it is an elliptical form. There are other cases, however, in which it is not readily apparent that a sentence presented out of context is elliptical or even that it allows a coherent interpretation. Consider, for instance, the sentence (adapted from Morgan 1973) *Bush imagines poached.* This sentence is interpretable only by providing a context relative to which *poached* can be taken as an elliptical form of a subordinate clause (e.g., it could be an answer to the question *Does anyone know how President Reagan likes his eggs?*), and only through an extraordinary feat of imagination could a person who was presented with it out of context guess a context that would allow the sentence to be understood at all. By contrast, recognizing that it is a normal answer to the indicated question and interpreting it when it is used as an answer to that question involve only ordinary knowledge of the language and require no particular exercise of the imagination.

The term **generative grammar** is often used in the technical sense that has been given to it by Chomsky: the construction of grammars that describe a language by specifying what its sentences are, i.e., by defining a set of sentences that is taken as comprising the language. The existence of sentences that are normal not absolutely but only relative to contexts is one of a number of reasons that I have for not doing generative grammar in the technical sense: it makes no sense to speak of such sentences either as unqualifiedly being or as unqualifiedly not being sentences of the language. A second reason that I have for not doing generative grammar in the technical sense is that a language (or even an **idiolect**—the linguistic system of a single person) normally provides not a single way of speaking and writing but a number of styles and registers, each with its own restrictions on the circumstances under which it is normal to use it. One's knowledge of a language involves some rules and vocabulary items that are restricted to particular styles and registers. "The language" can be identified neither with a set of sentences that are normal in one specific register/style (since that set would not reflect knowledge of the language that relates only to other styles and registers) nor with a set that lumps together indiscriminately sentences of all styles and registers. The latter set would be of no relevance to the question of what a speaker of English (or whatever the language is) knows; such a set (in which, for example, all of the sentences in (7) would be simply members, rather than, say, each being specified as appropriate to particular styles or registers) has the same sort of bizarreness as does a set of football scores that are given without any indication of which team each score corresponds to:

(7) a. The reader is invited to consult the works cited above.
   b. Any chance you could help me out?
   c. I need a chain about yay [gesture] long.
   d. Illinois Senator Paul Simon announced today in a Washington news conference that he would vote against military aid to Botswana.
   e. Single with everything hold the onion to go.

While the enterprise to which this book is devoted will thus not be generative grammar in the technical sense, it will be generative grammar in two looser senses: first, it will involve much of the descriptive machinery that is associated with linguists who claim (perhaps erroneously) to be engaged in generative grammar in the technical sense; and second, the grammars developed below can be regarded as specifying the membership of a set, though a set of something other than sentences: the rules to be developed in this book can be regarded as specifying not what sentences but what complexes of sentence, meaning, context, and style/register the given language allows.

To return to the topic of stigmata, I warn the reader in advance that while stigmata will always indicate deviance or abnormality, one will have to take into account the context in which the particular example is discussed in order to determine what is being called anomalous and what kind of anomaly is being ascribed to it. As mentioned above, it is sentences taken as structured objects rather than just as strings of words that will be judged normal or deviant, and the intended structure will occasionally be described in some detail but more often only hinted at, sometimes indicated in incomplete fashion by the use of brackets or other typographical devices that will be employed in an ad hoc way to indicate the structural details on which attention is focused. A number of different kinds of anomaly will be distinguished, and stigmata will generally be employed only to mark the sort of anomaly that is relevant to the point under discussion, other kinds of anomaly being ignored. For example, the sort of awkwardness that is manifested by structures in which (loosely speaking) "heavy" material occurs in the middle, as in (8), will be of central importance to some matters but only tangential to others:

(8) Mary said that she was tired to John.

Often, footnotes or parenthetical remarks will advise the reader of dimensions of deviance that are ignored in the employment of stigmata in various parts of the book.

Sometimes degrees of deviance will be indicated, using such stigmata as **, *, *?, ??, ? in a fairly informal way (** for extreme deviance, ? for mild deviance, the others for intermediate degrees of deviance). Where degrees of deviance are indicated, what will be significant will not be the specific stigma used on a given example but the relative deviance that is indicated by the choice of stigmata for the other examples with which it is compared. There thus need not be any inconsistency if, say, I mark the same example with * in chapter 4, with ? in chapter 8, and with ?? in chapter 12: perhaps in chapter 4 degrees of deviance are not at issue, in chapter 8 it is being compared with examples that are more deviant than it, and in chapter 12 it is being compared with examples that are less deviant. An additional stigma, %, will sometimes be employed to indicate dialect variation with regard to the normalness of the given example. For example, in (2c) above, *Anyone has a lot of money needs a tax shelter* was marked with % to indicate dialect variation in the acceptability of relative clauses in which both a subject relative pronoun and *that* are absent (cf. the standard *Anyone who/that has a lot of money . . .*). The use of % will in fact be very sporadic: while there is dialect variation on many points that will be taken up below, % will be employed only in the relatively few cases in which I have something to say about the variation in question.

c. *Syntax in Relation to Semantics*

The data that can properly play a role in studies of syntax are extremely diverse: they can come from any factual realm in which interactions between syntax and anything else are manifested. No complete catalog of types of data relevant to syntax is possible, since unpredictable future insights and discoveries may reveal the involvement of syntax in phenomena that syntax was not previously realized to be involved in.[4] Perhaps the richest and most accessible realm of facts that reflect interactions between syntactic structure and other things (such as logic, factual knowledge, and social organization) is facts about the meanings of sentences. Accordingly, a very large part of the data to be discussed in this book will be facts about the meanings of the various sentences taken up.

To start with some trivial examples illustrating that the meaning of a sentence depends not only on what words it contains but on how those words are combined, consider (1a–b):

(1) a. A dog bit a postman.
    b. A postman bit a dog.

The interpretations of (1a) and (1b) differ with regard to whose teeth were forcibly impressed on whose body: the dog's teeth on the postman's body or the postman's teeth on the dog's body. Consider now (2a) and (2b):

(2) a. Fido likes to bite.
    b. Fido was bitten.

In deciding on syntactic analyses for them, it is legitimate to consider not only "purely linguistic" data such as facts about what words can be added to them without reducing their acceptability, but also the fact that in (2a) *Fido* has the same semantic relationship to *bite* as *a dog* does in (1a) and that in (2b) it has the same semantic relationship to *bite* as *a dog* does in (1b).

Let us turn to the sentences in (3):

(3) a. Only the judge was annoyed at Sam.
   b. The judge was only annoyed at Sam.

Only bears a **focus;** i.e., it places one element of the sentence (*the judge* in the case of (3a), *annoyed* in the case of (3b)) in contrast with implicit alternatives; (3a) implies that the prosecutor and the defense attorney were not annoyed at Sam but is noncommital about whether the judge felt anything worse than annoyance (say, anger) toward Sam, whereas (3b), if pronounced with primary stress on *annoyed,* implies that the judge was not angry at Sam but is noncommital regarding whether the prosecutor and the defence attorney were annoyed at him.

In the two examples considered so far, *only* immediately precedes its focus. It is also possible for *only* to be separated from its focus. For example, if (3b) is pronounced with main stress on *Sam,* it is *Sam* that is the focus (i.e., the sentence then implies that the judge was not annoyed at the prosecutor, etc.). However, the possibilities for separating *only* from its focus are severely restricted by the syntactic structure of the sentence. For example, while (4a) can be interpreted with *the potatoes* as focus if *the potatoes* is given primary stress, (4b) does not allow *the potatoes* as focus, irrespective of where stress is placed:

(4) a. Sam only put salt on the potatoes.
   b. Sam put only salt on the potatoes.

The reason for this difference is that *put salt on the potatoes* in (4a) is a syntactic unit (a **constituent,** in the terminology to be adopted below), whereas *salt on the potatoes* is not (at least, not in (4); other sentences exist in which that sequence of words makes up a syntactic constituent). Thus *only* in (4a) but not in (4b) immediately precedes a constituent containing *Sam.* I will argue in §3b that *only* is required to immediately precede a constituent containing its focus. This is one of many cases in which the use of a linguistic element is governed by a rule that is sensitive to both syntactic and semantic characteristics of the sentence in which it is used. In such cases it will often be possible to use facts about the semantic interpretations of sentences to settle unclear details of syntactic structure; for example, in §3b facts about what placement of *only* a given focus allows will be used in choosing among alternative possibilities for the syntactic structure of certain examples.

There are also countless instances of different ways a given sequence of words can be interpreted that correspond to different structural relations among the parts of the sentence, e.g.,

(5) a. Visiting relatives can be a nuisance.
  b. The chicken is ready to eat.

There are two interpretations of (5a), with the paraphrases as 'Relatives who are visiting you can be a nuisance' and 'For you to visit relatives can be a nuisance'. In the former interpretation, *visiting* is a modifier of *relatives,* while in the second, *relatives* is the direct object of *visit.* The possible interpretations of (5b) can be paraphrased as 'The chicken is in a state appropriate for it to consume food' and 'The chicken is in a state appropriate for one to consume it as food'. In both these interpretations, *the chicken* is the subject of *ready,* but it is additionally the subject of *eat* in the one case and its direct object in the other. An account of the syntax of these sentences will not be satisfactory unless it provides an account of how their different semantic interpretations correlate with different syntactic relationships that their parts can have to one another.

d. *Syntax, Minds, and Brains*

I regard the phenomena taken up in this book as being primarily mental in nature. The judgments of normalness or deviance or of appropriateness to context, the meanings assigned, etc., that figure as data below reflect the knowledge and abilities of users of the language, and the rules and structures that are proposed below are hypotheses about what users of a language know and what faculties play a role in their use of language. How humans acquire their knowledge of a particular language and how they use that knowledge clearly are heavily influenced by their anatomy and physiology, especially by the anatomy and physiology of their brains and their auditory and visual systems. I find it plausible to suppose that there are neural structures specific to the acquisition, retention, and use of linguistic knowledge, though I find it extremely implausible to suppose (as many linguists appear to) that neural structures specific to language are responsible for the whole of language acquisition or the whole of language processing; rather, there is surely a division of labor between neural structures that are specific to language and structures not dedicated to linguistic knowledge (e.g., your general-purpose learning faculties don't turn themselves off while you are acquiring your native language).

Because of the fragmentary nature of what is known by linguists in general and by me in particular about how linguistic knowledge is acquired, the few remarks that I make in this book regarding language acquisition will be highly speculative. I do, however, occasionally invoke considerations of language acquisition in discussions of the relative plausibility of competing analyses.[5] The main role that considerations of language acquisition will play here will be that of providing estimates of the plausibility of certain possible analyses and certain theoretical points. For example, the popular idea that grammars must be nonredundant is quite implausible when viewed from the perspective of a scenario for language acquisition in which children extend the coverage of their internalized grammars by making minimal alterations in them. Under such a conception of language acquisition, a child might learn several highly specific rules before he hit on an insight that enabled him to learn a general rule that rendered them superfluous, but learning the general rule would not cause him to purge the now-redundant special rules from his mental grammar.

Considerations of language processing are likewise a potentially rich source of evidence bearing on the choice among alternative syntactic analyses, though likewise grossly underexploited. Besides helping us to identify the nature of the deviance of various examples (for example, by identifying the computational "garden path" that makes such sentences as *The horse raced past the barn fell* extremely difficult to understand), considerations of language processing are also sometimes relevant to general theoretical points. For example, in §6f it will be suggested that the existence of a plausible scheme of sentence understanding whose mechanisms crucially depend on **grammatical relations** such as "subject" and "direct object" provides some support for a conception of syntactic structure such as that of **relational grammar** (Perlmutter 1983), in which such relations are integral parts of syntactic structures and not (as they are for most transformational grammarians) merely parts of an informal metalanguage for talking about syntactic structures that those relations are not considered to be parts of.

NOTES

1. The * means "unacceptable" or "deviant" as an expression of the language under description. "Stigmata" such as * will be described further in §1b.

2. While the sentence is the unit on which the greatest amount of attention will be lavished in this book, I (unlike most linguists) take syntax to include principles constraining the combination of sentences and/or other units into larger units of discourse. At several points, phenomena will be taken up that depend on factors outside of the sentence in which the phenomenon occurs, e.g., the possibility of using certain pronouns and elliptical constructions may depend on the existence of an appropriate antecedent in an earlier sentence of the discourse.

3. In these examples, some notation is introduced that will recur frequently in the rest of the book. The "stigmata" * and % are explained later in this section. Similar examples are often grouped together through the use of / and (). The / is used to indicate alternative words filling a given position, e.g., (1b) represents both

of the examples *I will go to Boston soon* and *I will go to Boston tomorrow*. Examples differing with regard to the presence or absence of some item are represented with () around the item in question, e.g., *John thinks (that) Lenin was gay* represents both an example with *that* and an otherwise identical example without *that*. When the examples presented together through the use of / and () differ in acceptability, stigmata are combined with / and () in an obvious way, e.g., in (1b'), *soon/*tomorrow* indicates that the version with *soon* is normal and the version with *tomorrow* deviant, and in (3b) *(*at)* indicates that the version without *at* is normal and the version with it deviant. The symbol Ø indicates absence of an item, e.g., in (3b'), *at/*Ø* indicates that the version of (3b') with *at* is normal and the version without it deviant.

4. There is a common misconception among linguists that the data of syntax (or of linguistics in general, or of botany) constitute its subject matter. It should be obvious, however, that data can be relevant to a subject without being part of the subject, e.g., the subject matter of particle physics is subatomic particles, while the data are about phenomena involving heat, light, etc. in which subatomic particles can be held to play some role, but usually a very indirect role.

5. I am appalled at the lack of contact between the preaching of transformational grammarians about language acquisition and their practice of syntax. Transformational grammarians rarely bring considerations of language acquisition into discussions of particular linguistic phenomena other than as premises of arguments from ignorance, whether simpleminded ("It's unbelievably complicated, so it must be innate") or sophisticated ("The child does not [appear to] have access to data from which this could be learned, so it must be innate"). The positions on language acquisition that have been propounded by transformational grammarians (e.g., Chomsky 1965, 1968, 1974) are compatible with virtually any conception of the form and content of grammars, whether that of tagmemics, of stratificational grammar, of Prague-school structuralism, of Montague grammar, or of any of the many versions, past and present, of transformational grammar. The frequent large-scale changes in Chomsky's conception of the form of a grammar have not been accompanied by any corresponding change in his conception of the "language acquisition device." For a sketch of an approach to language acquisition that is consistent with only a limited range of conceptions of linguistic structure and linguistic knowledge, see McCawley 1983.

2. Overview of the Scheme of Syntactic Analysis Adopted Below

a. The Conception of Syntactic Structure

In the syntactic analyses to whose exposition and justification the bulk of this book is devoted, sentences will be regarded as objects for which diagrams such as (1) are appropriate:

(1)

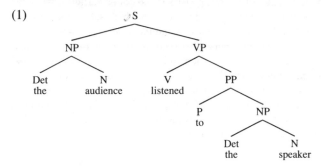

Such a diagram represents directly the following structural characteristics of the sentence:

(2) a. The minimal elements of which the sentence is composed (here, words, though morphemes, e.g., the *listen* and *-ed* of *listened,* could just as well be taken to be the minimal elements and indeed will be below);

   b. **constituent structure,** i.e., the grouping of those units into larger units;

   c. **categories** to which the various units belong, e.g., *to* here belongs to the category P (= preposition), *the speaker* to the category NP (= noun phrase), and *to the speaker* to the category PP (= prepositional phrase);[1] and

   d. the **linear order** relations in which the units stand, e.g., *to* precedes *the speaker,* and *listened* precedes *to the speaker.*

The various details of the structures to be presented will require justification, that is, a case will have to be made for recognizing those struc-

12

tures rather than alternative structures that might be proposed. If we are to assign to the sentence *The audience listened to the speaker* the structure represented in (1), we must be prepared, for example, to show that *listened to the speaker* behaves as a syntactic unit in that sentence and that *the audience listened* (which is represented in (1) as **not** being a unit) does not. Chapter 3 will be devoted largely to the question of how particular constituent structures can be argued for or against. The critical discussion of the notion of syntactic category that comprises chapter 7 will provide a partial answer to the question of how one can provide content to category notions such as are indicated by the labels on the nodes in (1), how one can justify recognizing that system or some other system of categories as having significance in syntax, and how one can justify assignments of particular syntactic units to one rather than another category.

The sort of object that can be represented by a diagram like (1) is known as an **ordered labeled tree.** Readers interested in an explicit characterization of the notion of an ordered labeled tree can consult the set of axioms defining that notion that are given in §2f. For present purposes, though, it will suffice to identify that notion with the information that a diagram like (1) represents: an ordered labeled tree consists of a set of **nodes** (both **terminal** nodes, i.e., nodes that are at the bottoms of "branches" such as the two nodes labeled Det/*the* in (1), and **nonterminal** nodes, i.e., nodes that have other nodes below them, such as the two labeled "NP" in (1)), along with the relation of **constituency** that the lines represent (e.g., the two lines in the lower right corner of (1) indicate that *the* and *speaker* make up the NP *the speaker*),² the relation of "preceding," indicated by the left-to-right alignment of the symbols on the page, and the category assignments, indicated by category symbols at the various nodes.

It should be stressed at the outset that there is no a priori reason why syntactic structure must take the form of ordered labeled trees. There are notions of syntactic structure that have played important roles in past and present syntactic research that are not included in (2), and some of these notions will indeed play a role in analyses to be developed below, notably:

(3) a. **Dependency** relations, i.e., the relation of an item to another item on which it is "dependent," e.g., an item that it "modifies," as in the sort of structure that traditional grammarians would have assigned to the example in (1):³

    the   audience   listened   to   the   speaker

   b. **grammatical relations,** such as "is the subject of" and "is the direct object of"; note that grammatical relations are represented only indirectly in (1): it is only in virtue of our knowledge of a generalization about English (namely, that when a S consists of a NP and a VP, the NP is the subject of the V of the VP) that we can infer from (1) that *the audience* is the subject of *listened;* and

c. **anaphoric relations,** i.e., the relation of a pronoun to its antecedent.

Although I will generally represent sentences by diagrams like that in (1), I will assume that structural information as in (3) can also play a role in syntactic analyses, and where appropriate I will supplement tree diagrams by ad hoc notational devices to represent other kinds of information.

b. Multiple Syntactic Structures; Derivations

Transformational grammar abounds in analyses in which a sentence is claimed to have multiple syntactic structures: a **surface structure,** in which the words and morphemes appear in the order in which they are pronounced, grouped in a way that corresponds to ways in which the sentence can be pronounced, and various **underlying structures** that involve units and ways of combining them that do not appear as such in surface structure. For example, there are a number of considerations that argue for setting up underlying structures in which tense markers are separate from the verbs that bear them in surface structure, as when *The audience listened to the speaker* is assigned an underlying structure such as (1):

(1)

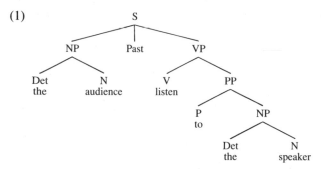

One reason for positing such a structure is the way that the phenomenon of **VP-deletion** affects Ss that have no auxiliary verb. VP-deletion is the optional omission of the sort of constituent that we have been calling a VP here (a verb plus its "objects," if any) when an identical VP occurs elsewhere in the structure:

(2) a. John has given $100 to the March of Dimes, and Mary has (given
          $100 to the March of Dimes) too.
     b. Since Amy is applying to Stanford, I'll bet Bert is (applying to
         Stanford) too.
     c. Roger thinks the Red Sox will win the pennant, and Lucy thinks the
         Tigers will (win the pennant).

However, when a VP that in the full form of the sentence would not have an
auxiliary verb is omitted, a form of *do* appears, bearing the tense that
would have been on the verb of the omitted VP (the ∅ here indicates the
location of the omitted VP):

(3) a.   The audience listened to the speaker, and the ushers listened to him
          too.
     a'. The audience listened to the speaker, and the ushers did ∅ too.
     b.   Although Tom doesn't play bridge, his wife plays bridge.
     b'. Although Tom doesn't play bridge, his wife does ∅.

The fact that the tense marker in (3a', b') is not deleted along with the VP
is a respect in which it behaves as if it is not part of the VP. If VP-deletion
is formulated as simply a deletion of one of two identical VPs, it will delete
the right material in the examples in (3) only if it applies to a structure in
which the tense is not contained in the VP, i.e., a structure such as is given
in (1).[4]

Positing underlying structures that are distinct from the surface structures of the sentences in question forces us to also posit rules expressing the
relationship between the underlying structures and the corresponding surface structures. Such rules are commonly referred to as **transformations,**
in view of the metaphor in which they are spoken of as "operations" that
"convert" the underlying structures into "derived" structures. I will indeed adopt much of the terminology that is based on that metaphor, though
occasionally interpolating warnings about respects in which the metaphor
should not be taken too seriously.

What I have said so far commits me to recognizing three transformations: one that deletes a repeated VP (**VP-deletion**), one that inserts a *do*
where there is a tense marker but no verb to attach it to (***Do*-support**), and
one that attaches the tense marker of any S to the V of that S (**Tense-
hopping**). In (4) I give the **derivation** of (3a'), using the common notation
in which the structures that a given transformation relates are connected by
an arrow over which the name of that transformation is written:[5]

(4)

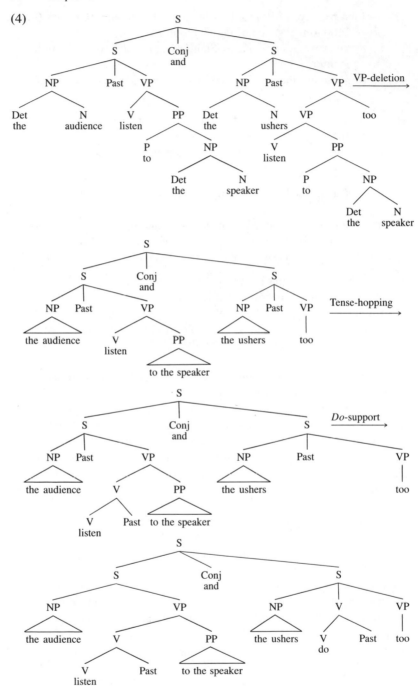

A particularly common situation in which there is reason to posit an underlying structure distinct from the surface structure of a sentence is that in which the sentence contains an **incomplete constituent.** Consider, for example, the following passive sentences:

(5) a. The Yankees were beaten 3–1 by the Red Sox.
   b. The flowers were removed from the vase by the maid.
   c. The Wright brothers were laughed at by everyone.
   d. Haig's resignation was talked about by many people.

Here the verb is followed by a different combination of elements than follows it in an active sentence. There is a (generally optional) prepositional phrase introduced by *by,* which is not permitted in the active (6a–a'), and the NP that is normally permitted or even required to follow the verb in an active sentence (6b–b''') is obligatorily absent in the passive:

(6) a.   The Tigers beat the Yankees 3–1 (*by the Red Sox).
   a'. The butler removed the flowers from the vase (*by the maid)
   b.   *The Red Sox beat 3–1.
   b'. *The maid removed from the vase.
   b''. *Everyone laughed at.
   b'''. *Many people talked about.

However, while what can follow the verb in the passive is different from what can follow it in the active, it is not **completely** different. What follows the passive verb is the same as what follows the active verb, but minus one NP and (optionally) plus one PP introduced by *by.* For example, in the active, *put* must be followed by not only a NP but also a "destination" expression (such as *in the vase* or *there*), and the destination expression is as obligatory in the passive as in the active:

(7) a.   The maid put the flowers in the vase.
   a'. *The maid put the flowers.
   b.   The flowers were put in the vase.
   b'. *The flowers were put.

In (5c–d), a preposition (*at, about*) appears without an object, whereas in an active sentence an object is required (see (6b''–b''')). This can be summed up by saying that the passive sentences have "incomplete" constituents: VPs (and in examples like (5c–d), also PPs) that lack a constituent that they "normally" contain.

A fairly straightforward way of accounting for the relation between the distributions of verbs in active sentences and their distributions in passive sentences is to assign to passive sentences underlying structures identical to those of corresponding active sentences and to posit a transformation that removes a NP from the VP, making it into a subject, combines *by* with the underlying subject and puts the resulting phrase at the end of the VP, and inserts *be* and the past participle marker (here written *-en*):[6]

(8)

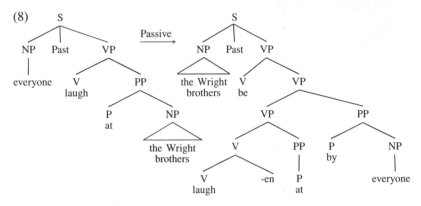

If the restrictions on what NPs, PPs, and other things each verb may combine with are a matter of underlying rather than surface structure, then the possibilities that each verb allows for "incomplete" passive VPs are determined by the possibilities that it allows for a complete active VP plus a rule calling for the removal of one NP from the VP in the derivation of a passive clause. More specifically, let us propose that the restrictions on what items each verb can combine with are formulated not just in terms of **some** underlying structure (recall that there may be several, e.g., the intermediate stages in a derivation like (4) are underlying structures) but in terms of **deep structure,** that is, the level of syntactic derivations that is furthest from surface structure. The kind of restriction that I am alluding to here is what various authors have called either **valence** or **strict subcategorization,** namely, restrictions on how many constituents an item can combine with "directly" and on what syntactic categories those constituents can belong to, for example, the requirement that *put* be combined with a NP and a PP, or more accurately, that *put* be the V of a [$_{VP}$ V NP PP] constituent. The traditional distinction between transitive and intransitive verbs is a rudimentary distinction of valence: the distinction of whether the VP of which the given V is the head may or may not contain a NP as well.[7] Henceforth, I will tacitly assume that each lexical item carries a specification of its valence as in (9), where the bracketed formula indicates the "frame" in which the item can be used:

(9) *put*, V, [＿＿ NP PP]   *kick*, V, [＿＿ NP]   *sleep*, V, [＿＿]

In the approach adopted here, it is only in deep structure that the items are restricted to those frames; there can be other syntactic structures (the surface structure and the intermediate stages of the derivation) in which constituents may be incomplete, that is, in which valence requirements need not be met.

Valence must be contrasted with a second type of restriction on what a lexical item can combine with, namely, that of **selection,** that is, a restriction on what can serve as each of the things that the given item is combined with, such as the requirement that the PP with which *put* is combined denote a "destination." Selectional restrictions are in fact generally restrictions not on the syntactic form of the expressions that a given item combines with but on their denotations. For example, the NP which serves as direct object of *subtract* must denote a number, but need not be a number in form; NPs of exactly the same form can differ with regard to whether they denote a number and accordingly differ in acceptability as object of *subtract:*

(10) a.   I subtracted 13.5 from 91.2.
      b.   I subtracted what I had just computed from 91.2.
      b'.   *I subtracted what I had just baked from 91.2.
      c.   Nothing greater than 30 should be subtracted from this number.
      c'.   *Nothing bigger than a breadbox should be subtracted from this
            number.

While meaning and denotation thus play a role in determining whether a selectional restriction is satisfied or violated, syntax also plays a role, namely, that of determining **which** constituent a given item imposes a selectional restriction on. Note that it is again deep syntactic structure that is relevant: in passive sentences like (10c–c'), the selectional restriction imposed by *subtract* is still on its deep structure direct object even though that NP appears in surface structure as the subject.

Note that both trees in (8) are given with the tense marker outside the VP, just as in the case of (1), which means that in passive as well as in active sentences there will be a separate step that combines the tense with the first verb. In adopting such an analysis, I am following a policy of identifying phenomena that recur in many types of sentence and describing each in terms of a rule that is general enough to cover the full range of sentences in which the phenomenon occurs and which interacts with rules for each of the specific sentence types. This policy is standard among generative grammarians and will be followed throughout this book; its effect is to require that the relation between deep and surface structure be stated in terms of what may be a large number of steps, with the steps being the same whether they appear in pristine isolation or in combination with other steps, for example, passive constructions will all have derivations involving a step like (8) regardless of what else the passive construction is combined with, which may be quite a bit, as in examples like (11):

(11) Extravagant claims are thought to be hard for people to be fooled by.

This sentence is in fact a straightforward combination of three syntactic constructions, and the rules for these constructions that will be given (in chaps. 4–5) will not need to be supplemented or altered in order to account for sentences like (11).

Another class of sentences that can be argued on the basis of facts about "incomplete constituents" to have underlying structures distinct from their surface structures is **WH-questions** such as *What did you buy?* In such questions an interrogative expression is followed by material that can be characterized most clearly in terms of a corresponding declarative sentence: what follows the interrogative expression is what would make up a corresponding declarative sentence except that (i) it lacks one item (namely, an item corresponding to the interrogative expression), and (ii) if the interrogative expression corresponds to something other than the subject, the word order after the interrogative expression is **inverted,** i.e., an auxiliary verb precedes the subject:

(12) a.   Who put the flowers in the vase?
      a'.   What did John put in the vase?
      a''.   Where did John put the flowers?
      b.   What was Jerry looking at?
      c.   What should we talk about?
      d.   Which diseases is this drug used in the treatment of?

The three questions (12a–a'') can all be answered with versions of *John put the flowers in the vase,* namely, versions in which the "new information" (*John* in the case of (12a), *the flowers* in the case of (12a'), *in the vase* in the case of (12a'')) is stressed and the items repeated from the question are either destressed or omitted entirely. In (12a), the interrogative expression *who* is the subject, and what follows it is a VP with normal (i.e., not inverted) word order. In the other examples in (12), the interrogative expression is something other than the subject, and in each case the subject (*John, Jerry, we, this drug*) is preceded by an auxiliary verb. Note that (12a', a'', b–d), in which the interrogative expression corresponds to an element of the VP, have correspondingly incomplete VPs, i.e., the VPs are not allowed to lack that element in "simple" sentences:

(13) a'.   *John put in the vase.
      a''.   *John put the flowers.

b.   *I wish Jerry would stop looking at.
c.   *They spent the whole evening talking about.
d.   *This drug has only been used in the treatment of.

In the accounts of these sentences that have been proposed in transformational grammar, deep structures are set up in which the various constituents are "complete," namely, structures in which the interrogative expression[8] is the direct object (in the case of (12a′)), the object of a preposition (as in (12b–d)), or the like. These deep structures do not have inverted word order. The relation between deep structure and surface structure is described in terms of a transformation that moves an interrogative expression to the beginning of the sentence and one which puts an auxiliary verb before the subject when an interrogative expression precedes the subject, in addition to the other transformations we have anyway, such as Tense-hopping and Do-support. Thus, for example, (12b) is described in terms of the following derivation, in which the first tree is the **deep structure** of the sentence, the last tree is its **surface structure,** and the other trees are **intermediate structures:**[9]

(14)

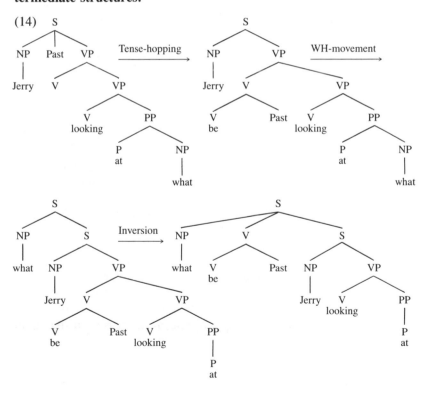

The transformations of a language specify how the various structures in a derivation may or must differ from one another; for example, the transformation of **WH-movement** specifies that if a derivation contains a structure with an interrogative expression in it, a subsequent structure in the derivation must have that interrogative expression outside and to the left of the S in which it occurs in the former structure;[10] this is precisely the way in which the second and third trees in (14) differ. The transformation of **Inversion** specifies that if a derivation contains a structure of the form "interrogative expression plus S," a subsequent structure must have the first auxiliary verb between the interrogative expression and the rest of the S; this is precisely the way in which the third and fourth trees in (14) differ.[11]

Note that these analyses describe only indirectly the constraints on what the various words of English can be combined with in surface structure. Restrictions on the ways in which verbs, prepositions, interrogative expressions, and so forth can combine in surface structure are not stated directly but are consequences of rules that really specify what are **possible derivations.** A VP in surface structure whose verb is *put* sometimes must also contain an object NP and a "destination" expression and sometimes must lack one or other of those expressions. Which situation obtains in a given surface VP is specified indirectly: *put* is required to be accompanied in deep structure by both constituents, and whether the corresponding surface VP contains both or only one of them depends on rules that call for various deep structure constituents to be manifested in surface structure elsewhere than in their deep structure position or (in cases that will be taken up later) to be given no surface manifestation at all.

I will conclude this section with remarks about some metaphors that figure prominently in the terminology and notation that is developed here. The arrow that is commonly used to link the successive stages of a derivation conforms to a popular metaphor according to which transformations are "operations" that "convert" an "input" into an "output." In the chapters that follow, I will in fact frequently use terms like "input" and "output" (e.g., I will speak of the second tree in (14) as the input to WH-movement and the third tree as the output of WH-movement) but will attempt to dissuade the reader from taking the "operation" metaphor too seriously, or from accepting an additional metaphor that carries with it what I regard as false and misleading suggestions, namely, the metaphor that takes the input to a transformation to be "prior to" or "more basic" than "its output and which accordingly takes the deep structure to be "basic" to the entire derivation.

What I regard as particularly objectionable in that metaphor is the idea that the surface structure and the intermediate stages in the derivation owe their existence to the deep structure that "underlies" them. That suggestion is particularly strong in much of the terminology that has been derived from the "operation" metaphor, as in the term "base rules" for rules that specify what deep structures are possible in the given language. "Base" in such terms as "base rules," "base structures," and "base generated" (none of which is used in this book) suggests the notions of "basic," "fundamental," "foundation," or "that on which everything else rests," and that structures other than deep structures are "derivative," "secondary," etc.

I will maintain below that acceptance of this last metaphor has been responsible for the readiness of many transformational grammarians to accept uncritically a number of ideas that ought to be subjected to critical scrutiny and indeed, as I will argue later, ought to be rejected. Among these are the idea that **combinatoric rules,** that is, rules specifying how units may combine with each other, should relate only (or at least primarily) to the level of deep structure, and the idea that the combinatoric rules for deep structure (the "base rules") should be "complete," that is, that they should enable one to construct the full range of possible deep structures for the given language without reference to other levels of syntactic structure. These ideas are particularly hard to avoid when one accepts a common vulgarization of the "operation" and "base" metaphors, namely, the metaphor in which the grammar is viewed as a sentence factory: a device that constructs sentences by assembling deep structures, putting them on an assembly line in which various alterations are performed on them, and having well-formed surface structures come off the other end of the assembly line.[12] In terms of that metaphor, the idea that the base rules are complete corresponds to the idea that you have to have something to put on the assembly line at the start, and the idea that combinatorics should be a matter primarily or entirely of deep structure corresponds to the proposition that you should avoid having items come off the assembly line that fail a quality control test and have to be junked. I will argue in chapter 10 that languages in fact abound in combinatoric rules that relate directly to surface structure and have nothing to do with deep structure, a state of affairs that conflicts sharply with what the assembly line metaphor leads one to expect. The claim made a few pages back that valence relates to deep structure thus does not entitle one to claim that other kinds of combinatoric restrictions also relate to deep structure or that there are no combinatoric restrictions relating to other structural levels, such as surface structure.

c. Rule Interaction; the Cycle

A transformation specifies how two stages in a derivation may or must differ. Derivations typically consist of more than two stages, and something must be said about how the full set of transformations that a grammar contains may interact so as to specify in general what derivations that language allows.

The first question that arises is whether it really **is** necessary for derivations to have more than two stages, that is, for them to have intermediate stages in addition to the deep structure and the surface structure. Couldn't we get along with a system of transformations that "apply simultaneously," in the sense that they simply specify details of the correspondence between deep and surface structure, without reference to intermediate stages? There is in fact a class of situations that force recognition of intermediate stages in derivations, namely, situations in which one transformation **feeds** another: those in which the combination of elements that meet the conditions for being the input to the transformation is not present in deep structure but only in some derived structure. One transformation feeds another in a given derivation if an application of the first transformation "sets up the conditions for" the application of the second.

As an illustration of feeding, consider the derivation of (1b), as contrasted with (1a):

(1) a. Who signed the petition?
    b. By whom was the petition signed?

According to what was said in §2b about questions and passives, (1a) and (1b) have the same deep structure. There is an application of Inversion [13] in (1b) but not in (1a), as a consequence of the application of Passive in (1b) but not (1a): the passive transformation has the effect of converting *who,* the underlying subject, into the object of the preposition *by,* and it is because *by whom* is not the subject of the passive clause that Inversion is applicable to the passive clause (recall that Inversion applies when a nonsubject interrogative expression precedes the subject). That is, in this derivation, Passive feeds Inversion. Moreover, the auxiliary verb that takes part in the inversion, namely, *was,* is not present in the deep structure but only in the stages of the derivation that are "after" (i.e., on the surface side of) the application of the passive transformation. Thus, the fact that Inversion applies in (1b) but not in (1a) is a consequence not of any difference in deep structure (since there is no difference) but rather of the difference between the structure to which Passive has not applied and that to which it has applied.

It is widely held by transformational grammarians (though no such assumption will be made here) that the transformations in any grammar have a fixed order of application. According to that conception of rule interaction (which is a natural concomitant of the "grammar as sentence factory" metaphor), each transformation gets its chance to apply in a derivation only after all preceding transformations have had their chance to apply. Passive might be rule number 7 in this list of transformations, WH-movement rule number 13, and Inversion rule number 18, and the sequence of steps in the derivation of (1b) sketched in the last paragraph would simply reflect this fixed order of application of the transformations that happen to play a role in it.

Note, however, that the necessity of allowing derivations such as the one just sketched provides no argument for the hypothesis that transformations have a fixed order of application, since any such derivation will be available as long as transformations can apply to the outputs of transformations, even if they apply irrespective of what other transformations have already applied. To argue for a fixed order of application of transformations (or for any other restriction on how transformations can interact), one needs to show that it **excludes** derivations that must be excluded. I will accordingly turn now to a well-known case in which transformations must be allowed to interact in one way rather than another and which has been widely used (incorrectly, I will maintain) as an argument for a fixed order of application of transformations. It is generally agreed that imperative sentences, as in (2), have deep structures with *you* as subject and that there is a transformation (let us call it **Imperative subject deletion,** or **ISD** for short) that deletes *you* when it is the subject of an imperative sentence:

(2) a. Open the door!
    b. Defend yourself!
    c. Tell me why you did that!

(See §21a for arguments in favor of such an analysis.) It is also generally agreed that there must be some difference in deep structure between imperative sentences and corresponding declarative (or interrogative, exclamative, etc.) sentences, and this distinction has generally been drawn simply by the ad hoc device of including in the deep structures of imperative sentences a symbol such as "IMP" that really amounts to a sign saying "I'm an imperative sentence." There are in fact a number of ways in which such a symbol could be incorporated into deep structures (a point that will assume some significance below), but for the moment let us just give the most popular way of fitting it into a deep structure, as in (3), intended as the deep structure of (2a):

(3)

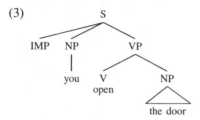

Let us see what the derivation of (2b) would be if this account of imperative sentences is combined with the popular analysis of reflexive pronouns (*myself, yourself,* etc.) in which they are taken to correspond to nonreflexive elements in deep structure and a transformation (call it **Reflexivization**) is posited that requires an underlying NP to be expressed as a reflexive pronoun if (roughly speaking) a preceding NP of the same clause has the same reference. Under the latter proposal, (4a) would have a deep structure looking like the surface structure of the ungrammatical (4b), and the reason that one would say (4a) rather than (4b) would be that the two occurrences of *you* in the same clause would have the same reference [14] and the second occurrence would accordingly have to be replaced by a reflexive pronoun:

(4) a.   You defended yourself.
    b. *You defended you.

The deep structure of (2b) would then be (5):

(5)

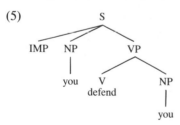

The conditions for Reflexivization and for ISD are both met in (5). However, if the first step of the derivation were an application of ISD, the structure derived would no longer meet the conditions for Reflexivization (we would have deleted one of the two coreferential NPs and there would thus no longer be the two coreferential NPs that provide the conditions for

Reflexivization), and the surface structure that we derived would then correspond to the ungrammatical (4b). We thus need to exclude somehow a derivation in which ISD applies to a structure like (5) without Reflexivization also applying.

There are in fact a large number of ways in which such a derivation could be excluded (see Pullum 1976:44–46 for details). The most popular way has been to invoke a fixed order of application for transformations: if Reflexivization is ordered before ISD, then ISD won't get a chance to delete the subject of the imperative sentence until Reflexivization has had its chance to turn into reflexive pronouns any other NPs that are coreferential with the subject. An alternative way of excluding the bad derivation emerges, though, if we consider one of the other ways in which the imperative marker might be fitted into deep structures. Specifically, suppose that it appears not inside the S in question (on a level with the NP and VP of that S) but outside that S, as in (6):

(6)

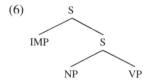

The difference between (6) and (3) appears at first to be completely trivial. It turns out, however, that (6) but not (3) allows the interaction between ISD and Reflexivization to be subsumed under a general principle about how rules interact. Consider the deep structure of (2b) under the hypothesis that structures like (6) and not (3) underlie imperatives:

(7)

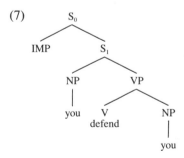

Note that S_1 meets the conditions for Reflexivization, but it does not meet the conditions for ISD, at least if we take the statement that ISD applies only to imperative Ss as meaning that it applies only to a structure containing IMP. Only S_0 contains IMP and thus meets the conditions for ISD.

To see the significance of these last observations, we must digress into the important notion of the **domain** of any particular application of a transformation. Consider (8a) and its presumable deep structure (8b): [15]

(8) a. John said that the petition was signed by 700 members of the faculty.

b.

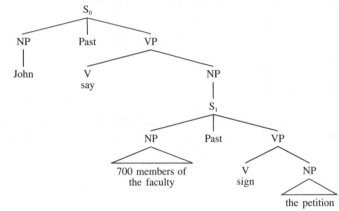

The derivation of (8a) involves an application of Passive, but not an application of it to the entire structure (8b). Rather, Passive applies to the embedded sentence S_1 exactly the same way that it would if S_1 were the entire syntactic structure rather than a constituent of a larger structure. Passive, like many other transformations, applies to a S, but not necessarily to a S that makes up the entire syntactic structure that it is at issue: the **domain** to which Passive applies in a derivation can in principle be **any** S, be it the whole or any part of the whole, just as long as that particular S meets the conditions for the application of the transformation.

We can then restate our conclusion about the derivation of (2b) by saying that if the underlying structure for imperatives is as in (6), Reflexivization and ISD apply to different domains, whereas if it is as in (3) they apply to the same domain. There is in fact a principle governing the application of transformations to different domains, namely, that when one domain to which transformations can apply is contained in another, the applications of transformations to the smaller domain precede the applications of transformations to the larger domain. If this principle (known as the principle of the **cycle,** or the **cyclic principle**) can be upheld, it will correctly predict the interaction between Reflexivization and ISD without any need to resort to a fixed order of application of transformations: Reflexivization will apply to S_1 before ISD gets a chance to apply to S_0, simply because S_1 is contained in S_0. Accepting that principle, we obtain (9) as the derivation of (2b):

(9)

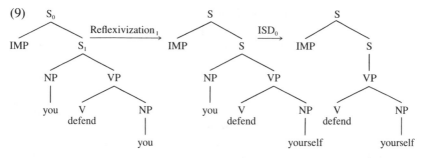

(In (9) I have introduced a notational device that will be used widely below: the use of subscripts to indicate the domain of a given application of a transformation, e.g., Reflexivization$_1$ means "application of Reflexivization to S$_1$.")

The principle of the cycle will in fact turn out to be our most powerful tool for predicting the way in which transformations interact with one another. Note, though, that minor differences between analyses can often affect whether the principle of the cycle will have any implications about the interaction of the transformations that are at issue, for example, the fairly minor change from (3) to (6) as the underlying structure of imperatives was sufficient to bring the interaction of Reflexivization and ISD under the purview of the cyclic principle. This is the case because fairly minor differences between analyses can affect how many different domains there are to which transformations might apply, and the more domains there are, the more the cyclic principle implies about the interactions of transformations. Accordingly, I will adopt a policy of examining the fine details of proposed analyses whenever there appears to be some restriction on the order in which transformations can apply and will seek analyses in which no stipulation of a fixed order of application of transformations need be made, that is, analyses in which the cyclic principle (and perhaps other principles governing how the steps in a derivation may interact) suffices to determine how applications of transformations may combine in derivations.

In chapter 6, after we have examined a fairly broad range of transformations and derivations and will thus have more of the perspective that one needs in order to be in a position to draw even tentative generalizations about what can make up a derivation and to evaluate those generalizations, we will examine in considerable detail the questions that we have raised in this section. For the present, let me just summarize briefly the position that will eventually be arrived at below. (i) The cyclic principle will do most of the work of predicting how transformations can interact, subject to the qualifications that (ii) a limited set of transformations (so-called **postcyclic** transformations) will have to be exempted from the principle, and (iii) not only Ss but also constituents of other categories will be admitted as domains to which transformations can apply. In addition, (iv) over and above the types of syntactic rules discussed so far, it will be necessary also to recognize restrictions on the surface shapes that sentences in the given language can take (see chap. 10); these restrictions will indirectly restrict the possibilities for combining transformations in a derivation, since the application or nonapplication of an "optional" transformation will sometimes make the difference between conformity to or violation of a restriction on surface structure, that is, restrictions on surface structures make particular instances of an optional transformation in effect obligatory or in effect inapplicable.

d. Deep Structure and Semantic Structure

Besides allowing the cyclic principle to correctly predict the way that ISD interacts with Reflexivization (indeed, the way that it interacts with all transformations that would apply to a domain in the position of S_1 in (7)), the analysis in which the imperative marker is placed as in (7) has an additional advantage over that in which it is placed as in (3), namely, that (7) is a closer approximation than (3) is to the semantic structure of an imperative like *Open the door!*: the meaning of *Open the door!* is not just a combination of three elements of meaning corresponding to "IMP," *you,* and the VP *open the door* but is rather the meaning of a sentence like *You open the door* or *You will open the door* combined with a notion of imperativeness. This point is even clearer with the parallel analysis of interrogative sentences that will be developed in chapters 8 and 14, in which there is an element of deep structure (Q) indicating that the sentence is interrogative. We will need to inquire whether that element combines into deep structures as in (1b) or as in (1c) (as the deep structure of (1a)):

(1) a. Did Edison invent the Cuisinart?

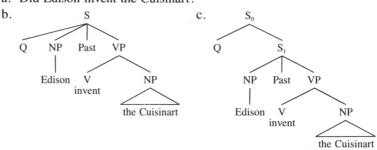

The structure in (1c) not only allows one to predict the interaction of Inversion (which applies to the domain S_0 because it is sensitive to Q) and such transformations as Passive whose conditions for application are met in S_1, which the structure in (1b) does not allow, but it also corresponds more directly to the semantic structure of (1a): (1a) asks whether it is true that Edison invented the Cuisinart, and (1c) but not (1b) contains a constituent (S_1) corresponding to the proposition that (1a) asks about.

The notion of "meaning" is sufficiently controversial and elusive that it would be rash, especially at this early a point in this book, to take a very specific stand on the relationship of meaning to syntactic structure. There are, for one thing, a number of distinct notions of meaning. For example, there are notions of "literal meaning" and of various kinds of conveyed meaning: *No man is an island* has a literal meaning in which it expresses the same sort of trivial truth as does *No coffee cup is an eyebrow,* but it also allows a metaphoric interpretation in which it expresses, roughly, the proposition that every person's fate affects the rest of humanity. And when it is uttered in certain contexts, the metaphoric interpretation can serve to convey, say, that the person to whom it is addressed should seek help. For the moment, I will simply adopt a policy of paying attention to relations between syntax and any of the kinds of meaning that can be distinguished and of attempting to identify respects in which details of particular kinds of meaning correlate more directly with one "level" of syntactic structure than with another, or with one particular syntactic analysis rather than with its competitors.

One respect in which the deep structures of the analyses developed below will correlate fairly closely with at least one notion of meaning is that they involve constituents that play a semantic role in the sentence but do not necessarily correspond to any constituent of surface structure. For example, according to the analyses that will be developed in chapters 4 and 5, (2a) will have a deep structure that is roughly as in (2b):

(2) a. The hostages are believed by the police to have been shot by the terrorists.

　　b.

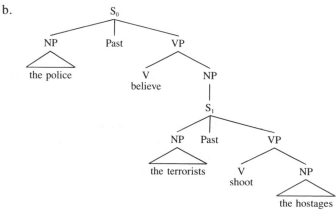

Note that the meaning of (2a) involves the proposition that the terrorists shot the hostages (it says that the police believe that proposition). The deep structure (2b) contains a constituent (S_1) that corresponds to that proposition, while no constituent of the surface structure can be held to contribute precisely that proposition (no more and no less) to the meaning of the whole sentence.

In the course of this book, I will bring into the discussion of the various syntactic analyses comments on the extent to which they allow for a close match between syntactic structure, especially deep syntactic structure, and semantic structure. It will develop that a very close match can be achieved. As evidence for or against putative syntactic analyses, I regard facts about interactions between syntax and semantics (indeed, interactions between syntax and anything) as on a par with "purely syntactic" facts (which is not to suggest that I think many facts are purely syntactic). Consequently, a conflict between the putative syntactic analysis of a sentence and the meaning of that sentence will count as evidence against the analysis. For example, the fact that (2a) has to do with the terrorists shooting the hostages and not with the hostages shooting the terrorists would provide an argument against an analysis in which (2a) was assigned a deep structure containing a S that corresponded to the proposition that the hostages shot the terrorists.

It remains to be seen, of course, whether there are cases in which syntactic considerations favored an analysis that semantic considerations would lead us to reject. If such cases exist, they discredit the suggested close match between deep structure and semantics. I leave it to the readers of this book to decide for themselves whether the semantic arguments that turn up with considerable frequency in the following chapters lead to any misrepresentation of syntactic facts or whether, as I would maintain, they help a syntactician to discover and account for syntactic facts that might otherwise escape detection.

e. Syntax in Relation to Linguistic Typology

This book is concerned both with **the syntax of** English and with **syntax,** the branch of linguistics whose subject matter is the syntaxes of languages and which is thus concerned with such general questions as those of what can go into the syntax of a language and of how the syntaxes of languages may differ from one another. Thus, in the course of working out the details of a large part of the syntax of English, we will often have occasion to raise questions about syntax in general and to propose and test general propositions of syntax that are relevant to the phenomena of English that are described. We will, for example, raise questions relating to the units in terms of which syntactic phenomena operate (e.g., is the structure of sentences appropriately described in terms of "grammatical relations" like "subject" and "modifier," as in my informal description of Passive in §2b, or do different notions provide a more satisfactory basis for describing syntactic phenomena?), or relating to the way in which syntactic phenomena interact with one another (for example, is the fact that the verb *be* in *The hostage was shot by the terrorists* agrees in number with *the hostage* and not with *the terrorists* merely a quirk of English, or is it a consequence of some general principle about how phenomena like agreement and passive structure may interact?).

The answers to such questions have implications about how languages may differ from one another. For example, the last question amounts to the question of whether it is possible for a language to be just like English except that the tense-bearing verb of the passive agrees with the underlying subject of the clause rather than with the surface subject. To answer questions about English, it will thus often be necessary to examine facts about other languages. That is, phenomena of English will generally be given analyses in which they are treated as reflecting a division of labor between language-particular rules and universal principles about language, and to fully justify an analysis, one needs not only to show that the analysis describes English accurately but also to verify both that the universal principles are universal and that all of the details of the putative rule of English are actually specific to English and not consequences of other facts of English plus universal principles.

In English *not* must precede its **focus** (the item, if any, that it contrasts with other things):

(1) a.   Not Bob but Alice won the prize.
    a'. *Bob not but Alice won the prize.
    b.   Alice, not Bob, won the prize.
    b'. *Alice, Bob not, won the prize.

That this detail of English word order is not universal can easily be demonstrated by pointing to languages in which a negative element must follow its focus, such as Turkish:

(2) a.   Ahmet değil Orhan gitti.
       (name) not   (name) went
       'Not Ahmet but Orhan went'
    a'. *Değil Ahmet Orhan gitti.

Thus, a linguist constructing an account of English sentences like those in (1) can be assured that the rules specific to English in his account must specify in some fashion or other that *not* precedes its focus. This, of course, still leaves considerable latitude regarding the exact nature of the rule(s), in particular, regarding how general they are: what we have said so far leaves it open whether the restriction on word order noted in (1) is a property just of *not* or of some more general class of words or of syntactic constructions.

Until we have explored a fair amount of syntax, it will be hard to give examples of universals that make details of language-particular phenomena predictable, since most of the universals cannot be stated without invoking ideas that cannot be introduced until later in this book. But let us take a look at one such example anyway, even though in doing so we will get considerably ahead of ourselves. In §2b I have already introduced the popular analysis in which English passive clauses are described in terms of a syntactic transformation that applies to the same structure that underlies the corresponding active S. The structure to which this transformation applies must involve a NP and a VP with the latter consisting of a verb and a NP and possibly additional material:

(3)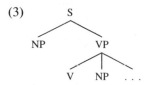

This statement of what the passive transformation may apply to makes no mention of certain other things that often occur in passive clauses, for example, the negative marker *n't* and adverbs such as *probably:*

(4) The hostage probably wasn't shot by the terrorists.

Linguists have in fact often given formulations of Passive that explicitly mention the optional presence of such elements in the structures to which it applies, thus formulating its conditions of application not in terms of the pristine structure (3) but rather in terms of something like (5):

(5)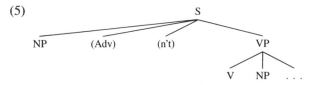

The latter formulations of Passive make it sound as if the presence of *n't* or of adverbs was potentially relevant to the application of Passive, in the sense that if the particular passive transformation of a given language did not explicitly provide for the presence of such elements, their presence would render Passive inapplicable.

I maintain, however, that a language in which such elements block the application of Passive is not possible.[16] Indeed, when the pristine form (3) of the conditions for application of Passive is combined with the rules for negation and for adverbs, certain universal principles will imply that passive sentences like (4) must be possible in English. The universals in question are: (i) that negative Ss have a deep structure of the form "negative element plus S," [17] (ii) that a sentence-modifying adverb (as opposed to adverbs that modify Vs or VPs, which will be discussed in chap. 19) likewise combines in deep structure with a S to form a larger S, and (iii) that (with some qualifications that do not apply here) transformations obey the cyclic principle. According to (i)–(ii), there are deep structures such as (6):

(6)

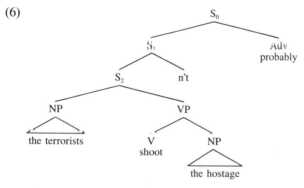

According to (iii), Passive gets a chance to apply to S_2 in (6) irrespective of the presence of *n't* and *probably* outside of S_2, and the normal rules for placement of *n't* and of adverbs apply to the passive clause derived from S_2 just as in the case of an active clause, which will then provide a derivation for (4).

Another interaction between universal principles and the syntactic rules of a particular language can be illustrated by considering English WH-questions, i.e., questions such as *Who is buried in Grant's tomb?* or *When did Caesar cross the Rubicon?* These questions ask the hearer to "fill in the blanks" (here, to fill in the blanks in "_____ is buried in Grant's tomb" and "Caesar crossed the Rubicon on _____"). The interrogative expression (such as *who, where,* or *for what reason*) with which a WH-question begins indicates the kind of information with which the blank is to be filled. As was pointed out in §2b, the interrogative expression must be followed by something having the shape of a corresponding declarative sentence except that it lacks any expression corresponding to the "blank" and begins with an auxiliary verb. One can thus describe English WH-questions by (i) positing a deep structure that is just like that of a declarative S except that it has an interrogative expression in place of one of the constituents,[18] and (ii) positing transformations that move the interrogative expressions to the beginning (WH-movement) and move a tense or an auxiliary verb to the position immediately after the interrogative expression (Inversion):

(7)

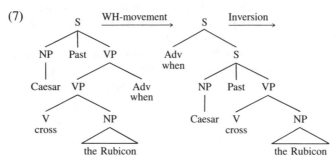

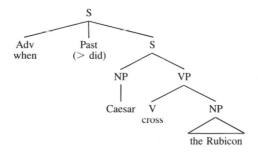

Note, however, that not all combinations of an underlying structure and derivation that conform to this informal sketch yield normal English WH-questions. For example, the questions by which one ought to be able to request that someone fill in the blanks in (8a, 8b) are not normal English:

(8) a.   Jascha Heifetz and _____ played the Kreutzer Sonata.
     a'.   *Who did Jascha Heifetz and play the Kreutzer Sonata?
     b.   Your mother attributed your low grades to _____ and laziness.
     b'.   *What did your mother attribute your low grades to and laziness?
     b".   ??To what and laziness did your mother attribute your low grades?

There is a characteristic shared by (8a) and (8b) that could reasonably be held responsible for the abnormality of the corresponding questions, namely, that in both cases the blank is part of a **conjoined** expression. Ross (1967a) has argued that not only is this the source of the abnormality of questions like (8a′, b′), but indeed a universal principle excludes the derivational steps that would otherwise relate deep structures like (8a, b) to such questions. Specifically, he argues that there is a universal constraint excluding derivational steps in which material is moved out of a conjoined expression. The oddity of (8a′, b′) can then be regarded as reflecting the interaction of that universal principle with a syntactic rule (WH-movement) that is specific to English. To form WH-questions corresponding to (8a, b), one is required by that rule of English to perform an operation that a universal principle of syntax rules out. The result is a class of questions that make perfect sense but cannot be asked in English because of a conflict between a requirement of English syntax and a universal syntactic principle.[19]

As an example of an issue that can be illuminated by considerations of language universals, consider the (highly controversial) question of what the syntactic status of auxiliary verbs is. According to one fairly popular view, English auxiliary verbs stand in the same relation to main verbs as "determiners" (such as *the, a, every*) do to the nouns with which they are combined. According to another fairly popular view, auxiliary verbs are verbs that combine with dependent verb phrases the same way that many main verbs do. In the former view, in (9a) the relationship of *is* to *drinking beer* is the same as that of *the* to *governor of Utah* in (9b), while in the latter view it is the same as that of *try* to *drinking beer* in (9c):

(9) a. (Fred) <u>is</u> drinking beer.
     b. <u>the</u> governor of Utah
     c. (Fred) <u>tried</u> drinking beer.

Since English auxiliary verbs are few in number and their syntax is somewhat idiosyncratic, it is not surprising that different linguists see different (incomplete) parallelisms between their behavior and that of other kinds of words. To determine whether either of the alleged parallelisms is significant or just represents flukes of English, it is useful to see whether there are universal correlations in the behavior of auxiliary verbs and the classes of words to which they are held to be parallel. For example, one of the parallels to which adherents of the first position attach importance is that of word order: auxiliaries precede main verbs and determiners precede head nouns. That position would receive strong support if it could be shown that such a correlation is universal: that in all languages auxiliary verbs have the same linear order relation to main verbs as determiners do to head nouns. It turns out, however, that there is no such correlation: the world abounds both in languages where determiners precede nouns but auxiliaries follow main verbs and in languages where determiners follow nouns and auxiliaries precede main verbs:

| | | Auxiliary | |
		before main V	after main V
Determiner	before N	English Russian	Japanese Turkish
	after N	Malay Swahili	Basque Somali

Thus, the fact that auxiliary verbs precede main verbs in English, viewed from a cross-linguistic perspective, appears to have no more connection with the fact that determiners precede nouns than it has with any other fact about English word order. By contrast, whether auxiliary verbs precede or follow main verbs in a language correlates strongly with whether main verbs in that language precede or follow their nonfinite dependent VPs. For example, in Swahili, just as in English, auxiliary verbs precede main verbs and main verbs precede their nonfinite complements:

(10) a. Alikuwa anasoma.
          he-was   he-reading
          'He was reading'.
      b. Amekwisha kwenda.
          he-finishes go
          'He has already gone'.
      c. Watoto hawawezi [kupigwa   jambo kama hili].
          children not-could be-punished matter like   this
          'Children could not be punished for such a matter'.
      d. Hajapata   kwenda kusafiri bado.
          he-not-gets go   to-trip   yet
          'He has not yet managed to travel'. (Examples from Ashton 1947:
             249, 271, 276)

Nearly all languages possessing one of these two characteristics also possess the other, irrespective of whether determiners in that language precede nouns (as in English) or follow them (as in Swahili). Thus, considerations of linguistic typology support the analysis of English auxiliary verbs that will be argued for in chapter 8, in which they fit into surface structures the same way main verbs that take nonfinite VPs as complements do:

(11) a.

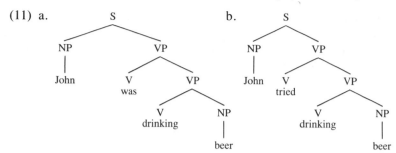

To the extent that an analysis of one language is given in terms that can be interpreted in other languages, the analysis has implications about what should be possible in other languages: it identifies factors responsible for the given phenomenon and implies that the same factors should favor corresponding phenomena in other languages.

∫ *Some Caveats and Addenda to the Preceding Sections*

CONCERNING §2A "Ordered labeled tree" is a species of what are called **graphs** in the branch of mathematics known as graph theory. In McCawley 1982, I give a set of axioms that distinguish ordered labeled trees from other "graphs." The axioms can be paraphrased as follows:[20]

(1) A tree consists of a set of objects (the **nodes**), two relations ("directly dominates" and "is to the left of") between the nodes,[21] and a function associating each node with a **label,** such that:

    i. There is a node (the **root** of the tree) that dominates every other node of the tree.[22] This axiom excludes a structure such as (2a).

    ii. The root is not dominated by any other node of the tree. This axiom excludes structures as in (2b).[23]

    iii. The tree has no "loops," i.e., a node can be directly dominated by at most one other node, whence there can be at most one path leading from a higher node to a lower node. This axiom excludes structures as in (2c).[24]

    iv. "Is to the left of" is a **partial ordering,** i.e., it is antisymmetric (if *x* is to the left of *y,* then *y* is not to the left of *x*) and transitive (if *x* is to the left of *y* and *y* is to the left of *z,* then *x* is to the left of *z*).

    v. If two nodes are **terminal,** i.e., do not dominate any other nodes, then one of them must be to the left of the other. That is, with respect to the terminal nodes, "is to the left of" is a **total ordering.**

    vi. If one node dominates another, then it is neither to the left nor to the right of it.

    vii. A nonterminal node is to the left of another nonterminal node if and only if every terminal node that it dominates is to the left of every terminal node that the other dominates. This axiom excludes structures as in (2d).

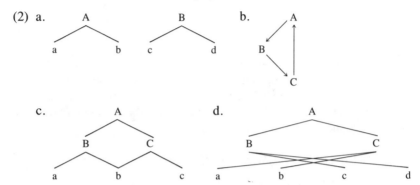

(2) a.   b.

c.   d.

    Axioms v–vii might be given in a simpler form if it were not that I want to allow for the possibility of **discontinuous constituent structure,** i.e., for trees in which a node dominates two items without dominating everything that is between them, as in (3):

(3)

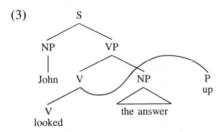

Structures such as (3) were widely accepted by descriptivist linguists in the 1940s and 1950s but have been almost uniformly rejected by transformational grammarians. Since I regard as preposterous the grounds on which transformational grammarians have rejected that type of structure (see Mc-Cawley 1982 for details), I harbor no prejudice against it. There are indeed several syntactic constructions for which there are strong arguments in favor of an analysis in terms of discontinuous structure, including parenthetical constructions (4a), nonrestrictive relative clause constructions (4b), and extraposed relative clause constructions (4c):

(4) a. Your brother, I'm fairly sure, won't want to help you.

b. Your brother, whom I don't trust, isn't a good person to ask.

c. Several persons have filed suits who were injured in the accident.

When those constructions are taken up below, I will present the arguments for a discontinuous structure.

While I regard the outright rejection of discontinuous structure as misguided, I note that continuous structures allow one to indulge in a typographical convenience, namely, that of representing the tree by a labeled bracketing, e.g., the information embodied in the diagram (5a) can be represented by the formula (5b):

(5) a.

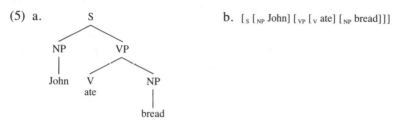

b. $[_S [_{NP}$ John$] [_{VP} [_V$ ate$] [_{NP}$ bread$]]]$

For convenience, I will in fact often use formulas like (5b) when referring to continuous structures; e.g., I will use $[_{VP}$ V AP$]$ as a shorthand device to refer to a verb phrase consisting of verb followed by adjective phrase.

I should also point out that the terms "tree" and "tree diagram" are by no means interchangeable, though their uncritical use often makes them seem interchangeable. The typographical objects that appear as (3) and (5a) are tree diagrams, and the abstract objects that they represent are trees. A tree diagram consists of symbols and lines, a tree consists of units and relationships among those units. It makes sense to say that a sentence is a tree, i.e., that it consists of units and relationships that satisfy the axioms (1), but it would make no sense to say that a sentence is a tree diagram. It is worth the while of an advocate of the former proposition to choose his words carefully so as to avoid giving the false impression that he is advocating the (absurd) other proposition.

We will have frequent occasion below to speak of the location of one node in a tree in relation to another. The terminology that has evolved for this purpose is an extension of kinship terminology, in which the various nodes are spoken of as female and the links between them as parent-child relations. This terminology can be illustrated in terms of the following tree:[25]

(6)

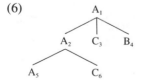

We speak of 1 as the mother of 2, 3, and 4; of 2, 3, and 4 as daughters of 1; of 2, 3, and 4 as sisters of one another; and occasionally of 3 as an aunt of 6, of 6 as a niece of 3, etc., though only "mother," "daughter," and "sister" are in common use as names of relations between nodes in trees. Often the kinship terms are combined with "left" and "right," as when we speak of 5 as a left sister of 6, or of 3 and 4 as right sisters of 2.

CONCERNING §2B Throughout §2b, I have spoken as if underlying syntactic structures consisted of exactly the same sorts of units and relations as make up surface structures. There are some respects in which it may be worthwhile to relax such a requirement. First, it is far from clear that the nodes of underlying trees must be assumed to have a full left-to-right order. While transformational grammarians have generally assumed that all syntactic structures are fully ordered and many influential analyses have been presented in such a way as to imply that the crux of the analysis is a difference in word order between deep and surface structures, there usually are equally acceptable alternative analyses in which the relevant difference between underlying and surface structure is one of constituent structure, with underlying word order being immaterial. The reader of this book should be prepared to see the relative importance of underlying constituent structure increase and that of underlying word order decrease as he advances through the book. I do not find it at all clear that **any** underlying word order need be posited for any language.

Second, while words in surface structure must have determinate morphological forms (e.g., if a noun has distinct singular and plural forms, it must be one or the other in surface structure), it will be argued in §11e that underlying structures must often be taken to be indeterminate with regard to inflectional categories, e.g., nouns in underlying structures must in many cases be left unspecified with regard to the singular/plural distinction. In such cases I will endeavor to make clear whether a unit written, e.g., *dog* is to be taken as singular or as neutral with regard to number.

The discussion of derivations here has sidestepped the important question of whether deep, intermediate, and surface structures should be regarded, as they are here, as separate entities, or instead as merely different parts of a single complex syntactic structure, as in such approaches as those of Jespersen 1937 and Perlmutter 1983, where deep and surface grammatical relations are represented together in the same complex structure.

CONCERNING §2C While the discussion of rule interaction in this section has been entirely in terms of a rule's interaction with **other** rules, everything that was said applies equally to interactions between different applications of the same rule. If a single transformation is in principle applicable to several domains within a single complex syntactic structure, one must raise the question of whether its application to one domain presupposes its application to another domain, whether its application to the one might destroy the conditions for its application to the other, and so forth.

EXERCISES

    1. a. In the last tree in §2b(14), indicate the mother, the sisters, and the daughters of the lower S node.

       b. Represent that tree in the alternative notation that uses labeled brackets.

    2. For each of the following verbs, give a selection of examples illustrating what kinds of constituents it can be combined with in active Ss, and give the relevant examples to check whether its distribution in passive Ss conforms with the informal statement of §2b (i.e., that in the passive it combines with what it combines with in the active, minus one NP):

       a. give   d. ascribe
       b. report   e. deprive
       c. accuse   f. elect

When the active VP contains two NPs, does it matter which one is missing from the passive VP?

    3. Using the model of §2b(14), give in full the presumable derivations of the following sentences:

       a. By whom was the petition signed? (= §2c(1b); give a derivation that conforms to what was said there about that example)

       b. Which students did the Bargle Foundation offer scholarships to?

       c. Which students did the dean say that the Bargle Foundation offered scholarships to?

       d. To which corporations did Smith offer himself as a consultant?

       e. Put yourself in my place.

Make the structures and derivational steps as parallel as possible to those of examples dealt with in this chapter that illustrate the same syntactic phenomena.

NOTES

    1. In chaps. 2–6 of this book, the choice of categories and the assignment of units to categories will be somewhat arbitrary; it will be considerably less so starting with chap. 7, where a critical reappraisal of the notion "syntactic category" is undertaken and an explicit, though fairly unconventional, policy on the nature of syntactic categories is adopted.

    2. One respect in which (1) and the tree diagrams to be given in the remainder of this book are unconventional is that each word and its category are represented

by a single node rather than in the more conventional way in which they are treated as distinct nodes; e.g., this book has diagrams like (i) where most textbooks of generative grammar would have (ii):

I reject (ii) as conflicting with the interpretation of the lines as meaning 'consists of': the noun in (ii) doesn't **consist of** *speaker*—it **is** *speaker*. Note that it is not just the fact that the line from N to *speaker* in (ii) does not "branch" that makes it abnormal to say "consist of," since it is quite normal to say that in the sentence *Birds fly*, the NP *birds* consists of the noun *birds* and the VP *fly* consists of the verb *fly*. For discussion of what led generative grammarians uniformly to adopt structures like (ii), see McCawley 1982b:184, where I attribute this puzzling state of affairs to the popularity in early transformational grammar of a notion ("rewriting rule") that is rejected here.

3. In traditional grammar, dependency **between individual words** was the principal structural notion that was exploited. The arrows in the diagram indicate that *to* is dependent on *listened,* that *speaker* is dependent on *to,* etc. See Percival 1976 for a discussion of how constituent structure came to replace dependency structure as the central notion of syntactic structure in American linguistics, Matthews 1981: chap. 4, for arguments that both constituent structure and dependency structure are essential to an adequate account of syntax, and Hudson 1984 for a detailed account of a number of syntactic phenomena within a somewhat nontraditional version of dependency grammar.

4. It should of course be kept in mind that (1) presents only one of several possibilities for exactly where in the underlying structure the tense might be: the only issue under discussion here is whether it is inside the VP or not, and in (1) I have made an arbitrary choice of one particular place that is not within the VP. A quite different choice of the underlying location of tense markers will in fact be argued for in chap. 8.

5. In (4), I also introduce a common notational device for leaving out details of structure: the triangle indicates, e.g., that *to the speaker* is a PP but does not indicate what its internal structure is (it does not indicate that it divides into *to* and *the speaker,* rather than dividing up in some other fashion). This device will be used both in cases in which the structure is so obvious that there is no point in spelling it out in detail (especially when one **has already** spelled it out in detail) and in cases where the structure is so unclear that it would be rash to attempt to give it in full detail.

6. The second tree in (8) differs in major respects from what other textbooks present as the surface constituent structure of passive clauses. I offer this structure here instead of other structures that readers might find less distressing, first in order

to stimulate the reader to think about the question of what the constituent structure of passives is and second because it is in fact right, as will be argued in chaps. 8 and 19; I regard the mitigation of readers' distress as insufficient grounds for the propagation of error.

7. This statement is not completely accurate, in that the traditional notion of "transitive" relates to a verb combining not just with any old NP but with a **direct object,** and verbs such as *be* and *become* that combined with a NP that had some relation to the verb other than that of direct object were not classed as transitive. In addition, such works as Hopper and Thompson 1980 develop a notion of transitivity according to which a verb is transitive to the degree to which its object is syntactically and semantically independent of it and denotes something that is conceived of as "affected."

8. Or something corresponding to the interrogative expression: the underlying forms of the interrogative expressions need not be exactly the same as their surface forms.

9. The analysis of auxiliary verbs is controversial. In chap. 8, I will take up the question of whether auxiliary verbs such as progressive *be* are heads of VPs, as is implicitly claimed in (14). The decision to have *what* and *was* in the last tree of (14) outside of the S from which they are extracted anticipates claims that will be argued for in subsequent chapters.

10. Here, as at many places in this chapter, the sketches given of the relevant transformations are greatly simplified. See chap. 14 for a more accurate formulation of this transformation.

11. The details of this are worked out in chaps. 8 and 14 in such a way that this transformation will invert the tense marker if there is no auxiliary verb in the underlying structure, which will leave the tense marker unattached and thus cause insertion of *do,* as in the discussion of (2) above.

12. Note, however, that whether one accepts the metaphor of a grammar as a sentence factory is independent of whether one identifies a grammar with a procedure that is employed in actual language use for constructing sentences. Most transformational grammarians take grammars to have a form that corresponds to the factory metaphor but maintain that sentences are produced in some fashion other than sheer replication of the assembly line (which is not to suggest that they have clear ideas as to what that fashion is). For example, most transformational grammarians recognize that the sequence of steps in a transformational derivation could not possibly correspond to the **temporal** sequence of corresponding mental events, since, e.g., one normally starts uttering a sentence before one has fully decided what one is going to say, and thus construction of a whole deep structure cannot yet have been completed when construction of the surface structure begins.

13. Henceforth I will follow the practice of capitalizing the names of transformations, in conformity with the fact that their names behave syntactically as proper nouns.

14. I ignore here cases in which, by use of stress and appropriate gestures, one can make two occurrences of *you* in the same sentence differ in reference:

Yóu [points to Alice] defended yóu [points to George].

15. In (8b) I have ignored the *that* and have followed the common practice of treating the direct object clause *(that) 700 members of the faculty signed the petition* as being a NP as well as a S. These two matters, which do not affect the argument being made here, will be dealt with in chaps. 5 and 7. In (8b), I introduce the practice of subscripting the labels to facilitate ready reference to one S or another, with S_0 at the top of the tree and lower nodes bearing larger subscripts than higher nodes. The subscripts are not part of the tree but only an informal device for referring to parts of the tree.

16. I emphasize that this is a statement about **syntax:** that there is nothing in the syntax of any language to exclude negative passives. This leaves open the possibility that the **morphology** of a language might exclude such a combination: if a language marks both passive and negation by inflections on the verb, there is no a priori guarantee that the morphology of the language will provide for negative passive forms.

17. The discussion here relates to "simple negation," not to "contrastive negation," as in (1)–(2), in which there is a "focus."

18. Actually, it will also have a Q, as in the treatment of questions sketched in §2c, but that point will be ignored here.

19. To a limited extent it is possible to move the whole coordinate expression to the beginning, as in (8b″), which, while not fully normal, is less deviant than (8b′).

20. To facilitate comprehension by linguists, these axioms are stated in terms of notions directly relevant to linguistics rather than the somewhat different notions that are more common in graph theory.

21. Note that only the nodes, not the branches, are ordered, notwithstanding the appearance that diagrams give of representing left-to-right order among the branches as well as among the nodes.

22. "Dominates" is defined in terms of "directly dominates" in the obvious way: *x* dominates *y* if *x* directly dominates *y*, or directly dominates a node that directly dominates *y*, or directly dominates a node that directly dominates a node that directly dominates *y*, and so on.

23. In (2b), arrowheads are used as a makeshift device to indicate which node directly dominates which. The usual typographical convention is to print diagrams with the dominating node higher than the dominated node, but it is only in virtue of axiom ii that that convention can be used, and we thus cannot rely on that convention in illustrating a violation of axiom ii.

24. In §16a I will in fact admit a limited class of structures that violate iii. However, since the need for such structures will not arise for several chapters, I will ignore that possibility in the earlier chapters of this book.

25. The subscripts on the node labels in (6) are informal typographical devices for identifying the nodes. Note that the labels on the nodes are often insufficient identification, because a tree may contain several nodes with the same label.

||||||| 3. *Some Tests for Deep and Surface Constituent Structure*

a. General Remarks

This chapter is devoted to a survey of ways in which one can justify particular decisions about what the deep and/or surface constituent structure of given types of sentences is. I will begin by presenting justifications for some details of the structures offered in the last chapter and will then shift my focus from those particular structures to the more general questions of what it takes to justify (or to refute) claims about syntactic structure and what means are at our disposal for answering questions about syntactic structure.

Throughout the last chapter, syntactic structures were posited that involved constituents labeled VP (verb phrase), consisting of a verb plus its object(s), if any, or of a smaller VP and an adverb that modified it. Let us see what evidence can be found for the claim that the elements of a sentence do in fact group together in that way, e.g., that the grouping of the parts of the sentence *Barnes reviewed "Evita"* is as in (1a) and not as in (1b) or (1c):

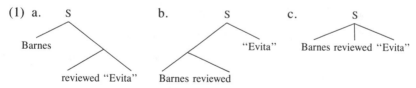

These structures embody different claims about what parts of the sentence make up syntactic units: (1a) embodies the claim that *reviewed "Evita"* is a syntactic unit but *Barnes reviewed* is not, (1b) that *Barnes reviewed* is a unit but *reviewed "Evita"* is not, and (1c) that neither is a unit. The question is considerably complicated by our decision in the last chapter to admit syntactic analyses having more than one level of syntactic structure: in principle, the question of how the elements are grouped together could have different answers for different levels of structure. For example, the sentence could, for all we know, have a surface structure like (1a) and a deep structure like (1c), and each of the tests that we employ can be expected to be of direct relevance to only one of a sentence's syntactic structures, not to all of them. I will make certain assumptions, however, that will simplify the enterprise somewhat. (These assumptions, of course, should be accepted only provisionally—they are possible bearers of blame if this enterprise should lead to inconsistent or counterintuitive results.) First, I assume that the different syntactic structures of a sentence do not differ without cause: they will be identical except in those specific respects in which the transformations of a language systematically allow underlying structures to differ from "derived" structures; and second, I assume that from the nature of different kinds of syntactic restrictions, one can draw tentative conclusions about the level of syntactic structure to which they are directly relevant (this vague statement will be clarified in the course of this chapter).

Let us then take up the question of the choice among the structures in (1). In the phenomenon of "VP-deletion," taken up briefly in the last chapter, constituents consisting of a verb and its object(s) behave as syntactic units:

(2) a. Barnes <u>reviewed "Evita"</u>, and Kerr did ∅ too.
  b. Hunt has <u>contributed millions to the Republican party</u>, and Stone has ∅ too.
  c. If Macmillan doesn't <u>publish your book</u>, I'm sure that Harper will ∅.

To justify using this phenomenon as a test for constituent structure, we have to show that constituent structure is relevant to the possibility of this sort of ellipsis. For example, if English simply allowed the omission of repeated material totally without regard to whether the repeated material makes up a constituent, then the acceptability of sentences like (2) would be of no relevance to establishing constituent structure. It is easy to see, however, that English does not allow unrestricted ellipsis:

(3) a. *Hunt has been <u>giving</u> $100,000 a year <u>to the GOP</u>, and Stone has been $1 million a year.
  b. *Mary <u>reported</u> the driver's license number <u>to the police</u>, and Alice did the make of his car.
  c. *Hunt <u>gave</u> $100,000 to the GOP, and Koch did $1 million to the Libertarian party.

The situation is complicated by the fact that English has several different ellipsis phenomena, and it is not always easy to tell which is which. I will argue, for example, that the ellipsis in (4a) ("VP-deletion") and that in (4b) ("Gapping") are distinct phenomena, applying under distinct conditions:

(4) a. Mary will buy a computer, and John will ∅ too.
  b. Mary will buy a computer, and John ∅ a CD-player.

Both involve deletion of a repeated verb, but with VP-deletion, in which the verb's objects are deleted along with it, an auxiliary verb (or at least, a tense inflection, realized as the corresponding form of *do*) must remain behind (5a), while with Gapping, in which an object must be left behind, all auxiliary verbs must be deleted (5b):

(5) a. *If Mary buys a computer, then John Ø too.
    b. *Mary has been looking at computers, and John has been Ø CD-players.

Moreover, Gapping is restricted to sentences in which the two clauses are conjoined with one another, while VP-deletion is not:

(6) a. If Mary buys a computer, John will Ø too.
    b. *If Mary buys a computer, then John Ø a CD-player.

While we are thus not yet in a position to say in general what ellipsis phenomenon any particular example illustrates, we can at least tentatively identify a phenomenon of VP deletion in which (i) without regard to whether the ellipsis site is conjoined with the "antecedent," (ii) a verb is deleted (iii) along with its object(s) if any, with the condition that (iv) an auxiliary verb or a tense must remain behind. The possibility of deleting a verb along with other material in an ellipsis of this sort can be used as evidence that the verb and the other material make up a syntactic unit, indeed, a VP.

We thus have evidence that at **some** stage of a syntactic derivation, a verb and its object(s) are grouped together as in the (1a) structure, and in view of the assumption made above, we can conclude that the structure is as in (1a) at all stages of the derivation, insofar as transformations do not disrupt that structure. The one transformation that we have alluded to that might conceivably disrupt that structure is Tense-hopping. Recall that (in view of the fact that tense markers do not participate in VP-deletion) we posited an underlying structure in which tense markers are outside the affected constituent, and a transformation (Tense-hopping) that combines the tense marker with the verb. However, saying that does not make clear whether the difference between the two structures is in the location of the tense marker or in the location of the verb, i.e., whether it is the tense marker or the verb that "moves." Assuming for the moment the arbitrary choice that was made of where the tense marker is in deep structure (we didn't **have** to treat it as a daughter of the S-node, and I will in fact argue in chapter 8 that it is not one) and that the combination of V and tense marker is itself a V, the output corresponding to the input (7a) might be either (7b), which conforms to the (1a) pattern, or (7b'), which does not:[1]

(7) a.

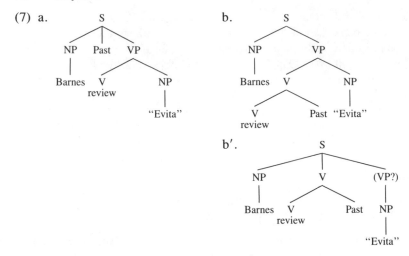

To choose between (7b) and (7b′) as the surface structure of *Barnes reviewed "Evita"* (this is not to suggest that these two are necessarily the only possibilities), we will have to look at something other than VP-deletion, since VP-deletion applies to a structure as in the input to Tense-hopping. Let us see if we can use the possibilities for coordinate conjunction as a test for constituent structure. Coordinate conjunction (often shortened to just "coordination" or "conjunction" or "conjoining") is a way of combining two or more units so that they share equally in a single syntactic role, as in the coordinate subject NP of (8a), the coordinate modifier of (8b), or the coordinate verb of (8c):

(8) a. His left leg, his jaw, and one of his fingers were fractured.
     b. The male and female employees are paid equally.
     c. I washed, rinsed, and dried the dishes.

English is unusual in that its devices for coordination are virtually unrestricted with regard to the category of the items conjoined; more commonly, a language will have, say, one way of conjoining NPs and a quite different way of conjoining Ss. As a first approximation to the considerably more complicated picture of conjoining that will be developed in chapters 9 and 16, let us suppose that wherever any simple syntactic constituent of a given category can occur, a coordinate conjunction of constituents of that category can also occur, and that coordination otherwise does not occur. We can then argue that certain combinations of elements are syntactic constituents if we can show that they occur as "conjuncts" of a coordinate structure. For example, we can argue that *Barnes reviewed "Evita"* has a constituent structure like (7b) and not like (7b′), on the grounds that *re-*

viewed "Evita," which is a syntactic unit according to (7b) but not according to (7b'), appears as a conjunct in the coordinate structures of (9):

(9) a. Barnes reviewed "Evita" and wrote an article about Baryshnikov.
    b. Barnes wrote an article about Baryshnikov and reviewed "Evita."

In the picture of coordination presented here, all coordinate structures are of the general shape (10a), i.e., two or more constituents of some category combine with a conjunction into a larger constituent of the same category, and (9a) must thus have a constituent structure such as (10b):

(10) a.   b.

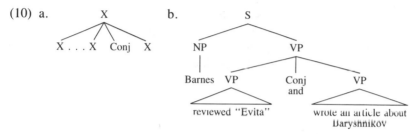

Since it is Tense-hopping that combines the tense and the verb, (10b) presumably represents a structure at a stage of derivation subsequent to the application of Tense-hopping, and since there does not appear to be anything that would change the constituent structure subsequently in the derivation, we can tentatively settle on (7b) as the surface structure of our example.

This test for constituent structure provides some confirmation for the unconventional structure for passive clauses that was proposed in chapter 2 and is repeated here in (11), since each of the VPs of (11) can in fact serve as a locus of conjoining:[2]

(11)

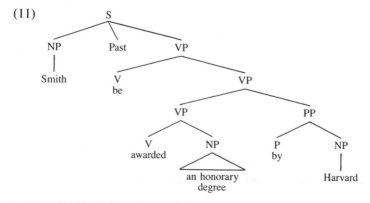

(12) a. Smith both <u>was awarded an honorary Ph.D. by Harvard</u> and was named a special assistant to the governor.

    b. Smith was both <u>awarded an honorary Ph.D. by Harvard</u> and named a special assistant to the governor.

    c. Smith was both <u>awarded an honorary Ph.D.</u> and offered an endowed chair by Harvard.

Further evidence that there is a VP constituent is provided by the placement of words such as *only* and *even* that have a **focus.** A focus is an item that is implicitly contrasted with other items; e.g., in *John drinks only beer,* the focus of *only* is *beer,* since *only* is used here to contrast *beer* with such other items as *wine* and *vodka,* i.e., *John drinks only beer* says that John doesn't drink wine, that he doesn't drink vodka, etc. *Only* need not immediately precede its focus; for example, *John only drinks beer* can be interpreted with *beer* as focus even though it is separated from it by *drinks.* Actually, it is necessary to distinguish a number of different ways of pronouncing that sequence of words, since the different pronunciations correspond to differences of focus:

(13) a. John only drinks béer. (focus = *beer*)
    b. John only drínks beer. (focus = *drinks*)
    c. John only drînks béer. (focus = *drinks beer,* i.e., he doesn't smoke pot or gamble)

It appears as if the focus must always bear primary stress. In subsequent examples, I will use underlining to indicate the intended focus, restrict my attention to pronunciations with stress appropriate to that focus, and give acceptability judgments only for interpretations in which the underlined item is the focus.

While *only* can be separated from its focus, as it is in (13a), it cannot be put in front of just any matter that precedes the focus:

(14) a.   John only put flowers <u>in the vase</u>.
    a'. *John put only flowers <u>in the vase</u>.
    b.   John only accused Bill of <u>negligence</u>.
    b'. John accused Bill only of <u>negligence</u>.
    b''. *John accused only Bill of <u>negligence</u>.

Only can appear at the beginning of a PP containing the focus, or, if there is indeed such a thing as a VP, at the beginning of a VP containing the focus. However, it can't appear before an item preceding the focus unless there is at least arguably a constituent beginning with that item and containing the focus; e.g., in (14b'') it is unlikely that *Bill of negligence* could be a constituent.

I will tentatively adopt the hypothesis that *only* can appear only as a left sister of a constituent containing the focus. *Only* is in fact subject to some other restrictions, e.g., that the constituent that it precedes may not be a S:

(15) *Only John drinks <u>beer</u>.

As long as these latter restrictions are not violated, the inadmissibility of *only* in a given position can be taken as evidence that that position does not begin a constituent containing the focus. For example, the difference in acceptability of *only* noted in (16) can be offered as evidence for the difference in constituent structure suggested in (17):

(16) a.   John drove only from Washington to <u>Baltimore</u>.
     b. *John drove only to Baltimore from <u>Washington</u>.

(17) a.

   b.

   The tests considered so far are much more directly relevant to establishing the surface structures of Ss than to establishing their deep structures, since it will turn out to be immaterial what the conjuncts of the coordinate structures or the constituent deleted by VP-deletion or the constituent containing the focus of *only* corresponds to in deep structure. For example, if the derivation of passive clauses proposed above is correct, the VP-deletion in (18a) involves deletion of a constituent (18b) that does not exist as such in deep structure (18c):

(18) a. Smith was awarded an honorary Ph.D. by Harvard, and Jones was
          Ø too.

b.

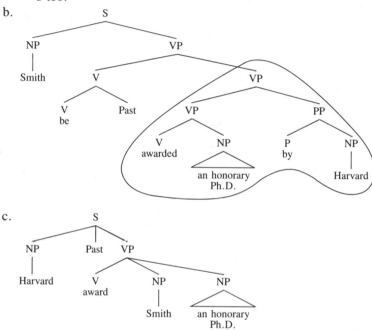

c.

Let us turn now to a valuable source of data relevant to establishing details of **deep** structure, namely, sentences involving idioms.

At least certain idioms that include a direct object NP (19) allow a passive form in which that NP appears as subject (20):

(19) a. They've pulled my leg many times.
      b. They let the cat out of the bag about John's plans.
      c. They took many liberties.
(20) a. My leg has been pulled many times.
      b. The cat was let out of the bag about John's plans.
      c. Many liberties were taken.

In "simple sentences," the pieces of an idiom are close together, while in various more complex sentences they can be separated from one another. Suppose we adopt the working hypothesis that the pieces of an idiom must be together in deep structure. Since there is nothing in principle to prevent transformations from treating parts of an idiom the same way that they treat comparable nonidiomatic units (e.g., treating *X's leg* in *pull X's leg* just like any other direct object NP), this hypothesis predicts that in "transformationally derived" structures it should be possible to get "idiom chunks" that are separated from the rest of the idiom.

The possibility of sentences with separated idiom chunks can then be used as justification for deep structures in which the idiom pieces are together. For example, the acceptability of (20) provides evidence that these sentences have deep structures in which *pull X's leg, let the cat out of the bag,* etc., are underlying constituents, as they are under the proposal that passive clauses have the same deep structure as active clauses. To turn these observations into an argument for such an analysis of passive clauses in general, we need to make one further assumption, namely that syntactic phenomena are uniform, i.e., that a particular syntactic construction has the same syntactic analysis irrespective of what items fill its various positions, e.g., irrespective of whether it contains items that make an idiom or items that exist independently of one another. With that extra assumption, which I will henceforth make,[3] the observations in (20) then provide an argument that **all** passive clauses have underlying structures in which the constituent corresponding to their surface subject is within the VP.

b. Some Syntactic Constructions Figuring in Constituency Arguments

The coordinate structures and VP-deletion structures that were taken up in the last section illustrate two syntactic constructions that have figured prominently in arguments as to what the constituent structure of various sentences is. These and other constructions that will be surveyed in this section do not differ systematically from those that are not taken up (facts about **any** syntactic phenomenon can in principle provide evidence about the deep and/or surface constituent structure of some class or other of sentences) but simply happen, perhaps by historical accident, to have been invoked in many such arguments.

i. Coordinate structures

An important qualification should be added to the use of coordination as a test for constituency in the last section, namely, that a given example may involve not just a simple coordinate structure but also one of a number of syntactic mechanisms that "deform" coordinate structures in various ways. Unless the details of those mechanisms are taken into account, incorrect conclusions may be drawn. For example, one might cite examples like (1) as a refutation of the argument given above that *reviewed "Evita"* is a constituent of *Barnes reviewed "Evita"* or even as an argument that *Barnes reviewed* is a constituent of it:

(1) Alice composes, and John performs, Philadelphia-style punk rock music.

However, it would be wrong to do so, since sentences like (1) involve not simple coordination of parts of sentences but rather coordination of whole Ss, supplemented by a mechanism (known as **Right-node-raising [RNR]**) that factors out identical final constituents from the conjuncts. As (2) shows, the shared final constituents need not even have the same syntactic role:

(2) Fred collects, and Ethel is a renowned authority on, Rembrandt etchings.

In the input to RNR in (2), *Rembrandt etchings* is the direct object in the one conjunct but part of an adjunct to a predicate noun in the other conjunct:

(3)

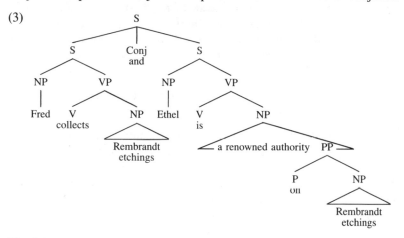

The following examples also make that point:

(4) a. Alice composes, and John is very fond of listening to, Philadelphia-style punk rock music.
    b. Alice is an admirer of, and John is a close friend of a critic who is writing an article about, Stevie Wonder.

The hypothesis that there is a transformation of RNR is the only obvious alternative to the counterintuitive proposition that *John is very fond of listening to* is a constituent of *John is very fond of listening to Philadelphia-style punk rock music*.[4]

The existence of the RNR transformation makes the implications of some examples unclear. For example, we are no longer in a position to conclude from the acceptability of (5a) (= §3a(12c)) that the *by*-phrase of passives is outside the minimal VP as in the structure proposed above (5b), since even if the structure were as in (5c), a derivation of (5a) involving a step of RNR would also be possible:

(5) a. Smith was both awarded an honorary Ph.D. and offered an endowed chair by Harvard.

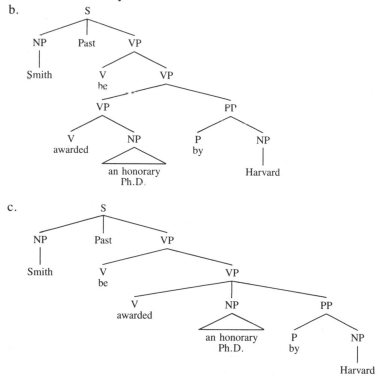

RNR is, however, of use in determining whether various combinations of items at the end of a S make up a single constituent, since the item extracted by RNR must be a constituent and not just a string of adjacent items. For example, the NP and PP at the end of (6a) presumably do not make up a single constituent, and while the PP can be extracted by RNR (6b), the two together cannot (6c):[5]

(6) a. Smith sells cars to insurance executives.
    b. Smith sells cars, and Jones rents trucks, to insurance executives.
    c. *Smith sells, and Jones rents, cars to insurance executives.

This characteristic of RNR has been useful in resolving some difficult questions of constituent structure, for example, the question of whether a "complementizer" such as *that* in (7a) is inside (7b) or outside (7b') the subordinate clause that it introduces:

(7) a. I wouldn't suggest that John was contributing too little.

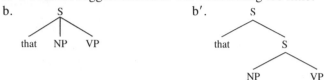

b. S — that NP VP

b'. S — that S — NP VP

c. I wouldn't even wonder whether, let alone suggest that, John was contributing too little.

Bresnan (1974) used examples such as (7c) to argue that the constituent structure is as in (7b') rather than (7b): if the NP VP part of a *that NP VP* sequence were not a syntactic constituent, then (7c), in which the NP and the VP but not the *that* are extracted by RNR, ought to have the same sort of oddity as does (6c).

A second important qualification to the use of coordination as a test for constituent structure is that there are sentences, as in (8), in which each conjunct consists of two constituents of the VP that do not comprise a single constituent as far as we can tell from other tests of constituency:

(8) a. John donated $50 to the Anti-Vivisection Society and $75 to the Red Cross.
   b. I put the potatoes in the pantry and the milk in the refrigerator.

Such sentences, however, are subject to a restriction that allows us to salvage a test for constituency, namely that they do not allow the first conjunct to be introduced by *both, either,* or *neither,* whereas conjoining of conjuncts that are otherwise constituents frequently does allow the use of those words:

(9) a.   John donated money both to the Anti-Vivisection Society and to the Red Cross.
   a'. ??John donated both $50 to the Anti-Vivisection Society and $75 to the Red Cross.
   b.   I didn't put either the potatoes or the milk in the refrigerator.
   b'. ??I didn't put either the potatoes in the pantry or the milk in the refrigerator.

ii. Cleft and pseudo-cleft constructions

English has two related constructions in which a constituent of a corresponding simpler sentence appears in predicate position. One is the **cleft** sentence, which has *it* as its subject and what appears to be a relative clause at the end:

(10) a.   John wants to look at your notes.
    a′. It's your notes that/which John wants to look at.
    a″. It's John that/who wants to look at your notes.
    b.   Ann bought a first edition of *Naked Lunch* for $500.
    b′. It was Ann that/who bought a first edition of *Naked Lunch* for $500.
    b″. It was a first edition of *Naked Lunch* that Ann bought for $500.
    b‴. It was for $500 that Ann bought a first edition of *Naked Lunch*.

The other construction is the **pseudo-cleft** sentence, in which what looks like an interrogative clause appears in subject position:

(11) a.   What John wants to look at is your notes.
    b.   What Ann bought was a first edition of *Naked Lunch*.

Note the use of *what*, which is normally an interrogative and not a relative pronoun, whereas clefts allow *which*, which can normally be only a relative pronoun unless it is combined with a noun:

(12) a.   What did John look at?
    a′. the portrait which/*what John was looking at
    b.   Which did John look at? (requires understood noun: *Which portrait,* etc.).

Cleft and pseudo-cleft constructions fulfill similar functions of "focusing" a constituent of the corresponding simpler sentence; i.e., (10a′) and (11a) both present the information contained in (10a) as an answer to an implicit question *What does John want to look at?,* though the two constructions differ considerably with regard to the class of cases in which they can be employed. In general, the cleft construction is more widely applicable, in that the predicate constituent of a cleft construction can be of any category that is otherwise admissible in predicate position (thus, not only NP but also PP, adjective phrase, and adverbial phrase), while the pseudo-cleft construction is more restricted in this regard; and (though there is much regional and individual variation on this point) the pseudo-cleft construction for many speakers requires *what,* and correspondingly the predicate element is restricted to constituents of types that can serve as answers to a question with *what:*

(13) a.   It's Alice that John was talking to.
    a′. %Who John was talking to is Alice.
    b.   It's to Cleveland that John drove the truck.

b'.   % Where John drove the truck is to Cleveland.

c.   It's because he was tired that John yelled at you.

c'.   % Why John yelled at you is because he was tired.

d.   It was very carefully that Marge handled the sulfuric acid.

d'.   % How Marge handled the sulfuric acid was very carefully.

e.   ? It was deathly afraid of flying that John became.

e'.   What John became was deathly afraid of flying.

f.   It was for a good reason that I stopped you.

f'.   *Why I stopped you was for a good reason.

g.   It was for two hours that his speech lasted.

g'.   *How long his speech lasted was for two hours.

These two restrictions on the pseudo-cleft construction are of course related: some of the constituent types that may not appear in predicate position in the pseudo-cleft either have no corresponding interrogative expression at all or (in the case of dialects that demand *what*) correspond to some interrogative expression other than *what*.

The only case taken up so far in which a pseudo-cleft is more acceptable than a corresponding cleft is (13e), where the focused constituent is an adjective phrase. An important additional case of that type is that in which the focused constituent is a *that*-clause or an infinitival clause:

(14) a.   ?? It's that he wants to quit school that Fred told us.

a'.   What Fred told us is that he wants to quit school.

b.   ?? It's to submit her manuscript to *Fortune* that Alice intends.

b'.   What Alice intends is to submit her manuscript to *Fortune*.

The oddity of (14a, b) reflects not a restriction specifically on the cleft construction but the more general constraint against subordinate clauses in the middle of a surface constituent,[6] illustrated in (15):

(15) a.   Bill told that lie to Alice.

b.   *Bill told that Fred had quit school to Alice.

b'.   Bill told Alice that Fred had quit school.

Since the focused constituent is at the end of the pseudo-cleft construction but in the middle of the cleft construction, such a constraint would restrict the occurrence of a clausal focused constituent in the cleft construction but not in the pseudo-cleft.

In either case, however, only a single constituent, not a sequence of two or more separate items, may occur as the focused item, and it is this characteristic that gives cleft and pseudo-cleft constructions considerable utility as a test for constituent structure:

(16) a.   I gave a watch to my brother.
    a'.   *It was a watch to my brother that I gave.
    a".   *What I gave was a watch to my brother.
    b.   Jack threw the wrappings into the wastebasket.
    b'.   *It was the wrappings into the wastebasket that Jack threw.
    b".   *What Jack threw was the wrappings into the wastebasket.
    c.   I saw Venus through a telescope last Tuesday.
    c'.   ??It was through a telescope last Tuesday that I saw Venus.

This fact can be used, for example, to argue that *from NP to NP* in (17a) is a constituent:

(17) a. Johann Sebastian Bach lived in Leipzig from 1723 to 1750.
    b. It was from 1723 to 1750 that Johann Sebastian Bach lived in Leipzig.

    The reason that I have contrasted the possibilities for cleft and for pseudo-cleft constructions is to provide a rationale for choices of one rather than the other of them as having a bearing on a particular question. For example, in deciding whether the *for NP to VP* combination of examples like (18a) forms a constituent, we must look at pseudo-cleft constructions like (18b) rather than cleft constructions like (18c), because (18c) will be unacceptable regardless of whether *for NP to VP* makes up a constituent, since clausal focused constituents in cleft constructions violate the "internal S constraint":

(18) a.   I hate for people to play radios on buses.
    b.   What I hate is for people to play radios on buses.
    c.   *It's for people to play radios on buses that I hate.

The acceptability of (18b) provides an argument that *for people to play radios on buses* is a constituent in (18a); the unacceptability of (18c), which one might conceivably offer as evidence for the contrary conclusion, actually shows nothing, since it would be unacceptable irrespective of whether *for people to play radios on buses* is a constituent.

iii. Various anaphoric devices

    Personal pronouns such as *he, she, it,* and *they* are one of several types of **anaphoric devices (ADs),** that is, words, expressions, and constructions that refer to an **antecedent** elsewhere in the sentence or discourse and take their reference from that antecedent. In some cases one can argue for one syntactic analysis over another on the grounds that the one but not the other provides a constituent that can serve as antecedent for some AD. For example, the interpretation of *it* in (19a) provides evidence for an analysis in terms of an underlying structure such as (19b) in which the auxiliary verb is outside of its surface clause:

(19) a. I may be wrong, but I doubt <u>it</u>.

b.

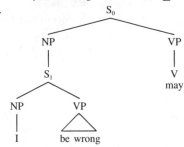

The *it* refers not to the proposition that I **may** be wrong but to the proposition that I **am** wrong. Under an analysis in which *I may be wrong* has a deep structure like (19b), there is a constituent, namely S_1, that is a semantically appropriate antecedent for the *it* of (19a).

I will argue in chapter 11 that ADs differ from one another in their syntactic and semantic properties. In particular, for some ADs, deep and not surface constituent structure is relevant, while for others it is surface and not deep constituent structure that is relevant. For establishing the antecedents of personal pronouns, it turns out to be deep structure that is relevant, so that (19a) is directly relevant to establishing the deep though not the surface constituent structure of *I may be wrong*. The AD that will figure in the greatest number of arguments below is, however, one to which surface and not deep constituent structure is relevant, namely, the omission of repeated VPs, alternatively regarded as the use of a phonologically zero VP pronoun, that was discussed in §3a and is further illustrated in (20):[7]

(20) a. Frieda <u>finished the assignment</u>, but Walter didn't Ø.
      b. I didn't think I'd <u>get here on time</u>, but I did Ø.
      c. Anyone who wants to Ø can <u>come along on the trip</u>.
      d. While you were <u>playing poker</u>, I was Ø too.

As an illustration of the use that will be made of zero VPs later in this book, consider the way that it can be used in arguing that certain kinds of adverbs are adjuncts to VPs. The possibility of sentences like (21b–b′) argues that both *play poker* and *play poker on Saturdays* in (21a) are VPs, and thus (21a) must have a surface constituent structure like (21c):

(21) a. John plays poker on Saturdays.
      b. John <u>plays poker</u> on Saturdays, and Bill does Ø on Sundays.

b′. John <u>plays poker on Saturdays</u>, and Bill does Ø too.

c.

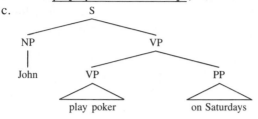

iv. Placement of elements with focus

There are a small number of elements besides *only* that have a focus and can be separated from their foci. I leave it to the reader to verify that everything said in this chapter about where *only* can occur in relation to its focus also applies to *even*. *Too* and *also* likewise have a focus but differ from *only* and *even* in that whereas *only* or *even* normally must precede its focus, *too* or *also* must follow its focus except that *also* may precede a VP or S that it is attached to.⁷

(22) a. John <u>kicked</u> Sam too.
     b. John admires <u>Hitler</u> also.
     b′. John also admires <u>Hitler</u>.

This difference among the various focus-bearing elements implies that *too* and *also* will yield information about constituent structure in different classes of cases than will *only* and *even*. Facts about *only* and *even* can often provide information as to where a constituent begins. For example, it is not always clear whether an adverb that immediately precedes a transitive verb is a modifier of the verb or of a VP of which that verb is the head. In the latter but not the former case, the verb is the first element of a constituent that contains the direct object of the verb. The observations in (23) provide evidence that *stupidly* in (23a) is a VP-modifier while *mildly* in (23b) is a V-modifier, so that the constituent structures differ as in (24a–b):

(23) a. John stupidly only informed <u>Mary</u>.
     b. *John mildly only reprimanded <u>Mary</u>.
     b′. John only mildly reprimanded <u>Mary</u>.

(24) a.   b.

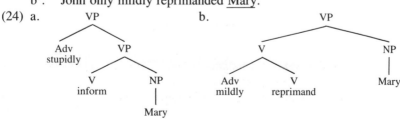

That is, if *only* has *Mary* as its focus, it is placed in (23a) as if the adverb is outside of a constituent containing *inform* and *Mary,* while in (23b–b′) it is placed as if the smallest constituent containing *reprimand* and *Mary* also contains the adverb.

Facts about elements that follow their foci (*too* and sometimes *also*) are of relevance to establishing where a constituent ends. For example, it is often not obvious whether a given V NP PP sequence is simply a VP in which the three items are sisters or contains a [$_{VP}$ V NP] constituent of which the PP is a modifier. If *too* with the verb as focus can appear between the NP and the PP, then that position must be the end of a [V NP] constituent and the PP must be outside that constituent. It is not as easy to construct plausible examples in this case as it was when we were working with *only,* since here the focus must be the verb, and it is often difficult to construct examples where the verb (NB, just the verb, not the whole VP) is implicitly contrasted with alternatives. The difference between (25a) and (25b) (where the implicit contrasts are, say, between sending a copy of the book to me and showing one to me, and between writing a poem for me and reciting it for me) provide evidence that *send X to Y* has a constituent structure as in (26a) and *recite X for Y* has a structure as in (26b):

(25) a. *He <u>sent</u> a copy of his book too to me.
　　　b. He <u>recited</u> the poem too for me.

(26) a. 　　　　　　　　　　　　　　　b.

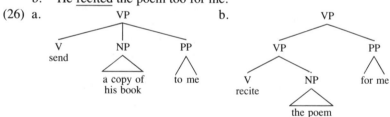

To illustrate the use of the constructions considered in this section as tests for constituent structure, let us consider their implications for the constituent structure of such sentences as:

(27) a. John picked up the money.
　　　b. John ran up the stairs.

Let us first test whether the *up + NP* combinations can be conjoined with similar combinations:

(28) a. *John picked <u>up the money and out a coin</u>. (cf. John picked up the money and picked out a coin.)
　　　b. John ran <u>down the corridor and up the stairs</u>.

The *up + NP* combination of (27b) behaves like a unit in allowing conjoining with something similar, while that of (27a) does not. Sentences as in (29) illustrate the application of RNR to such combinations:

(29) a. *John picked, and Mary hoisted, up some heavy weights. (cf. John picked up, and Mary hoisted up, some heavy weights.)
　　 b.　John ran, and Bill walked, up the stairs.

Again, *up* + *NP* behaves like a unit in a combination as in (27b) but not in one as in (27a).

The following examples show what happens when one makes such a combination the predicate constituent of a cleft construction:

(30) a. *It was <u>up the money</u> that John picked.
　　 b.　It was <u>up the stairs</u> that John ran.

Again, the *up* + *NP* combination of (27b) behaves like a unit and that of (27a) does not.

There is no way to test the possibility of replacing these combinations by ADs, since there is no AD whose meaning could plausibly represent the combinations that we are testing. (Note that this does not imply that they are not constituents—we have no assurance that there need be a full inventory of ADs to match all the different types of constituents that there are.) Let us thus turn to the final class of constructions considered in this section: those involving *only* or other focus-bearing elements. The following examples illustrate what happens when an *only* that has as its focus the NP of an *up NP* combination is put before the verb or before the *up:*

(31) a.　John only picked up the money (*not out a coin too).
　　 b.　John only ran up the stairs (not down the corridor too).
(32) a. *John picked only up the money.
　　 b.　John ran only up the stairs.

In both cases, *up the stairs* of (27b) displays behavior characteristic of the focus of *only,* but *up the money* of (27a) does not: the focus in *John picked up the money* can be *the money* but not *up the money* (note the unacceptability in (31a) of a contrasting phrase that would match *up the money* rather than just *the money*), while *up the stairs* can be contrasted with *down the corridor* in (31b), and *only* can precede *up* in (32b), just as it should if *up* there is a preposition with the focus as its object, while it cannot precede it in (32a).

The four tests that yielded any results thus confirm a well-known analysis (Fraser 1976, Bolinger 1971), according to which *pick up the money* is a **Verb-particle construction,** with a structure as in (33a) or (33a′), in which the NP and the "particle" do not comprise a constituent, while *run up the stairs* consists of a verb and a prepositional phrase:

(33) a.

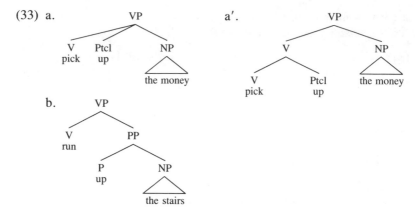

b.

This conclusion is confirmed by the interaction of these constructions with a number of other syntactic phenomena. For example, prepositions normally can accompany their objects when an interrogative expression is moved to the beginning of a question (34a), and in this respect (27b) but not (27a) behaves as if *up* is a preposition and the following NP is its object:

(34)   a.   To which person did you give the money?
     b.   *Up how much money did John pick?
     b'.   Up which staircase did John run?

c. "Funny" NPs

I will use the term "funny NPs" here as an informal name for NPs that have restricted distributions. In §3a I took up one type of funny NP, namely, NPs that are parts of idioms, e.g., *my leg* and *the cat* in *pull my leg* and *let the cat out of the bag*. Two other examples of funny NPs are the "existential *there*" of *There's someone outside* and the "ambient *it*" of *It's raining*.[9] Funny NPs of all kinds are useful in establishing that two parts of a sentence (the funny NP and the material that "supports" it) make up a deep structure unit; this will often provide the basis of an argument that an embedded S of some sort must be posited in the deep structure of a given class of sentences. In each case the argument will allude to a restriction on the use of the funny NP in simple sentences and will maintain that complex sentences in which the funny NP occurs must have underlying structures in which the same restriction holds as in simple sentences. For example, when existential *there* occurs in a simple sentence, it is restricted to the position of the subject of the sentence:[10]

(1)   a.   There occurred a disaster here.
     a'.   *A disaster occurred there here.

b.   There is nothing wrong with you.

b'.   *Nothing is there wrong with you.

b".   *Nothing is wrong with you there.

This observation can be used in arguing that sentences like (2a) have an underlying structure containing an embedded S of the sort that *there* could be the subject of, as in (2b):[11]

(2) a. John believes there to be a man outside.

b.

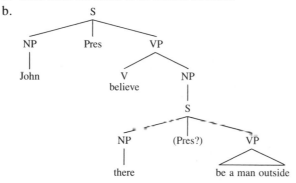

In chapter 4, I will argue that existential *there* is not present in deep structure, and that there is a transformation ("There-insertion") replacing the subject of one kind of existential sentence by *there* and moving the underlying subject into the VP (e.g., *There is a man outside* will have the same deep structure as *A man is outside*). In conjunction with that analysis, the restriction on existential *there* leads to the conclusion not that (2b) is the deep structure of (2a) but rather that it is an intermediate stage in its derivation, the deep structure being instead more like (3):

(3)

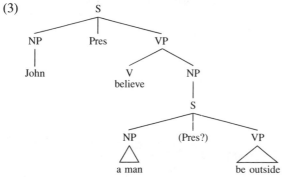

Ambient *it* occurs only in combination with a limited set of verbs and predicate adjectives that express "environmental conditions" (especially, but not exclusively, weather):

(4) a. It was raining/snowing/thundering/pouring.
    b. It was hot/cold/pleasant/delightful/unbearable/disgusting/uncom-
        fortable in the attic.
    c. I like/enjoy/hate it here.
    d. It's third down and twelve to go.
    e. It's intermission now.
    e'. It's 4:00.

In most instances ambient *it* is the subject of its clause either in surface structure or in what is arguably the deep structure (as in the case of *The lake makes it pleasant here,* which allows an analysis in which the deep structure direct object of *make* is a sentence *It is pleasant here* whose subject is ambient *it*). There are, however, a few clear cases like (4c) in which ambient *it* is not the subject of a clause under any well-supported analysis.[12] In either case, however, there are words that "support" the ambient *it* (*rain, hot,* etc. in the case of an ambient *it* subject, *like,* etc. in the case of an ambient *it* object), and sentences in which ambient *it* and its support are separated from one another can be used as the basis of arguments for deep structures in which they are together and thus for a transformation that separates them. For example, the acceptability of sentences as in (5) provides an argument for an underlying structure in which the NP and VP of *NP happen to VP* comprise a S of deep structure and for a transformation that breaks that S up:

(5) a. It happened to rain/snow on the day of the picnic.
    b. It happened to be hot/pleasant/delightful on the day of the picnic.

That is, for the sentences in (5) to have deep structures in which *It rain* or *It be hot* occur as constituents, ambient *it* must not be the deep structure subject of *happen* but rather the deep structure subject of *rain* or *(be) hot,* and a movement transformation must detach it from the embedded S of which it is the subject and make it into the derived subject of *happen.*

(6)

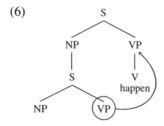

Details of this derivation will be given in §5b.

Examples involving funny NPs can bring out distinctions among combinations that are otherwise hard to distinguish. For example, there are two fairly obvious possibilities for the derivations of sentences like those in (7):

(7) I made John open the window.
   I led/got/caused/prompted John to open the window.

One is to posit a deep structure in which the verb has a S as its direct object, and a transformation ("Raising to object," (8)) breaking up the embedded S by moving its subject into the main S:

(8)

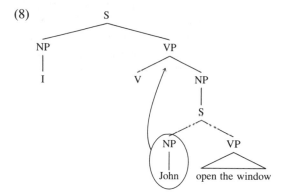

The other is to posit a deep structure in which the verb has an object NP in addition to an embedded S, and a transformation ("Equi-NP-deletion," (9)) deleting the subject of the embedded S if it is identical with the object of the main verb: [13]

(9)

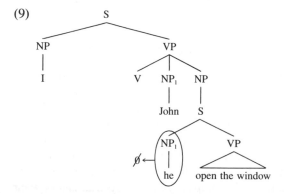

We have no grounds to suppose that one of these hypotheses would cover all the examples in (7), and we can in fact show that some of the verbs in (7) demand the (8) analysis and others the (9) analysis if we look at examples in which a funny NP follows the verb. Sentences involving ambient *it* provide evidence that *make, get,* and *cause* require the Raising analysis of (8) while *lead* and *prompt* require the Equi-NP-deletion analysis of (9):

(10) a.   The witch doctor made it rain by doing a rain dance.
    a′.   I got/caused it to rain by praying to St. Polycarp.
(11)   *I led/prompted it to rain by praying to St. Polycarp.

That is, with a deep structure as in (8), there is nothing to prevent the embedded S from being one whose subject is ambient *it,* in which case the ambient *it* becomes the derived object by Raising-to-object, thus yielding sentences as in (10). However, with a deep structure as in (9), supplemented with the assumption that *lead* and *prompt* are not included in the small set of verbs (such as *like*) that support ambient *it* as a deep structure object, if the embedded S had ambient *it* as its subject there could not be the application of Equi-NP-deletion that the (9) analysis requires, since the NP of the main S then could not be identical to the subject of the embedded S, and thus the conditions for Equi-NP-deletion could not be met. We then have an explanation of the unacceptability of the examples in (11).

The same distinction among these verbs can be brought out by examples involving existential *there:*

(12) a.   I made there be total silence.
        I got/caused there to be total silence.
    b.   *I led/prompted there to be total silence.

The facts involving idiom chunks differ from one idiom to another:

(13) a.   *I made the cat get out of the bag.
    a′.   I caused/??got the cat to get out of the bag.
    b.   *I led/prompted the cat to get out of the bag.

The difference in acceptability of the sentences in (13a–a′) brings out a reason why it is sometimes difficult to assess the implications of data involving funny NPs, namely that the embedded S posited in a given analysis may be subject to additional restrictions beyond the purely syntactic restrictions that the analysis imposes. For example, while the (8) analysis does not itself impose any restriction on the embedded S beyond the fairly trivial requirement that it be of [NP VP] form, perhaps some of the verbs that participate in the construction impose semantic restrictions of their own on what the embedded S can denote. Thus, the unacceptability of (13a) does not necessarily imply that *make* is excluded from the (8) construction—perhaps *make* imposes a restriction that is violated by *the cat gets out of the bag,* say, a restriction that the embedded S denote something "under the control of" the individual denoted by its subject NP.

A clear instance in which a verb imposes a semantic constraint on its complement S is illustrated by sentences with the main verb *cease:*

(14) a. *The cat ceased to get out of the bag.
   b.   John ceased to be angry at me.
   b'.   John ceased to yell at me.
   b".   *John ceased to have a fit of anger.
   b'''.   John ceased to have a fit of anger every time he saw me.
   b''''.   John ceased to have fits of anger.
   c.   *The bomb ceased to explode at 10:00.
   c'.   The bombs ceased to explode at 10:00.
   d.   There ceased to be any reason to remain here.
   d'.   It ceased to be pleasant here.

To determine whether the NP and VP of *NP cease to VP* make up an underlying S, one should look at examples in which the NP is "funny" and the VP contains material that normally supports that NP. While (14a) is such an example, its unacceptability does not in this case provide an argument that the NP and VP do not make up an underlying S, since *the cat gets out of the bag* violates a semantic constraint illustrated in (14b–c'), namely, that the complement of *cease* denote a state rather than an event. The acceptable sentences in (14) are those in which the embedded S can be interpreted as denoting a state. For example, (14b') refers not to an event of yelling but to the state describable as *John yells at me:* (14b') means that it is no longer the case that John (regularly) yells at me. The contrast between (14b") and (14b'''–b'''') is between an embedded S referring to a single fit of anger (unacceptable) and one referring to regularly repeated fits of anger (acceptable); in (14c–c'), the contrast is between an embedded S referring to a single explosion (unacceptable) and one referring to a state in which repeated explosions occur (acceptable).[14] The examples in (14d–d') involve funny NPs in complement Ss that denote a state rather than an event, and their acceptability establishes that the NP and VP of *NP cease to VP* do make up an underlying S.

EXERCISES

1. What do the possibilities for VP-deletion tell you about the constituent structure of the following examples?
   a. John gave a book to Mary.
   b. John washed the dishes for Mary.
   c. Ann filled the pool with a hose.
   d. Ann filled the pool with water.

e. Sam hammered the metal flat.

f. Sam gave a lecture drunk.

2. Determine whether facts about conjoining confirm the conclusions you reached in exercise 1.

3. Using examples with coordinated constituents, test the correctness of each of the following possibilities for the surface constituent structure of NPs:

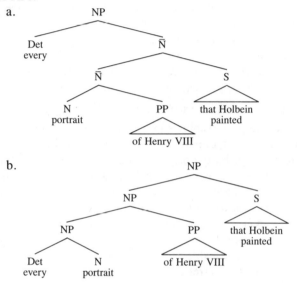

Treat the symbol N̄ (which will be introduced more formally in chap. 7) as simply meaning something that consists of a noun plus adjuncts and/or modifiers that it may have.

4. Using facts about "funny NPs," check whether §3c(8) or (9) can be taken as the analysis of sentences involving the verbs underlined below:

    a. Mary <u>let</u> John sell the car.

    b. Bill <u>had</u> the tailor lengthen the sleeves.

    c. George couldn't <u>induce</u> Mary to go to the concert with him.

    d. The robbers <u>compelled</u> John to give them the money.

    e. The autopsy <u>showed</u> the victim to have died of cyanide poisoning.

    f. Mary <u>prevented</u> John from selling the car.

5. Apply the tests of §3b to determine whether each of the following examples contains a verb-particle construction or a verb plus a prepositional phrase. Do not overlook the possibility that a particular example might be both, i.e., that it is ambiguous between an interpretation corresponding to the one structure and an interpretation corresponding to the other:

   a. John <u>took off</u> his shoes.

   b. Libya <u>borders on</u> Egypt.

   c. We <u>looked at</u> the announcement.

   d. They <u>looked over</u> the table.

   e. I <u>threw out</u> the garbage.

   f. We were <u>working on</u> the furnace.

   g. Amalgamated Frammis has <u>taken over</u> Consolidated Implements.

6. Make up examples to show that verb-particle constructions differ from V PP combinations with regard to each of the following:

   a. The possibility of putting the particle or preposition **after** the NP (e.g., *John picked the money up*).

   b. The possibility of having the NP position filled by a pronoun (e.g., *He ran up it*).

   c. The possibility of putting an adverb between the verb and the particle or preposition (e.g., *John ran frantically up the stairs*).

NOTES

1. The parentheses and question-mark in (7b′) indicate unclarity as to whether the constituent in question retains its status as a VP when it loses its verb. The possibility of "tree pruning," that is, of the elimination of nodes as they become "nonfunctional" in the course of the derivation, will be taken up in §7c.

2. The coordinate structures in (12) are given in the form *both X and Y* to make clear where the coordinate structure begins: the *both* of *both X and Y* (likewise the *either* of *either X or Y*) immediately precedes the first conjunct.

3. The assumption will be weakened somewhat in chap. 22, where we will consider mechanisms for extending a syntactic construction beyond the class of cases that it "properly" applies to.

4. For the surface constituent structure of sentences involving RNR, see chap. 16. In this passage I have deviated from my usual practice of illustrating the outputs of the various transformations, because in this case the derived constituent structure is of a different type from the structures considered so far in the book, and I prefer postponing discussion of structures of that type until later in the book.

5. There is in fact some dialect variation on this point. See Grosu 1976 for discussion of dialects and idiolects that allow RNR more freely than does the variety of English assumed here.

6. This constraint will be discussed in detail in §10c, where attention will be paid to how exactly "S" and "in the middle of" must be understood. For example, the constraint must exclude *that*-clauses and infinitives but not expressions such as *(John's) insulting her* in the middle of clauses:

It was John's insulting Mary that offended Roger the most.

7. Note that (as illustrated in (20)) a zero VP can precede its antecedent; so can a personal pronoun, as in *While he talked, John smoked a cigar*. The conditions

under which an AD can precede its antecedent are discussed at length in chap. 11. Note also that, as pointed out in §3a and further illustrated in (20c, d), the clause whose VP is deleted need not be conjoined with the clause containing the antecedent—either can be subordinate to the other, or both can be subordinate to some third clause.

What is relevant to "derived anaphoric devices" such as the zero VP discussed here is actually not surface structure but what is known as **shallow structure:** a level of syntactic structure that falls short of surface structure by virtue of, e.g., having tense markers outside of the VPs in which they appear in surface structure. A more precise characterization of the notion of shallow structure is given in §6c.

8. Actually, to a limited extent, *only* or *even* can follow its focus:

John owns three shirts only.
Alice likes snake meat even.

Such examples, which are discussed in some detail in Ross and Cooper 1979, will be ignored below.

9. In calling existential *there* a NP, I am following a policy that I will impose arbitrarily in the first few chapters of this book, that of applying the term "noun phrase" not only to expressions such as *the roof of the house,* whose **head** (here, *roof*) is a noun, but also to expressions that serve as a subject or as a direct or indirect object, irrespective of their internal structure. I will review this policy and amend it somewhat in chap. 7, where I will adopt a more critical attitude toward syntactic categories than I take in the earlier chapters.

10. *There* in all the examples in (1) is to be interpreted as existential *there*, not as the locative *there* (meaning "(at/in) that place") of such sentences as *A disaster occurred there.*

11. The parenthesized "Pres" in the embedded S of (2b) reflects unclarity as to whether that S should indeed have a tense marker. I will eventually argue (§8b) that some nonfinite Ss have underlying tenses and others do not, and that the infinitival complement of *believe* does have an underlying tense (here, Pres).

12. I owe this and many other observations about ambient *it* to Bolinger 1977.

13. We are in no position to say that these are the only possibilities. I restrict attention here to those possibilities mainly to facilitate the exposition.

14. Actually, (14c′) has two possible interpretations, both of which fit this description. In one interpretation *at 10:00* modifies the main clause and the sentence means that explosions had been going on until 10:00 but no more occurred after 10:00. In the other interpretation it modifies the subordinate clause, and the sentence means that there used to be an explosion at 10:00 every night but that that ceased to be the case (say, the bombers changed their schedule so that the bombs now went off at 9:30 instead of 10:00).

IIIIII *4. Some Subject-Changing Transformations*

a. Passive

In this chapter, I will discuss five transformations that move a subject NP
into the VP and insert something in its place. In the next chapter these
transformations will play a role in justifying analyses in which various infinitive and participial expressions are derived from underlying Ss. Positing
those underlying Ss will be necessary because the infinitive or participial
expression can be a VP such as is derived by one of the subject-changing
transformations, and the hypothesized S will be needed in order to provide
a domain for that transformation to apply to. For example, *John wants
to be loved by everyone* will require an underlying structure with an embedded S *everyone love him* so that there will be something that the passive
transformation can apply to to yield the VP *be loved by everyone.*

Before taking up these transformations, I must say a word about tenses
and auxiliary verbs. The analysis of tenses and auxiliary verbs that I will
ultimately argue for (in chap. 8) presupposes a number of important points
that will be discussed at various points in chapters 4–7. Rather than present a makeshift analysis that does not make those presuppositions and
then reject it in favor of the right analysis, I prefer to ignore tenses and
auxiliaries as much as possible until I reach the point where I can give an
analysis that can be taken seriously. I will accordingly omit tenses and auxiliaries from the structures that are given, while issuing a promissory note
to be redeemed for an analysis of tenses and auxiliary verbs that can be
combined in a satisfactory fashion with the analyses that are developed in
this chapter. Where reference to auxiliary verbs is unavoidable (e.g., in the
discussion of passive clauses, where one of the crucial elements of the phenomenon, namely, passive *be,* is an auxiliary verb), I will say only what is
necessary about auxiliary verbs to make my points.

Passive clauses in English involve an auxiliary verb *be* combined with a
VP that is in the past participle form. The *be* follows any other auxiliary
verbs:

(1) a.   Sam may have been arrested for selling drugs.
   a′. *Sam may be had arrested for selling drugs.
   b.   Dinner is being served.
   b′. *Dinner is been serving.

Auxiliary verbs impose specific morphological requirements on what follows them, e.g., *may* (like other "modal auxiliaries" such as *must, should, can*) can be followed only by a "bare infinitive"; progressive *be* only by a verb in the *-ing* (present participle) form; and *have* and passive *be* only by a past participle. Thus, the acceptable (1b) has progressive *be* preceding passive *be* (the *-ing* of *being* shows that the *is* is a progressive *be,* and the past participle form of *served* shows that the *being* is a passive *be*), while the unacceptable (1b′) has passive *be* preceding progressive *be*.

The VP of a passive clause lacks one of the NPs with which its verb could be combined in an active clause:

(2) a.   The judge sentenced Bill to 20 years' hard labor.
   b′. Bill was sentenced Ø to 20 years' hard labor.
   b.   Everyone laughed at the Wright brothers.
   b′. The Wright brothers were laughed at Ø.
   c.   They gave Schwartz up for lost.
   c′. Schwartz was given Ø up for lost.

The passive VP optionally contains an expression *by NP* whose NP could serve as the subject of the given verb in an active clause:

(3) a.   The judge/*bottle sentenced Bill to 20 years' hard labor.
   a′. Bill was sentenced to 20 years' hard labor by the judge/*bottle.
   b.   His arrogance/*bicycle exceeds his ignorance.
   b′. His ignorance is exceeded by his arrogance/*bicycle.
   c.   The president's speech/*reputation took up an hour.
   c′. An hour was taken up by the president's speech/*reputation.[1]

We can account for these observations by treating active and passive Ss as having identical deep structures and positing a transformation that applies in the derivation of passive Ss, replacing the subject by one of the NPs in the VP, inserting *be* before the VP, and either deleting the underlying subject or combining it with *by* and putting the resulting combination at the end of the VP:

(4)

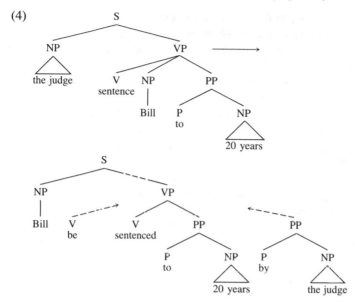

The dotted lines in (4) serve to maintain neutrality with regard to how exactly *be* and *by the judge* fit into the structure, e.g., whether they are daughters of the original VP node, whether they are daughters of the S node, or whether they combine with what is left of the original VP into a larger VP. It is in fact a constituent structure of the last type that will be argued for below:

(5)

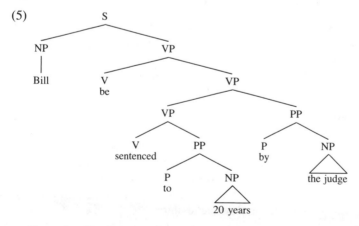

Since the Passive transformation removes one NP from the VP, this analysis accounts for the fact that the verb in the passive combines with everything that it does in the active, minus one NP, and since it makes the underlying subject the object of the *by,* it accounts for the fact that the object of the *by* must be something that can serve as the subject of the verb in an active S. Whether anything need be added to our analysis in order to account for the fact that passive *be* cannot precede auxiliary verbs will depend on the analysis of auxiliary verbs that it is combined with. It will in fact turn out that the analysis of auxiliary verbs developed in chapter 8 will combine with the analysis of passives developed here in such a way as to leave only one possibility for where passive *be* can appear in relation to other auxiliary verbs. In combination with some other treatments of auxiliary verbs, however, it would be necessary to add to the formulation of Passive a stipulation that *be* be inserted in a position between the last auxiliary verb and the main verb.

The constituent structure in (5) is accepted by virtually no transformational grammarians. Something like it is required, however, if the inserted *be* and *by* are to fit into surface configurations that their respective parts of speech otherwise allow. Prepositions occur only in the $[_{PP}$ P NP] combination (except where the NP has been extracted from a PP, as in (2b)); of the various combinations in which verbs occur, only $[_{VP}$V VP] (e.g., *He tried writing poems*) could accommodate a verb that precedes another verb, as passive *be* does; and of the combinations in which PPs occur, only $[_{VP}$ V . . . PP] and $[_{VP}$ VP PP] (as in *he [[sliced the meat] with a cleaver]*) are possibilities here.

The structure proposed in (5) is supported by the fact that each of the VPs posited is available as a locus of conjoining:

(6) a. John [[failed miserably] and [was laughed at by everyone]].
    b. John was [[taken for a fool by everyone] and [subjected to much ridicule by his relatives]].
    c. John was [both [regarded with total contempt] and [subjected to much ridicule]] by his relatives.

In (6a) we have conjoining of something corresponding to the topmost VP of (5), in (6b) conjoining of something corresponding to the middle VP, and in (6c) conjoining of something corresponding to the lowest VP. In chapter 19, I will take up facts about the distribution and interpretation of adverbs that provide additional support for the proposed structure.

The status of *by* + *NP* as a constituent is clear from the following examples in which it behaves as a syntactic unit:

(7) a. By whom has this book been read? (example from Emonds 1976:66)

b. John was attacked neither by a robber nor by a terrorist.

c. A letter was sent to Mary by John.

c′. A letter was sent by John to Mary.

In (7a), *by* accompanies the interrogative word as it moves to the beginning of the interrogative S, the way that prepositions are generally allowed to accompany their objects when the object is moved (*To whom did John show the book?*). If the NP that follows *by* in a passive S were not the object of *by*, there would be no reason for the *by* to participate in this movement. In (7b), two *by* + *NP* expressions are conjoined. In (7c–c′), a *by* + *NP* combination is permuted with a PP the way that adjacent prepositional phrases normally can be permuted (e.g., *Mary talked with John about politics; Mary talked about politics with John*).

The informal statement of Passive given above does not make clear how, if at all, it applies to VPs that contain more than the bare minimum of a V and one NP. Examples have in fact been given in (2) in which a passive is formed from a VP containing more than that bare minimum. When a VP consists of a verb, a NP, and something other than a NP (e.g., a PP), generally the NP can become the subject of a passive but any NPs inside the other constituent cannot, though with many idioms of the form V NP PP a passive with the object of the preposition as subject is reasonably acceptable:

(8) a.   Everyone threw coins into the fountain.

a′.   Coins where thrown Ø into the fountain by everyone.

a″.   *The fountain was thrown coins into Ø by everyone.

b.   Honest Oscar sold a car to my brother for $200.

b′.   A car was sold Ø to my brother for $200 by Honest Oscar.

b″.   *My brother was sold a car to Ø for $200 by Honest Oscar.

b‴. *$200 was sold a car to my brother for Ø by Honest Oscar.

c.   The FBI kept tabs on my brother.

c′.   Tabs were kept Ø on my brother by the FBI.

c″.   ?My brother was kept tabs on Ø by the FBI.

Where a verb is combined with two NPs (indirect and direct objects), the possibilities for passives depend on the type of indirect object and are subject to considerable dialect variation, e.g., (9a″) sounds more normal in British than in American English:

(9) a.   Honest Oscar sold my brother a car for $200.

a′.   My brother was sold Ø a car for $200 by Honest Oscar.

a″.   %A car was sold my brother for $200 by Honest Oscar.

b.   Fred bought Ethel a birthday present.

b′.   ?Ethel was bought Ø a birthday present by Fred.

b″.   ??A birthday present was bought Ethel Ø by Fred.

c.   (colonel to troops) Okay you guys, kill me some Commies!

c′.   ??The colonel was killed Ø several Commies by his troops.

c″.   *Several Commies were killed the colonel Ø by his troops.

The indirect object of expressions such as *sell my brother a car* (what we may call **to-dative** constructions in virtue of paraphrases in which *to* introduces the indirect object: *sell a car to my brother*) can be converted into the subject of a passive. The indirect object of expressions such as *buy Ethel a birthday present* (what we may call **for-dative** constructions in virtue of paraphrases in which *for* introduces the indirect object: *buy a present for Ethel*) generally does not make a fully acceptable subject of a passive, though *for*-dative constructions differ with regard to how deviant the passive is.[2]

The acceptability of passives in which the object of the preposition in a V PP combination becomes the subject varies from one combination to another:

(10) a.   This bed has been slept in Ø.

b.   The Wright brothers were laughed at Ø by everyone.

c.   ?This bus is gotten on Ø by hundreds of people every day.

d.   ??B flat is modulated into Ø after 8 bars by this étude.

e.   *A monster was turned into Ø by Dr. Jekyll.

No attempt will be made here to identify the factors responsible for these differences; for worthwhile discussion of that topic, see Davison 1980 and Rice 1987. The following rough generalization, at least, seems to emerge from (8)–(10): except for those speakers who accept *A car was sold to my brother,* the NP that becomes subject of the passive is the first NP after the verb; if that NP is not the object of a preposition, it is available for conversion into the subject of a passive, though if it is the object of a preposition, additional conditions must be met for it to become subject of a passive.[3]

One additional restriction on the NP that is to become subject of the passive emerges from a consideration of the following examples:

(11) a.   Many people intend to buy cars.

a′.   *Cars are intended to buy Ø by many people.

b.   The storm seems to have damaged the transmitter.

b′.   *The transmitter is seemed to have damaged Ø by the storm.[4]

c.   A bomb exploded outside City Hall.

c′.   *City Hall was exploded outside Ø by a bomb.

d.   Riots occurred in Poland.

d′.   *Poland was occurred in ∅ by riots.

In each of these cases the verb and the NP that is to be made into the subject are not in the same VP. The NP is either in a VP embedded in that of which the verb is the head ((12a); cf. (11a, b)) or in an adverbial expression outside that VP ((12b); cf. (11c, d)):

(12) a.   b.

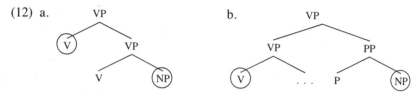

We will say that the V and the NP that is to be made into the subject must be **VP-mates:** the lowest VP node that dominates one of them must also be the lowest VP node that dominates the other.

The informal description given above of Passive left unclear what underlies **reduced passives,** in which no *by*-phrase appears. A common treatment of reduced passives in transformational grammar has been to assign to them deep structures having some sort of "indefinite" subject such as *someone,* to have Passive form a *by*-phrase no matter what the underlying subject is, and to have an additional transformation that deletes *by*-phrases that have the "indefinite" NP in question, e.g., if *someone* is taken to be the underlying subject of reduced passives, then (13a–c) all have the same deep structure, and the derivation of (13c) differs from that of (13b) only to the extent of including a step in which *by someone* is deleted:

(13) a. Someone attacked John.
     b. John was attacked by someone.
     c. John was attacked.

The identification of the "indefinite" underlying subject presents a major problem, though. *Someone* isn't indefinite enough, as can be seen from (14):

(14) a.   We have been outvoted.
     a′.   ?Someone has outvoted us.
     b.   The Earth was formed 4 billion years ago.
     b′.   Someone formed the Earth 4 billion years ago.
     c.   My brother was drowned in a boating accident.
     c′.   ?Someone drowned my brother in a boating accident.

d.   Chomsky's *Syntactic Structures* was written in 1956.

d′.   Someone wrote Chomsky's *Syntactic Structures* in 1956.

Someone is human and singular. Its singular number makes (14a′) odd and not a paraphrase of (14a): it generally takes a set of persons and not just a single person to outvote us. The humanness of *someone* prevents (14b′) from being a paraphrase of (14b): (14b) is consistent with a materialistic view of the origin of the Earth, but (14b′) says that there was a Creator. In (14c), no one need have been responsible for your brother's death, whereas (14c′) brings in a murderer. Finally, (14d′) implies that someone other than Chomsky wrote *Syntactic Structures,* while (14d) is neutral with regard to its authorship (it is consistent with Chomsky having written it but could also be used even if the author were really someone else, just as many people persist in applying the name *Purcell's Trumpet Voluntary* to a composition that they know is really by Jeremiah Clarke).

If reduced passives are to be analyzed as having underlying subjects, the underlying subject must be something more indefinite than any expression of English is: it must be neutral with regard to whether it refers to one individual or more than one, with regard to whether it refers to human or nonhuman entities, and with regard to whether its referent is the same as or different from other individuals mentioned in the discourse. I will invoke a deus ex machina at this point and simply assume that such an element, hereby christened UNSPEC, is available, and will set up deep structures having UNSPEC as subject in the case of reduced passives:[5]

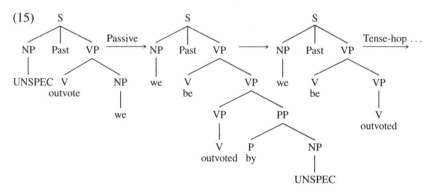

UNSPEC is subject to the constraint that it must not appear in surface structure; i.e., all occurrences of it must be eliminated in the course of a derivation if a well-formed surface structure is to result. There are other places where it will be necessary to invoke UNSPEC in underlying structures; for example, UNSPEC will be the underlying subject of the infinitive in sentences like *John is easy to talk to*.

One further matter that should be dealt with in this sketch of English passives is the alternative word orders found in sentences as in (16):

(16) a.   The demonstrators were ordered to disperse by the police.
    a'.   The demonstrators were ordered by the police to disperse.
    b.   ?I was told that pigs have wings by my teachers.
    b'.   I was told by my teachers that pigs have wings.
    c.   Smith was sentenced to 5 years' hard labor by the judge.
    c'.   Smith was sentenced by the judge to 5 years' hard labor.

The analysis as worked out so far in this section provides only for the word order in (16a, b, c), in which the *by*-phrase follows all constituents of the VP. How can this analysis be modified to provide for the word order of (16a', b', c'), in which the *by*-phrase is between the verb and another constituent of the VP? There are two fairly obvious possible answers to this question: (i) alter the passive transformation so that it provides for two (or more?) positions into which the *by*-phrase can be inserted, or (ii) retain the present form of Passive, but supplement it with a rule that converts the word order of (16a, b, c) into that of (16a', b', c'). The latter possibility has two variants—either (iia) posit a transformation that can move the *by*-phrase into the VP under certain circumstances or (iib) posit a transformation that can move certain constituents of the VP to the right of a *by*-phrase. It turns out that a transformation as in (iia) must be posited anyway to account for the word orders found in (17):

(17) a. John sent to his mother <u>the statue that he had spent the whole summer carving</u>.
    b. I arrived on Dec. 12 <u>in a city that I had always wanted to visit</u>.
    c. They continued for several months <u>to occupy the house</u>.

In each of these cases a "heavy" constituent of a VP either follows a constituent of the VP that it "normally" would precede (compare (17a) with the normal [V NP PP] word order of *John sent the statue to his mother*) or follows a constituent that modifies the whole VP (in (17b) *on Dec. 12* modifies *arrive in a city that I had always wanted to visit* and in (17c) *for several months* modifies *continue to occupy the house*). This transformation, which will be taken up in §15b, is known (misleadingly, since the moved constituent need not be a NP but can be a PP or a S or a nonfinite VP) as **heavy-NP-shift.** I will thus assume henceforth that sentences such as (16b) have derivations as in (17):

(18)

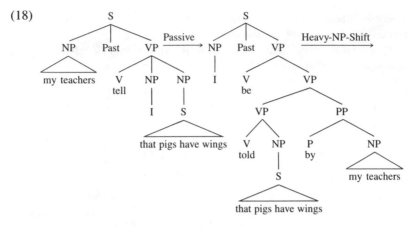

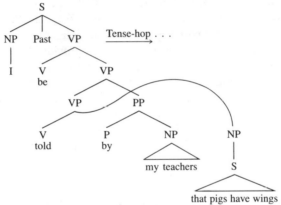

In the interests of accuracy, I have given the output of Heavy-NP-shift in (17) with the discontinuous structure that I will later argue that it has; i.e., Heavy-NP-shift makes certain heavy constituents of a VP follow certain constituents that they precede in its input, but does not alter the constituent structure.

b. There-*Insertion*

Existential *there* has an extremely restricted distribution. In relatively simple sentences, it occurs only in the position of the subject:[6]

(1) a.   There was a riot in Philadelphia last week.
    a'. *Someone caused there a riot in Philadelphia last week.
    b.   There occurred a tragic event yesterday.
    b'. *We experienced there a tragic event yesterday.

In certain more complex sentences it can appear in the position of a direct object; e.g., (2a) has a surface structure completely parallel to that of such sentences as *We believe Smith to be the culprit,* namely, (2b):

(2) a. We believe there to be an error in this proof.
  b.

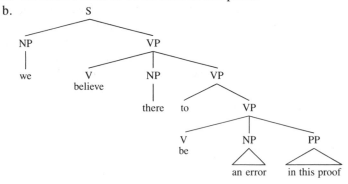

However, existential *there* can occupy that position only in constructions in which the direct object can be argued to be the subject of a subordinate S in underlying structure; e.g., (2a) can be argued to have an underlying structure (not its deep structure but, in virtue of the analysis of *there* to be given below, an intermediate stage of the derivation) in which *there* is part of an underlying embedded S *There is an error in this proof* in which it occupies subject position:

(3)

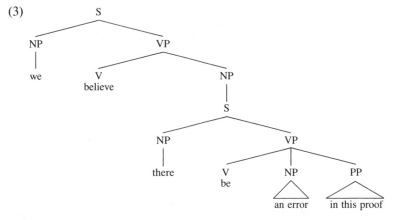

In the VP of which *there* is apparently the surface subject, a verb is directly followed by a NP that could otherwise serve as subject of that verb:

(4) a. There is a unicorn in the garden.
  a′. A unicorn is in the garden.

b. There occurred a tragic event yesterday.
b′. A tragic event occurred yesterday.
c. Deep within him there smoldered an unquenchable desire.
c′. An unquenchable desire smoldered deep within him.

The most common treatment of existential *there* in transformational grammar has been to account for these facts by means of a transformation (**There-insertion**) that inserts existential *there* in subject position (under certain conditions that will be sketched below) and moves the original subject into the VP in a position immediately following the verb, for example:

(5)

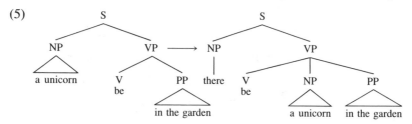

There-insertion is subject to the following conditions: First, the verb must have an appropriate meaning, typically one that ascribes existence or "visibility" to the subject:

(6) a. There arose/*ended a commotion.
    b. At the top of the hill there stood/*tottered a flagpole.
    c. Deep within him there burned an undying passion.
    d. To every action there corresponds an equal and opposite reaction.
    e. Behind that respectable façade there lurked a twisted mind.

As one might guess from the diversity of the verbs in (6), there are a fairly large number of verbs that allow *There*-insertion, notwithstanding a surprisingly widespread belief among linguists that only a few verbs allow it; indeed, there are well over a hundred such verbs. It should also be noted that the full range of uses of *be* allow *There*-insertion, even though not all of them fit the above semantic characterization of "*There*-insertion verbs":

(7) a. There is a unicorn in the garden.
    b. There is a child sick here.
    c. There was a man running down the road.
    d. There was a man executed yesterday.
    e. There's a meeting going to be held at 5:00.

Second, generally the verb may not be followed by another NP:[7]

(8) a.   There barked a dog.
    a′. *There shouted a man a curse.

b.   There were three persons successful.
b'. ??There were three persons successes.
c.   There are few students able to play the piano.
c'. *There are few students [competent pianists].

Third, to treat all instances of existential *there* as derived through an application of *There*-insertion, one must make the transformation obligatory in the important case of "pure existential" sentences with *be:*

(9) a.   There is a Santa Claus.
    a'. *A Santa Claus is.

Alternatively, the ungrammaticality of sentences like (9a') may reflect a condition not on the applicability of *There*-insertion but on the derived structure contexts in which *be* may occur: that *be* requires an additional constituent within its VP.

Fourth, *There*-insertion is often held to be subject to a restriction that the underlying subject be "indefinite," in view of contrasts in acceptability such as are noted in (10):

(10) a.   Yesterday there occurred a tragic event.
     b.   Yesterday there occurred two tragic events.
     c. *Yesterday there occurred that tragic event.
     d. *Yesterday there occurred every event of importance in John's life.
     e. *Yesterday there occurred the riot.
     f. *Yesterday there occurred Harry's attempt to seduce Elaine.

Giving an accurate characterization of the relevant understanding of "indefinite," however, is not easy. One cannot simply exclude the application of *There*-insertion when the subject NP is a proper noun or has *the, this, that, every,* etc. as determiner. There are, for example, several classes of sentences in which, in contrast with (10c, e), a subject NP with *the* or *that* does not inhibit *There*-insertion:

(11) a.   Mary: Who could we give our old lawnmower to?
           John: Well, there's that student next door, there's the guy who works for your uncle, . . .
     b.   Yesterday there occurred the most tragic event in decades.
     c.   There was the smell of rum on his breath.

There are reasonable grounds for claiming that examples like (11a), in which "definite" NPs are given as a list of answers to an explicit or implied question, illustrate a different phenomenon from the *There*-insertion that figured in the preceding examples.[8] For example, Milsark (1974) notes that such sentences are subject to the restrictions that the verb be existential *be* and that the underlying VP contain nothing besides that *be:*

(12) a. Mary: Did anything strange happen?
        John: *Well, there occurred the riot, . . .
    b. Mary: Did you notice anything strange?
        John: *Well, there was Fred on the roof, . . .

Examples such as (11b) can be held to show that "indefinite" must be given a semantic rather than a syntactic interpretation, in view of their allowing paraphrases containing what is by any standards an indefinite NP ('an event more tragic than any in decades', with an indefinite article). Examples such as (11c), which are discussed with considerable insight in Woisetschlaeger (1983), are much harder to characterize as "indefinite" without great arbitrariness.

    For the present, I will leave unresolved the question of what exactly the restriction on the underlying subject NP is that is reflected in examples like (10). I note that whatever the relevant distinction is, it is at least partly semantic, in view of the fact that "generic" and "existential" uses of bare plural NPs behave differently:

(13) a. There are books out of stock.
    b. Books are out of stock.

While (13b) allows both generic ('Books generally are out of stock') and existential ('Some books are out of stock') interpretations, (13a) has only the existential interpretation, and thus only one of the two senses of a sentence like (13b) can be allowed to undergo *There*-insertion.

c. Quantifier-float

The term **quantifier** refers to a class of words that introduce NPs (i.e., they are included in what we have been referring to as "determiners") and indicate how much or what part of something a given "propositional function" is true of:

(1) a. John played all of the Chopin études.
    b. Many philosophers play chess.
    c. Each student gave a talk in the seminar.
    d. Most linguists play musical instruments.

For example, (1a) says that the propositional function "John played x" is true for all values of x in the class "the Chopin études," and (1b) says that the propositional function "x plays chess" is true of many values of x in the class "philosophers." *All, both,* and *each* have a property that distinguishes them from the other quantifiers,[9] namely, that they can also occur in a position in which they appear to function syntactically as adverbs:

(2) a. All/Most of the Chopin études give me great pleasure.
  a'. The Chopin études all/*most give me great pleasure.
  b. Each/One of the guests made a speech.
  b'. The guests each/*one made a speech.
  c. Both of Tom's hands were filthy.
  c'. Tom's hands both were filthy.

In such examples, *all, both,* and *each* retain the semantic function of quantifiers, e.g., (2a: *all*) [10] says that "*x* gives me great pleasure" is true for all values of *x* in the class "the Chopin études." When adverbial *all, both,* or *each* is at the beginning of a VP, it is always interpreted in relation to the subject NP; e.g., (3a) allows only the paraphrase "All the boys waved at the girls," not "The boys waved at all the girls," and (3b) allows only the paraphrase "Each of the visitors gave the children a dollar," not "The visitors gave each of the children a dollar":

(3) a. The boys all waved at the girls
  b. The visitors each gave the children a dollar.

Each can also occur after a direct object NP, in which case it is ambiguous between an interpretation that relates to an indirect object NP and one that relates to the subject NP, or it can be between indirect and direct object NPs, in which case it has an interpretation relating to the indirect object NP:

(4) a. The visitors gave the children a dollar each.
  b. The visitors gave the children each a dollar.

That is, (4a–b) both allow an interpretation 'The visitors gave each of the children a dollar', and (4a) additionally allows the interpretation noted above for (3b). These extra possibilities are not available for *all* and *both*. In the remainder of this section I will ignore the word orders in (4).

I will account for the occurrence of *all/both/each* in adverbial positions and their semantic interpretation when used adverbially by positing a transformation (called **Quantifier-float**) that optionally removes *all/both/each* from a subject NP and moves it into an adverbial position. Saying exactly what Quantifier-float does will consist largely in saying what exactly the "adverbial position" is into which the quantifier is moved. The following examples provide evidence that the combination of a "floated" quantifier and a following VP is a syntactic constituent, presumably itself a VP, so that the effect of Quantifier-float is as in (5d):

(5) a. The neighbors either [all like punk rock] or [all want to annoy me].
  b. What the children did was [all make obscene gestures].

c. I want your friends to [all/each/both apologize to me].

d.

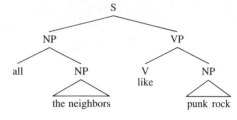

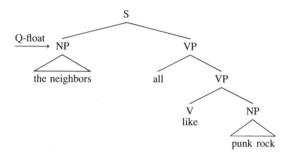

The examples discussed so far have not involved auxiliary verbs. Where there are auxiliary verbs, floated quantifiers generally can occur before, between, or after them: [11]

(6) a.   The children all were singing.
    a′.   The children were all singing.
    b.   The children all have been vaccinated.
    b′.   The children have all been vaccinated.
    b″. ?The children have been all vaccinated.
    c.   We all have been robbed many times.
    c′.   We have all been robbed many times.
    c″.   We have been all robbed many times.
    c‴.   We have been all given eviction notices many times.
    d.   The neighbors all must have been sleeping.
    d′.   The neighbors must all have been sleeping.
    d″.   The neighbors must have all been sleeping.
    d‴.   The neighbors must have been all sleeping.

By contrast, main verbs generally cannot be followed by floated quantifiers:

(7) a.   *His parents admire both Billy Graham.
    b.   *The speakers denounced each the president.
    c.   *The guests enjoyed all every dish they were served.

Certain sentences that appear at first glance to have a floated quantifier following a main verb demand an analysis in which the quantifier is floated not from the subject of that verb but from the understood subject of an embedded S. For example, (8a, b) have deep structures corresponding not to (8a', b') but rather to (8a'', b''):

(8) a.   They hope both to win prizes.

   a'. Both of them hope [they will win prizes].

   a''. They hope [both of them will win prizes].

   b.   The boys intend all to return.

   b'. All of the boys intend [they will return].

   b''. The boys intend [all of them will return].

For example, the derivation of (8b) will be roughly as in (9):

(9)

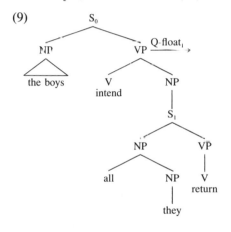

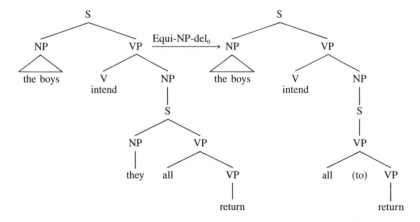

According to this proposal, the quantifier in (8a, b) gets to follow the verb of the main S not by being moved in relation to that verb but through deletion of the NP that (e.g., in the second tree in (9)) stood between it and that verb. Note that the claim that the deep structures of (8a, b) correspond to (8a″, b″) rather than to (8a′, b′) accords with what they mean, e.g., in (8b) the intention is that all of them return.

There is one additional case in which a floated quantifier follows a main verb, namely, that in which the main verb is *be* or the possessional sense of *have*.

(10) a.   The children are all hungry.
      b.   The speakers are all renowned philosophers.
      c.   % Your friends have all a lot of money.

These are in fact the main verbs that in general behave like auxiliary verbs with regard to the phenomena (such as Inversion: *Are the children hungry?*) that characterize auxiliary verbs, and they count as main verbs mainly because they are the **only** verbs of their clauses. It is thus reasonable to conjecture that their position in relation to floated quantifiers can be accounted for in the same way the position of true auxiliary verbs (as in (6)) can, and the analysis of auxiliary verbs to be given in chapter 8 will in fact account for examples like those in (10) (including the dialect variation in the acceptability of examples like (10c), which will correlate with variation in the acceptability of other examples in which main verb *have* is treated like an auxiliary verb).

There are several conceivable accounts of the multiple positions of the quantifiers in (6). (i) Perhaps Quantifier-float applies not only in the pristine form suggested above, where it makes a quantifier an adjunct to a VP, but can also put the quantifier in a position where it is separated by one or more auxiliary verbs from the VP. (ii) Perhaps Quantifier-float retains its pristine form but is supplemented by an additional transformation that permutes auxiliary verbs and floated quantifiers. (iii) Perhaps we can reanalyze auxiliary verbs in such a way that the pristine form of Quantifier-float will cover cases in which a floated quantifier precedes an auxiliary verb. For example, since I will ultimately argue that in the underlying structure each auxiliary verb is the main verb of its own S, each auxiliary verb will contribute to the deep structure a S that could in principle be a domain for the application of Quantifier-float. I will in fact argue in chapter 8 for an analysis meeting this last description, in which different positions of quantifiers in relation to auxiliary verbs will reflect differences with regard to what domain Quantifier-float applies to.

Before leaving the topic of Quantifier-float, I should note that not all sentences in which a quantifier follows a NP reflect that particular transformation. Note that *all* or *both* can follow a pronoun even if that pronoun is not the subject of its clause:

(11) a.   Arrau played them all.
    a'.   *Arrau played the Beethoven concertos all.
    b.   Arrau played them both.
    b'.   *Arrau played the Brahms concertos both.
    c.   I have listened to them all.
    c'.   *I have listened to the Beethoven sonatas all.

The word order in (11a, b, c) cannot be attributed to an application of Quantifier-float, since Quantifier-float, at least as we have encountered it so far, is not sensitive to whether the NP from which the quantifier is detached is a pronoun or a "full" NP. I maintain rather that the word order "pronoun *all/both*" is a variant of the word order "*all/both* NP" that is found in such expressions as *all my friends* or *both his hands*. Hitherto I have paid no attention to whether *of* appears in expressions such as *all (of) my friends* and *both (of) his hands*. Forms with and without *of* are both possible, except when *all/both* is combined with a pronoun, in which case only the form with *of* is possible:

(12) a.   All (of) his books have received good reviews.
    a'.   All of them have received good reviews.
    a''.   *All they/them have received good reviews.
    b.   Arrau played both of the Brahms concertos.
    b'.   Arrau played both of them.
    b''.   *Arrau played both them.

This gives us reason to conjecture that *they all, they both,* and so on fill the gap left by the unacceptable *all they,* and the like, i.e., that there is a transformation moving the quantifier of a Quantifier + Pronoun combination into a position after the pronoun. Confirmation for this conjecture is provided by the fact that *each,* which does not allow omission of *of,* likewise does not occur in the Pronoun + Quantifier combination: [12]

(13) a.   The *Times* reviewed each of/*∅ his books.
    a'.   *The *Times* reviewed them each.

I thus conclude that there is a transformation (**Quantifier-pronoun Flip,** in the terminology of Maling 1976) that postposes a quantifier to a sister pronoun, applying only to structures in which quantifier and NP are combined without any *of.* This conclusion, incidentally, implies that a sentence like (14a) has two different derivations (and correspondingly, two different surface structures), one involving Quantifier-float and one involving Quantifier-pronoun Flip:

(14) a. They all received good reviews.

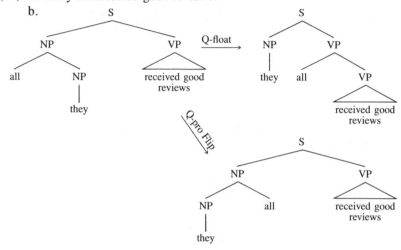

d. Extraposition

The last two transformations to be discussed in this chapter will require that this book get slightly ahead of itself, since both presuppose ideas about embedded Ss that are not developed until chapter 5. Specifically, we will assume here that the grammatical roles filled by NPs (e.g., that of subject) can also be filled by embedded Ss or, more correctly, by combinations of an embedded S and a **complementizer** such as *that* or *for . . . to.*

Let us consider, in particular, examples in which such a constituent figures as subject:

(1) a. <u>That John quit his job</u> surprised me.
   b. <u>That Fred is a lousy teacher</u> is obvious.
   c. <u>For you to leave so soon</u> would inconvenience us.
   d. <u>For John to quit his job</u> would be unthinkable.

Corresponding to each of these sentences there is a roughly synonymous [13] sentence that differs from it in having the complementizer + S combination at the end and an *it* in its place in subject position:

(2) a. It surprised me that John quit his job.
   b. It is obvious that Fred is a lousy teacher.

   c. It would inconvenience us for you to leave so soon.

   d. It would be unthinkable for John to quit his job.

We must take up two questions regarding this hypothesized transformation. First, under what conditions does it apply? And second, what is the derived constituent structure that it gives rise to? To answer the first question, let us start by enumerating the factors that could conceivably influence the applicability of Extraposition. For example, it might depend on what kind of embedded sentence we have. In (2) we have examples of extraposed *that* complements and *for-to* complements, but what about "possessive *-ing* complements" such as *John's quitting his job?* What about NPs that might be analyzed in terms of an embedded S other than a complement per se, e.g., "nominalizations" such as *John's resignation from his job?* What about relative clauses? The applicability of Extraposition could conceivably depend on what material the complement S is combined with. In (2) there are examples in which the VP is of the form [V NP] or [*be* AP], but what about VPs of forms other than those two? Does Extraposition apply only to **subject** complements, or does it also apply, e.g., to sentential direct objects?

Extraposition does not apply to possessive *-ing* complements or to nominalizations, though it does apply to interrogative complements:

(3) a.   John's quitting his job would surprise me.

     a'. *It would surprise me John's quitting his job.

     b.   John's resignation from his job came as a surprise.

     b'. *It came as a surprise John's resignation from his job.

     c.   Whether Bill can join us isn't clear.

     c'. It isn't clear whether Bill can join us.

The asterisks in (3a', b') refer to pronunciations in which there is no intonational break between the VP and the extraposed item and in which the main stress is on the last major word (here, *job*). There are acceptable sentences consisting of the same sequence of words but with the main stress on *surprise* and the following words pronounced on a low pitch. Such sentences involve not Extraposition but **Right Dislocation,** which can move not just a complement S but any sort of NP to the end, leaving in its place a corresponding pronoun:

(4) a. He's just bought a new cár, my uncle.

     b. It's unbéarable, the weather in Syracuse.

     c. It came as a surpríse, John's resignation from his job.

It is also possible to move restrictive relative clauses to the end of the sentence, though in this case nothing is left behind to fill the place of the moved item:

(5) a.   A man who was wearing a black cloak entered.
    a'. A man entered who was wearing a black cloak.
    b.   Anyone who wants to come over is welcome.
    b'. Anyone is welcome who wants to come over.

It will be argued in chapter 13, however, that "Extraposition of relative clauses" is a distinct phenomenon from the Extraposition dealt with hitherto in this section. In particular, it gives rise to a very different derived constituent structure. In anticipation of that result, I will adopt the policy of restricting the term "Extraposition" to the extraposition of complement Ss except where, by using terms such as "Extraposition of relative clauses" or "Extraposition of PPs," I will explicitly refer to other phenomena. The reader may wish to verify for himself that extraposed relative clauses behave differently from extraposed complements with regard to the phenomena taken up in (13)–(14) that provide grounds for our conclusions about the place of extraposed complement Ss in derived constituent structure.

For Extraposition of subject complements, the form of the VP is immaterial, subject to the qualification that Extraposition is avoided when it gives rise to certain awkward combinations that are generally avoided. For example, if there is both a subject complement and an object complement, extraposition of the subject complement gives rise to a derived structure in which the object complement is in the middle of the sentence:

(6) a.   That the corkscrew had blood on it proves that the butler is the
        culprit.
    a'. *It proves that the butler is the culprit that the corkscrew had blood
        on it.

Sentences having a S in the middle of a constituent are avoided regardless of whether Extraposition plays any role in them; e.g., while most sentences have cleft counterparts (7a–a'), the cleft construction is avoided when the "clefted" constituent, which occurs in the middle, is a S:

(7) a.   John sang "Melancholy Baby."
    a'. It was "Melancholy Baby" that John sang.
    b.   John believes that pigs have wings.
    b'. *It's that pigs have wings that John believes.

The following are some apparent instances of extraposition of direct object complements, and even of an indirect object complement (example from Jespersen 1937:§22.2):

(8) a. I took it for granted that George would help us.
   b. John regrets it that he quit his job.
   c. I can't help it that I'm madly in love with Edith.
   d. He never gave it a thought that Bolshies are human beings.

Some of these sentences have no nonextraposed counterparts (9a, c, d). However, the existence of the related sentences given in (9a′–a″, c′, d′) argues that the embedded Ss in question are in fact object complements:

(9) a. *I took that George would help us for granted.
   a′. What I took for granted was that George would help us.
   a″. I took only one thing for granted, namely, that George would help us.
   c. *I can't help that I'm madly in love with Edith.
   c′. What I can't help is that I'm madly in love with Edith.
   d. *He never gave that Bolshies are human beings a thought.
   d′ The one thing that he never gave a thought was that Bolshies are human beings.

Extraposition of object complements is fairly restricted, with many verbs not allowing their complements to be extraposed:

(10) a. My boss thinks (*it) that I'm indispensable.
   b. Ted denies (?it) that he had a fight with his wife.
   c. Smith conjectures (*it) that Japanese is a Dravidian language.

In some cases, Extraposition of an object complement makes a difference with regard to the meaning of the sentence. For example, while (11a) is neutral as to whether the Yankees actually won the pennant, (11b) presupposes that they did in fact win it (at least, for those speakers for whom (11b) is acceptable):

(11) a. Harry predicted that the Yankees would win the pennant.
   b. %Harry predicted it that the Yankees would win the pennant.

The most that can be said here about the extraposition of object complements is that it is irregular but is favored by two factors, namely, "factive" interpretation of the complement, as in (11b), and position of the complement in the middle of the VP, as in (9a, d), where Extraposition allows one to avoid surface structures in which an embedded S is in the middle of the VP.[14]

There is no consensus regarding the surface structure of sentences involving extraposed subject complements. All of the following have been proposed at some time or other:

(12) a.   (Ross 1967b)   b.   (Emonds 1976)

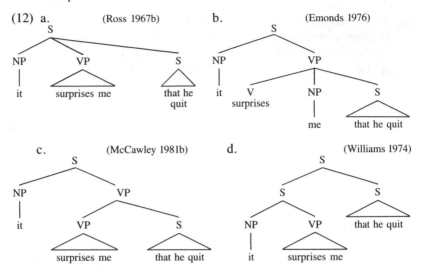

c.   (McCawley 1981b)   d.   (Williams 1974)

What little evidence can be marshalled in support of a choice among these alternatives favors (12c).[15] Both the original VP and the combination of it with the extraposed subject complement behave as units with regard to conjoining:

(13) a. It both surprised Alice and shocked Susan that John quit his job.
     b. It both surprised Alice that John quit his job and shocked her that
        he didn't seem concerned.

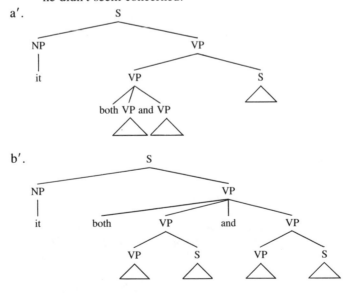

Reinhart (1983:50–52) provides the following examples in which movement transformations treat a combination of VP or AP and extraposed subject complement as a unit:

(14) a. I warned you that it would upset Rosa that you smoke, and <u>upset her that you smoked</u> it certainly did.
      b. <u>Unlikely that she would pass</u> though it was, Rosa still took the exam.

Determining whether a similar conclusion for extraposed object complements is warranted is left as an exercise.

e. Tough-*movement*

Sentences like those in (1) contain an "incomplete" VP:

(1) a. John is difficult for me to dislike.
     b. John is impossible for me to work with.
     c. These buttons are a bitch for anyone to sew onto overalls.
     d. The Kreutzer sonata is impossible to play on your violin.
     d'. Your violin is impossible to play the Kreutzer sonata on.

In each case the infinitive VP lacks a NP that otherwise may or must be present:

(2) a. I dislike John/*∅.
     b. I work with John/*∅.
     c. I sewed buttons/*∅ onto the overalls.
     d. I play (études) on your violin.
     d'. *I play the Kreutzer sonata on.

The missing NP corresponds to the surface subject of *be impossible/difficult,* etc. in the sense that the meanings of the sentences in (1) relate to my disliking John, to my working with John, to anyone sewing these buttons onto overalls, etc. Indeed, they allow close paraphrases[15] in which such a sentence appears intact as the subject of *be difficult,* etc.:

(3) a. For me to dislike John is difficult.
     a'. It is difficult for me to dislike John.
     b. For me to work with John is impossible.
     b'. It is impossible for me to work with John.
     c. For anyone to sew these buttons onto overalls is a bitch.
     c'. It is a bitch for anyone to sew these buttons onto overalls.
     d. To play the Kreutzer sonata on your violin is impossible.
     d'. It is impossible to play the Kreutzer sonata on your violin.

The form of the incomplete VP in sentences like (1) and the relationship of such sentences to their counterparts in (3) has generally been accounted for by transformational grammarians in terms of an analysis in which the sentences in (1) have deep structures essentially identical to those in (3) and there is an optional transformation (often called ***Tough*-movement**) that removes a NP from the complement of *difficult* etc. and makes it a derived subject. Several versions of *Tough*-movement have achieved some popularity, and there is no consensus as to a choice among them. In the version of *Tough*-movement proposed in Rosenbaum 1967, *Tough*-movement applies to a structure that has undergone Extraposition (as in (3a′, b′)) and replaces the *it* by a NP extracted from the VP of the complement S; combined with the conclusions about Extraposition arrived at in the last section, that proposal would yield derivations as in (4), ignoring for the moment the tense and the *for . . . to:*

(4)

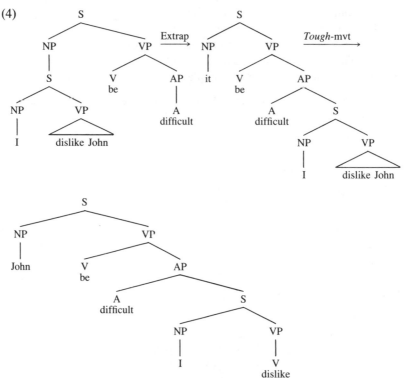

The version of *Tough*-movement proposed in Postal 1971 applies to a structure with a S in subject position (as in (3a)), replacing that S by one of its constituent NPs and concomitantly moving the residue of the embedded S to the end of the VP.[17] The derivations under Postal's proposals differ from (4) principally in the absence of the intermediate stage: for Postal, *Tough*-movement does not involve an intermediate step of Extraposition.

The principal argument that Postal offered against Rosenbaum's proposal was directed not against the derivation given in (4) but against a similar derivation that followed the consensus of mid-1960s transformational grammarians in taking extraposed complements to be daughters of the S-node (cf. §4d(12a)). With that constituent structure, Rosenbaum's version of *Tough*-movement would result in a surface structure in which *difficult for me to dislike*, etc. was not a constituent, but the available evidence shows that it is one; e.g., it can undergo VP-deletion or topicalization, be conjoined with an AP, or be the predicate constituent of a pseudo-cleft sentence:

(5) a. John is difficult for me to dislike, and Frieda is Ø too.
     b. Reliable, John isn't, but difficult for me to dislike he has always been.
     c. John is both witty and difficult for us to dislike.
     d. What John has always been is [impossible for anyone to work with].

However, if Rosenbaum's proposal is combined with the version of Extraposition adopted in §4d, it is consistent with the acceptability of the examples in (5). To my knowledge, there is in fact no substantial basis for a choice either way between the versions of *Tough*-movement with and without the intermediate step of Extraposition. In this book I will remain agnostic regarding the choice between them and will simply adopt the one that I happen, through historical accident, to be used to, namely Postal's version, which does without the intermediate stage in (4).

Two constraints on the application of *Tough*-movement should be mentioned here. First, the NP extracted from the embedded S cannot be its subject:

(6) a.   It's difficult for John to read your handwriting.
     a'. *John is difficult to read your handwriting.

Second, *Tough*-movement requires an appropriate predicate element: it is permissible only with a predicate adjective (or predicate NP) that expresses how easy or difficult the action denoted by the complement S is (or at least marginally, the extent to which there are obstacles to performing it), and not all predicate elements whose meanings fit this description in fact allow it, e.g., *possible* does not:

(7) This book is $\left\{\begin{array}{lll} \text{tough} & \text{?barely possible} & \text{*praiseworthy} \\ \text{easy} & \text{a snap} & \text{*kind} \\ \text{simple} & \text{a breeze} & \text{?legal} \\ \text{hard} & \text{a bitch} & \text{?illegal} \\ \text{difficult} & \text{a piece of cake} & \text{?necessary} \\ \text{impossible} & \text{a pain in the ass} & \text{?essential} \\ \text{*possible} & & \end{array}\right\}$ to read.

Some of the examples above (e.g. (7)) have not contained any overt subject of the infinitive. I will treat such examples the way that I treated reduced passives in §4a, namely, by positing an underlying subject ('UNSPEC') that is obligatorily deleted in the course of the derivation.

There is one major respect in which the treatment of *Tough*-movement given in this section is an oversimplification. Berman (1973) presents evidence that in at least some *Tough*-movement sentences the underlying predicate constituent is not simple (e.g., *hard*) but complex (e.g., *hard for John*; *John* is then an "object" of the adjective rather than the subject of the infinitive) and that the NP of the predicate constituent controls deletion of the subject of the embedded S, so that the deep structure is as in (8a) and the surface structure as in (8b):

(8) a.

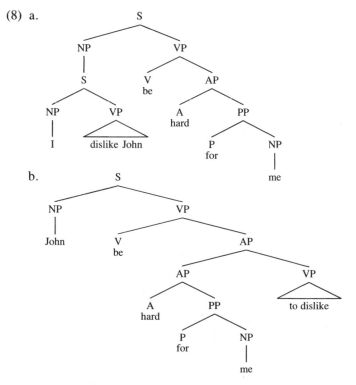

However, this issue will not be pursued here, since it has little bearing on the uses of *Tough*-movement that will be made below.

I will take no stand here on the relationship between *Tough*-movement and the construction involving prenominal adjectives illustrated in (9):

(9) a.   *Ulysses* is a difficult book to read.
    b.   Nancy is an easy person to get along with.
    c.   Oscar was a stupid person to invite.
    c'. *Oscar was stupid to invite.
    d.   Pickled garlic was an unusual thing to ask for.
    d'. *Pickled garlic was unusual to ask for.

As (9c, d) indicate, a considerably broader range of adjectives allow that construction than allow the *Tough*-movement construction proper.

EXERCISES

1. Give the deep structures and derivations for the following sentences according to the analyses developed so far in this book:
    a. The culprits all were caught by the police.
    b. It is believed that Lenin was gay.
    c. There was a prisoner shot by the guards.
    d. Those books both are hard for us to read.
    e. Extravagant claims are easy for people to be fooled by.

2. Find 6 verbs other than those discussed in the text that allow *There*-insertion, and give example sentences that demonstrate that they allow it.

3. Check the correctness of the claim made in §4d that subject complements can be extraposed regardless of the internal form of the VP. Be sure to give a broad selection of the different forms of VPs that can be combined with a sentential subject.

4. a. The illustrations given above of Quantifier-pronoun Flip all had *they* as the pronoun. Test how general the rule is by making up examples using other personal pronouns and demonstrative pronouns.
    b. Give examples to show whether Quantifier-pronoun Flip can apply when *almost all* is the quantifier.

5. Construct examples from which one can determine whether extraposed **object** complements are Chomsky-adjoined to the VP, i.e., whether their surface position in the constituent structure is as in §4d(12c).

6. a. Give the derivation that, according to the analyses developed so far in this book, the following sentence should have:

There are many persons difficult for us to talk to.

b. In much of this book, it is assumed that sentences with the same deep structure have the same meaning. Show that the above sentence poses a problem for that assumption, i.e., show that among the sentences that (according to the analyses in this chapter) are supposed to have the same deep structure as that sentence, there is at least one that is clearly different from it in meaning. Your answer should include a succinct statement of the difference between the meanings of the sentences. (The resolution of this problem constitutes exercise 4b of chap. 18.)

7. In what respects are sentences with *worth,* such as *This book is worth ordering a copy of,* like the *Tough*-movement sentences considered in this chapter, and in what respects are they unlike them?

8. Conceivably sentences like (i) could be analyzed as instances of *Tough*-movement (cf. (ii)):

i. This novel took me 3 years to write Ø.
ii. It took me 3 years to write this novel.

Alternatively, one might want to analyze them (as some have) as having a deep structure of the form below, with the subject of S_0 controlling deletion of a NP in the VP of S_1 (NB: not deletion of the subject of S_1).

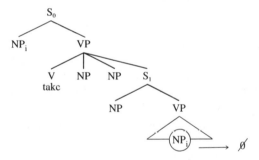

Construct examples involving funny NPs that have a bearing on the choice between these alternatives.

9. Examples like the following are among the diverse counterexamples given in Bolinger 1974 to the generalization that the NP that becomes subject of the passive is the first NP after the verb in the active:

This paper has been written on one side of.
We were made a fuss over.
Several houses were set fire to recently.

Suggest how either the examples could be made to conform to the generalization or the generalization could be weakened (though not rendered vacuous) so as to accommodate those examples, and construct additional examples that will test the correctness of your suggestion(s).

10. For any language other than English (your native language, if that is not English),

    a. Give a rough description of the class of sentences that is most closely analogous to English passive sentences.

    b. Make up analogues to a selection of the examples given in §4a. Where discrepancies arise between your language and English (i.e., where one of the two languages allows something that the other one does not), suggest a generalization about how your language differs from English and make up examples that will test that generalization. (Do not write more than a couple of pages on this question: this is an assignment for a syntax course, not a request for an M.A. thesis.) Note: in this and all subsequent assignments that call for data in foreign languages, follow the model of §2e(2, 10) for presenting the examples.

NOTES

1. The * versions of (3c–c′) are acceptable if the meaning is that the discussion of the president's reputation took up an hour. This is an instance of the parallelism claimed here: the acceptability of either interpretation of (3c′) matches that of the corresponding interpretation of (3c). A qualification must be added to the statement that the *by*-phrase is optional, since without the *by*-phrase (3c′) is in fact quite odd:

    i. ??An hour was taken up.

The oddity of (i) is due to its pointlessness: time is always taken up by anything that takes place, and thus no information is conveyed by saying that time is taken up unless some indication is given of what it is taken up by. Here as elsewhere, the statement that something is optional does not imply that it is immaterial whether the option is taken. In many cases an option that a language makes available to its users defeats a user's purposes and for that reason is avoided.

2. This brief discussion does not even hint at the remarkable syntactic and semantic diversity that is to be found in English dative constructions, details of which are given in Green 1974.

3. This statement and the preceding discussion presuppose that *John was sold a car* corresponds to an active form *(They) sold John a car* and *A car was sold to John* corresponds to *(They) sold a car to John,* and not vice versa. That assumption is shown to be correct when one considers verbs that allow only one of the two active forms:

    A passerby reported the accident to the police.
    *A passerby reported the police the accident.
    The accident was reported to the police by a passerby.

    *The police were reported the accident (to) by a passerby.
    The judge spared the defendant the ordeal. (example from Dowty 1979)
    *The judge spared the ordeal to/from/of/. . . the defendant.
    The defendant was spared the ordeal by the judge.
    *The odreal was spared (to/from/of/. . .) the defendant by the judge.

The unacceptable passive form is in each case the one that (according to the above assumption about which passives correspond to which actives) corresponds to the unacceptable active form.

    4. This sentence should not be confused with the completely normal *The transmitter seems to have been damaged by the storm.* The latter sentence is not a passive of (11b) but rather involves application of Passive to the embedded S, i.e., it consists of *seem* plus *the transmitter has been damaged by the storm.*

    Languages in fact differ with regard to whether passives of structures as in (12a) are possible: Timberlake (1982) and Keenan and Timberlake (1985) report that Lithuanian and Turkish allow analogs to (11a′).

    5. Since a serious treatment of tenses is not given until §8a (it must wait until we have covered certain material in chaps. 5–7 that the analysis of tenses presupposes), tenses will be omitted from most of the structures given in chaps. 4–7. However, in this section, tenses are included in the structures and an application of Tense-hopping is indicated in the derivations, to remind the reader that a full account of the sentences discussed here will have to include tenses.

    6. The existential *there* treated in this section must be distinguished from locative *there*. Locative *there* can be paraphrased as *that place* (or *in/to/. . . that place*), whereas existential *there* cannot. Paraphrases (i′, ii′) can be given for (i, ii), whereas no such paraphrases are available for (1a, b):

      i. John lives there.
      i′. John lives in that place.
      ii. John went there.
      ii′. John went to that place.

Existential *there* can be combined with *here,* while locative *there* cannot:

      iii.   There is some food here.
      iv. *There, we live here.

    7. One does, however, find such examples as *There were few persons still his friends* (Paul Deane, personal communication). The acceptability of this example is enhanced both by the intervening adverb *still* and by the fact that *his friends* here expresses an "ephemeral" rather than a permanent property. This latter distinction is invoked by Milsark (1974) in accounting for such contrasts as:

    There were several persons sick/*tall.

    8. The treatment of *There*-insertion so far has implicitly assumed that there is **only one** *There*-insertion transformation. Milsark (1974) argues that besides *There*-insertion constructions having the underlying subject immediately after the verb, as

in the examples cited in this section, there is a separate construction having the underlying subject at the end of the VP, as in *There stood on the lawn a huge bull-dog.* Lakoff (1987) argues that there are a large number of *There* constructions that are distinct but related, in the sense that more "basic" constructions serve as proto-types on which less basic constructions are modeled, with some but not all of the syntactic and semantic conditions on the more basic construction carrying over to the less basic one.

9. This characteristic is shared by "hedged" versions of *all* such as *almost all:*

The students almost/practically/virtually/nearly all failed the exam.

All can in addition be used as an adverb meaning "completely," as in *I was all tired out* (≠ **All of me was tired out*). Sentences like (i) are ambiguous between an interpretation in which *all* is a floated quantifier (*All of the biscuits were soggy*) and one in which it is the adverb (*The biscuits were completely soggy*); if *all* is not adjacent to a word that the adverbial sense could modify, only the interpretation as a floated quantifier is possible (i'):

    i. The biscuits were all soggy
    i'. The biscuits all were soggy.

10. When I wish to refer to one specific example of a set that is grouped to-gether by means of () or /, I will use the notation that is introduced here, e.g., (2a: *all*) means "the version of (2a) that has *all.*"

11. Different positions of floated quantifiers often correspond to differences in meaning, specifically to a difference in what the "scope" of the quantifier is. For example, (6c″) has a meaning referring to all of us being robbed together, whereas (6c–c') have meanings referring to each of us individually being robbed many times. Such correspondences between the positions of quantifiers and their seman-tic interpretations will be accounted for in chap. 18.

12. This fact was first noted in Maling 1976. The transformation referred to here as Quantifier-pronoun Flip was first proposed by Postal (1974:109–18), under the name "Quantifier Postposing."

13. The principal respect in which the synonymy is not exact is that the embed-ded S counts as "old information" in (1) but as "new information" in (2); e.g., (1a) would be a normal thing to say if John's quitting his job is already under discussion but would be abnormal if it serves to introduce John's quitting into the discus-sion. In the latter case, (2a) is normal. More generally, in English and most other languages (though not all languages [see Tomlin and Rhodes 1979 for ample dem-onstration that Ojibwa behaves otherwise]), old information must precede new in-formation unless special devices (such as the destressing of old information in *It surprised me that John quit his job*) are used to mark an item as new or as old information. This principle influences a speaker's choices among the options that the language makes available.

14. See Bolinger 1977 for enlightening discussion of differences in meaning between object complements with and without extraposition.

15. The term **Chomsky-adjunction** is used for a step in which an $[_x$ X Y] or $[_x$ Y X] configuration results from adjunction of an item of category Y to an item of category X. We will thus describe Extraposition as Chomsky-adjoining the complement S to the VP, and Quantifier-float as Chomsky-adjoining the quantifier to the VP.

16. The paraphrases are not exact as regards the "topic" of the sentence; e.g., (1d) contrasts the Kreutzer sonata with other compositions, (1d') contrasts your violin with other instruments, and (3d) contrasts playing the Kreutzer sonata on your violin with doing other things. See Lasnik and Fiengo 1974 for other respects in which the two sets of sentences may fail to be exact paraphrases.

17. In the latter version, *Tough*-movement is what relational grammarians call an "Ascension": a derivational step in which part of a constituent takes on the grammatical function of that constituent (here, part of a subject clause takes on the function of subject). According to that proposal, it is predictable that the residue of the embedded S is "demoted" to status as a VP-constituent lacking any true "grammatical relation" to its clause.

⁞⁞⁞⁞⁞⁞ 5. Complements

a. Full Complements

In the following examples, something identifiable as a sentence plus markers of subordination serves as subject of a clause.

(1) a. <u>That Reagan got so many votes</u> surprised me.
   <u>That Bill can't handle the job</u> is obvious.
   b. <u>For it to start raining now</u> would be a disaster.
   <u>For John to believe such a lie</u> is unthinkable.
   c. <u>Smith's refusing our offer</u> took us by surprise.
   <u>Germany's invading Poland</u> set off World War II.
   d. <u>Children drinking wine</u> is unheard of here.
   <u>Otto already knowing Marcia</u> is something we hadn't counted on.
   e. <u>How the cat got into the pantry</u> isn't clear.
   <u>Whether Schwartz will be fired</u> hasn't been decided yet.

   In (1a), the subject has the form *that* + S, where the S can be any declarative sentence. That the whole expression *that* + S and not just the S is the subject is shown by the fact that it is that whole expression that corresponds to the subject in such sentences as:

(2) a. <u>What</u> surprised me is <u>that Reagan got so many votes</u>.
   b. <u>The only thing</u> that surprised me is <u>that Reagan got so many votes</u>.
   c. Did <u>anything</u> surprise you in the results of the 1980 election? Only
      <u>that Reagan got so many votes</u>.

The constituent structure of *that NP VP* can be argued to be as in (3a) and not as in (3b), i.e., the S retains its identity as a unit separate from the *that*:

(3) a.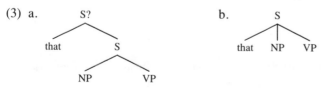

For example, the S can serve as the locus of conjoining, as in (4a), which

109

presumably involves a constituent with the structure as in (4a′), and can be factored out from the rest of the sentence by Right-node-raising (4b):

(4) a.   That the price of gas went up and the price of gold went down isn't surprising.

a′.

b.   I didn't even ask whether, let alone assert that, the governor would soon resign.

Note in addition that the main verb in (4a), *isn't*, takes a singular number agreement form (replacing it by *aren't* would result in ungrammaticality), whereas a similar sentence in which each conjunct has its own *that* allows plural number agreement:[1]

(5) That the price of gas went up and that the price of gold went down aren't surprising.

This sentence differs in meaning from (4a): (5) says that the rise in the price of gas and the fall in the price of gold are each individually not surprising, whereas (4a) says that their conjunction is not surprising. If these examples are discussed in terms of structures as in (3a), they can be treated as reflecting a difference between a conjoined S used as a subject (4a = 6a) and conjoined subjects, each of which is a S (5 = 6b):

(6) a.   b.

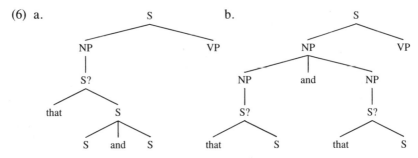

The subject in (6a) is singular, just like any sentential subject, while the subject in (6b) is plural, just like most conjoined subjects.

   Facts parallel to those in (2) can be cited as evidence that the underlined expressions in (1b–c) are likewise syntactic constituents. Their internal constituent structure, however, is not so obvious, and a diverse range of structures for "*for-to* complements," as in (1b), have been proposed, of which those in (7) are a sample:

(7) a. S?   b.   S   c.   S

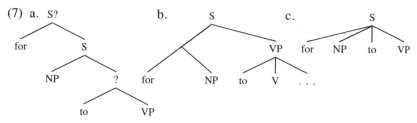

The possibilities for conjoining provide evidence for the (7a) structure; i.e., (8a) provides evidence that *for* is separate from the remainder of the construction, (8b) provides evidence that the combination of *to* and VP is a constituent, and (8c) provides evidence that the VP with which the *to* is combined retains its identity as a constituent.

(8) a. For either [John to tell Bill such a lie] or [Bill to believe it] is outrageous.

    b. For John either [to make up such a story] or [to repeat it] is outrageous.

    c. For John to either [make up such a story] or [repeat it] is outrageous.

Note, incidentally, that according to this conclusion, *to* is an adjunct not of the **verb** but of the verb **phrase,** contrary to the popular belief that *to* is an inflectional marker on the verb.

The VP in (1b–d) bears no tense marker. The NP and VP plus the missing tense are in each case what would make up an independent sentence.[2] Not every NP and VP that could make up an independent S can occur in these constructions. First, the underlined constructions in (1b–d) do not admit a modal auxiliary verb:

(9) a. *For it to will start raining soon is something to worry about.

      *For you to must shine your boss's shoes is outrageous.

      (Cf. For you to have to shine your boss's shoes is outrageous.)

    b. *Smith's maying refuse our offer worries me.

      (Cf. That Smith may refuse our offer worries me.)

    c. *Students canning sue their professors is a recent development.

      (Cf. Students being able to sue their professors is a recent development.)

Second, in the "Poss -*ing*" complement of (1c), the NP may not be *this, that, here, there,* nor any of the constructions listed in (1):

(10) a. *This's annoying George amuses me.

      (Cf. That this annoys George amuses me.)

   b. *Here's being a good place to hide the money was not suspected.

      (Cf. That here was a good place to hide the money was not suspected.)

   c. *Germany's invading Poland's meaning a world war was obvious to everyone.

      (Cf. That Germany's invading Poland meant a world war was obvious to everyone.)

However, these facts do not reflect syntactic restrictions on these constructions but rather morphological gaps in the paradigms of words that figure in them. Modal auxiliary verbs have no nonfinite forms, and *this, that, here, there,* and clauses do not have genitive case forms. The oddity of (9) is not a peculiarity of the complement constructions in (1b–d) but is shared by parallel examples formed with any other construction involving the infinitive or the *-ing* form of a verb, and the oddity of (10) is shared by any construction involving the genitive form of a NP:

(11) a. *With John maying know about your past, you should watch what you say to him.

      (Cf. With John possibly knowing about your past, . . .)

   b. *[Here's history]$_{NP}$ is very interesting.

      (Cf. This place's history is very interesting.)

   b. *This's implications are amazing.

      (Cf. The implications of this are amazing.)

One cannot exclude the examples in (10) by any restriction on deep structure, since sentences with the same deep structure but having a derivation in which something else becomes the subject of the embedded S are normal, e.g., *George's being annoyed by this amuses me*, in which Passive applies to the embedded S. We are free to take the constructions in (1b–d) as involving an underlying embedded declarative S that is subject to essentially no syntactic restrictions; as with all syntactic constructions, the surface structures will be constrained by the morphology: each word in the sentence must allow the morphological form that the surface form of the construction demands.

The hypothesis that (1b–d) have an underlying structure with an embedded S is confirmed by the fact that the NP of *for NP to VP* or *NP('s) VP-ing* can be a funny NP, with the VP providing the material required for the occurrence of the NP:

(12) a. For <u>the cat</u> to <u>get out of the bag</u> would be disastrous.
　　b. <u>Your leg</u> being <u>pulled</u> didn't surprise me.
　　c. For <u>it</u> to <u>rain</u> now would spoil the day completely.

Likewise, the NP and VP can make up a transformationally derived structure:

(13) a. John's being fired by the manager came as no surprise to any of us.
　　b. For there to be an error in the proof would be horrible.
　　c. For it to get out that Sam has a prison record would only add to his problems.
　　d. Your children all being arrested was a real shock.

The subject of the sentences in (13) is composed not just of any NP and any VP but of the NP and VP that would result from applying Passive, *There*-insertion, Extraposition, or Quantifier-float to an underlying S. Under the hypothesis that there is an embedded S and that all Ss can serve as domain for the application of transformations, the existence of sentences like those in (13) is predicted. Without that assumption, it is hard to see, for example, what would insure that *there* could be combined only with VPs of the form that is derived by *There*-insertion.

The examples in (1e) are the only instances given so far of an embedded nondeclarative S, here an interrogative S. A couple of differences between independent questions and the embedded interrogatives of (1e) should be noted. Only independent questions have Inversion (i.e., auxiliary verb before subject), and embedded yes-no questions are introduced by *whether* or *if,* which is not used in independent questions:

(14) a.　How did the cat get into the pantry?
　　a'.　*How the cat got into the pantry?
　　b.　I wonder whether/if Schwartz will be fired.
　　b'.　*Whether/*If Schwartz will be fired?
　　b".　Will Schwartz be fired?

The various expressions illustrated in (1) also can serve as direct objects:

(15) a. I didn't expect <u>that Reagan would get so many votes</u>.
　　　Everyone claims <u>that Bill can't handle the job</u>.
　　b. I prefer <u>for people to call me in the evening</u>.
　　　We would hate <u>for you to do all that work for nothing</u>.
　　c. Most of my relatives opposed <u>Linda's marrying Rex</u>.
　　　Hardly anyone predicted <u>Truman's winning of the 1948 election</u>.

d. I heard <u>George yelling at his wife</u>.
I saw <u>Mark being beaten up by three goons</u>.
e. Tom asked <u>whether anyone had seen Geraldine</u>.
This hypothesis explains <u>why birds have feathers</u>.

The constructions in (1c−e) can in addition serve as objects of prepositions, though the *that* clauses and *for-to* complements of (1a−b) cannot:

(16) a. *I'm ashamed of <u>that I neglected you</u>.
   b. *We're content with <u>for the cleaners to return the drapes next week</u>.
   c. Most of my relatives are shocked at <u>Linda's marrying Rex</u>.
   d. It would lead to <u>some noble gentleman marrying her</u>. (Hardy, *Tess,* cited by Jespersen)
   e. Bush is worried about <u>whether he can get the Armenian vote</u>.

That-clauses and *for-to* complements do, however, occur in sentences like (17):

(17) a. I'm ashamed that I neglected you.
   a′. I'm delighted that Marty finished his thesis.
   b. We're content for the cleaners to return the drapes next week.
   b′. I'm eager for you to visit us.

While no overt preposition precedes the embedded S in (17), the meanings of these sentences are parallel to those of sentences in which a preposition follows the adjective (e.g., (17a) might be paraphrased as *I'm ashamed of my neglectful treatment of you*), and indeed a preposition appears overtly when the embedded S is replaced by a pronoun or is made into the predicate element of a pseudo-cleft sentence:

(18) a. Aren't you ashamed that you neglected me?
     Of course I'm ashamed of/*∅ that.
   a′. What I'm ashamed of/*∅ is that I neglected you.
   b. Are you content for the cleaners to return the drapes next week?
     Yes, I'm content with/*∅ that—I don't need them until then.
   b′. What I'm most eager for/*∅ is for you to visit us.

This observation argues that the sentences in (17) have underlying structures in which the preposition has a sentential object and are parallel in underlying structure to sentences in which the same adjective is followed by a preposition and a nonsentential object:

(19) a. I'm ashamed of my past.
      b. Everyone's delighted about/at/over that development.
      c. We're content with the results.
      d. I'm eager for adventure.

I will henceforth assume such an underlying structure for the sentences in
(17) and will accordingly need to posit a transformation deleting a preposition whose object is a *that* or *for-to* complement:[3]

(20)

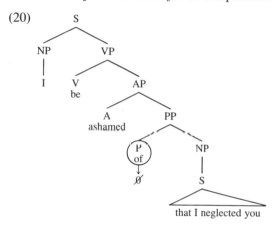

In the remainder of this book, I will use the following terminology. A
complement is a S (or better, a combination of S and possibly a marker of
subordinate status such as *that*) that stands in the grammatical relation of
subject, direct object, or indirect object of something.[4] I will take "object"
here in a broad sense that will cover the embedded Ss of (16)–(17), for
example. I will speak of *that I neglected you* as an object of *ashamed* in
(17a). A **complementizer** is an element that marks a constituent as a complement, e.g., *that* in (15a). There is no consensus regarding the application of the word "complementizer" to markers of subordinate status that
are inflectional (the genitive marker, *-ing,* and possibly *to*). For the time
being, I will speak of such elements also as complementizers, reserving the
right to alter that decision after their status becomes clearer.
    I will postpone until chapter 7 any serious discussion of the category of
the constituents in (3), (4), (6), and (7) that were marked with question
marks. For the present I will arbitrarily treat complementizers as "modifiers," that is, as combining with items of some category (S in the case of
that and *for,* VP in the case of *to,* NP in the case of *-'s*) to yield a constituent of the same category:[5]

(21)

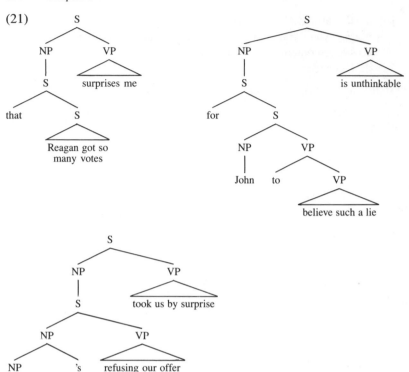

Several different positions have been taken on the issue of how complementizers fit into deep structure, the principal ones being: (a) that they do not occur in deep structure at all but are inserted by a transformation whose effect depends on the predicate element of a higher S (e.g., *deny* allows insertion of *that* but not of *for . . . to* into its complement); (b1) that they appear in deep structure in "Comp position," i.e., as adjuncts to the complement S, and *to, -ing,* and *-'s* are moved by a transformation from Comp position into their surface positions as adjuncts to a VP, a V, and a NP, respectively; (b2) that they appear in deep structure in their surface position (thus, with *to* as an adjunct to the VP); and (c) various combinations of the above, e.g., that *that* and *for . . . to* work as in (b1) but *-'s -ing* as in (a). Two problems are created by (b2) that are avoided under the other alternatives. First, (b2) demands a complication in analyses that involve transformationally inserted verbs, as in the treatment of passive Ss adopted in §4a, where passive *be* is inserted by a transformation. Note that in the derivation of (22) that would be forced on us if *-ing* were a deep structure adjunct of a verb, *-ing* would have to be moved from the main verb to the inserted *be*, since the main verb would be the only deep structure constituent available to bear the *-ing*.

(22) I was delighted at Smith's being awarded a prize by the committee.

Second, under the analysis of auxiliary verbs to be argued for in chapter 8, in which auxiliary verbs in deep structure are outside the Ss in which they appear, it will be possible to adopt a pristine form of the passive transformation, in which it applies to a [s NP VP] structure and (among other things) adjoins a *be* to the whole VP. However, if *to* is a deep structure adjunct to the whole VP, the transformation would have to treat the *to* as if it were not there and adjoin the *be* to the lower VP in derivations of sentences like (23):

(23) For Smith to be denied tenure is unthinkable.

I will accordingly eliminate (b2) from further consideration.

For present purposes, I will arbitrarily adopt (b1) and will thus treat (22)–(23) as having derivations as in (24), with steps in which *to, -'s,* and *-ing* are moved from Comp position to their surface positions:[6]

(24) a.

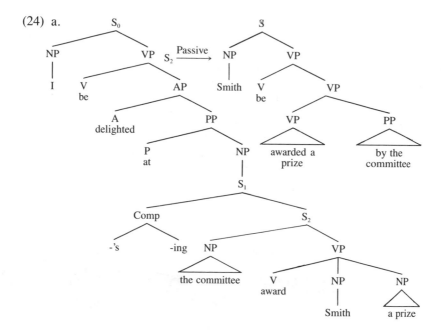

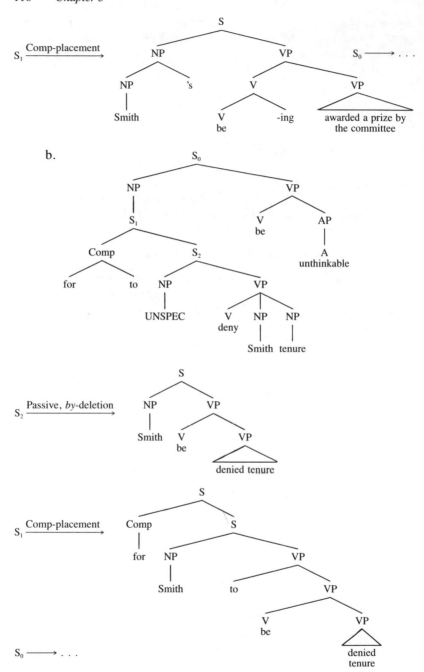

It should be kept in mind that no justification has been given for the tacit assumption made in this section that all the "complementizers" identified so far form a single syntactic category. If any reason presents itself for not treating all "complementizers" as fitting the same way into deep structure, we are perfectly free to modify our assumption (b1) in the direction of (c).

b. Reduced Complements

Let us now turn to cases in which a position where a full *for-to* complement or *-'s -ing* complement could appear is occupied by a VP in the *to*-infinitive or *-ing* form that lacks an overt subject:

(1) a. I am amazed <u>to find that this barbecued rattlesnake is delicious</u>.
       George expects <u>to be named chairman</u>.
       Alice is eager <u>to get to Toledo by noon</u>.
    b. I regret <u>having left</u> without <u>saying goodbye to you</u>.
       I'm ashamed of <u>having left without saying goodbye to you</u>.
       Amy enjoys <u>reading detective stories</u>.
(2) a. The money appears <u>to have been stolen</u>.
       The price of tantalum is likely <u>to go up next year</u>.
    b. George kept/continued <u>asking me for money</u>.
       Suddenly the students began <u>shouting obscenities</u>.

In each of these sentences the nonfinite VP not only is in a position in which (perhaps with different lexical items in the main clause) a full complement clause could occur but also has a form that the VP of a full complement clause can have. Accordingly, many linguists have analyzed these VPs as being reduced forms of full complements, with derivations that involve the deletion or extraction of the subject NP from a complement S. To see how exactly these sentences could be analyzed in terms of embedded full Ss, let us begin with the sentences in (1).

In each sentence in (1), the understood subject of the nonfinite VP refers to the same entity as does the subject of the main clause: the sentences refer to **my** finding that the barbecued rattlesnake is delicious, to **George's** being named chairman, etc. In many of these cases, parallel sentences exist in which the VP has an overt subject, perhaps with a different complementizer:

(3) George expects that he will be named chairman.
    Alice is eager for us to get to Toledo by noon.
    I regret my having left without saying goodbye to you.
    I regret that I left without saying goodbye to you.
    I'm ashamed that I left without saying goodbye to you.

The most obvious way to treat the nonfinite VPs in (1) as derived from underlying Ss is to set up an underlying structure having, in place of that VP, a S consisting of that VP combined with a subject NP that corresponds to that of the main clause, and to posit a transformation, generally called **Equi-NP-deletion,** that deletes the subject of the embedded S. To make this proposal explicit, we need to decide what exactly the deleted NP should be. If the underlying structures are to represent the meanings of the sentences in question correctly, that NP will have to be one **coreferential** to the main subject, i.e., a NP purporting to refer to the same entity as does the main subject.

There are several possibilities as to **which** such NP is the appropriate one. Should the hypothesized underlying subject be identical in form as well as reference to the main subject (i.e., should it be *George?*)? Should it consist of *the* or *that* plus an appropriate common noun (*the/that man*)? Should it be a personal pronoun (*he*)? The embedded S posited in sentences like (1) has often been taken to contain a NP identical to the main clause subject, but that policy is semantically unacceptable in many instances. For example, the meaning of (4a) cannot be paraphrased by (4b) (it is not possible for every contestant to win, and (4a) can be true without every contestant expecting that that impossibility will turn out true), while by contrast, it is accurately paraphrased by (4c), at least where (4c) is given an interpretation in which *he* has *every contestant* as antecedent, indicated here by the makeshift device of matched subscripts:

(4) a. Every contestant expects to win.
   b. Every contestant expects [every contestant will win].
   c. Every contestant$_i$ expects [he$_i$ will win].

I adopt provisionally the version of the Equi-NP-deletion analysis in which the missing NP in the hypothesized embedded S is a personal pronoun with the main clause subject as its antecedent (or, more generally, with the **controller** of the deletion as its antecedent; cases will be taken up shortly in which the deletion of the lower subject is "controlled" by something other than the subject of the main clause).

The following examples provide evidence that the sentences in (1) in fact have underlying structures involving embedded full Ss:

(5) a. Sam doesn't expect to be easy for those punks to intimidate.
   b. I was amazed to be informed that I had won $1000 in the lottery.
   c. George expects to be named chairman by the president.
   d. Alice is eager to be given a promotion.
   e. The boys are ashamed of all having left at the same time.
   f. I regret having been made to betray you.

Under the assumption that the derivations of sentences like *Sam is easy for those punks to intimidate* and *George was named chairman by the president* involve transformations (*Tough*-movement and Passive) that apply to a S and turn an item in its VP into its subject, the sentences in (5) require underlying structures that serve as domains to which those transformations apply, e.g., (5a) requires an underlying structure containing a S of the form "Those punks intimidate X" for *Tough*-movement to apply to, and (5c) requires an underlying structure containing a S of the form "The president names X chairman" for Passive to apply to. The Equi-NP-deletion analysis provides precisely such embedded Ss.

The proposed derivation for the sentences in (1) is given plausibility by the existence of analogous sentences as in (3) that have a full complement such as is posited here in the underlying structure. By contrast, the examples in (2) do not have corresponding forms with a full complement S:

(6) a. *The money appears for the jewelry to have been stolen.
     b. *The price of tantalum is likely for interest rates to go up next year.
     c. *George continued his brother's asking me for money.
     d. *Suddenly the students began the faculty's shouting obscenities.

This suggests that the sentences in (2) **do not** have derivations involving Equi-NP-deletion. The hypothesis that the predicate elements in (1) allow Equi-NP-deletion to delete the subject of an object complement under the control of the main subject, while those in (2) do not, is confirmed by the fact that only those in (2) allow a funny NP as subject with its supporting material in the nonfinite VP. For example, the predicate elements of (2) allow idiom-fragments, existential *there,* and ambient *it* as surface subject to be supported by material in the dependent VP, but those of (1) do not:

(7) a. My leg appears to have been pulled.
         The cat is likely to get out of the bag.
         My leg kept being pulled as long as I hung around with those jokers.
     b. There appears to be an error in the proof.
         There is likely to be a riot if Macnamara is made a trustee.
     c. It appears to be raining torrentially.
         It is likely to snow all day today.
         It kept snowing all night long.
(8) a. *My leg expected to be pulled.
         *The cat is eager to get out of the bag.
         *Aspersions expected to be cast on Smith's honesty.
     b. *There expected to be an error in the proof.
         *There is ashamed/eager to be a riot if Macnamara is made a trustee.
         *There were amazed to be doubts in my mind about his honesty.

  c. *It expected to be raining torrentially.
      *It was eager/ashamed to rain cats and dogs.
      *It regretted having snowed all night long.

The differences between (7) and (8) will be accounted for if the sentences in (2) are treated in such a way that the surface subject is not just coreferential with the underlying subject of the nonfinite VP, as in the case of (1), but indeed **is** its subject. Suppose that the sentences in (2) have deep structures in which the verb is combined with a sentential subject and that their surface structures are derived by a step (**Raising**) that breaks up the embedded S, making its subject into the derived subject of *appear, be likely,* etc. and moving the remainder of it into the VP,[7] as in the simplified partial derivation indicated in (9):

(9)

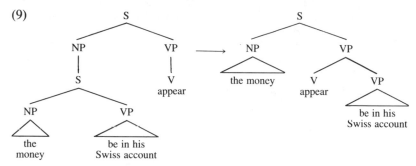

The precise details of the derivations of the sentences in (2) (as well as of those in (1)) will depend on an important matter that we have so far neglected, namely, that of how complementizers figure in the derivations of sentences like (1)–(2). Suppose that we adopt a policy of identifying the complementizers of reduced complements as much as possible with complementizers that occur in full complements. We then presumably must identify the examples in (1a) and (2a) as having *for-to* for the underlying complementizer, and those in (1b) and (2b) as having either *-'s -ing* or accusative + *-ing*. We must accordingly revise (9) in such a way as to provide for a *for-to* complementizer.

The only difficulty in making such a revision is in deciding what happens to the *for*. I will adopt here the treatment of *for* that will apply with the greatest generality to the full range of reduced complements to be taken up here, namely that in which the deletion or extraction of the subject of a *for-to* complement leaves behind a [*for to* VP] combination, and the *for* of such a combination is deleted. Thus, derivations involving Equi-NP-deletion into a *for-to* complement will be as in (10) and derivations involving **Raising** from such a complement will be as in (11), of which (9) is a simplified version:[8]

(10)

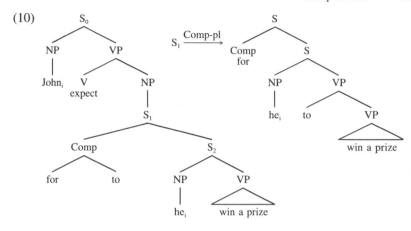

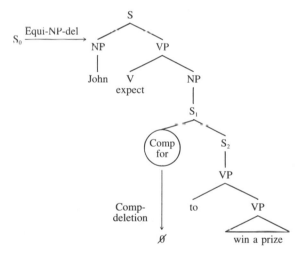

(11)

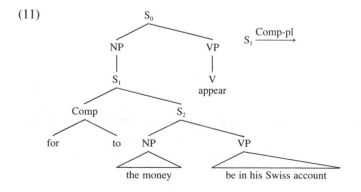

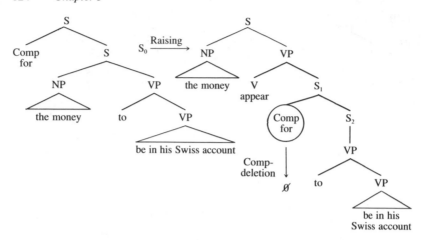

Note that for deletion of *for* in (11) to apply under the same conditions as in (10), Raising must be taken to have a somewhat different effect than it seems to have in (9): rather than consisting of movement of the lower VP into the higher VP, it consists in replacement of the complement (here, S_1) by its subject, with concomitant movement of the remainder of the complement, including the *for,* into the higher VP.[9]

Under the hypothesis that the predicate elements in (2) have sentential subjects that are broken up by Raising, the occurrence of funny NPs as surface subjects of those items is predicted: there is nothing to prevent the complement from being a S that has ambient *it,* existential *there,* or an idiom fragment as its (derived) subject, and the hypothesized step of Raising yields a derived structure in which the funny NP is in subject position in the main clause. By contrast, under the analysis argued for in the case of (1), no derivation of sentences with funny NP subjects (8) is possible, since there is no way to achieve the coreferentiality that is required for the application of Equi-NP-deletion that their derivations would have to involve. For example, if *for the cat to get out of the bag* were the deep structure complement of *eager,* its subject *the cat* would not be a personal pronoun and furthermore could not be coreferential with the subject of *eager:* even if *the cat* here were interpreted as having a reference (say, as referring to the secret that is revealed), it could have that reference only as a part of the expression *the cat (be) out of the bag,* and an occurrence of *the cat* as deep subject of *eager* would not be part of (a second occurrence of) that expression. Similarly, with the deep structure proposed here, *there* could be the surface subject of *expect* or *eager* only if *There*-insertion applied on the main clause, but that would result in such surface forms as *There expected three students to find an error in the proof* rather than sentences like (8b).

This proposal as to the difference between *expect/eager/*. . . and *appear/likely/*. . . in addition provides an account of a subtle but important difference between the semantic interpretations of sentences as in (12) and sentences as in (13):

(12) a. Most of the survivors appear to have been rescued.
     b. 500 Americans are likely to die in accidents this weekend.
(13) a. Several candidates expect to win the election.
     b. No one regretted having signed the petition.

The sentences in (12) allow both an interpretation in which the **scope** of the quantified NP is the whole sentence and one in which the scope is the hypothesized subordinate clause. For example, (12b) can be interpreted either with **wide scope,** as in (14a), that is, as saying that there are 500 Americans, each of whom is likely to die in an accident, or, more plausibly, with **narrow scope,** as in (14b), that is, as saying that it is likely that there will be 500 accident victims (which does not imply that any specific persons are likely candidates for accidents the way that (14a) does):[10]

(14) a. $(\exists: 500 \text{ American})_x$ [likely (x will die in an accident this weekend)]
     b. likely [$(\exists: 500 \text{ American})_x$ (x will die in an accident this weekend)]

By contrast, the sentences in (13) do not allow narrow scope interpretations, i.e., interpretations that refer to the proposition that several candidates will win the election or the proposition that no one signed the petition. For example, (13b) does not refer to regrets that no one signed the petition but in fact presupposes that some people did sign it and says that none of them regrets having done so. The sentences in (12) have deep structures in which *Most of the survivors have been rescued* (12a), and *500 Americans will die in accidents this weekend* (12b) figure as subordinate clauses, and their semantic interpretations are simply combinations of the meaning of the embedded sentence with the meaning of *appear, likely,* etc. However, in (13) the embedded sentence must have a pronominal subject (*They will win the election, He signed the petition*), and the quantifier is then not part of the embedded S.[11]

Let us now turn to some sentences in which a verb is followed by a NP in addition to an infinitive expression:

(15) a. Tom forced/persuaded/urged Dick to give him the money.
     b. The police believe George to be the culprit.

Alice expects the Yankees to win the World Series.
Einstein showed space to be curved.

While the sentences in (15a) have the same surface shape as those in (15b), differences in the possibility of combining them with funny NPs provide grounds for assigning the sentences in (15b) deep structures of a different shape from those in (15a):

(16) a. *The IRA persuaded there to be terrorists involved in the bombing.
    *The man next door urged my leg to be pulled.
    *Someone should force it to rain.
  b. The police believe there to be terrorists involved in the bombing.
    I don't expect my leg to be pulled.
    These photographs show it to have been raining at the time of the crime.

The difference between *force/persuade/urge* and *believe/expect/show* is parallel to that between *expect* and *appear.* In (15a) there is a NP that is in the main clause in deep structure and controls deletion of the subject of a complement clause (though here that NP is the direct object, whereas in the case of *expect* it was the subject), and in the other case (15b) the corresponding NP is an underlying constituent of a complement clause and takes on a role in the main clause (here the role of object, whereas with *appear* it was the role of subject) by being moved from the complement clause into the main clause:

(17) a.

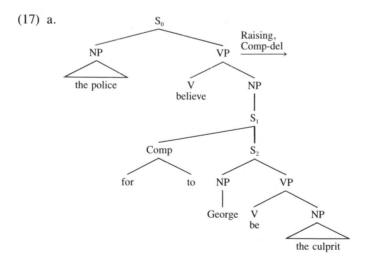

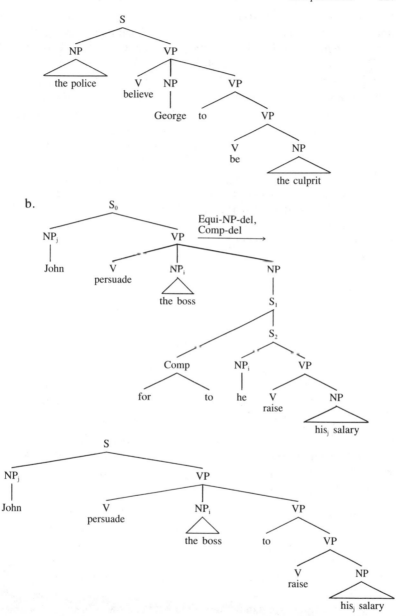

The transformations corresponding to the derivational steps given in (17a) and (17b) are commonly known as **Raising** and **Equi-NP-deletion,** a

terminological practice that presupposes that they are the same transformations as are involved in sentences with *appear* and *expect,* respectively. I
will remain neutral in this book with regard to whether "Raising to subject"
(as with *appear*) and "Raising to object" (as with *believe*) are instances of a
single phenomenon (and thus to be described in terms of the same transformation), as well as with regard to whether "Subject-controlled Equi-NP-
deletion" (as with *expect*) and "Object-controlled Equi-NP-deletion" (as
with *persuade*) are instances of a single phenomenon. Where the presup-
position that they are the same might be pernicious, I will use ad hoc names
to distinguish between them, as I did in the preceding sentence.

The difference in underlying structure posited in (17) is reasonable in
view of what *believe* and *persuade* mean: *believe* expresses a 2-place relation (a relation between a person and a proposition, as in corresponding
sentences with a *that*-complement: *The police believe that George is the
culprit*), whereas *persuade* expresses a 3-place relation (a relation among
two persons—persuader and persuadee—and something—it is not quite
correct to call it a proposition—of which the former person persuades the
latter). *Persuade* exhibits the three-place structure overtly when it occurs
with a *that* clause:

(18) a. Joan persuaded thc boss that the Yankees couldn't win the Series.
      b. Joan persuaded the boss that he should raise her salary.

As has often been noted, this treatment of the difference between *believe*
and *persuade* provides a natural account of the fact that while (19a) and
(19a′) are roughly synonymous (as synonymous as *Dr. Grimshaw treated
Otto* and *Otto was treated by Dr. Grimshaw*), (19b) and (19b′) are not:

(19) a.   The police believe Dr. Grimshaw to have treated Otto.
      a′. The police believe Otto to have been treated by Dr. Grimshaw.
      b.   Agncs persuaded Dr. Grimshaw to treat Otto.
      b′. Agnes persuaded Otto to be treated by Dr. Grimshaw.

In (19b) Agnes's persuasion is exercised on Dr. Grimshaw, in (19b′) on
Otto, which fits the deep structures required under the 3-place analysis of
persuade, in which the deep structures of (19b–b′) differ with regard to
whether *Dr. Grimshaw* or *Otto* is the deep object of *persuade.* By contrast,
under the analysis proposed here, (19a′) has the same deep structure as
(19a).[12]

The same difference can be identified between the following examples:

(20) a.   Mary talked John into going back to school.
      a′. Mary restrained John from shooting himself.
      b.   Mary prevented/kept John from shooting himself.

The verbs in (20b) allow as their surface objects existential *there* and idiom chunks, whereas those in (20a−a') do not:

(21) a.   *The mayor talked there into being a riot.
  a'.   *Mary restrained John's leg from being pulled.
  b.   The mayor kept there from being a riot.
  b'.   Mary prevented John's leg from being pulled.

The deep structures thus presumably differ along the following lines, with *John* controlling deletion of the embedded clause subject in (20a−a') and the *John* of the embedded clause being raised into main clause object position in (20b):

(22) a.

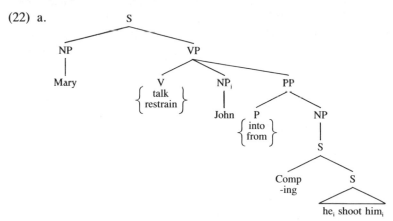

  b.

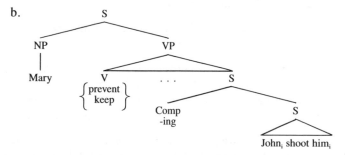

There is some unclarity as to what structure should intervene between the VP node and the lower S node in (22b), e.g., whether the S should be treated as object of a preposition the way that it is in (22a). *Prevent* allows the embedded S to take the form of a -'s -*ing* complement, but does not in that case allow *from*; and no related sentence exists in which the complement of *keep*[13] retains its identity as a constituent:

(23) a.   Mary prevented (*from) John's shooting himself.
     b. *Mary kept (from) John's shooting himself.

Tentatively I will assign to both *keep* and *prevent* deep structures in which the embedded S is the direct object and there is no preposition. Raising will be optional with *prevent* and obligatory with *keep,* and insertion of *from* will have to be made a concomitant of Raising.[14]

In the above discussion I have without comment spoken of *John* in (20b) and *George* in (15b) as the surface direct object of the verb. The proposition that these NPs are surface constituents of the main clause is in fact a matter of considerable controversy, with Postal (1974) arguing that they are (indeed, that they are derived direct objects of the higher verb) and Chomsky (1973) arguing that they are not: that the NP in question is in the embedded S in surface structure as well as in deep structure. I will make no attempt to present Chomsky's side in this dispute, since his account of the facts in question involves an approach to syntax and semantics that could be compared with the approach pursued here only at the expense of a digression that for this book would be inordinately long. The interested reader is referred to Chomsky 1973 and subseqent works for the details of that approach and to Bach 1977 for a critical evaluation of both approaches.

As evidence for the status of the NP in question as derived direct object of the main verb, let us compare sentences with *believe* and sentences in which a verb is followed by a NP that is clearly not a surface constituent of the main clause:

(24) a.   Mary believes George to be the culprit.
     b.   Mary favors Greenland being admitted to the UN.

The NP following *believe* is available for conversion into the subject of a passive clause, while the NP following *favor* is not:

(25) a.   George is believed by many people to be the culprit.
     a'. *George to be the culprit is believed by many people.
     b. *Greenland is favored by many people being admitted to the UN.
     b'.   Greenland being admitted to the UN is favored by many people.

The NP VP sequence following *believe* cannot serve as the predicate constituent of a pseudo-cleft sentence (26) nor be conjoined (27), whereas the sequence following *favor* can:

(26) a. *What Mary believes is George to be the culprit.
     b.   What Mary favors is Greenland being admitted to the UN.
(27) a. *Mary believes both George to be the culprit and greed to be the
           motive.

b. Mary favors both Greenland being admitted to the UN and Congress repealing the Hatch Act.

The position immediately after the verb is a fairly normal site for insertion of parenthetical material in the case of *favor* but not of *believe;*[15] with insertion of parenthetical material between the NP and the nonfinite VP the situation is reversed:

(28) a. *Mary believes, of course, George to be the culprit.
    a'. ?Mary believes George, of course, to be the culprit.
    b. ?Mary favors, of course, Greenland being admitted to the UN.
    b'. *Mary favors Greenland, of course, being admitted to the UN.
    c. *Mary forced, of course, George to pay the bill.
    c'. Mary forced George, of course, to pay the bill.

These are exactly the facts that we would expect if *George* in (24a) is the surface object of *believe* (i.e., if sentences like (24a) have a surface constituent structure like that of sentences with *force*) while not *Greenland* but *Greenland being admitted to the UN* is the surface object of *favor* in (24b).

(29) a.

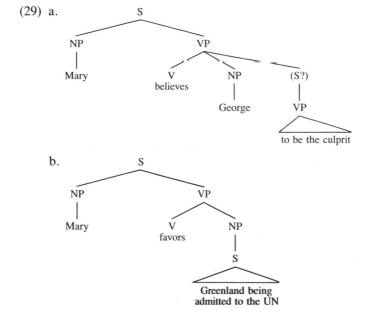

George to be the culprit **does not act like a syntactic unit with respect to any of the phenomena discussed, while** *Greenland being admitted to the UN* **does with respect to all of them, and** *George* **in (24a) acts like a VP-**

mate of *believe* with regard to the one syntactic phenomenon discussed so far (passivization) for which that was a condition. Similar arguments can be given that *John* in (20b) is the surface object of *prevent* or *keep*.

c. Exceptionality; Rule-Government

Some of the transformations discussed in the last section require that the structure to which they apply be not merely of a particular gross shape but also have a lexical item that allows the application of that particular transformation. For example, of the verbs that take a nonfinite sentential direct object, some do and some do not allow Raising, and some do and some do not allow Equi-NP-deletion. Indeed, all four combinations of allowing or not allowing the one and allowing or not allowing the other are attested:

(1)	Raising	Equi
believe (*for-to*), prevent (*-'s -ing*)	+	−
expect (*for-to*)	+	+
regret (*-'s -ing*), hope (*for-to*)	−	+
advocate (*-'s -ing*)	−	−

Let us look at examples that will verify some of the entries in (1). We have already shown that *believe* allows Raising, so we only need show that it excludes the application of Equi:[16]

(2) *John believes to be a genius.

Expect behaves like *believe* in most respects, but allows Equi:

(3) a. John expects there to be a revolution in Albania.
       John expects someone to help him. (Allows narrow-scope inter-
          pretation)
     b. John expects to win the prize.

Regret allows (optionally, in this case) Equi-NP-deletion:

(4) John regrets (his) having insulted Mary.

Sentences like (5a) are instances not of Raising but of an Accusative *-ing* complement whose subject remains in the complement S in surface structure, in view of the unavailability of the complement subject and availability of the entire complement as the derived subject of a corresponding passive clause (5b–b′), i.e., *regret* does not allow Raising:

(5) a.   John regrets Mary having sold the car.
     b.   *Mary is regretted having sold the car by John.
     b′.   Mary having sold the car is regretted by John.

Advocate can be shown in the same way not to allow Raising, and it does not allow Equi either:

(6) a.　George advocated Edith being named treasurer.
　　a'.　*Edith was advocated being named treasurer by George.
　　b.　George$_i$ advocated his$_i$/*∅ being named treasurer.

For Raising or Equi to be applicable to a given S of the appropriate shape, it is not sufficient that there be a verb just anywhere in the S that allows the application of that transformation—that verb must occur as the "predicate element" of the given S. For example, the presence of *believe* is not sufficient to make Raising applicable in (7a), nor is the presence of *regret* sufficient to make Equi applicable in (7b):

(7) a.　*John hopes Bill to believe Mary to be innocent.
　　b.　*Mary believes to regret having offended you.

Following the terminology of Lakoff (1965), I will speak of the verb in the predicate position of a given S as **governing** the application of such transformations as Equi and Raising to that S and of transformations whose application is contingent on the presence of an appropriate lexical item in that position as **governed** transformations.[17] In (7a), *hope* governs the applicability of Raising to the main S, and since *hope* does not allow Raising, the application of Raising to that S is disallowed even though a verb that allows it is present elsewhere in the structure; likewise, in (7b), *believe* governs the application of Equi to the main S, and since *believe* does not allow Equi, the application of Equi to that S is excluded despite the presence of *regret,* which allows it, in the embedded S.

　　Another governed transformation, one of considerably less generality than Raising and Equi, figures in the syntactic behavior of the verb *want.* Let us contrast *want* with *believe.* Both verbs appear followed by a NP and an infinitival VP in surface structure, and in both cases the evidence points to the NP and VP making up an underlying embedded S:

(8) a.　John believes there to have been a riot yesterday.
　　a'.　John wants there to be a riot.
　　b.　John believes the cat to be out of the bag.
　　b'.　John doesn't want the cat to get out of the bag.
　　c.　The police believe a terrorist to be responsible for the bombing.
　　c'.　John wants a terrorist to shoot the governor.

In (8a–a'), existential *there* occurs and only the infinitival VP contains the material that supports it; in (8b–b'), the verb is followed by part of an idiom, of which the remainder occurs in the infinitival VP; and in (8c–c') *a terrorist* allows an interpretation in which the embedded S is its scope (besides one in which the whole S is its scope); for example, (8c) allows an interpretation in which what the police believe is that there is a terrorist responsible (though there need not be any particular terrorist that they believe to be responsible) and (8c′) allows an interpretation in which John's desire is that a terrorist (any old terrorist) shoot the governor.

Nonetheless, there are a number of differences between *want* and *believe:*

(9) a.   *What John believes is (for) George to be the culprit.
    a′.   What John wants is for the Yankees to win the World Series.
    b.   *John believes firmly (for) Jesus Christ to be God.
    b′.   John firmly believes Jesus Christ to be God.
    b″.   John wants passionately for the Yankees to win the World Series.

In (9a′,b″), the complement of *want* begins with *for.* By contrast, in the more common sentences in which the complement immediately follows *want,* no *for* is allowed in standard English (though it is fairly common, for example, in Scottish, Appalachian, and Ozark English):

(10) John wants (% for) the Yankees to win the World Series.

Believe does not allow an overt *for* under any circumstances. In view of the alternation between forms in which *want* is accompanied by *for* and forms in which it lacks *for,* it is difficult to decide what is responsible for the oddity of analogs to the examples that show that the NP following *believe* is its surface direct object:[18]

(11) a.   *What everyone wants is John to resign.
     b.   ?Everyone wants both John to resign and Alice to be named his
            successor.
     c.   *Everyone wants, of course, John to resign.
     c′.   ?Everyone wants John, of course, to resign.

Perhaps (11a–c) are odd because *want* in these cases requires Raising and thus *John to resign* is not a surface constituent in *Everyone wants John to resign,* or alternatively, there might be no Raising with *want* but merely a deletion of *for* when it immediately follows *want,* and (11a–c) would then be odd by virtue of their lacking the *for* even though the conditions for its deletion are not met.

I will arbitrarily choose the latter account of *want,* noting that the case for either of the two alternatives is not particularly strong.[19] The deletion of *for* posited here is then a governed transformation: *want* allows it but very few other verbs do. This deletion must not be confused with the deletion of *for* that applies when the subject of a *for-to* complement is deleted or extracted; the latter deletion is in fact ungoverned, i.e., it applies without regard to what verb is in predicate position. This means that while (12a) is closer to (12b) than to (12c) with regard to the words that make up its surface form, its derivation is closer to that of (12c), differing only in that the governed deletion of *for* applies in (12a) but not in (12c):

(12) a. I want John to be happy.
 b. I believe John to be happy.
 c. I prefer for John to be happy.

It is actually not just verbs that govern applicability of transformations. For example, predicate adjectives differ from one another in whether they allow Raising-to-subject:

(13) Diane is likely/*probable to win the prize.

It is thus necessary to revise the above characterization of "governor" to allow for predicate adjectives as governors. One way of doing this is simply to give a disjunctive definition: the governor in a structure [$_S$ NP [$_{VP}$ V X]] is the V unless the V is *be* and the X is an AP, in which case it is the A of the AP. A second way requires a significant alteration of our underlying structures but provides some important insights that would otherwise be missed. Suppose that copula *be* were not included in deep structures (and thus that there was a transformation inserting copula *be*). Predicate adjectives would then be in the same deep structure position as any other governors, i.e., the governor would in every case be the head of the XP of a [$_S$ NP XP] structure.

This proposal implies that transformations having an adjective as governor have to apply before the insertion of copula *be*. Only before insertion of *be* is the adjective in the position of the governor—after insertion of *be*, it is the *be* and not the adjective that is in that position. This provides an explanation of why the surface structure of clauses with *Tough*-movement is as in (14a) and not as in (14a'): the derivation must be as in (14b), with Extraposition and *Tough*-movement applying prior to *be*-insertion, since *Tough*-movement is a governed transformation and thus must apply at a stage of the derivation when the "predicate" element is something that allows it (e.g., *easy*, but not *be*):

(14) a.

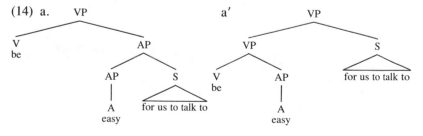

b.

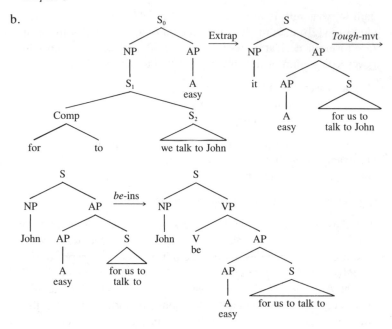

Since for most of the topics treated in this book it will be immaterial whether copula *be* is included in deep structures, the deep structures given below will generally not be like that of (14b); i.e., copula *be* will be included in the deep structures presented below even though it strictly speaking need not, in fact, should not, be there.

I note in addition that the characterization of "governor" given above implies that many transformations will be ungoverned. For example, since movement of interrogative pronouns applies to a structure that is of the form [Comp S] rather than to one of the form [NP XP], no element of the structure to which it applies meets the condition for being its governor.

A further respect in which lexical items can differ from one another becomes apparent when one attempts to determine whether *try* takes a subject complement and Raising or an object complement and Equi-NP-deletion and finds that the criteria given in §5b yield conflicting results. In most respects, *try* in fact behaves like *want, expect,* and other transitive verbs that take nonfinite sentential objects and allow deletion of the subject of the complement by Equi-NP-deletion. For example, it does not allow a funny NP as its subject (15):

(15)　a.　*My leg tried to be pulled.
　　　b.　*There tried being errors in the proof.
　　　c.　*It tried to rain this morning.

A quantifier on its subject can only have wide scope; e.g., (16a) can only be interpreted as meaning that "*x* tried to keep calm" is true of most of the survivors, and not as anything that combines *try* with "most of the survivors keep calm":

(16) a. Most of the survivors tried to keep calm.
     b. No one tried kicking the machine.

Likewise, it can be used in a pseudo-cleft construction with *what* corresponding to the nonfinite VP, like *expect* and *regret* and unlike *appear* and *keep:*

(17) a.   What Fred tried was to put everything in one suitcase.
     b.   What Amy expected was to be given a bonus.
     b′.   What Ron regretted was not having said goodbye to you.
     c.   *What Bob appears is to have caught a cold.
     c′.   *What the children kept was singing songs.

However, it differs from *expect* and *regret* (and in this respect is like *appear* and *keep*) in not allowing any alternative surface form in which a subject of the complement sentence appears overtly in addition to its own subject:

(18) a.   *Fred tried for him/himself/Ethel to put everything in one suitcase.
     a′.   *Fred tried that he would put everything in one suitcase.
     b.   *Roger tried his/your mixing some vinegar with the soy sauce.

Since (15)–(17) provide such strong evidence that the surface subject of *try* is its deep subject and not a deep constituent of its complement, the most appealing way of dealing with this apparently anomalous conjunction of properties is to treat *try* as having an object complement and Equi-NP-deletion but impose on it an additional condition that will exclude derivations of (18a, b). What I propose as this additional condition, following Lakoff (1965: §6.2), is that *try* not merely requires that Equi-NP-deletion apply when its conditions of application are met but indeed requires that the conditions for application be met. I will speak of Equi-NP-deletion as being **Superobligatory** when its governor is *try*.

An alternative characterization of the special property of *try* suggests itself, namely, that it requires that in deep structure its subject and the subject of its complement be conreferential. In the cases discussed so far, the deleted subject of the complement of *try* is in fact the deep subject of the complement, and thus either version of the constraint would have correct implications for those examples. To choose between the two versions, we thus need to consider derivations in which the complement sentence undergoes a subject-changing transformation, either removing from subject position a pronoun coreferential with the subject of *try* (19) or causing such a pronoun to assume subject position (20):

(19) *Officer Krupke$_i$ tried for Creepy Calabresi to be arrested by him$_i$.
(20) a. Sam tries to be easy for us to get along with.
   b. Wilma was trying to seem to be unconcerned.
   c. The boys tried to all leave at the same time.

Such examples give one grounds to conclude that the relevant condition is not coreferentiality of the two subjects in deep structure but applicability of Equi-NP-deletion at the intermediate stage of the derivation at which that transformation applies to the S whose predicate element is *try:* the deep structure coreferentiality of the two subjects is not enough to make (19) acceptable, and the deep structure subject of the complement in (20) is something other than the pronoun that Equi-NP-deletion is to delete.

There are thus at least four possibilities for what a governor requires of the application of a particular governed transformation:

(21) a. Inapplicable: Sam$_i$ believes himself$_i$/*∅ to be a victim of circumstances.
   b. Optional: Sam$_i$ regretted his$_i$/∅ having offended you.
   c. Obligatory: Sam$_i$ hoped (for Amy/*him$_i$/*himself$_i$) to be vindicated.
   d. Superobligatory: Sam$_i$ tried (for *Amy/*him$_i$/*himself$_i$) to steal a hubcap.

d. Control

We have taken up a number of cases in which the subject of a nonfinite complement was deleted if coreferential with a certain NP in the main clause (and which in certain cases, e.g., the complements of *try* and *force*, **had** to be coreferential with that NP):

(1) a. Sam$_i$ tried/hoped [∅$_i$ to cheat me out of $50].
   b. Joan persuaded the boss$_i$ [∅$_i$ to raise her salary].

In this section I will deal briefly with the question of what NP can serve as the **controller** for Equi-NP-deletion, that is, the NP that the subject of a subordinate S must be coreferential with in order to be deleted.

In (1a), there is only one NP outside of the complement S in which the deletion takes place, and thus if any NP is to control the deletion, that one must be it. In (1b), however, there are two NPs outside of the complement

S, *Joan* and *the boss,* that would come into consideration as possible controllers, if we assume only that the controller must be a constituent of a superordinate S. While only the (deep) object of *persuade* can control deletion of the subject of the complement of *persuade* (2), there are other verbs that occur in similar syntactic structures but whose **subjects** are the controllers for Equi-NP-deletion:[20]

(2) a. Joan_i persuaded the boss_j $[\emptyset_{j/*i}$ to go to Bermuda].
   b. The boss_j was persuaded by Joan_i $[\emptyset_{j/*i}$ to go to Bermuda].
(3) a. John_i promised Alice_j $[\emptyset_{i/*j}$ to empty the garbage].
   b. John_i vowed/swore to God_j $[\emptyset_{i/*j}$ to stop taking cocaine].
   c. John_i offered to Alice_j $[\emptyset_{i/*j}$ to paint her car].

The meaning of (3a) relates to John, not Alice, emptying the garbage, that of (3b) to John, not God, giving up cocaine, and that of (3c) to John, not Alice, painting the car. Control by the object, as in (2a), is decidedly more common than control by the subject, as in (3); e.g., *force, challenge, encourage, advise, ask, tempt, dare, order,* and many other verbs behave like *persuade,* while there are few verbs other than those in (3) for which control works as with *promise.* Which NP in a [NP [V (P) NP S]] combination serves as controller for deletion of the subject of the S appears to be predictable from the meaning of the V, i.e., I know of no minimal pair for control: two verbs with roughly the same meaning, one having its subject as controller, the other its object. However, specifying which verbs work the one way and which ones the other is tricky and will not be attempted here; the interested reader is referred to Bach 1979.

There are also cases in which the subject of a subject complement is deleted under the control of a NP within the main VP:

(4) a. $[\emptyset_i$ getting a low grade] didn't bother John_i.
   b. $[\emptyset_i$ running away] was cowardly of Derek_i.
   c. $[\emptyset_i$ driving recklessly] gives some people_i thrills.
   d. $[\emptyset_i$ punching Harry] led to Susan_i's downfall.

Note that in (4d) the presumable controller is not even a major constituent of the main S but is part of a larger NP; at least, though, even in that case, the controller is a constituent of the immediately superordinate S. Unlike the cases of Equi-NP-deletion considered up to now, the deletion of the complement subject in sentences like (4) is generally optional:

(5) a. His_i getting a low grade didn't bother John_i.
   b. His_i running away was cowardly of Derek_i.
   c. ?His_i driving recklessly gives Fred_i a thrill.
   d. Her_i punching Harry led to Susan_i's downfall.

(6) a. John$_i$ tried (*his$_i$) putting cinnamon in the stew.
   b. John$_i$ intends (for *him$_i$/?himself$_i$) to remodel the house.

There is also a phenomenon often referred to as **Super-Equi-NP-deletion** (Super-Equi, for short), in which deletion of the subject of an embedded S appears to be controlled not by an element of the next higher S but by something in a still higher S:

(7) a. John$_i$ hinted [that it was likely [that [Ø$_i$ buying himself a new hat] would prove unwise]].
   b. It appeared to John$_i$ [that it was a foregone conclusion [that it would be illegal [Ø$_i$ to nominate himself for a Nobel Prize]]].

This description of examples like (7) is in fact controversial. Kimball (1971) maintained that alleged instances of Super-Equi involved a deep structure in which the S immediately superordinate to the deletion site contained a "dative" NP and that that NP was the controller for ordinary Equi-NP-deletion; e.g., under Kimball's analysis, the deep structure of (7a) contains *[he$_i$ buy him$_i$ a new hat] would prove unwise for him$_i$*, ordinary Equi deletes the subject of *buy* under the the control of the *him* of *unwise for him*, and another rule deletes the latter *him* under the control of *John*. This issue will not be pursued here; the interested reader should consult Kuno (1975), Jacobson and Neubauer (1976), Richardson (1986), and the references cited in those papers.

There are in addition subjectless nonfinite VPs that may require the recognition of uncontrolled deletion:

(8) a. Making paper airplanes is fun.
   b. To tell lies is cowardly.

Two possibilities for the analysis of such examples immediately suggest themselves: either they involve some sort of underlying "generic" subject that is deleted without any controller,[21] or an underlying subject is deleted under the control of some understood element. Under the latter proposal, (8b) might be assigned an underlying structure something like that proposed by Kimball for (7), i.e., *[for one$_i$ to tell lies] is cowardly of one$_i$*, with ordinary Equi deleting the subject of the complement and some special rule deleting the main clause occurrence of *one*. I know of no solid grounds for a choice between these two possibilities. In either event, some sort of "generic" element would have to be set up in the underlying structure, and in fact *one* and its colloquial equivalent *you* are the prime candidates for the underlying subject of these complements, since when the nonfinite VP contains a pronoun that would require the understood subject as antecedent, the pronoun takes a form corresponding to *one* or "generic" *you:*[22]

(9) a. Praising 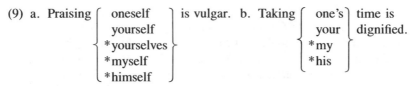 is vulgar. b. Taking one's/your/*my/*his time is dignified.

However, as Thompson (1973) notes, not all nonfinite VPs without controllers have interpretations that are consistent with *one* as underlying subject, and Thompson's examples (10a, b) appear not to allow variants in which a pronoun has the understood subject as antecedent: [23]

(10) a.   Senator Claghorn voted in favor of (our/*one's) opening up trade with Albania.
     b.   Trapping muskrats bothers Mary.
     b'.   ??Catching muskrats in one's traps bothers Mary.

I thus tentatively conclude that there must be a variety of possible underlying subjects for nonfinite VPs aside from the pronoun that is deleted under identity with a controller: *one* is one possible underlying subject, but not the only one.

In addition to deletion of subjects of complements under the control of particular elements of the main clause, there is also deletion of the subjects of certain adverbial expressions under the control of a main clause element:

(11) a. Before $\emptyset_i$ leaving the office, John$_i$ phoned Mary.
     b. You$_i$ shouldn't listen to the radio while $\emptyset_i$ studying.
     c. John$_i$ wore a tuxedo [$\emptyset_i$ to impress Mary].
     d. Mary$_i$ irritated John by [$\emptyset_i$ ignoring him].

The controller in **Adverbial Equi,** as this deletion is sometimes called,[24] is generally the main clause subject, though there is some individual variation on this point; e.g., Grinder (1976:87) finds (12) ambiguous as to whether it refers to Louise or Don leaving home:

(12) a. Louise saw Don while leaving home.
     b. Drivers score only if they zap you$_2$ when $\emptyset_2$ jaywalking. (*AOA Orientation Map,* Hong Kong)

This phenomenon appears at first to be uncontrolled, since the main clause verb seems to be immaterial to its applicability; e.g., substituting another verb for *leave* in (11a) or for *wear* in (11c) cannot make Adverbial Equi inapplicable. It is not completely clear, though, that the governor, if any, for Adverbial Equi would be the main clause verb. In §8e and chapter 19, it will be argued that *before, while,* etc. are prepositions with sentential objects and appear in deep structure in the combination [S [$_{PP}$ P S]]. Whether the characterization of "governor" proposed in §5c is applicable here depends on a technical point in its interpretation, namely, whether the first S of this combination should be taken as matching the NP of the [NP XP] combination of §5c. If it is in fact applicable, then it is the P (i.e., the "subordinating conjunction") that will be the governor. Since in fact different Ps differ with regard to whether Adverbial Equi is possible (and if so, also with regard to whether it is obligatory), I tentatively conclude that it is actually the P that is the governor:

(13) a.   ??John complained unless getting special treatment.
    b.   John got rich despite (his) having had hardly any education.
    b′.   John got rich before (our/*his) returning to Ohio.
    c.   John became disillusioned while (*his/*our) working for the government.
    d.   John won't be named chairman, irrespective of his/your/?∅ being the best candidate.

e. Additional Forms of Complements

This chapter has so far taken up only the most common forms that complements in English can have. This final section will be devoted to brief remarks on some other possible forms of complements.

Besides indicative *that*-clauses such as have figured prominently in this chapter, English also has subjunctive *that*-clauses:

(1) a. The king decreed that the rebels be drawn and quartered.
    b. I requested that John help me.

I tentatively identify the difference between the two types of *that*-clauses as consisting at least in part in whether the complement has an underlying tense (indicative) or is tenseless in deep structure (subjunctive).

That-clauses often allow alternative forms in which the *that* is omitted:

(2) a. John said (that) Alice would be here tomorrow.
    b. Bill is ashamed (that) he insulted you.

Omission of the *that* is generally possible when the *that*-clause immediately follows the verb or adjective of which it is the object. Its omission from a nonextraposed subject complement is highly deviant, and its omission from a subjunctive *that*-clause or from a *that*-clause that is separated from the verb or adjective by intervening material is mildly odd:

(3) a.   That/*∅ Bush will be elected is unlikely.
    a′. It is unlikely that/(?)∅ Bush will be elected.

b. ?The king decreed the rebels be drawn and quartered.

b'. ?I requested John help me.

c. John said sarcastically that/?∅ he was glad he had such good friends.

c'. Frank assured us yesterday that/?∅ the trouble was over.

Besides the complementizers discussed so far, a couple of other words have limited uses as complementizers:

(4) a. Did you read <u>where</u> the governor is expected to be indicted for taking bribes?

b. It seems <u>as if</u> we've met before.

b'. I feel <u>as though</u> nothing could stop me.

c. It would be a good idea <u>if</u> you hired a bodyguard.

d. %I hate <u>when</u> people keep me waiting.

d'. I hate it <u>when</u> people keep me waiting.

The complement here has the appearance of an adverbial clause but functions as a complement rather than as a modifier, since it is restricted to the position of a complement (i.e., it cannot be moved into an unambiguously adverbial position) (5a); it cannot be omitted (5b); it pronominalizes in a way that complements sometimes do (5c); and in the case of the *if*-S and *when*-S expressions of (4c–d), it can match the *what* of a pseudo-cleft construction (5d):

(5) a. ?If you hired a bodyguard, it would be a good idea.
   *As if we've met before, it seems.
   *Where the governor's expected to be indicted, did you read?
   When people keep me waiting, I hate ?it/*∅.

b. *Did you read?
   *It seems.

c. Did you read that/*there?
   It seems so.

d. What would be a good idea would be if you hired a bodyguard.
   What I hate (*it) is when people keep me waiting.

There are also constructions involving nonfinite VPs in different forms from those considered above, namely, the bare infinitive form (6) and the past participle form (7):

(6) a. John wouldn't let me help him.

b. They made me sign the contract in triplicate.

c. Mary saw John cross the street.

(7) a. The governor had all the students arrested and fingerprinted.

   b. Nancy had the whole of "Paradise Lost" committed to memory.
   c. We finally got the dishwasher repaired.

In addition, there are a variety of constructions involving VPs in the *-ing* form whose status as instances of the reduced complement constructions discussed in §5d is controversial: [25]

(8) a. We finally got the dishwasher running.
    b. George kept the top spinning.
    c. George left Mary wondering about his sanity.
    d. Pavarotti had the whole audience cheering.
    e. Mary saw John crossing the road.
    f. RCA recorded Horowitz playing the Liszt b-minor sonata.

No attempt will be made here to sort out the details of these constructions.
   There are cases in which less than a VP can be argued to be a reduced complement S. For example, there are several arguments for treating sentences like (9a) as reduced forms of sentences like (9b): [26]

(9) a. John wants a lollipop.
    b. John wants to have a lollipop.

For example, they support adverbial expressions that are interpreted as modifying the hypothesized complement S, as in (10a), which has a meaning corresponding to a deep structure (10b), in that *until next summer* gives not the time at which my wanting takes place but the time when (in my wish) I am to have Tom's apartment:

(10) a. I wanted Tom's apartment until next summer.
     b.

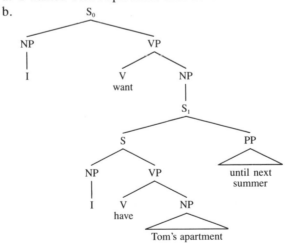

Indeed, such sentences can have two time adverbials that normally would contradict one another but which can co-occur provided that one of them modifies the main S and the other one modifies the hypothesized embedded S:

(11) Last week Tom wanted my apartment next summer, but now he wants it in October.

The hypothesis that *want* allows the deletion of *have* from its complement (actually, from the VP that remains after Equi-NP-deletion deletes the subject of the complement) implies that the posited embedded S (S_1 in the case of (10b)) can serve as the locus of S-modification (as in (10a)) or of conjoining, that it can be the scope of a quantifier, and that it can pronominalize the way that Ss do.

These predictions are confirmed. Consider first the conjoined NP in (12):

(12) Mary wants either a Cadillac or a Rolls-Royce.

According to the proposal under discussion, the derivation of (12) could involve a deep structure with either conjoining of the main S or conjoining of the embedded S:

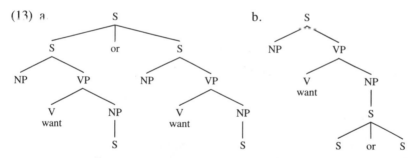

(Constructing derivations of (12) with each of these deep structures is left as an exercise.) Each of the two deep structures corresponds to a meaning that (11) can express: (13a) corresponds to the meaning in which either Mary wants a Cadillac or she wants a Rolls-Royce—the speaker doesn't know which one she wants—and (13b) corresponds to the meaning in which her desire is that she have one or other of the two kinds of car. There is a similar ambiguity in (14), which can mean either that there is a recipe for shredded pig's ears that John wants or that John has a desire to the effect that he have a recipe for shredded pig's ears:

(14) John wants a recipe for shredded pig's ears.

These two iterpretations are the same as those of *John wants to have a recipe for shredded pig's ears* and correspond to whether S_0 or S_1 in a structure like (10b) is the scope of the quantified NP *a recipe for shredded pig's ears*. Finally, in (15), the pronoun must be the one that corresponds to a S such as *he has a mistress,* not the one that corresponds to a feminine singular NP such as *a mistress*.

(15) John wants a mistress, but his wife won't allow it/*her.

If *John wants a mistress* is analyzed in terms of an embedded S *he have a mistress,* there is then a constituent that matches the object of *allow* in (15) (*allow* requires a sentential object) and thus can serve as antecedent for the *it*.

In McCawley 1974, it is argued that a fairly large number of verbs allow deletion of verbs from their complements, though they differ with regard to what verb(s) they allow to be deleted; e.g., if *John promised Mary a Rolls-Royce* involves Equi-NP-deletion plus deletion of the verb of the complement, the deleted verb would have to be *give.* See also Borkin 1975 and Ruwet 1979 for discussion of cases that have often been treated in terms of deletion of *be* from a nonfinite complement, as in the proposal in which (16a) has the same deep structure as (16b) and its derivation involves deletion of *be:*

(16) a. We believe John guilty.
     b. We believe John to be guilty.

This issue will not be pursued here.

EXERCISES

1. Give derivations for the following sentences in accordance with the analyses developed so far:
   a. John likes to be praised by the boss.
   b. John seems to want to know a lot.
   c. John wants to seem to know a lot.
   d. Mary kept being persuaded by John to do silly things.
   e. The judge declared it to be illegal for strikers to throw bombs.
   f. The boys tried to all win prizes. (NB: not "The boys all tried to win prizes.")
   g. The boys both were afraid to go outside.
2. a. Find three English verbs not discussed in this chapter that can be the V in a VP of the form V + nonfinite VP, and for each one

give at least two kinds of evidence as to whether it behaves like *seem* (i.e., it has a deep structure sentential subject and allows Raising) or like *want* and *hope* (i.e., it has a deep structure sentential object and allows Equi-NP-deletion).

b. Do the same for three English adjectives not discussed in this chapter that can be used in APs of the form [A *to* VP] or [A P VP-*ing*]. (NB: when an adjective takes an -*ing* complement, a preposition is required, as in *ashamed of having lost the money*).

3. Give the two derivations of §5e(12) that were sketched in the text.

4. For each of the following examples find facts that allow one to decide whether the underlined NP is raised out of a complement S (consisting of it and the nonfinite VP) or is an underlying constituent of the main S and controls deletion of the subject of the complement S:

   a. You are in danger of losing all your money.

   b. The contract proved to be a forgery.

   c. We can depend on the Tribune to expose crooked politicians. (example from Emonds 1976:76)

   d. Susan is bound to notice that something is wrong.

   e. The manager accused John of padding his expense account.

5. Show that the *one* posited as the underlying subject of sentences like §5d(8)–(9) cannot be identified with the "UNSPEC" that was posited as the underlying subject of reduced passives.

6. It is occasionally suggested that in a sentence of the form X *helped* Y *to do* Z the underlying subject of the infinitive is X *and* Y (or better, a pronoun having the same reference as X *and* Y). Find facts that support or conflict with this proposal.

7. One occasionally encounters the suggestion that the NP deleted by Equi-NP-deletion is not the subject of its clause at the point in the derivation at which it is deleted, but rather that it is moved into the higher S by Raising and is deleted from a position in that S (e.g., under that suggestion, in the derivation of *John intends to go home,* Raising yields an intermediate stage *John$_i$ intends him$_i$ [to go home]*). Find at least one good reason for rejecting that proposal.

8. a. For any language other than English (your native language, if that is not English), describe the principal forms that complement clauses take.

   b. If the language has complementizers, either give arguments like those of §5a, showing that both the Comp-S combination and the S of that combination are constituents, or say why such arguments cannot be given.

   c. Pick any class of sentences discussed in this chapter that have close analogs in your language, and say in what respects their syntax agrees or disagrees with that of the English sentences. (NB: Don't write more than about 2 pages on this question; a really complete answer could be a Ph.D. thesis.)

NOTES

1. It is in fact also possible to have *isn't* in (5), in which case it has the meaning of (4a). When a subject of the form *that S and that S* takes singular number agreement, its deep structure is as in (6a), with a single complementizer and a conjoined S, and the complementizer is "spread" over the conjuncts. This is one of a number of cases in which English allows something that is combined with a conjoined structure to be spread over all of the conjuncts. In that case the surface structure of (5) will be not (6a) but:

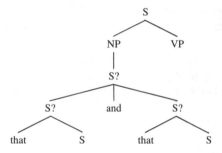

2. There is one class of cases in which they do not correspond exactly to an independent sentence:

i.   For John to have gone home at 2:00 this afternoon is unthinkable.
ii.   *John has gone home at 2:00 this afternoon.

I will argue in chap. 8 that the *have* of examples like (i) corresponds not to the *have* of a correspondingly independent S but rather to a past tense, as in (iii), that is, I will adopt an analysis in which (i) involves not an embedded present perfect but rather an embedded simple past tense:

iii. John went home at 2:00 this afternoon.

3. The conditions under which this deletion takes place will be taken up in §7b.
4. In relational grammar, a constituent standing in one of these relations is called a **term.** The definition given here thus restricts the application of the term complement to "terms" and excludes, e.g., embedded Ss that serve as modifiers.
An example of a sentential indirect object was given in §4d:

He never gave it a thought that Bolshies are human beings too.

Two factors conspire to make sentential indirect objects rare. First, indirect objects usually must denote "affected persons," and Ss denote propositions rather than persons. And second, indirect objects usually occur in the middle of a VP, while embedded Ss are most normal at the beginning or end (not the middle) of the structures in which they are embedded; note that Extraposition applies in the above example and serves to put the sentential indirect object in final position.

5. In the bulk of the recent transformational literature, constituents consisting of a complementizer and a S are labeled not S but S̄. In chap. 7 I will take up the question of whether *it rained* and *that it rained* belong to the same syntactic category, and, if not, whether the difference in category is of the sort represented by the bar of the "X-bar" conception of syntactic categories.

6. While the use of the term "Comp-placement" in (23) suggests that a single rule is responsible for the placement of *to*, *-'s*, and *-ing*, it is not a foregone conclusion that that need be the case. Indeed, while it is clear that placement of *to* and *-ing* must be in the cycle, placement of *-'s* may have to be postcyclic in order to allow the transformations that will be discussed in §5b to apply the same way to *-s* *-ing* complements as they do to *for-to* complements.

7. An analysis of these sentences as having an underlying sentential subject was first proposed in Jespersen 1913.

8. The parenthesized $(S_1 ? S_2 ?)$ in the last tree of (11a) indicates uncertainty as to whether either or both of the lower S nodes should remain in the derived structure. In §7c we will take up the possibility of "tree pruning," that is, of loss of nodes as a side effect of derivational steps that render them "nonfunctional."

9. Raising is what is known in Relational Grammar as an **Ascension:** a transformation in which a grammatical relation that a constituent stands in is taken over by a part of that constituent (here, the status of the complement S as subject of the main S is taken over by its own subject), with concomitant demotion of the remainder of that constituent to a status as a **chômeur,** i.e., as having lost its grammatical relation to something else. In English, chômeurs always take a surface position as constituents of the VP.

10. The formulas in (14) are simplified versions of those presented in McCawley 1981a. That in (14a) can be given the informal paraphrase "There are 500 Americans x such that it is likely that x will die in an accident this weekend." As in McCawley 1981a, I assume a system of **restricted** quantifiers, that is, that each quantifier must be supplied with an expression (here, "American") that tells what the admissible values of its variable are. In the framework of **unrestricted** quantifiers that is usually assumed in works on formal logic but which I argue against in McCawley 1981a, all bound variables are assumed to all have the same domain of values, and apparent restrictions on the value of the variable are simulated by combining the quantifier with a complex propositional function, e.g., by representing *All politicians are crooks* by "For all x, (if x is a politician, then x is a crook)."

11. The astute reader will have noticed that *They will win the election* is not the expectation of the candidates in (13a): each of the candidates in question expects that **he** will win, not that **they** will (all) win. The semantics thus demands that the embedded sentence contain something like the logician's bound individual variable (the x of x *will win the election*), which corresponds more closely to a singular pronoun than to a plural one. The use of the plural pronoun in *The candidates expect that they will win* is dictated by the syntactic requirement that a pronoun have

the person, number, and gender of its antecedent. I will argue in §11e that underlying structures must be admitted in which at least some pronouns are unspecified for person, number, and gender.

12. Caution must be exercised, however, in using facts such as the interpretations of the sentences in (19) in deciding whether a verb has a 2-place or a 3-place underlying structure. Schmerling (1979) points out that the interpretation of sentences can depend not only on their structure but also on one's beliefs about the "scene" that the sentence describes. One assigns "actors" to all the roles in the scene even when the sentence does not really refer to all of them. For example, Schmerling argues that *allow* is a 2-place verb not only when it occurs in sentences like i–ii that demand a 2-place analysis, but even in sentences like iii–iv, which often receive interpretations like those of (19b–b') (i.e., interpretations differing with regard to whether Dr. Grimshaw or Otto is the person that receives permission for something) and might be taken (incorrectly, according to Schmerling) as showing that *allow* can also be a 3-place verb like *persuade:*

    i. We allowed there to be some confusion.
    ii. I won't allow my leg to be pulled.
    iii. Agnes allowed Dr. Grimshaw to treat Otto.
    iv. Agnes allowed Otto to be treated by Dr. Grimshaw.

In Schmerling's analysis, giving permission is only one of many ways of allowing something, but when a sentence containing *allow* refers to a scene that involves giving permission, one tends to assign the role of "recipient of permission" to the grammatically most prominent possible filler of the role, which is to say, Dr. Grimshaw in iii and Otto in iv.

13. This discussion relates only to the sense of *keep* that means roughly "prevent," not to the sense that appears in such sentences as *John kept the audience laughing.*

14. This use of *from* appears to be restricted to verbs implying "cause not" such as *keep, prevent,* and *stop.*

15. This remark relates only to the use of *believe* with an infinitive complement. In such sentences as *Mary believes that George is the culprit,* insertion of parentheticals between *believe* and the *that*-clause causes no awkwardness.

16. In many other languages, the equivalent of *believe* allows Equi-NP-deletion, as in the French counterpart of (2):

    i. John croit être un genie.

Indeed, even English *believe* allows it in a limited range of cases:

    ii. They skim the surface of melange and believe thereby to attain grace. (Frank Herbert, *Children of Dune,* p. 43

17. This use of "govern" and its derivatives should not be confused with the quite different sense of "govern" that is introduced in Chomsky 1981 and subsequent works; the word will not be used in the latter sense in this book. Both of these technical senses of "govern" are adaptations of the use of the word in traditional

grammar (Matthews 1981:246–55), where, e.g., the German verb *helfen* is spoken of as governing the dative case in its object.

18. Another type of example whose implications are unclear is the passive sentence. The possibility of using sentences like (i) to argue that the NP following *want* is not its sister (thus, that *want* does not have Raising-to-object) is weakened by the fact that *want* resists Passive (ii) except in certain specialized uses (iii):

   i.   *John is wanted to resign by many persons.
   ii.   ?Higher pay is wanted by many workers.
   iii.   Creepy Calabresi is wanted by the FBI for armed robbery.

19. See Postal 1974 for an alternative analysis in which absence of *for* with *want* is always a concomitant of Raising, and sentences like (9a', b″) are accounted for in terms of a restriction that makes Raising, which for Postal is normally obligatory with *want,* inapplicable in those cases. The case that Postal makes for Raising with *want* is much weaker than the powerful case that he makes for Raising with *believe.*

20. Combinations of asterisks and subscripts here are used to indicate which interpretations are possible or impossible; e.g., (2a) allows an interpretation relat ing to the boss going to Bermuda but not one relating to Joan going to Bermuda.

21. To say that the deletion of such a NP is uncontrolled is not to say that it is unrestricted. Note that many nonfinite subjectless VPs do not allow interpretations parallel to those of (8); e.g., *John hates playing cards* does not admit an interpretation in which the understood subject of *play* is "generic" but only one in which it refers to John.

22. The asterisked forms in (9) are in fact acceptable if the "topic" of the given stretch of discourse is a person or persons to whom the pronoun in question could refer; e.g., in a stretch of discourse that deals with Harry's boasting, the version of (9a) with *himself* is acceptable provided the understood subject of *praise* is taken as referring to Harry. I conjecture that the deletion of the understood subject in such cases should be identified with Super-Equi.

23. Thompson notes that (10b) is ambiguous between controlled and uncontrolled deletion, as illustrated by alternative ways that it could be continued:

   i.   . . . . She thinks it's not feminine.
   ii.   . . . . She is circulating a petition to have it made illegal.

24. For further discussion of Adverbial Equi, see Williams 1974, Elliott, Legum, and Thompson 1969, Grinder 1976, and McCawley 1984.

25. See Akmajian 1977 and Gee 1977 for valuable discussion of "perception verb" constructions such as (6c) and (8e).

26. For further details of these arguments, see McCawley 1974, Partee 1974, and Ross 1976.

a. Feeding and Bleeding

According to the analysis developed in chapter 5, (1a) has a deep structure as in (1b), aside from the complementizer, which is omitted here; in its derivation, Passive applies to S_1, yielding the intermediate structure (1c), and Equi-NP-deletion applies to S_0, deleting he_i;[1]

(1) a. John wants to be admired by everyone.

b.

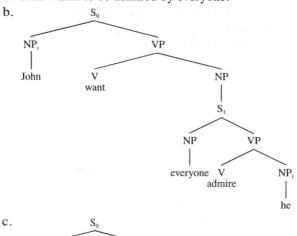

c.

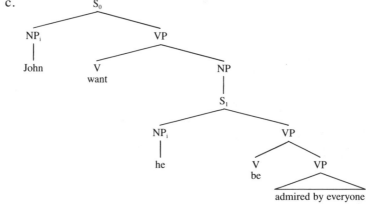

Note that the condition for the application of Equi-NP-deletion to S_0 (namely, that the subject of S_1 be coreferential with the subject of S_0) is not met in (1b) but is met in (1c), that is, the condition for the application of Equi-NP-deletion to S_0 comes to be fulfilled through the application of Passive to S_1. In such cases we will speak of one rule application **feeding** another; here, the application of Passive to S_1 feeds the application of Equi-NP-deletion to S_0, or, for short, Passive$_1$ feeds Equi-NP-deletion$_0$.

Consider now the derivation of (2a) that conforms to the analysis of chapter 5, in which the deep structure is (2b) and Passive applies to S_1 to yield the output (2c):[2]

(2) a. John doesn't want anyone to be hurt by him.

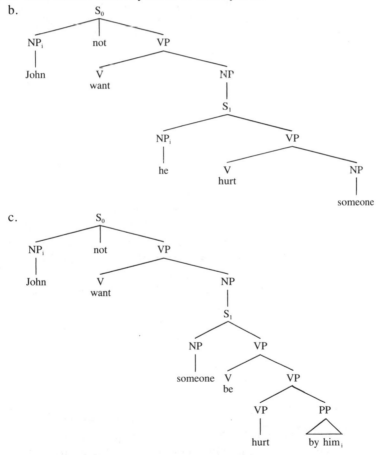

Here, although the condition for the application of Equi-NP-deletion is met in (2b), it is not met in (2c), that is, the application of Passive to S_1

destroys the conditions for the application of Equi-NP-deletion to S_0, and Equi-NP-deletion indeed cannot be applied to S_0 in a derivation that involves the step from (2b) to (2c). In such cases we speak of one rule application **bleeding** another. Here, Passive$_1$ bleeds Equi-NP-deletion$_0$.

The terms "feed" and "bleed," introduced in Kiparsky (1965), are part of a system of terminology for relations between rule applications in a given derivation, not only rule applications that actually occur in the derivation but also those that fail to occur, such as the application of Equi-NP-deletion to S_0 in (2).[3] These terms will figure prominently in the remainder of this chapter, which is concerned with how transformations may interact in derivations, i.e., with working out the principles that determine what feeding and bleeding relationships are possible in derivations.

Two caveats before delving into some aspects of that question. First, it is important to recognize that feeding and bleeding are relationships not between rules but between rule applications in a given derivation. For example, in the derivation of (3) there are two applications of Passive, and it is only its application to the most deeply embedded S that feeds the application of Equi-NP-deletion:

(3) It is believed by many people that John wants to be admired by everyone.

Linguists do occasionally speak of one rule feeding another, but that usage is derivative from the usage just described: if a linguist says, say, that Passive feeds Agreement, what he probably means is that whenever both rules are potentially applicable to a given domain, the application of the one to that domain feeds the application of the other. Second, I will use the term "feed" not only in cases where the application of one rule makes the other rule applicable at all, but also in cases where the application of the one rule affects what the other rule does in the given case. Thus, in the derivation of (4a) we will say that Passive$_1$ feeds Raising$_0$ (calling the embedded S S_1 and the main S S_0) because, though Raising is applicable to S_0 even when Passive is not applied to S_1, as in (4b), Passive affects whether it is *Holmes* or *the solution* that Raising$_0$ makes the derived subject:

(4) a. The solution seems to have been found by Holmes.
    b. Holmes seems to have found the solution.

b. *Schemes of Rule Interaction*

We have already given a rough sketch of a principle that will form a large part of the answer to the question of how rules may interact in a derivation, namely, the principle of the cycle. That principle says (at least in its pristine form—an important qualification will have to be added in §6c) that when one domain is contained in another, applications of rules to the former domain precede applications of rules to the latter, so that, e.g., in the examples given in the last section, any application of rules to S_1 will precede any application of rules to S_0. In the two cases taken up in the last section, that principle implies exactly the interaction between Passive and Equi-NP-deletion that we observe: in both cases, the input to $Equi_0$ is not the deep structure but rather the structure resulting from application to S_1 of whatever rules are going to apply to it (here, only Passive).

The principle of the cycle tells us how an application of a rule to S_1 will interact with an application of a rule to S_0, but it tells us nothing about how it will interact with an application of another rule to S_1. For example, it tells us nothing about the feeding and bleeding that can be observed in cases where there appears to be only one S, as in (1a), with the presumable deep structure (1b), where Passive feeds Quantifier-float, i.e., Passive applies to a structure in which the conditions for Quantifier-float are not met (since *all* can be floated only from a subject NP) to yield an output (1c) to which Quantifier-float can apply:

(1) a. The workers all were praised by the manager.

b.

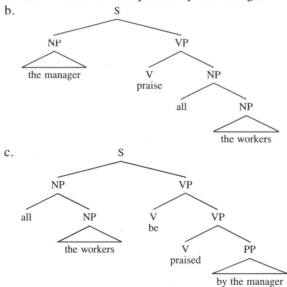

Likewise, in (2a), with the presumable deep structure (2b), Passive bleeds Quantifier-float:

(2) a.   The manager was praised by all the workers.

    a'. *The manager $\begin{Bmatrix} \text{all was} \\ \text{was all} \end{Bmatrix}$ praised by the workers.

b.

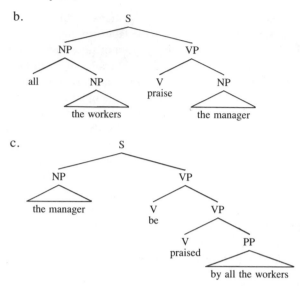

c.

What is of interest here is not that (2a) is acceptable but that (2a′) is un-acceptable, i.e., with a deep structure as in (2b), Passive can apply to yield the structure (2c), to which Quantifier-float is inapplicable, but it must be kept from applying to a structure to which Quantifier-float has already applied, so as to exclude a derivation of (2a′).[4]

Let us list some ways in which transformations applying to a single domain might conceivably interact and see which of them are consistent with the interactions that we observe in (1)–(2) and other examples. A first possibility is that the application of transformations to a given domain is **simultaneous,** i.e., that the given structure is converted in one fell swoop into a structure that differs from the first one in all respects specified by all the transformations whose conditions for application are met in the first structure. This possibility fails miserably in (1)–(2): it implies that there can be no feeding such as is observed in (1), since only rules whose conditions of application were met in (1b) would apply, and it implies that one or other version of (2a′) should be possible, since (2a′) is what would result if Passive and Quantifier-float, whose conditions for application both are met in (2b), both applied.

A second possibility is that the application of transformations to any given domain is **random sequential,** in the sense that the application of transformations to the domain is a sequence of steps, each consisting of the application of **any** transformation whose conditions for application are met in the output of the preceding step. This second possibility provides derivations for (1a) and (2a) but incorrectly also provides a derivation for (2a′).

Random sequential application allows, e.g., for the desired derivation of (1a), since the conditions for application of Passive are met in the deep structure (1b), and the conditions of the application of Quantifier-float are met in the output of Passive. In the case of (2b), since the conditions of application for both Passive and Quantifier-float are met in the deep structure, random sequential application allows the derivation to begin with an application of either transformation. If the derivation begins with an application of Passive, all is well, since the conditions for Quantifier-float are not met in the output, and (2a) results. However, if the derivation begins with an application of Quantifier-float, there is nothing to prevent Passive from then applying to the output of Quantifier-float, in which case the unacceptable (2a') results.

A third possibility is to posit what has generally been accepted in transformational grammar, namely a fixed **order** of application of the transformations, with each transformation allowed to apply only when its "turn" is reached. Note that since we wish to allow derivations in which Quantifier-float applies to the output of Passive (1a) but exclude derivations in which Passive applies to the output of Quantifier-float (2a'), if there is a fixed order of application in which Passive precedes Quantifier-float, we will get exactly the derivations that we want in these cases. While this third possibility is thus apparently consistent with the facts that we have taken up so far, it also appears to allow for an extraordinary amount of variation in language, namely, variation with regard to the order that is imposed on a given set of rules, and there is little evidence that any such variation actually exists. For example, as it stands, the third proposal for rule interaction seems to imply that there could be a dialect of English that was just like the variety of English under discussion except that Passive and Quantifier-float were in the opposite order, which would imply that (2a') was acceptable and (2a) unacceptable in that dialect. No such dialect is known to exist, and it is very doubtful that such a dialect is even possible.

The three schemes of rule interaction just sketched of course come nowhere near exhausting the possibilities, since there are for example other schemes in which these possibilities are combined with each other and/or supplemented by additional principles. For example, possibilities two and three are combined in the suggestion of Anderson (1969, 1974) that rules are subject to a partial rather than a total ordering and that their application is sequential but only partially random, in that the partial ordering must be respected. And possibilities one and two are combined in the detailed scheme developed by Koutsoudas, Sanders, and Noll (1974), for whom a derivation consists of a sequence of steps in which the rules whose conditions for application are met in the output of the preceding step are applied simultaneously. Among the principles that have been combined with all three of these schemes of rule application is the **Elsewhere Principle** (due originally to Panini, ca. 500 B.C., and reintroduced in Anderson 1969, Kiparsky 1973, and Koutsoudas, Sanders, and Noll 1974): when the conditions of application for one rule are a special case of those for another rule, the latter (more general) rule is inapplicable in those cases in which the conditions for the former (more specific) rule are met, i.e., specific rules preempt the application of general rules.

No attempt will be made here to survey the full range of conceivable schemes of rule interaction and their implications. Readers who are interested in pursuing this question in all the detail that it deserves are referred to Pullum (1976), the definitive treatment of this topic. For the remainder of this book, I will adopt a fairly agnostic position on how rules applying to the same domain interact. I will argue, in fact, that there are far fewer cases in which rules apply to the same domain than is generally alleged, so that the question of how rules applying to the same domain interact arises much less frequently than is generally thought.

In a large proportion of the cases that are alleged to require the fixed ordering of transformations of proposal three, a perfectly satisfactory alternative analysis is available in which the domain to which one of the transformations applies is not identical to but is properly contained in the domain to which the other applies, and the principle of the cycle predicts correctly how the two transformations interact. To take one especially popular putative example of a fixed order of application of transformations, consider the interaction observed in examples like (3) between the transformations responsible for the reflexive pronoun ("Reflexivization") and for the absence of the subject ("Imperative subject deletion" = ISD):

(3) Defend yourself/*you.

According to a widely accepted analysis, (3) has a deep structure like (4), involving a symbol that marks the sentence as imperative, and the derivation involves applications of Reflexivization, which converts into a reflexive pronoun a NP that is coreferential with the subject of its clause,[5] and of ISD, which deletes a second person subject in the presence of the imperative marker:

(4)

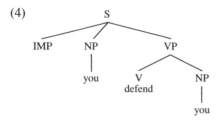

Note that with the deep structure (4) and the assumed transformations, the rules cannot apply in random sequential fashion. The conditions for the application of both Reflexivization and ISD are met in (4), and of the two derivations that random sequential application would allow, one yields the desired *Defend yourself* (namely, the derivation in which Reflexivization applies to (4) and then ISD applies to the output of Reflexivization), but the other yields the unacceptable **Defend you* (namely, the derivation in which ISD applies to (4), yielding an output to which Reflexivization is no longer applicable, since the subject NP to which the second *you* is co-referential has been deleted). This result argues against random sequential application of the assumed transformations but is consistent with a fixed order of application in which Reflexivization precedes ISD.[6]

An extremely minor change in the proposed deep structure changes this situation drastically, however. Suppose that the "IMP" appears not as a constituent of but as a sister of the S in question:

(5)

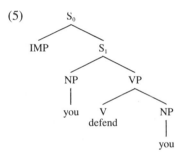

With respect to almost everything, (5) and (4) are no more than minor typographical variants of one another. However, the principle of the cycle yields many implications when applied to (5), though none when applied to (4). In particular, the principle of the cycle, in conjunction with deep structures like (5), implies that ISD (which is sensitive to the presence of "IMP" and whose conditions for application thus could not be met in S_1 but only in S_0) can apply to structures derived by any of the transformations that affect declarative sentences (i.e., any transformations that would apply to the domain S_1 in (5)), and thus that it is possible to form imperatives in which a subject *you* is deleted from a S that has undergone Passive or *Tough*-movement (or Reflexivization). As (6) shows, this implication is correct:

(6) a. Don't be surprised by what I'm going to say.
    b. Please be easy for them to deal with.

Where the approach that posits deep structures like (4) must specify an ordering of transformations in which Reflexivization, Passive, and *Tough-*

movement are ordered before ISD, an approach with deep structures like (5) is able to predict their interactions without assuming any fixed ordering of the transformations, i.e., the approach with (4) must make do with a description of how these transformations interact, while the approach with (5) provides an **explanation** of their interaction.

In the following chapters, I will pursue a research program of seeking analyses that exploit the principle of the cycle to predict the interactions of the transformations that are posited. I will regard the program as successful if the analyses that it leads to are on other grounds desirable, for example, if the rules can be stated in their pristine forms and the deep structures posited accurately represent the meanings of the sentences. (On the last criterion, (5) is preferable to (4): semantically, *Defend yourself* is not a combination of IMP with two separate elements *you* and *defend you* but is rather an order or request that you defend yourself, i.e., it is a combination of the meaning of "IMP" with the meaning of the posited S_1.) I will regard the program as a failure if it forces one to accept objectionable analyses, e.g., an analysis in which the statement of the conditions under which some rule applies requires complications that are avoided under alternative analyses, or one that misrepresents the meanings of the relevant sentences. An analysis will be presented in §18a, incidentally, that will allow the interaction between Passive and Quantifier-float noted in (1)–(2) to be predicted from the principle of the cycle, namely, an analysis in which quantified NPs in deep structures are outside the Ss that they appear in in surface structure, so that the principle of the cycle will predict that applications of transformations to the "matrices" (such as *the manager praised x*) with which a quantified NP is combined will precede applications of transformations to structures that contain the quantified NP. Until we work out that analysis, however, we must continue to regard (1)–(2) as a serious problem that must be solved by any approach to rule interaction that does without a fixed order of application of transformations.

c. *The Cycle*

By all rights, this section should consist mainly of arguments for accepting the principle of the cycle. The section will in fact be mostly devoted to discussion of **what** principle of the cycle should be adopted, and indeed only one real attempt at an argument for accepting such a principle will be made.

The reason for the absence of such arguments in this section is that to give a solid argument for something, one must be clear about what it is to be an argument against, and there happens to be no alternative position on the relationship between rule applications on different domains that has achieved even the status of a respectable straw man, let alone that of a serious contender to the cyclic principle. Accordingly, the best arguments that can be offered for the cyclic principle must to some extent be arguments from ignorance: demonstrations that the principle successfully accounts for the observed rule interactions, especially those that are fairly intricate, combined with statements that no alternative principle is known to account satisfactorily for how rules apply to structures that contain multiple domains of rule application. Rather than presenting such arguments here, perhaps the most useful thing I can do is simply urge the reader to consider some of the more involved derivations given in this book and ponder how the various transformations could be made to interact correctly without reliance on the principle of the cycle.

There are many supposed arguments for the cyclic principle that rely on the fact that certain sentences demand derivations in which an application of one transformation is "sandwiched" between applications of another transformation in a way that the cyclic principle allows. For example, in the derivation relating (1a) to the deep structure (1b), $Raising_2$ feeds Equi-NP-deletion$_1$, which in turns feeds $Raising_0$, and in the derivation relating (2a) to the deep structure (2b), $Passive_1$ feeds Raising-to-object$_0$, which in turn feeds $Passive_0$:

(1) a. John happened to want to seem to understand economics.

    b.

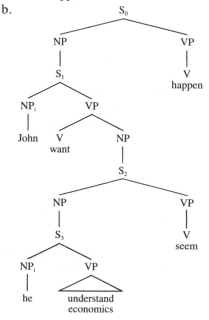

(2) a. The bagel is believed by Marvin to have been eaten by Seymour.

b.

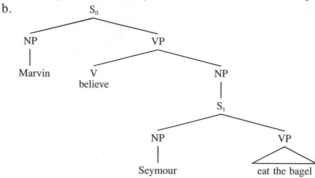

However, the necessity of such derivations provides an argument for the cyclic principle only to the extent that one can exclude other schemes for rule interaction that also allow such derivations. There is one obvious logical possibility for a scheme of rule interactions in which such derivations are allowed, namely, the possibility that the sequence of steps in a derivation is unconstrained both with regard to what transformation applies in any step and what domain it applies to in that step. Any serious argument for the cyclic principle will have to rest on facts relating not only to what derivations it allows but also to what derivations it excludes.

Let us then, before turning to the questions with which this section will be mainly concerned, give one argument for the cyclic principle, an argument showing that the principle correctly excludes certain derivations that an alternative scheme (namely, that of totally random rule application) allows. The cyclic principle (but not the straw man alternative with which it is being compared) excludes derivations in which application of a rule to a domain feeds or bleeds application of a rule to a domain properly contained within the latter domain. The possibility of such a derivation arises when we consider possible interactions between Reflexivization and Raising-to-object (RO). In the oversimplified sketch of Reflexivization given in the preceding section, it was stated that the antecedent of a reflexive pronoun must be the subject of the S to which Reflexivization applies. This statement of the conditions for Reflexivization is in fact overly restrictive, since a reflexive pronoun in English can have an object NP as its antecedent (3a), but in any event Reflexivization must be restricted so that a NP in a VP cannot be the antecedent of a reflexive pronoun in a lower VP (3b) (cf. (3b'), where the antecedent is presumably not the object of *force* but the underlying subject of the infinitive):

(3) a. Mary asked John$_i$ about himself$_i$.

b. Mary promised John$_i$ to defend him$_i$/*himself$_i$.
b'. Mary forced John$_i$ to defend himself$_i$.

Now consider the possibilities for RO and Reflexivization (4a–a') in the structure (4b):

(4) a. We believe Bill$_i$ to hate himself$_i$.
a'. *We believe Bill$_i$ to hate him$_i$.
b.

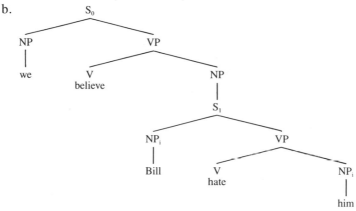

If the application of transformations were totally random, there would be nothing to rule out a derivation in which RO$_0$ bleeds Reflexivization$_1$: note that application of RO to S$_0$ would move *Bill* into such a position that, as in (3b), it could not serve as antecedent in an application of Reflexivization. The cyclic principle, however, rules out such a derivation: Reflexivization would apply to S$_1$ before RO had its chance to apply to S$_0$. Thus, random application of transformations incorrectly allows derivations for both (4a) and (4a'), whereas the cyclic principle correctly allows only a derivation for (4a).[7]

Having given one argument for "the" cyclic principle, let us turn to the question of **what** cyclic principle we should adopt. In what has been said so far in this book about the principle of the cycle, we have sidestepped the two important issues of what exactly the domains are to which transformations apply, and of whether the cyclic principle governs the application of **all** transformations or only of certain kinds of transformations.

With regard to the first issue, we have spoken so far as if the domains to which transformations applied were precisely the Ss that figure in the underlying structure of a sentence. It is far from obvious that only Ss can be domains of application of transformations. For example, note that in the application of Equi-NP-deletion in the derivations of sentences like (5), nothing outside the VP of the main clause plays any role in determining whether the transformation is applicable, or on the effect of the transformation:

(5) John forced Mary$_i$ [(she$_i$ → ∅) to empty the garbage].

There is thus nothing in principle to prevent one from taking the domain to which "object-controlled Equi-NP-deletion" applies to be not a S of the shape (6a) but a VP of the shape (6b):

(6) a. [$_S$ NP [$_{VP}$ V NP$_i$ VP]]]
    b. [$_{VP}$ V NP$_i$ [$_S$ NP$_i$ VP]]

Likewise, there is nothing in principle to prevent one from taking the **Dative-movement** transformation that is often posited in the derivations of sentences like (7a) (cf. (7a′), in which the transformation has not applied)[8] to be a VP of the shape (7c) rather than a S of the shape (7b):

(7) a. Mary sold John the candlestick.
    a′. Mary sold the candlestick to John.
    b. [$_S$ NP [$_{VP}$ V NP [$_{PP}$ to NP]]]
    c. [$_{VP}$ V NP [$_{PP}$ to NP]]

There are also several transformations that could be taken to have a NP rather than a S as domain of application, e.g., the optional replacement of *the* by a dependent NP that will be proposed in chapter 12 as part of the account of NPs like those in (8):

(8) a. the denunciation of Smith by Jackson
    b. Jackson's denunciation of Smith

To make the cyclic principle precise, we must thus specify what exactly the possible domains of application of transformations are (only Ss? only Ss and NPs? VPs as well? constituents of all categories?) and clarify whether we should retain our tacit assumption that all domains of application are "cyclic domains," e.g., whether we should interpret the cyclic principle as implying that the application of the NP movement transformation of (8) must precede the application of any transformations to the S in which the NP is contained.

Surprisingly, very little attention has been devoted to these questions, with virtually all published discussion of domains and the cycle restricted to the question of whether NPs as well as Ss are cyclic domains. Only in Williams (1974) is anything approaching the proposition that all constituents are cyclic domains taken up seriously, though as I pointed out in McCawley 1977, when viewed from a certain perspective, Montague grammar can also be interpreted as regarding all constituents as cyclic domains.

Since the existing literature thus provides little on which one can base an answer to these questions, I will, provisionally, simply adopt the answer that best fits my research program of making the cyclic principle do the greatest amount of work, i.e., I will provisionally assume (i) that every syntactic constituent is a cyclic domain (in the sense that the cyclic principle will be taken as implying that applications of transformations to any constituent must precede applications of transformations to anything that the given constituent is contained in, irrespective of the categories of the two constituents) and (ii) that the domain to which any transformation applies will be the smallest constituent containing all material relevant to its application, so that e.g., the domain to which Dative-movement or Object-controlled Equi-NP-deletion applies will be a VP and the domain to which the NP movement of (8) applies will be a NP. Note that these two answers do in fact maximize the amount of work done by the cyclic principle: they maximize the class of cases in which the cyclic principle will say which of two applications of transformations must precede the other.

Let us turn now to the question of whether all transformations are subject to the principle of the cycle. It turns out that some transformations must be exempted from the cyclic principle, as can be seen easily from the following example. Suppose that **all** transformations applied according to the cyclic principle. Then there would be no derivation relating sentences like (9a) to the presumable deep structure (9b):

(9) a. John bought a car, and Mary did too.
    b.

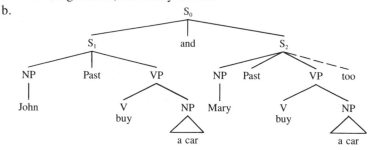

In S_1 and S_2 the conditions for Tense-hopping are met.[9] Thus, the application of Tense-hopping to S_1 and S_2 would precede any application of a transformation to S_0. Since S_0 is the smallest constituent containing the two occurrences of *buy a car,* that means that Tense-hopping would attach Past to the two occurrences of *buy* before VP-deletion had a chance to apply. But then VP-deletion could not delete *buy a car,* the stage of the derivation to which it might apply would no longer contain two occurrences of *buy a car* but only two occurrences of *buy-Past a car:*

(10)

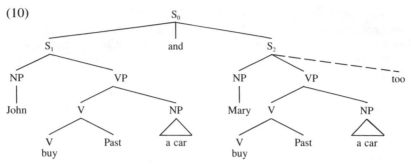

Thus, if VP-deletion is simply the deletion of a repeated VP, and (9a) has (9b) as its deep structure, the application of Tense-hopping to S_1 and S_2 will have to follow the stage of the derivation at which VP-deletion gets its chance to apply to S_0.

This is an anomaly from the point of view of the cyclic principle in its pristine splendor, and either of the two transformations involved here could in principle be held responsible for the anomaly: one could say that the derivation from pristine cyclicity is either that VP-deletion must apply earlier than it "ought to" or that Tense-hopping must apply later than it ought to. More precisely, one could propose either that VP-deletion is **precyclic** (i.e., that it applies prior to the application of all transformations that conform to the cyclic principle) or that Tense-hopping is **postcyclic** (i.e., that it applies after the application of all transformations that conform to the cyclic principle). I will reject the former of these possibilities and adopt the latter, not because of any really clearcut arguments against the one or in favor of the other, but simply on the grounds that taking VP-deletion to be precyclic would subvert the entire program of exploiting the cyclic principle. If VP-deletion were precyclic, then so also would be the vast bulk of the transformations taken up above or in the following chapters, and the cyclic principle would tell us nothing about the interactions of the transformations that we are most interested in. To see this, note that all transformations that feed a precyclic transformation must themselves be precyclic, and that all transformations that change subjects (e.g., Passive, *Tough*-movement, and *There*-insertion) feed VP-deletion:

(11) a. Tom was arrested by the FBI, and Dick was too.
     b. Bill is hard for us to get along with, but Agnes isn't.
     c. We said that there was a leak in the boat, and in fact there was.

By contrast, taking Tense-hopping to be postcyclic does not appear to force one to take any other transformations to be postcyclic, and thus under that alternative the cyclic principle continues to have rich implications for the interaction of transformations. I accordingly rate the second horn of our dilemma the less objectionable one and will henceforth adopt the conclusion that we must weaken the cyclic principle to the extent of admitting a set of postcyclic transformations, with Tense-hopping among them.

The argument just given is in fact valid only for the case of Tense-hopping that combines tenses with main verbs;[10] it is easy to see that it does not carry over to the combining of tenses with auxiliary verbs, in view of the lack of parallelism between (9a), where a tense is "stranded" by the deletion and consequently appears attached to *do,* and (12), where the tense cannot be stranded but must appear in combination with the auxiliary verb:

(12) a. Tom was arrested by the FBI, and Dick was/*did Ø too. (= (11a))
    b. The FBI has bugged my office, and the KGB has/*does Ø too.

It is thus necessary to divide what we have so far lumped together under the name "Tense-hopping" into two transformations: a postcyclic one that combines a tense with a main verb (and for which I will retain the name **Tense-hopping**), and a cyclic one that combines a tense with an auxiliary verb (henceforce to be called **Attraction-to-tense**).

Besides Tense-hopping (in the narrower sense in which we are now using that term), the transformations that are known to be postcyclic are *Do*-support, the deletion of prepositions before complement Ss, the deletion of *for* before *to,* and the irregular deletion of *for* after *want.* Pullum (1976) makes some tentative suggestions as to what kinds of transformations can in principle be postcyclic and makes one proposal that I find particularly attractive, namely that a postcyclic transformation must be **local** in the sense (Emonds 1976) that it can involve only two constituents, which must be adjacent with regard both to linear order (nothing intervenes between them) and to constituent structure (they either are sisters or are aunt and niece).[11] The four transformations listed above meet this description.

Pullum's proposal heavily restricts the possibilities for interactions among postcyclic transformations: the smaller the parts of a syntactic structure that can be involved in the application of two transformations, the less opportunity there is for them to interact in any way. There is indeed only one case that I know of where the possibility of interactions among postcyclic transformations even arises, namely that of Tense-hopping and *Do*-support. *Do* must be adjoined to precisely those tenses that cannot undergo Tense-hopping. But that interaction is predictable if one assumes the Elsewhere Principle (§6b). Tense-hopping applies to the configuration (13a) and *Do*-support to the more general configuration (13b),[12] and thus by the Elsewhere Principle the application of *Do*-support is excluded in those cases where Tense-hopping applies:

(13) a.   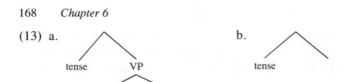   b.

The level of structure that is the output of the cyclic transformations and the input to the postcyclic transformations is often called **shallow structure.** We will thus henceforth assume the following picture of levels and sets of transformations: [13]

(13)

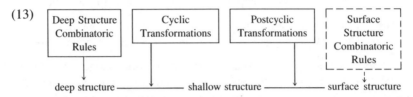

In this diagram, each box represents a set of rules, and the arrow coming out of each box indicates what that set of rules constrains. The arrow may point either to a structural "level," in which case the rules constrain what structures can occur at that level, or to a line connecting two levels, in which they constrain the relationship between the two levels, e.g., the cyclic transformations specify what deep structures may correspond to what shallow structures.

d. Root Transformations

This section is devoted to a notion that, as a result of some quirks of history, is often confused with the notion of postcyclic transformation. It is taken up at this point largely because I believe that the reader will be less likely to confuse the two notions if he sees them taken up together in a context that makes clear that they not only are distinct but are indeed unrelated.

Of the transformations that we have taken up so far, exactly one, namely Inversion, has been subject to the restriction that it applies only in main clauses (i.e., independent questions), not in subordinate clauses (i.e., dependent questions):

(1) a.   What did George talk about?
     b.   Ann asked what George talked about.
     b'.   *Ann asked what did George talk about.

By contrast, the other transformations that we have taken up so far have applied without regard to whether the domain to which they were potentially applicable made up the whole sentence or was embedded in a larger structure. For example, the applicability of Passive in such a sentence as (2a) is not affected when the structure underlying that sentence is embedded in a larger sentence like (2b):

(2) a. The bomb was planted by terrorists.
   b. The newspapers report that the police are convinced that the bomb was planted by terrorists.

The term **root transformation** has been introduced by Emonds (1970, 1976) to refer to transformations whose application is restricted, as in the case of Inversion, to main clauses.[14]

The two postcyclic transformations that we have taken up so far, namely Tense-hopping and *Do*-support, clearly are not root transformations:

(3) a. The State Department refused to confirm the rumor that an ambassador had told a reporter from *Le Monde* that George Washington owned slaves.
   b. It is widely recognized that George Washington owned slaves, but the State Department refuses to confirm the rumor that an ambassador had told a reporter from *Le Monde* that Thomas Jefferson did Ø too.

In (3a), a tense marker gets attached to the following verb just as well in a deeply embedded subordinate clause as it does in a main clause, and in (3b) we see that deletion of the verb to which a tense would otherwise be attached can affect a deeply embedded clause, and that clause can be the domain to which *Do*-support applies, inserting a *do* to serve as bearer of the tense.

Since Tense-hopping provides such a clear example of a postcyclic transformation that is not a root transformation, it is hard to see how the notions could be confused. Such confusion does however exist, as a result of terminological practices in which different linguists in the late sixties and early seventies distinguished "cyclic" transformations from some other kind of transformations, not appreciating that the "other kind" differed from one group of linguists to another. The "other kind" was postcyclic transformations for one group, root transformations for a second group, and something called "last-cyclic transformations" (which is of at most historical interest and will not be taken up in this book) for a third group. Confusion among these three terms was engendered by linguists' failure to make clear which of (at least) three distinctions they had in mind when they argued about whether such-and-such transformation is "cyclic."

Both the notion of postcyclic transformation and that of root transformation will play a role in the chapters that follow, and each notion will be given the appropriate name wherever it arises.

e. Obligatory and Optional Transformations

In the preceding sections, a distinction has implicitly been drawn between **optional** and **obligatory** transformations. Passive provides a fairly clear example of an optional transformation, in the sense that when a derivation contains a structure that meets the conditions for the application of Passive, the derivation is normally allowed but not required to have an application of Passive, e.g., both (1a) and (1a′) have the deep structure (1b), and their derivations (involving *There*-insertion$_1$ and RO$_0$) are identical up to the point where Passive applies in the one derivation but not in the other:

(1) a.   There is believed by many experts to be an error in the argument.
　　 a′. Many experts believe there to be an error in the argument.
　　 b.

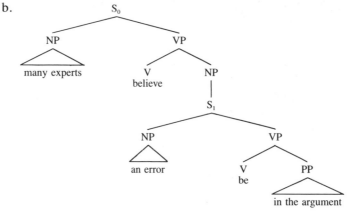

Tense-hopping provides an equally clear example of an obligatory transformation, in the sense that when a derivation contains a structure that meets the conditions for Tense-hopping, the derivation is required to have an application of that rule. For example, the deep structure (2b) can figure in a derivation of (2a), involving an application of Tense-hopping, but not in a derivation of (2a′) or (2a″), to give the only apparent things that one might get without an application of Tense-hopping:[15]

(2) a.   John enjoys tennis.
    a'.   *John does enjoy tennis.
    a".   *John -s enjoy tennis.
    b.

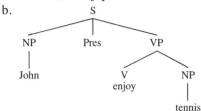

The characterizations just given of "optional" and "obligatory" are far too imprecise to be of much use. Let us attempt to say more precisely what the terms mean. Note that the characterization of "optional" just given is in conflict with the common practice of calling a rule optional even when there are instances in which some factor extraneous to the conditions of application of the rule happens to exclude derivations in which there is no application of the rule. For example, corresponding to (3a) and (4a), whose derivations involve applications of Passive, there are no sentences like (3b) and (4b), whose derivations are like those of (3a) and (4a) except for the nonapplication of Passive:

(3) a.   John forced Mary to be examined by Dr. Grimshaw.
    b.   *John forced Mary for Dr. Grimshaw to examine her.
(4) a.   Mike's being bothered by this is ridiculous.
    b.   *This's bothering Mike is ridiculous.

Here, failure to apply Passive results in violation of one or other constraint on derivations: in (3), violation of the constraint that the complement of *force* must undergo Equi-NP-deletion, and in (4), violation of the constraint that in surface structure all words must be in forms that their morphology allows (*this* has no genitive form).

We will speak of Passive as being optional notwithstanding the existence of cases where one "has to apply Passive," in that what is wrong with the derivations that yield (3b) and (4b) is the violation of the constraints just mentioned, not the nonapplication of Passive that gave rise to those violations. If application of Passive is the only way to avoid these violations in derivations with the given deep structures (and one must make a systematic search of the syntactic devices of English before one is in a position to say that it is), that is true only by accident. There are many cases in which there are two or more optional transformations, the application of any of which could suffice to avoid violation of a particular constraint. For example, the oddity of (5a–a′) (which reflects the fact that a conjoined NP with a personal pronoun as one conjunct and a nonpronoun as the other conjunct has no genitive form) could be avoided not only by passivizing the embedded S (5b) but also by "dislocating" the offending NP, as in (5c):

(5) a.   *You and Nancy's annoying Tom is ridiculous.
    a′. *Your and Nancy's annoying Tom is ridiculous.
    b.   Tom's being annoyed by you and Nancy is ridiculous.
    c.   You and Nancy, your annoying Tom is ridiculous.

To call a transformation optional is simply to say that the rule in itself allows both for derivations in which its conditions for application are met and it is applied, and for derivations in which its conditions for application are met but it is not applied. This is completely neutral with regard to whether there is anything else that in a given case might rule out one or both of these alternatives. This may be a good point at which to remind the reader of something that has largely been lost sight of in this chapter, namely, that a grammar is **not** a procedure for constructing sentences by assembling a deep structure and converting that deep structure into a surface structure, and the notion of derivation that is assumed in this book does not commit one to the latter conception of a grammar.

In the conception of a grammar assumed in this book, neither deep structure nor surface structure, nor any other linguistic level, has any "priority" in relation to other levels. A grammar specifies what derivations a language allows, by means of rules of which some (the "combinatoric" rules) specify what structures are allowed on particular levels, and others (the "transformations") specify how the stages in a derivation may or must differ from one another. In speaking, or in understanding speech, one mentally constructs a derivation,[16] assembling structures on all levels simultaneously, in such a way that (if all is successful) the structures and the relations among them conform to the rules of the grammar. An optional transformation does not direct the language user to flip a mental coin in choosing between two alternative structures; rather it simply makes available to him two possibilities that he is free to use as he puts together syntactic and semantic structures, and it carries no guarantee that even one of those two possibilities, let alone both of them, will be of any use to him in a given case.

The notion of "obligatory transformation" is fairly unproblematic in orthodox transformational grammar, where a fixed order of application of transformations is assumed: if the conditions for the application of transformations are met at the point in the derivation where the rule gets its chance to apply to the given domain, it must apply, in the sense that the derivation is excluded if the rule is not applied. The notion requires some further explication, however, when it is combined, as it is here, with a picture of rule interaction that does not assume a fixed order of application of transformations. Under either conception of rule interaction, the notion of obligatoriness is constrained by the notion of "getting a chance to apply" that is in force. For example, in view of the principle of the cycle, what is directly relevant to the application of an obligatory transformation to a given domain is not whether in deep structure that domain meets the conditions for application but whether it meets them in a stage of the derivation that follows the application of any cyclic transformations to domains contained with it. However, in the approach that is followed here, we have to contend with the possibility that more than one transformation might "get a chance to apply" at a given stage of a derivation. Nothing that has been said so far excludes, for example, the possibility that a single structure might meet the conditions for application of two or more obligatory transformations. Perhaps (i) "obligatory" should be interpreted according to a literal understanding of "must apply whenever its conditions for application are met," which would imply that all the obligatory transformations whose conditions for application are met by a given structure apply simultaneously. Alternatively, (ii) one might require that rules apply one at a time and allow any one of the obligatory transformations whose conditions for application are met at a given stage of a derivation to be the rule that applies at that stage. Or (iii) one might merely require that at the end of the application of the cycle to a given domain there be no obligatory transformation whose conditions for application are met by that domain. Each of these three possibilities restricts the class of admissible derivations less than does the preceding one; for example, (ii) is less restrictive than (i) because it allows for the possibility that one obligatory transformation might bleed another one, and (iii) is less restrictive than (ii) because it allows for the possibility that an optional transformation might bleed an obligatory one. I know of few instances in which a structure meets the conditions for application of more than one obligatory cyclic transformation (S_2 on p. 224, to which both Raising and Tense Replacement apply, is one such case) and none in which the choice among (i)–(iii) matters. I will accordingly leave this question unresolved until cases arise where its answer makes a difference

It is worth noting that whether a given transformation is obligatory or optional can depend on what other rules the grammar is to contain and on how exactly one formulates its conditions of application. A transformation that is **de facto** obligatory, in the sense that no derivations are well formed in which its conditions for application are met but it is not applied, need not be classed as obligatory in the technical sense if the derivations in which it is not applied can be held to be ill formed for some other reason such as, say, that the surface structures violate some combinatoric constraint on surface structure. For example, while *Do*-support is de facto obligatory, the ill-formedness of derivations in which it is applicable but is not applied could be attributed to violation of the morphological requirement that tenses in surface structure be attached to verbs. If *Do*-support were not applied in the derivation of (6a), a surface structure would result in which a tense was in a configuration that its morphology did not allow:

(6) a.   Sarah doesn't like Proust.
    b. * Sarah -sn't like Proust.

There is thus no apparent obstacle to treating *Do*-support as technically optional, notwithstanding the fact that it indeed "must apply" when it can.

One can even seriously entertain the possibility that no transformations need be regarded as obligatory: perhaps in all cases where nonapplication of a transformation is excluded, nonapplication results in violation of some independently necessary constraint. With the analyses adopted here, it seems to be impossible to maintain this last position, since, for example, Tense-hopping apparently must be taken to be obligatory in order to avoid spurious derivations of such nonsentences as (2a'). Likewise, the treatment of Reflexivization in §6b requires that it be obligatory. If it were optional, there would be a spurious derivation for (7: *him*), since it could fail to apply on the lower S, and RO could move the potential antecedent to a position where it no longer met the conditions for Reflexivization.

(7) We believe John$_i$ to hate himself$_i$/*him$_i$.

Note that there is no general constraint against surface structures in which a personal pronoun and its antecedent are in the configuration of (7):

(8) We promised John$_i$ to help him$_i$.

Reflexivization also illustrates how whether a transformation is optional or obligatory can depend on details of what are taken as its conditions for application. In the analyses developed in this book, "indices" (such as the subscript in (7)–(8)) indicate the purported reference of NPs, and when the applicability of a transformation is contingent on two constituents being identical, a difference in the indices of otherwise identical NPs renders it inapplicable. In some versions of transformational grammar, however, syntactic structures are taken to be unspecified for purported reference, and transformations that here are regarded as obligatory and contingent on identity of indices are regarded as optional. Thus, Lees and

Klima (1963) took (9a) and (9b) to have identical deep structures and to differ in whether the option of applying a certain optional transformation was taken or not:

(9) a. John hates himself.
    b. John hates him.

In the approach adopted here, (9a–b) have deep structures that differ with regard to whether the two NPs have identical or distinct indices, with the deep structure of (9a) meeting and that of (9b) failing to meet the conditions of application of an obligatory transformation of Reflexivization.

f. The Cycle and Language Use

It is far from obvious how the cyclic principle relates to the mental events that are involved in a language user's production and understanding of speech. This section will be devoted to a rough sketch of an approach to the understanding of language that is a fairly plausible hypothesis as to the sort of computation that goes on in people's heads and which turns out to embody a recognizable variant of the cyclic principle.

The approach in question, due to Lakoff and Thompson (1975a, 1975b), has the following characteristics: (i) Syntactic analysis is done "in real time," that is, words and phrases are assigned roles in a syntactic structure as soon as the hearer hears them—the hearer does not wait until he has heard the whole sentence before he starts doing a syntactic analysis. (ii) The syntactic analyses are **relational** in nature, that is, they consist of specifications of the grammatical relations (such as "is the subject of") that hold between the parts of a sentence. (iii) The analysis proceeds by steps of provisional assignment of grammatical relations and of revision of already assigned grammatical relations. (iv) The analysis yields a structure that is closely analogous to a deep structure rather than to a surface structure.

More specifically, the analysis works as follows. Consider the sentence (1):

(1) The hostages are believed by the police to have been killed.

Let us assume that besides being able to carry out the scheme of analysis about to be described, hearers can identify all the words in question and can identify NPs as being NPs. (The procedure to be sketched takes NPs as given and fits them into a syntactic structure.) The analysis begins by positing a sentence S_0. The first NP that is encountered (here, *the hostages*) is tentatively assigned the role of subject of S_0, and the first verb that is encountered after it (here, *are*) is tentatively assigned the role of predicate of

S_0. The next word encountered is *believed,* which is the past participle of a verb. The combination of a form of *be* and a following past participle triggers a reassignment of grammatical relations: the verb of which the past participle is formed takes over from *be* the role of predicate of S_0, and the NP currently assigned the role of subject of *be* is reassigned the role of object of the "main" verb (here, *believe*). The procedure so far can be summarized in the following table, in which entries in lower lines indicate revisions made on the entries in the upper lines:

(2)

the hostages	are	believed
Subj of S_0	P of S_0	———
———		believe
Obj of S_0		P of S_0

Next comes *the police.* If the S currently under analysis (here, S_0) has been identified as passive (i.e., if a NP previously identified as its subject has been reassigned the role of object), the NP of a *by + NP* combination may be assigned the role of subject of the S, and I assume that the option of so analysing it is taken here. (There is also the possibility of assigning it other roles, such as a locative or a time specification, as in *He was shot by the lakefront* or . . . *by 10:00.* For expository ease, I ignore such alternative possibilities here.)

We now encounter *to have.* The predicate of the S under analysis is at this point *believe,* and *believe* belongs to a class of verbs that, when followed by *to* and a verb in the infinitive form, trigger the following reassignment of grammatical relations: (i) a new S (here called S_1) is posited and takes over the status of "the S under analysis"; (ii) the object of *believe* is reassigned the role of subject of S_1; and (iii) S_1 is assigned the role of object of S_0. The analysis so far is as follows:

(3)

S_0	the hostages	are	believed	by	the police	to	S_1
	Subj of S_0 Obj of S_0	P of S_0	——— believe				
			P of S_0		Subj of S_0		
	Subj of S_1						Obj of S_0

Leaving aside *have,* which can be worked into the analysis in a fairly straightforward way, we reach *been killed* and do the same reanalysis that we did in the case of *are believed: be* is first assigned the role of P of S_1 but is then supplanted in this role by *kill,* and the role of *the hostages* is reassigned from subject of S_1 to object of S_1. If we retain only our final assignments of grammatical relations, we then have the following structure, which is a close approximation to the deep structure that would be set up under the analyses developed in chapters 3–5:

(4)

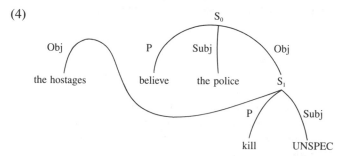

In this diagram, "Subj," "Obj," and "P" are labels not of nodes but of branches, and the curved lines are an informal way of indicating that left-to-right order should not be regarded as significant. The content of (4) is that S_0 is made up of *believe* as its predicate, *the police* as its subject, and S_1 as its object, with S_1 made up of *kill* as its predicate, *the hostages* as its object, and UNSPEC as its subject (the step that would assign UNSPEC that role was not given in the procedure sketched above, but could easily be filled in).

The various steps of reassignment of grammatical relations amount to the steps in a derivation with (4) as deep structure. Moreover, the interaction of these steps is precisely in accord with the cyclic principle: the initial assignments of grammatical relations correspond roughly to the surface structure, and in each reassignment of grammatical relations, either a more deeply underlying structure for the same S is recovered or a derived structure for an embedded S is posited and the task is changed to that of recovering an underlying structure for the latter S. Note in particular that in the application of Lakoff and Thompson's procedure to (1), *the hostages* is successively assigned the status of subject of S_0, of object of S_0, of subject of S_1, and of object of S_1, via steps that correspond to Passive on S_0, to RO on S_0, and to Passive on S_1. Moreover, the structures that are directly relevant to the various reassignments of grammatical relations are in most cases neither surface structures nor deep structures but intermediate structures in derivations, e.g., in the step that assigns to *the hostages* the role of subject of S_1, it is completely immaterial that *the hostages* is the surface subject of S_0: what is relevant is only that at that stage of the procedure it is the object of S_0.

EXERCISES

1. Give derivations for the following sentences, ignoring tenses but giving full attention to complementizers:
   a. The boys all seem to be hated by their teachers.
   b. Your brothers happen to both be admired by Lucy.
2. a. Construct a derivation in which Raising-to-subject on a particular S feeds Q-float on that S.
   b. Construct one in which Tough-movement on a particular S feeds Equi on the next higher S.
   c. Construct one in which Passive bleeds Inversion.
   d. Determine whether Quantifier-float can feed VP-deletion.
3. Because Extraposition is optional, there is sometimes more than one possibility as to **which** domain it applies to. Show that the sentence

   John believes it to be obvious that God is dead.

allows two different derivations (with slightly different surface constituent structures), one where Extraposition applies on the lowest possible domain and one where it applies on a higher domain. Assume that Extraposition of object complements, like that of subject complements, yields a derived structure

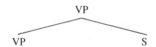

Give the two surface structures in full detail.
4. a. Provide an argument that the transformation deleting prepositions before *that*-clauses and *for-to* complements must be postcyclic.
   b. Do the same for *Do*-support.
   c. Do the same for the transformation that deletes *for* before *to*.
   d. Explain the cryptic remark in chap. 5, n. 6 about attachment of -*'s* to subjects of *'s -ing* complements.
5. Suppose that (contrary to what you are likely ever to have been told) in deep structure the plural morpheme is part of the Det and that it is moved into its surface position by a transformation something like Affix-hopping. Construct an argument, directly analogous to the one (on pp. 165–66 of this chapter) that Tense-hopping is postcyclic, showing that this transformation must also be postcyclic. In the role played by VP-deletion in the earlier argument, use the transformation that replaces a repeated $\bar{\text{N}}$ by *one*.

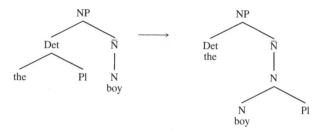

6. Decide whether each of the following is a root transformation, and give appropriate examples to justify your conclusion.
  a. Preposing of VP in such sentences as
     They said that John would win the prize, and <u>win it</u> he has.
  b. VP-deletion.
  c. Optional inversion accompanying preposed direct quotations, as in
     "You're insane," <u>shouted John</u> in a menacing tone.
  d. Extraposition of relative clauses.
  e. Inversion after preposed negatives, as in:
     Never before had he seen such stupidity.
     Under no circumstances will I talk to them.
  f. Deletion of *for* after *want*.
  g. Any other transformation whose status as a root transformation has not been taken up.

NOTES

1. In most of the structures presented in this chapter, tenses, auxiliary verbs, and complementizers will be omitted for simplicity's sake. The omissions do not affect the points being made.

2. *Someone* appears in place of *anyone* in (2b), in accordance with the analysis to be adopted in §17a, according to which the *any* of sentences like (2a) is the form that *some* takes when it is in the scope of a negation. The position of *not* in (2b) is a makeshift and should not be taken seriously. A serious proposal regarding the deep structure location of *not* is made in §8b and elaborated in chapter 17.

3. This terminology is further systematized in Koutsoudas, Sanders, and Noll (1974).

4. Which version of (2a′) would result would depend on how exactly Passive would affect a structure that had a VP-modifier, which is a possibility that we have not considered in our discussion of Passive so far. I reject as a cop-out the suggestion that (2a′) be excluded by gerrymandering the details of Passive so that it would be simply inapplicable to such a structure.

5. For a more accurate statement of the conditions of application of Reflexivization, see §11f.

6. These observations are of course perfectly consistent with other schemes of rule application, e.g., simultaneous application or the combined simultaneous/random scheme proposed by Koutsoudas, Sanders, and Noll.

7. This argument is weak not only because it argues only against a straw-man alternative but also because even that straw man can be rescued by combining it with an idea that has considerable independent interest and much popularity, namely, the idea that in the output of movement transformations, the position previously occupied by the moved item is filled by a **trace,** i.e., a phonologically null constituent that functions syntactically as a pronoun whose antecedent is the moved item (Wasow 1979, Chomsky 1981). Under that conception of movement transformations, the above argument collapses, since the antecedent of the reflexive could then be the trace rather than *Bill,* and RO would not bleed Reflexive no matter what sequence the rules applied in.

8. To simplify exposition, an arbitrary choice has been made regarding which of (7a) and (7a′) is closer to deep structure. The few arguments that I know of that allegedly choose between an analysis that derives a structure like (7a) from one like (7a′) and an analysis that derives a structure like (7a′) from one like (7a) have shaky foundations.

9. The dotted line in (9b) indicates that no serious claim about the place of *too* in the constituent structure is intended. I in fact argue in §17e that in examples like (9b), *too* is Chomsky-adjoined to the VP.

10. The argument that Tense-hopping is postcyclic is due to Akmajian and Wasow (1975). The transformation that combines *-ing* and the past participle morpheme with their host verbs is, like Attraction-to-tense, cyclic. A possible case of precyclic transformations will come up in chapter 18, where some reasons will be given for taking "Negative incorporation" (which, e.g., combines *not* and *anyone* into *no one*) to be precyclic.

11. Emonds's definition of "local" required in addition that one of the two constituents involved be of a "lexical" rather than a "phrasal" category.

12. The basis of this claim will be presented in chap. 8.

13. The inclusion of the box labeled "surface structure combinatoric rules" anticipates conclusions arrived at in chap. 10.

I have inadvertently neglected to include in this section discussion of a principle that will play an important role in chapters 17–18 of this book, namely, the principle of **strict cyclicity.** This principle excludes de facto violations of the cyclic principle by imposing a narrow interpretation on what it is for a transformation to apply to a particular domain: if one potential domain *Y* for the application of transformations is contained in another domain *X,* then if all the material relevant to some application of a transformation is contained in *Y,* only *Y* and not *X* can count as the domain for that application of a transformation. This stipulation has the effect of preventing one from "returning to" *Y* after cyclic transformations have applied to *X.* See McCawley 1984 for discussion of alternative conceptions of "strict cyclicity" that have played a role in the literature and of the implications of the version of the principle that is adopted here.

14. Two caveats must be made regarding the interpretation of "main clause." First, when Ss are conjoined, each of the conjunct Ss has the main or subordinate status of the whole coordinate structure, e.g., in *Where did he go and when will he be back?* both *Where did he go?* and *When will he come back?* are main clauses. Second, direct quotations of main clauses count as main clauses, e.g., in *I'm sure that Bill asked Ann, "When will he come back?"* we must treat *"When will he come back?"* as a main clause, notwithstanding its being embedded in a larger structure. See Hooper and Thompson (1973), Green (1976), and Goldsmith (1981) for discussion of whether the transformations that Emonds identifies as applying only in main clauses really are restricted to main clauses.

15. *Do* in (2b) is unstressed; *John dóes enjoy tennis* is of course acceptable.

16. The construction may well be only partial, i.e., the speaker or hearer may well construct only as much of the derivation as he needs to for his purposes of the moment. The derivations given here purport to represent the linguistic structure that is accessible to the language user but do not embody the claim that he avails himself of all of that structure in each instance in which he uses the given sentence.

7. *Syntactic Categories*

a. Factors Influencing Syntactic Behavior

In the syntactic analyses presented so far in this book, I have represented the various constituents as belonging to particular syntactic categories but have made no attempt to say in general what a syntactic category is or what it is for two items to belong to the same syntactic category. This chapter is intended to partially remedy that deficiency.

Since different syntactic constituents have different syntactic properties, some categorization of items must play a role in a syntactic description. The following examples illustrate differences in the ways in which items having the same or close to the same meaning may combine with other items:[1]

(1) a.   John is old enough/*sufficiently to get married.
　　a'.   John is sufficiently/*enough old to get married.
　　b.   John opened the box carefully.
　　b'.   John opened the box with care.
　　b".   John carefully opened the box.
　　b"'.   *John with care opened the box.
　　c.   Mary realizes/*aware(s) that no one can help her.
　　c'.   Mary is aware/*realize that no one can help her.
　　d.   Margaret is very similar to her mother.
　　d'.   *Margaret very resembles her mother.
　　d".   *Margaret is similar to her mother very much.
　　d"'.   Margaret resembles her mother very much.

With the possible exception of the difference between *sufficiently* and *enough* noted in (1a–a') (which is an unclear case because of difficulty in deciding what part of speech *enough* should be assigned to), these differences in syntactic behavior are concomitants of differences in the "part of speech" (or as we will say henceforth, the **lexical category**) of the words in question. Two systematic differences between verbs and adjectives are illustrated by (1c–c', d–d"'), namely, that adjectives but not verbs require the copula *be* when used in predicate position and that degree expressions (such as *very (much)*) precede or follow the phrase that they modify depending on whether the **head** of that phrase (i.e., the word on which the other parts of the phrase "depend") is a verb or an adjective. There are also differences in the form that the degree phrase takes: *very* vs. *very much*. In (1a–a′, b–b′) we see that adverbs (*sufficiently, carefully*) are allowed to precede the phrases that they modify, but synonymous expressions (the hard to categorize *enough* and the prepositional phrase *with care*) must occupy other positions.

Lexical category is as much a notion of morphology as one of syntax, in that what an item is inflected for provides sufficient grounds for assigning it to a lexical category, e.g., an English word that is inflected for tense and for agreement with its subject in person and number is a verb regardless of any other facts about its behavior.[2] The differences in syntactic behavior of the different lexical categories serve in part to allow compliance with morphological requirements, e.g., the use of *be* with predicate adjectives insures that something will be available to support the tense inflection that finite clauses are required to have.

In my informal statement of the differences among (1d–d‴), I spoke of the phrases *similar to her mother* and *resemble(s) her mother* and the fact that the head of the one is an adjective and that of the other a verb. It is in fact common for a phrasal constituent of a construction to be subject to restrictions on the lexical category of its head:

(2) a.　John seems (very) displeased with me.
　　a′.　*John seems cursing me.
　　b.　They named Alice manager of their Toledo office.
　　b′.　*They named Alice responsible for their Toledo office.

Let us accordingly recognize **lexical category of the head** of a constituent as a factor relevant to the syntactic behavior of that constituent, and let us also tentatively adopt the following position on syntactic categories: (i) there are a number of factors (hopefully, a small number) that can play a role in the syntactic behavior of constituents of syntactic structures, and (ii) a syntactic category is simply a combination of those factors, i.e., to say that two items belong to the same syntactic category is simply to say that they agree with respect to the factors that determine their potential syntactic behavior.

The above discussion of (2) has brought up something that might be a second factor distinguishing items with regard to their syntactic behavior, namely, the distinction between a lexical item and a phrasal unit having that item as head. There is of course an obvious respect in which, e.g., the transitive verb *resemble* and a phrase *resemble her mother* of which it is head differ syntactically, namely, that the former but not the latter can be combined with an object NP:

(3) a.   Margaret <u>resembles</u> her great aunt Matilda.

    b. *Margaret <u>resembles her mother</u> her great aunt Matilda.

This difference, though, could very well be regarded as semantic rather than syntactic, since (3b), whatever its syntactic status, would evidently correspond to an ill-formed semantic structure: *resemble* expresses a two-place relation,[3] and (3b) has more NPs than *resemble* can accommodate semantically. Even so, there are a number of syntactic phenomena in which a phrasal unit plays a role that its head by itself cannot play, and these provide a reason for drawing a category distinction that is already implicit in our terminology, which distinguishes V from VP and A from AP.[4] For example, "VP-deletion" is indeed the deletion of a repeated VP, not just of its V:[5]

(4) a.   If Margaret understands this poem, then Alice does too.

    a'. *If Margaret understands this poem, then Alice does the other poem.

    b.   Although Alec gave money to the Red Cross, Nancy didn't.

    b'.   Although Alec gave money to the Alumni Fund, Nancy didn't give/*∅ books to the library.

Similarly, the preposing of verb phrases and adjective phrases illustrated in (5) never affects just the verb and adjective of a phrase that also contains an "object" of the verb or adjective:[6]

(5) a.   Bill said he would buy a motorcycle, and buy a motorcycle he did.

    a'. *Bill said he would buy a motorcycle, and buy he did a motorcycle.

    b.   Ashamed of his past Dudley isn't.

    b'. *Ashamed Dudley isn't of his past.

    A caveat should be inserted regarding the use of the terms "phrase" and "phrasal" here, namely, that (in conformity with the terminological practices of transformational grammar and the earlier chapters of this book, but contrary to older terminological practices) a single word counts as a "phrase" when it has no "objects," e.g., *Birds fly* and *I'm hungry* contain a V that makes up a VP (*fly*) and an A that makes up an AP (*hungry*). Note that this policy is in accord with the way that the deletions and movements of APs and VPs noted in connection with (4)–(5) work:

(6) a. Although Alec <u>sang</u>, Nancy didn't ∅.

    b. Bill said he would sing, and <u>sing</u> he did.

    c. <u>Hungry</u> I'm not.

Following partially the notational practice introduced in Chomsky 1970a, let us use symbols of the form $\overline{\text{X}}$ (read "X bar") to mean "phrasal unit whose head is of category X."[7] Thus we will henceforth write $\overline{\text{V}}$ and $\overline{\text{A}}$ for what we have hitherto called VP and AP (and will thus say "$\overline{\text{V}}$-deletion" for what we have hitherto called VP-deletion). What else we can apply symbols of this form to will depend on precise details of what is a phrasal unit and what is a head, e.g., whether it is appropriate to write $\overline{\text{P}}$ for what we have hitherto called PP will depend on whether prepositional phrases should be counted as phrasal units and whether the preposition should count as the head.

The discussion so far has not made clear what the symbol $\overline{\text{N}}$ should be applied to, e.g., whether it should be applied to any or all of the constituents marked with ? in (7), supposing for the moment that the constituent structure is actually as indicated:

(7)

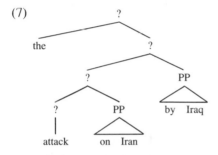

It can easily be seen that a three-way category distinction must be made, among the noun (*attack*), the whole NP (*the attack on Iran by Iraq*), and phrasal units within the NP (*attack on Iran* and *attack on Iran by Iraq*), and it is to these last units that, in virtue of analogies with $\overline{\text{V}}$ and $\overline{\text{A}}$ that will be discussed shortly, I will apply the term $\overline{\text{N}}$. Consider the phenomenon that is usually (and incorrectly) described as a replacement of a repeated noun by *one*. By examining NPs in which the noun is accompanied by PP adjuncts, one can see that it is in fact a phrasal unit that is replaced by *one*:[8]

(8) a. The <u>students</u> of physics are smarter than the students/*ones of chemistry.

   a'. The <u>students of physics</u> who play chess are smarter than the ones who play bridge.

   b. The <u>attack</u> on Iran by Iraq was more destructive than the attack/?one on Angola by South Africa.

   b'. The <u>attack on Iran</u> by Iraq was more destructive than the one by Israel.

b″. The <u>attack on Iran by Iraq</u> in June was more destructive than the one in September.

c. Newton's <u>theory</u> of planetary motion is more interesting than his theory/*one of light.

c′. The <u>theory of light</u> that Newton developed was more interesting than the one that Huyghens proposed.

The antecedent of *one* can be a N-headed phrasal unit such as *student of physics, attack on Iran, attack on Iran by Iraq,* or *theory of light,* but not a noun that does not make up a whole phrasal unit, as illustrated in (8a), (8c), and possibly (8b). (I conjecture that the greater acceptability of *one* in (8b) than in (8a, c) reflects greater ease in interpreting *attack* in (7) as making up a phrasal unit.) However, *one* cannot have a whole NP as antecedent:

(9) a. *Alice read <u>every book on the reading list</u>, and George read one too.

b. *Toscanini recorded <u>Wagner's Faust overture</u>, and Fürtwängler recorded one too.

(If possible at all, (9a) would have to be interpreted with *book* or *book on the reading list* as the antecedent of *one*.) Thus, if $\bar{N}$ is interpreted in such a way as to take in expressions like *student of physics* but not whole NPs, then the transformation under discussion can be described as replacement of a repeated $\bar{N}$ by *one*.[9]

The antecedent of *one* or of a deleted $\bar{V}$ need not be a minimal $\bar{N}$ or $\bar{V}$ but can involve modifiers over and above the basic material of an $\bar{N}$ or $\bar{V}$:

(10) a. Tom <u>lived in Vienna</u> for two years and Mary did ∅ for three years.

a′. Tom <u>lived in Vienna for two years</u> and Mary did ∅ too.

a″. George <u>plays Beatle songs on a violin whenever he gets drunk</u>, and Marvin does ∅ too.

b. The <u>theory of light</u> that Newton proposed was more interesting than the one that Huyghens proposed.

b′. The <u>theory of light that Newton proposed</u> that at first was laughed at was more interesting than the one that met with instant acceptance.

These larger expressions fit the informal definition of $\bar{X}$ given above, provided that we take the addition of modifiers to a constituent as not affecting its status as a phrasal unit or what its head is, so that, e.g., *live in Vienna for two years* is a phrasal unit with *live* as its head, just as *live in Vienna* is. "Modifier" must here be understood as **not** including "Determiners": while *theory of light that Newton proposed* must count as an $\bar{N}$, **the** *theory of light that Newton proposed* must not.

By identifying as $\bar{\text{N}}$ the expressions that we have, we also thereby make $\bar{\text{N}}$ analogous to $\bar{\text{V}}$ and $\bar{\text{A}}$ with regard to what it can consist of. Vs, As, and Ns express **predicates,**[10] i.e., properties or relations. The constituents that we have identified as minimal $\bar{\text{X}}$s contain an item (the "X") that expresses a predicate, plus other items expressing the things that its subject is presented as standing in the given relation to. For example, in (1c–c′), the verb *realize* and the adjective *aware* both express a certain relation between a person and a proposition, and the $\bar{\text{V}}$ or $\bar{\text{A}}$ contains an expression denoting the latter proposition as well as containing the V or A. Likewise, the adjective *related* and the noun *relative* make the same contributions to the meanings of (11a) and (11b):

(11) a. Genevieve is related to my oboe teacher.
 b. Genevieve is a relative of my oboe teacher.

The $\bar{\text{A}}$ *related to my oboe teacher* and the $\bar{\text{N}}$ *relative of my oboe teacher* both consist of a word (*related, relative*) expressing a certain two-place predicate and additional material that provides content for the second "place" of that predicate. If we stretch the term "object" to take in relationships such as that of *my oboe teacher* to *related* in (11a) and *relative* in (11b), we can say that a minimal $\bar{\text{X}}$ consists of a head of lexical category X plus that item's "objects," if any.

"Predicate" is a notion of **logical category,** and logical category must in fact be added to the two dimensions of syntactic categorization identified so far if the dimensions are to suffice to distinguish NP from $\bar{\text{N}}$ and to distinguish S from other categories such as $\bar{\text{V}}$. I tentatively identify NPs as constituents that correspond to logical **arguments** of predicates, i.e., to the things of which a predicate is predicated, so that, e.g., *that John quit* and *the boss* in (12) are NPs in virtue of their expressing the logical arguments of the predicate *surprise:*

(12) That John quit surprised the boss.

This tentative identification of "NP" with "argument" can actually be accepted only as a first approximation if the account of what it is to be a NP is to agree with the consensus among transformational grammarians that extraposed complements like *that John quit* in (13a) are not NPs (even though they correspond to logical arguments) and that a "predicate NP" like *a lawyer* in (13b) is a NP (even though it does not correspond to an argument: *lawyer* expresses a predicate that is predicated of Sophie):

(13) a. It surprised the boss that John quit.
 b. Sophie is a lawyer.

These judgments of NP-hood are not mere visceral feelings on the part of linguists but correspond to syntactic phenomena in which predicate NPs and nonextraposed complements behave the same way that typical NPs do, while extraposed complements do not, e.g.:

(14) a.   What Sophie is is a lawyer.
      b.   What surprised the boss is that John quit.
      c. *What it surprised the boss is that John quit.

I hold that "NP" is not a "classical" category, to which an item either belongs plain and simple or does not belong plain and simple, but rather a **fuzzy category,**[11] to which items can belong in different respects and/or to different degrees, and that the category NP has (at least) the following dimensions:

i.   **Semantic.** An item is semantically a NP if it expresses an argument of the predicate element with which it is combined.
ii.   **Internal syntactic.** An item is a NP in internal syntax if it has a form typical of items that express logical arguments, i.e., if it is a pronoun or proper name or of the form Det N̄.
iii. **External syntactic.** An item is a NP in external syntax if it occurs in a position typical of items that express logical arguments, i.e., if it occurs in subject or object position, or as object of a preposition.

An alternative, not completely equivalent, statement of the idea of iii is:

iii'. An item is a NP "by inheritance" if it occupies an "argument position" in the sense that either (a) it is a logical argument and has not been moved from its deep structure position or (b) it has replaced an item that is a NP by (a) or (b).

One case in which iii and iii' classify things differently is that of predicate NPs, which are NPs on the criterion of iii, since they fill the NP position of the [v̄ V NP] configuration, but not on the criterion of iii', since they do not correspond to logical arguments and have not replaced anything that does. I have no firm conclusion as to whether iii or iii' or both need be admitted into our repertoire of category notions.

How these dimensions of NP-hood apply in particular cases will depend, of course, on how the meanings of sentences are analyzed into predicates, arguments, and other semantic constituents. In applying them, I will take the position that the prepositions that introduce adverbial expressions express predicates in most cases, e.g., in *John writes poems in his room,* both *write* and *in* express predicates, namely a two-place relation between a person and something that he writes, and a two-place relation between an event (here one of John writing a poem) and the place where it occurs.

Poems and *his room* are NPs on the semantic dimension in virtue of their status as arguments of these two predicates, besides being NPs in both internal and external syntax.

In the examples discussed so far in this section, the predicates that have figured in their meanings have not only received overt expression but have been expressed by words that are in "standard" positions for predicates. There are also cases where predicates are without any overt expression, as in (15a), where the meaning involves the same predicate that is expressed by *at* in (15b) or *on* in (15c) (a predicate expressing the relation between an event and the time at which it occurs, or between a proposition and a time at which it is true) but no preposition occurs overtly:

(15) a. John wrote a poem (*on/*at) last Tuesday.
　　 b. John began writing at 2:00.
　　 c. John wrote a poem on Tuesday.

I will speak of *last Tuesday* as possessing semantic NP-hood in this case in virtue of its status as argument of the understood *on/at,* and as possessing an intermediate degree of external syntactic NP-hood in virtue of the absence of the preposition that would otherwise make its semantic role explicit. I will apply the dimensions this way in cases in which the predicate of which something is an argument is manifested in something other than a "predicate position," e.g., where a relation such as the "understood *at/on*" of (15a) is expressed by an inflectional morpheme rather than by a separate word.

We can then recognize the italicized items in (16), hitherto all indiscriminately labeled NP, as peripheral members of the category NP in virtue of their meeting some but not all of the above criteria for NP-hood:

(16)	Semantic	Internal syntactic	External syntactic	By inheritance
That John left shocked us.	+	−	+	+
It shocked us *that John left*.	+	−	−	−
It shocked us that John left.	−	+	+	+
There was a man outside.	−	−	+	+
Sophie is *a lawyer*.	−	+	+	−
He went home *that day*.	+	+	intermed.	+?

Where the category "NP" has been invoked in the description of phenomena, it will be necessary to specify which dimensions of NP-hood are relevant, and thus what part of the periphery of the category is to be taken in. For example, external syntax but not internal syntax appears to be relevant to whether an item can appear in "focus" position of a pseudo-cleft sentence.

I will close this section by stating emphatically that the syntactically relevant properties that have been taken up in this section are by no means all that there are; indeed, another has already been taken up, namely, exceptionality features, such as were discussed briefly in §5c. Others may be taken up below, as the occasion arises.

b. A Reappraisal of the Categories Proposed So Far

Let us now reexamine the putative syntactic categories that figure in chapters 1 through 6 in light of the conception of syntactic category adopted in the preceding section.

S. The category "S" is, like NP, the fuzzy syntactic category corresponding to a logical category, namely that of proposition. The internal structure most typical of constituents that express propositions is [NP $\bar{\mathrm{V}}$]. The periphery of the category includes items that express propositions but have a different internal syntax; this takes in both items as in (1a–a'), which exhibit a reduced form of [NP $\bar{\mathrm{V}}$] and perhaps should be regarded as being Ss in internal syntax to an intermediate degree, and items as in (1b–b'), which do not exhibit even a distorted form of that internal syntax:

(1) a.   John wants <u>to go home</u>.
    a'. With <u>the bus drivers on strike</u>, we'll have to form a car pool.
    b.   <u>The more, the merrier</u>.
    b'. John made nasty remarks about Mary, and <u>vice versa</u>.

Reduced Ss differ in the degrees to which they are reduced, with the reduced embedded Ss of (1a–a') sharing more of the internal syntax of full Ss than do complements that are reduced down to just a NP, as in *John wants a new house*.

PP. It is not obvious what (if anything) should count as the head of a prepositional phrase. If we regard the preposition as the head, we can interpret PP as $\bar{\mathrm{P}}$, though we must guard here against basing such a judgment on an equivocation over the term "object." What is normally called the "object" of a preposition is often its object in the sense of §7a (e.g., in *George Washington was born in 1732*, a two-place relation between an event and a time is expressed by *in,* and *1732* indicates the time that fills the second place). However, *Carthage* in *the destruction of Carthage* does not have

that object relation to *of,* since *of* there does not express a predicate. I will in fact categorize as $\bar{\text{P}}$ even expressions such as *of Carthage,* but I emphasize that that policy is justified only if we can maintain (as I will, at least tentatively) that semantically empty instances of a lexical category take on the same syntactic relations as do semantically contentful members of the category.

I will in addition (following Jespersen [1924:89]) treat so-called "subordinating conjunctions," as in (2), as prepositions with sentential objects, and will consequently take expressions such as *before he left* to be $\bar{\text{P}}$s:

(2) a. John phoned me <u>before</u> he left.
    b. Sam worked at a second job <u>until</u> he had paid off his debts.
    c. I'll help you <u>if</u> you'll tell me what the problem is.
    d. <u>Although</u> Debbie likes Ed, she is very inconsiderate of him.
    e. <u>While</u> you're making the coffee, I'll set the table.

The words in many cases are homophonous with and synonymous with prepositions as normally understood, as illustrated by the following parallels to (2a–b):

(3) a. John phoned me before his departure.
    a'. John phoned me before the football game.
    b. Sam worked at a second job until the summer.
    b'. Sam worked at a second job until his arrest.

In other cases (2c–e) they have the sorts of meanings that could be expressed by prepositions if the "object" were expressed by an ordinary NP rather than by a S, e.g., *while you were singing* can be paraphrased by *during your singing,* and the contribution of *while* to the meaning of the one expression is the same as that of *during* to the meaning of the other.

"**AUX.**" The category name "AUX," though not used in this book, has figured widely in analyses of English auxiliary verbs, though its meaning varies considerably from one author to another. It was introduced in Chomsky (1957) to designate the whole sequence of auxiliary verbs that occurs in a given S, e.g., in Chomsky 1957, *must have been* was an AUX. In the works of many subsequent authors (e.g., Akmajian, Steele, and Wasow 1979), however, it has been used to mean "tensed auxiliary verb" (so that, e.g., *must have been* would not be an AUX but the *must* of that combination would be one). It will be argued in chapter 8 that the constituent structure assumed in the former analysis is incorrect, so the problem of categorizing the (nonexistent) constituent that the analysis posits vanishes. It will also be argued there that auxiliary verbs (whether tensed or tenseless) are verbs and each is the head of its own $\bar{\text{V}}$ except insofar as it has been removed from that $\bar{\text{V}}$ by Inversion.

Adverb. Traditional definitions of "adverb" all amount to "modifier other than adjective." They thus make it a wastebasket for modifiers. At least, though, the traditional definitions point to a factor that can serve as a basis for classification of modifiers if it is used systematically rather than in the haphazard way in which it has figured in traditional schemes of parts of speech, namely, the category of what is modified. (Adjectives modify nouns and NPs; "adverbs" modify everything else.) The various items that have been classed as adverbs in fact differ among themselves with regard to what they can modify and, correspondingly, in the surface positions that they can occupy:

(4) a.   *Completely the invaders were destroying the fort.
    a′.   *The invaders completely were destroying the fort.
    a″.   The invaders were completely destroying the fort.
    a‴.   The invaders were destroying the fort completely.
    b.   ?Intentionally John was insulting Mary.
    b′.   John intentionally was insulting Mary.
    b″.   John was intentionally insulting Mary.
    b‴.   John was insulting Mary intentionally.
    c.   Probably a war will break out.
    c′.   A war probably will break out.
    c″.   A war will probably break out.
    c‴.   *A war will break out probably.[12]

Here *completely* modifies a V, *intentionally* a $\bar{V}$, and *probably* a S. It thus may be appropriate to introduce terminology that expresses distinctions with regard to the category of what is modified, e.g., we may wish to apply terms such as "Ad-V," "Ad-$\bar{V}$," and "Ad-S" respectively to the three "adverbs." Such categories figure prominently in the tradition of **categorial grammar** (e.g., Ajdukiewicz 1935), the first syntactic approach in which a policy was adopted of classifying modifiers systematically on the basis of the category of what they modify.

The last paragraph has dealt with notions of adverb that relate to syntactic functions. However, the question of what adverbial syntactic functions must be recognized is independent of the question of whether a lexical category corresponding to the traditional term "adverb" must be posited. Note in this connection that the lexical category "adjective" is not restricted to items that are functioning as modifiers of Ns, $\bar{N}$s, or NPs, as in (5a)—it also takes in predicative uses as in (5b), where *happy* strictly speaking does not modify anything:

(5) a. I've written a poem about a happy man.
    b. John is happy.

In chapter 8 we will make use of the proposition that morphology provides a prima facie case for membership in a lexical category, e.g., because *have* (whether it is used as an auxiliary verb or as a main verb) is inflected like a verb, it for that reason belongs to the category V. Since adverbs in English have no inflectional morphology, we cannot assign items to a putative lexical category "Adverb" on the basis of how they are inflected. There is, however, one detail of morphology that provides some support for the recognition of such a category, namely the fact that the suffix -*ly* is common among adverbs of several of the classes that differ with regard to what they modify (note, e.g., that all three of the adverbs in (4) have the suffix -*ly*).

Let us in fact tentatively accept **both** a lexical category "Adverb" **and** a set of notions "ad-X" that distinguish modifiers with regard to what they modify. (We must be careful, of course, not to confuse the lexical category Adverb with the category Ad-V.) If there is a lexical category Adv(erb), is there also a corresponding phrasal category "Adverb phrase" consisting of phrasal units having an Adv as head?[13] Adverbs can be combined with degree expressions, as in (6):

(6) a. extremely quickly
    b. quite disgustingly

However, since the degree expressions are modifiers of and not "objects" of the adverbs, expressions as in (6) provide no grounds for recognizing a category $\overline{\text{Adv}}$ (Adverb phrase): a modifier combines with an item into an expression of the same category as that item, and thus *extremely quickly* cannot be classed as an Adverb phrase unless *quickly* itself can be so classed. Jackendoff (1977:78) has observed that adverbs usually do not admit objects, even if they are close counterparts of adjectives or verbs that do admit objects (7a–b), but that there is a small range of adverbs that do admit objects (7c):

(7) a. fearfully (*of snakes)
    b. angrily (*at Bill)
    c. fortunately/unfortunately/luckily for us

I accordingly tentatively recognize a phrasal category $\overline{\text{Adv}}$, though I note that it will often be difficult to determine whether a particular occurrence of an adverb instantiates it, since not all positions that admit adverbs will admit the relatively few adverbs that can take an object and thus allow the position to be identified unambiguously as filled by an $\overline{\text{Adv}}$.

Det and **Conj.** For these two categories one can also seek a basis in notions of logical category. **Det** corresponds to the logical category of quantifier, i.e., an element of logical structure that specifies for how much or for which part of a domain a propositional function is true (in *Some politicians are honest,* the quantifier *some* indicates that "x is honest" is true of a nonempty part of the domain defined by "politician"). **Conj** corresponds to the category of those logical "operators" that specify how many of a set of propositions are true (e.g., *and* specifies that all of the propositions in a given list are true).[14]

The relation of Det and Conj to lexical category is unclear because of the unclarity of the notion of lexical category when one gets beyond N, A, V, and P. I in fact hold that "Det" does not correspond to a separate lexical category but includes items of the lexical categories A and N, as well as, perhaps, some items without a lexical category. I take lexical category differences among determiners to be responsible for differences in the surface form of NPs such as in (8):

(8) a.   every$_A$ book
     a'.   a lot$_N$ of books
     b.   každaja$_A$ kniga (Russian)   'every book'
     b'.   mnogo$_N$ knig   'many books'

The assignment of lexical categories is clearer in highly inflected languages such as Russian, where the word for "every" takes adjectival inflection and agrees in case and gender with the noun with which it is combined, while the word for "many" does not agree with the noun but rather requires that the noun be put into the genitive plural. The lexical category differences among determiners are relevant to how they are allowed to combine with other elements in surface structure but are not, as far as I know, relevant to their combinatoric possibilities in deep structure.

As in the case of NPs, there are also Dets that do not have the logical function that defines the category but appear in positions that are typical of items that have that function. For example, a NP in genitive form that replaces an underlying *the,* as in *Iran's attack on Iraq,* derived from a structure that also underlies *the attack on Iraq by Iran* by a step in which *Iraq* replaces *the,*[15] is a peripheral member of the fuzzy category Det:

(9)

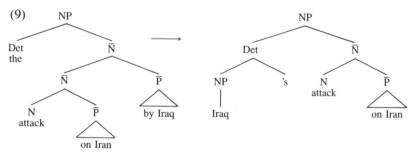

The semantically empty articles that appear on predicate NPs (10) are likewise peripheral members of the category Det, since they too do not have the semantic function that defines the category but do occur in a position typical of items with that semantic function:

(10) a. Janet is a̱ lawyer.
   b. Scott is ṯẖe̱ author of *Waverley.*

Complementizer. Items have been classed as **complementizers** partly on the basis of their function (combining with an embedded S that can fill an argument position) and partly on the basis of their occurrence in "complementizer position" (in English, the position as left sister of an embedded S). Some elements that have the function of complementizers are realized as verbal inflections (e.g., *-ing*) and hence do not occur in complementizer position. It may be appropriate to recognize a lexical category "Complementizer," though in some languages the function of complementizer is sometimes fulfilled by elements of major lexical categories, e.g., the Japanese complementizer *koto* can be regarded as a noun and the complement S has the appearance of a relative clause modifying *koto.*

The category "Comp" is often discussed in connection with a putative category "$\overline{\text{S}}$," with the combination of Comp and S assigned to the category $\overline{\text{S}}$. This terminological practice raises two questions: first, is there reason to draw a category distinction between S and $\overline{\text{S}}$, and second, if so, is the distinction of such a nature as to justify the name $\overline{\text{S}}$ for the combination of Comp and S?

There appear to be cases where a distinction between S with Comp and S without Comp must be drawn. For example, a distinction must be drawn between sentential complements that are objects of prepositions, where the preposition is deleted and a complementizer appears in surface structure (11a), and Ss combined with prepositions in adverbial constructions, where the preposition is retained and no complementizer appears (11b):

(11) a. Bill is anxious (for → ∅) that you get home safely.
   b. I left before (*that) Joan arrived.

This distinction can at least be drawn neatly in terms of a class of cases where a P has an $\overline{\text{S}}$ object (11a) and one where it has a S object (11b). The question, however, is whether there is reason to take that to be the distinction rather than, say, to make the relevant rules sensitive to presence vs. absence of a complementizer instead of to the putative distinction between S and $\overline{\text{S}}$.

The symbol $\overline{\text{S}}$ suggests a category which is to S as $\overline{\text{V}}$ is to V and $\overline{\text{A}}$ is to A. It is hard to see any such parallelism. S is not a lexical category, and the relation of a Comp to the S with which it is combined has nothing in common with the relation of object NPs and $\bar{P}$s to the V with which they combine into a $\bar{V}$. The only halfway plausible parallelism between "$\bar{S}$" and "bar" categories is that in which the Comp is regarded as the head and the S as its object, in which case not $\bar{S}$ but $\overline{\text{Comp}}$ would be the appropriate name.[16] Rather than pervert the use of the bar by employment of the symbol $\bar{S}$, I will provisionally simply take presence vs. absence of a complementizer to be an additional factor to which syntactic rules can be sensitive, and in cases where that factor plays a role I will simply introduce symbols ad hoc to distinguish between categories that will otherwise be lumped together under the symbol "S."

It may be useful to conclude this section by pointing out some differences between the conception of syntactic categories adopted in this book and the conceptions generally adopted in transformational grammar. Transformational grammarians generally take syntactic categories as provided by "base rules," which specify how elements may combine in deep structure. Under that policy, two items belong to the same syntactic category if and only if they combine in the same way with other items in deep structure, and an item in surface structure (or in any intermediate stage of the derivation) belongs to some category if and only if its counterpart in deep structure belongs to that category. That policy implies that a constituent cannot change category in the course of a derivation, and that items introduced in the course of a derivation belong to no category at all (because an item has to have a deep structure counterpart if it is to have a category).

By contrast, the conception of category advanced in this chapter has no special connection with the notions of "base rules" (= deep structure combinatoric rules) or of "deep structure," does not preclude change of category in the course of a derivation, and treats transformationally inserted items on a par with any other items in the application of category notions. For example, under the approach advanced here, anything consisting of a preposition and a NP is a $\bar{P}$, regardless of whether the preposition is present as such in deep structure, is inserted in the course of a derivation, or replaces an item of a different lexical category.

No examples of this last possibility have been given so far, but one can easily be given. The extended sense of possession that is expressed by *have* can also be expressed by *with* in a postnominal modifier:

(12) a.   a man who has a scar on his face
     a'. a man with a scar on his face
     b.   a plan which has no prospects for success
     b'. a plan with no prospects for success

c. several persons who have serious problems
c′. several persons with serious problems

The expressions introduced by *with* appear in positions that can be occupied by reduced relative clauses (e.g., *a person (who is) under the influence of drugs*) but are not derivable from relative clauses simply through deletion of relative pronoun and *be,* since the expressions with *with* cannot occur as predicate $\bar{\text{P}}$s:

(13) a. *John is with a scar on his face.
   b. *The MX missile project is with no prospects for success.
   c. *Your neighbors are with serious problems.

However, they can be treated as reduced relative clauses if *with* is taken as optionally replacing *having* in reduced relative clauses, e.g., (12a′) would be derived from *a man having a scar on his face* (a reduced form of (12a)) by replacement of *having* by *with*.[17] Under the policies of this chapter (and the remainder of this book), this step would change the category of the expression from $\bar{\text{V}}$ to $\bar{\text{P}}$, since the lexical category of the head changes (*have* is a V, *with* a P) and the other factors remain constant (the replacement does not change the status of the constituent as "phrasal"), and syntactic category names are only informal abbreviations for combinations of syntactically relevant factors.

Under the approach of this chapter, there is no need to suppose that all syntactic categories that figure in the surface structures of a language also figure in its deep structures. For example, it allows for the possibility of a language in which there are $\bar{\text{P}}$s in surface structure but not in deep structure, all Ps being inserted as adjuncts to NPs in the course of derivations. (Under the policies of orthodox transformational grammar, all categories that appear in surface structure must also appear in deep structure.)

In addition, our policy allows for constituents that are unspecified for one or other of the syntactic factors. For example, it allows for the possibility of constituents whose heads belong to no lexical category at all. An instance of precisely this will be presented in chapter 8, where an analysis will be presented involving structures in which a tense marker is the head of a phrasal unit. Since tense markers belong to no lexical category, the phrasal units will be labeled $\bar{\text{0}}$, using the makeshift of a 0 to indicate absence of lexical category.

Another novel possibility that this conception of syntactic category makes available is that of a word belonging simultaneously to two different lexical categories (e.g., of *blue* in *a pale blue shirt* being simultaneously an A and a N); in §22b it will be argued that there are phenomena which require analyses of that type.

c. *Tree Pruning*

Through deletions and extractions, an underlying S may be converted into less than what would normally make up a S:[18]

(1) a. John$_i$ try [for he$_i$ to escape] $\xrightarrow{\text{Equi}}$ John try <u>to escape</u>

   b. [For John to admire courage] seem $\xrightarrow{\text{Raising}}$
       John seem <u>to admire courage</u>

   c. any person [who owns a car] $\xrightarrow{\text{RCR}}$ any person <u>owning a car</u>
       a building [which is on 43rd St.] $\xrightarrow{\text{RCR}}$ a building <u>on 43rd St.</u>

Ross (1969) raised the question of whether these constituents remain Ss after the deletion or extraction and provided some arguments that they do not and thus that these derivational steps have a side effect of **tree pruning,** that is, of removal from the structure of nodes and labels that are rendered "nonfunctional" by the given derivational steps.

The idea that nodes are lost as they become nonfunctional has enjoyed widespread popularity since the appearance of Ross's paper, despite the fact that few phenomena have been adduced where it might matter whether tree pruning occurs and that hardly anything has been written on the topic since the appearance of Ross's paper.[19]

In combination with the conception of syntactic category adopted here, the idea of tree pruning takes on a new character. Removal of the subject of a S makes it less than fully a S on the dimension of internal syntax (since it is no longer of the form [NP $\overline{\text{V}}$]), though it remains equally much of a S on the other two dimensions. Thus, from the point of view taken here, supposed tree pruning should manifest itself solely in interactions between a derivational step that changes the internal syntax of a constituent and a rule that is sensitive to internal syntax.

I have too few cases that I can point to with confidence as fitting this description for me to be able to say anything very concrete about tree pruning or its counterpart in the approach taken here. Let me at least give two reasonably clear examples, one a case where tree pruning as understood by Ross clearly takes place, and a second where it clearly does not.

Ross observes that while Latin predicate adjectives are in the nominative case, adnominal adjectives such as might be derived by RCR take whatever case the head N bears:

(2) a. Marcus amat feminam [quae pulchra est].
         'Marcus loves a woman who is beautiful (Nominative)'
    b. Marcus amat feminam pulchram.
         'Marcus loves a beautiful (Accusative) woman'

Under the (reasonable) assumption that the case of Latin nouns is not copied onto constituents of lower Ss, if RCR applies in the derivation of (2b) it must be accompanied by tree pruning, so that the adjective will not be prevented from taking on the case of the noun.

Consider now the failure of Inversion to apply in (3a), as contrasted with the parallel (3b–c), in which a preposed negative expression requires Inversion:

(3) a. With no job, Sam is miserable.
 b. At no time was Sam miserable.
  * At no time, Sam was miserable.
 c. Never had he been subjected to such cruelty.
  * Never, he had been subjected to such cruelty.

If *with no job* in (3a) is treated as a reduced form of an adverbial clause *with [he has no job]*, the lack of Inversion in (3a) will be parallel to other cases in which a negative element is subordinate to the putative Inversion site, provided that the negative element counts as subordinate even after the reduction of the embedded S:

(4) a. Since he has no job, Sam is miserable.
  * Since he has no job is Sam miserable.
 b, To people who have no jobs, Bert has been very unkind.
  * To people who have no jobs has Bert been very unkind.

Another respect in which the negation in (3a) acts as if it is in a subordinate clause is that it does not support occurrences in the main clause of "negative polarity items" like *a red cent*, i.e., items that normally require a negation in the same clause or a superordinate clause (cf. §17b).

(5) a. * With no job, Sam would give you a red cent.
 b. At no time did Sam give me a red cent.
 c. * To people who have no jobs, Bert would give a red cent.

There thus appears to be no tree pruning in the reduction of *he has no job* to *no job*. Note, though, that both of the phenomena discussed here are sensitive to the scope of negation, thus, to a characteristic of semantic structure. According to the conception of syntactic categories adopted here, the reduction of the embedded S affects its status as a S on the dimension of internal syntax but not on those of semantics and external syntax. The apparent lack of tree pruning evidenced in (3) and (5) may thus merely show that the dimension of S-hood that is affected by the reduction of the S is not the one that is relevant to the phenomena that come into the picture here.

The purported cases of tree pruning that have been discussed in the literature so far have almost all related to pruning of a S-node. One can easily imagine cases, however, in which pruning of a $\bar{V}$-node might take place. For example, suppose that one deletes or extracts the V that is the head of a $\bar{V}$. Does the latter constituent remain a $\bar{V}$? The conception of syntactic category presented in §7a suggests that it does not—if you re-move the V of a [$_{\bar{V}}$ V $\bar{A}$] combination, say, the remainder no longer has a V as a head. It indeed is not clear that it has **any** head. There are some facts, however, that suggest that such constituents do indeed remain $\bar{V}$s. Consider first cases in which "$\bar{V}$-deletion" deletes not a $\bar{V}$ but a $\bar{P}$, an $\bar{A}$, or a NP.

(6) a. Alice is <u>a first-rate lawyer</u>, and Ted is ∅ too.
   b. The post office is <u>on 43rd St.</u>, and the bank is ∅ too.
   c. Alice is <u>afraid of snakes</u>, and Ted is ∅ too.

As Akmajian and Wasow (1975) note, not just any repeated $\bar{P}$, $\bar{A}$, or NP can be deleted, but only one that is combined with a copula *be:*[20]

(7) a. *Alice became <u>a first-rate lawyer</u>, and Ted became ∅ too.
   b. *Alice is <u>a first-rate lawyer</u>, and ∅ is what we need.

Akmajian and Wasow account for these facts by positing a transformation that extracts a *be* from its $\bar{V}$. Under that proposal, supplemented by the assumption that what remains retains its status as a $\bar{V}$, the permissible dele-tions **are** deletions of repeated $\bar{V}$s:

(8)

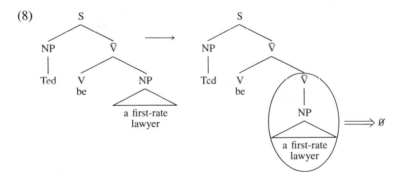

The second relevant case is that of deleted *be*'s in certain nonfinite con-structions, e.g., the absolute construction with *with:*

(9) a. With Mary still in Florida, Fred must be lonely.
   b. With Mexico City currently the world's largest city, I'm surprised that your company doesn't have an office there.

One strong argument for positing an underlying *be* in such sentences is that one thereby gets an explanation of why adverbs can appear in combination with constituents that normally do not support adverbs:

(10) * I've just returned from <u>currently the world's largest city</u>.

But then what is the category of such constituents as *currently the world's largest city* in (9b)? One might suggest NP because the constituent consists of a modifier and a NP. But that would be a mistake, since the adverb modifies not the NP but the underlying *be NP* constituent. The problem of assigning a category to such constituents is important in the context of this book, where I will argue (§10a) that each language has a system of combinatoric rules to which its surface structures must conform. If we can justify saying that *currently the world's largest city* remains a $\overline{\text{V}}$ even after the deletion of *be*, there is no problem fitting examples like (9b) to the surface combinatoric rules: they instantiate the familiar $[_{\overline{\text{P}}}\ \text{P S}]$ and $[_{\text{S}}\ \text{NP}\ \overline{\text{V}}]$ configurations. The problem, though, is whether we can identify *currently the world's largest city, etc.*, as $\overline{\text{V}}$s without perverting the conception of category presented in §7a. Perhaps the best thing to say in both these cases is that the head of a constituent remains its head even if it is deleted or extracted, and thus that to have a V as its head, a constituent need not **contain** a head. (If the head is **replaced,** however, the replacing item takes on the role of head.)

There is an additional case in which it may be necessary to recognize a phrasal constituent without an overt head, though here there is probably not deletion of the head but rather just a head with an empty phonological form. Specifically, in view of some respects in which adverbial uses of *yesterday, today, tomorrow, next Tuesday,* etc. behave like prepositional phrases, a case can be made for treating them as $\overline{\text{P}}$s with a zero P. First, such items differ from such true adverbs as *soon, recently,* and *frequently* in not being completely normal when placed at the beginning of a $\overline{\text{V}}$:

(11) a. John will $\left\{ \begin{array}{l} \text{soon} \\ *\text{tomorrow} \\ *\text{next Tuesday} \end{array} \right\}$ finish his assignment.

  b. Nancy must $\left\{ \begin{array}{l} \text{recently} \\ *\text{yesterday} \\ *\text{last Friday} \end{array} \right\}$ have gone to Florida.

In this respect, their behavior parallels that noted by Jackendoff (1972: 94–95) for $\overline{\text{P}}$s:[21]

(12) a. John was $\left\{ \begin{array}{l} \text{carefully} \\ *\text{with care} \end{array} \right\}$ slicing the bagels.

b. ??We will for several hours be discussing linguistics.

c. ??Ed in Atlanta was hit by a truck.

Second, in their adverbial uses, *yesterday,* etc., have the meanings of objects of prepositions, e.g., if yesterday was September 6, then (13a) conveys the same information as (13b):

(13) a. John went home yesterday.

b. John went home <u>on</u> September 6.

In either case the sentence says that a certain event (John's going home) occurred on a certain day, with the relation between the event and the day expressed by *on* in (13b) and by no overt word in (13a). Third, *yesterday,* etc., in other constructions occupy the positions of NPs (i.e., they are NPs in external syntax), including the position of object of a P:

(14) a. Yesterday was a beautiful day.

The king has declared tomorrow to be a holiday.

b. From last Tuesday until yesterday, I was in Boston.

I can't get there before tomorrow.

After today, you can reach us at Fred's house.

If adverbial uses of *yesterday,* etc., are treated as $\bar{\bar{P}}$s with a zero P (in this case, a zero allomorph of the *on* of *on Tuesday*), these facts will be accounted for:

(15)

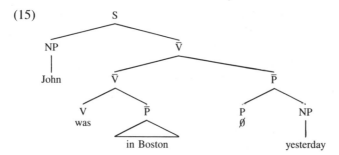

By contrast, *soon, frequently, recently, currently,* etc., are adverbs and not NPs (with or without zero Ps) and thus are allowed in pre-$\bar{V}$ position but cannot normally be the object of a P. The one case in which such a word appears as object of a P, namely, the common expression *until recently,* can be treated as an idiom in view of the unacceptability of *recently* as the object of any other P:

(16) a. *Between recently and next month, a lot of mice will have been caught.

b.   The houses of yesterday/*recently were sturdily built.
c.   ??Fred has been drinking heavily since recently.

I note finally that under the policies adopted in this chapter, saying that an expression is a $\overline{P}$ in surface structure is not the same as saying that a $\overline{P}$ underlies it, since a derivational step in which a P is replaced by something of a different lexical category will result in a surface constituent belonging to a category other than $\overline{P}$. Thus, in saying that *recently* or *carefully* is not a $\overline{P}$ in surface structure, I am not ruling out an analysis in which it is derived from an underlying $\overline{P}$ (such as "since a recent time" or "with care"): irrespective of what underlies those words, they belong to the lexical category Adv and are the heads of whatever phrasal unit they might make up. In an adverbial use of *last Friday,* the role of the underlying P as head is not taken over by something of a different lexical category, and thus the surface category remains $\overline{P}$. In making this point I am not advocating an analysis that derives *carefully* from *with care,* etc., but am simply insisting that any proposal of that sort be judged on its merits and not incorrectly assumed to be in prima facie conflict with the conception of syntactic categories adopted here.

EXERCISES

1. For each of the underlined constituents, determine on what dimensions (if any) it is a NP. Where the application of a dimension to any of the examples is unclear, say in what way:
   a.   They were pulling <u>your leg</u>. (in the idiomatic sense)
   b.   John isn't <u>Mary's husband</u>—he's just living with her.
   c.   A mouse ran out from <u>under the sink</u>.
   d.   John does most of his work at <u>home</u>.
   e.   <u>Under the bed</u> is a stupid place to hide the money.
   f.   Only <u>your brother</u> passed the exam.
   g.   Only <u>your brother</u> passed the exam.
   h.   If Lucy is tired, she'll say <u>so</u>.

For f–g, assume the constituent structure at the right.

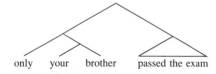

only   your   brother   passed the exam

2. Find at least three words or expressions whose syntactic categorization is problematic, other than those taken up in this chapter, and say what the difficulty in categorizing them is.

3. Say what problem the following examples pose for the treatment suggested in §7b of the distinction between what some linguists call S and S̄:

Bill hopes you will be considerate.
Denise is surprised you were angry.

4. Examine three syntactic constructions taken up so far that can contain a S, and make up appropriate examples to determine whether it is necessary to distinguish between "S" and "S̄" in an account of the construction.

NOTES

1. Sentences (1a–b‴) are modeled after examples in Jackendoff (1972:94, 1977:73) and (1c–d‴) after examples in Lakoff 1970.

2. It should be emphasized that languages differ from one another with regard to what inflection each lexical category bears, e.g., in English, only verbs are inflected for tense, but in Japanese, both verbs and adjectives are. This may also be a good place to point out that traditional schemes of parts of speech cannot always be accepted in toto. There is substantial agreement among traditional grammarians regarding the application of the terms "noun, verb, adjective, preposition" (though not with regard to their definitions), but there is no consensus as to what other parts of speech there are or as to the basis for drawing part of speech distinctions. For worthwhile criticism of traditional systems of parts of speech (but not, regrettably, for an alternative that is much of an improvement), see Jespersen (1924; chaps. 4–6).

3. *Resemble* actually **can** express a three-place relation, with the third place being the dimension of resemblance: *Margaret resembles her mother in her love of music*. However, none of the NPs in (3b) could fill that role.

4. The terminology unfortunately suggests an additional parallel that is not correct: the phrasal category that corresponds to N as VP corresponds to V is not what we have so far been calling NP but rather the (so far nameless) category illustrated by *destruction of the city* in *the destruction of the city*. This point will be clarified below.

5. The examples are chosen so as to be unambiguously instances of VP-deletion rather than of Gapping. While Gapping in simple cases does delete just a verb (e.g., *Margaret plays golf and Alice ∅ tennis*), it operates under very different conditions than VP-deletion does. Gapping but not VP-deletion requires the antecedent clause to be **conjoined** with the clause in which the deletion takes place, Gapping but not VP-deletion deletes the tense marker, and the material deleted by Gapping is not in general just a verb but rather everything in a clause other than one constituent before the verb and one after it:

　　*If Margaret plays golf, then Alice tennis.
　　Alec gave money to the Alumni Fund, and Nancy books (*to the library).

6. Some A + PP combinations allow the A to be separated from the PP much more readily than does *ashamed of his past*.

(?) Prudent John isn't in financial matters.

In combinations like *prudent in financial matters,* the PP does not provide an object of the A, the way it does in *ashamed of his past,* but is a modifier of a whole AP or VP, i.e., the two combinations differ roughly as follows:

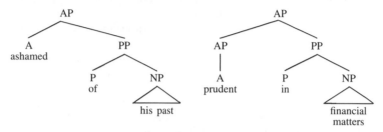

The following examples illustrate further consequences of this difference (*afraid of X, hostile to X,* and *concerned about X* work like *ashamed of X*):

> John is afraid of nothing in financial matters.
> *John is afraid in financial matters of nothing.
> John is afraid of and hostile to policemen.
> ?John is concerned about and prudent in financial matters.
> His past, John is ashamed of.
> Snakes, John is afraid of.
> *Financial matters, John is prudent in.

7. The chief discrepancies between bars as they are used here and as they are used in Chomsky 1970 are that (i) Chomsky (and most proponents of "X-bar syntax") recognize multiple bars (in symbols such as $\bar{\bar{N}}$, with the number of bars corresponding to the depth to which the head is embedded in the constituent), whereas bars are used here in such a way that multiple bars make no sense; (ii) in this book, modifiers are treated as giving rise to nested $\bar{X}$ configurations like $[_{\bar{N}}$ *new* $[_{\bar{N}}$ *theory of light*$]]$ or $[_{\bar{V}}$ *willingly* $[_{\bar{V}}$ *risk defeat*$]]$, while for Chomsky such nesting of categories is excluded; and (iii) Chomsky identifies NP with $\bar{\bar{N}}$ (in general, X-bar syntacticians identify NP as N plus some number of bars), whereas in this book NP is treated as not fitting into the "bar" framework at all.

8. This point is taken from Jackendoff (1977:58). Jackendoff, however, adopts a somewhat different analysis of many of the examples discussed below, in virtue of his adherence to a policy (cf. n. 7) that forbids nesting of $\bar{N}$s such as figures in the analyses proposed below.

9. This transformation is subject to the conditions that the head be a count noun, not a mass noun, and that *one* appear with more than just an article:

> The water in the lake is cleaner than the water/*one in the river.
> Mary has a car, and John has a car/*one too.
> If you buy a piano, you'll need to have the piano/*one tuned twice a year.

10. This is an oversimplification, since there are types of adjectives that cannot be used in predicate position and have only indirect connections with predicates,

e.g., *a **mere** child, her **former** husband, an **electrical** engineer, an **occasional** visitor.* See Levi (1973, 1978) for discussion of such adjectives.

11. On fuzzy categories, see Rosch 1978, Lakoff 1987. The characterization of "NP" here fits Rosch's conception of the structure of categories, in which each category has a "core" consisting of its most prototypic members (here, items expressing logical arguments, having forms such as Det N̄, and occurring in positions like "subject" position) and a "periphery" consisting of items showing characteristics that are typical of the core members.

12. The * relates to the pronunciation in which *probably* bears the primary stress and is part of the same intonational unit as the preceding words. If *probably* is pronounced on a low pitch and the primary stress and terminal intonational contour are on *out,* the sentence is fine. The acceptability of such a pronunciation is a further respect in which *probably* differs from *completely* and *intentionally:* the latter adverbs do not allow such a pronunciation.

13. One should resist the tendency to confuse "Adverb Phrase" with the more common term "Adverbial phrase." An Adverb Phrase is a phrasal unit whose head is an adverb. An adverbial phrase is a phrasal unit, irrespective of the category of its head, that is used adverbially. Far more adverbial phrases have prepositions as their heads than adverbs.

14. Only "coordinating conjunctions" are treated here as "Conj." "Subordinating conjunctions" are treated as prepositions with sentential objects.

15. This analysis will be justified and elaborated in chap. 12.

16. Chomsky 1986 indeed reinterprets "S̄" as $\overline{\overline{\text{Comp}}}$.

17. Alternatively, these examples could be given an analysis that posits *with* in the deep structures of all and allows replacement of *be with* by *have,* as in the treatment proposed in Fillmore 1966 (cf. also Fillmore 1968:77–80).

18. RCR = Relative clause reduction, which will be taken up in §12b.

19. Hankamer 1974, G. Horn 1974, Anderson 1976, and Todrys 1979 are the only works that I know of that add anything to what is found in Ross's short and quite programmatic paper.

20. They also note that the *be* cannot be in a progressive form:

> *John was being obnoxious, and Mary was being ∅ too.

Accordingly, they state the rule illustrated in (8) as inapplicable when the *be* is a niece of a progressive *be.*

21. There actually are some types of P̄ that are quite normal when placed before a V̄:

> John has for many years been a Republican.
> John has on many occasions voted for Republicans.

I do not know of any neat way to distinguish between these P̄s and the ones in (11).

|||||| 8. Auxiliary Verbs

a. Possible Sequences of Auxiliary Verbs

We are now in a position to deal in detail with English auxiliary verbs, which I have postponed a serious discussion of until this chapter, since the analysis to be developed here leans heavily on ideas presented in chapters 5 through 7.

English allows up to four auxiliary verbs in a clause:[1]

(1) a. Fred plays tennis every day.
   b. I <u>may</u> spend my vacation in Jamaica.
      It <u>has</u> rained every day for the last week.
      The workers <u>are</u> demanding higher pay.
      Alice's car <u>was</u> stolen recently.
   c. Tom <u>must have</u> arrived by now.
      My book <u>has been</u> selling well.
      The house <u>is being</u> remodeled.
   d. Nietzsche <u>may have been</u> influenced by Abelard.
      Politicians <u>have been being</u> assassinated for years.
   e. George <u>must have been being</u> interrogated by the police at that very
      moment.

Auxiliary verbs are also subject to restrictions that limit the sequences in which they can occur and the forms with which they can combine. Note in particular the following restrictions, which we will attempt to account for below.

(i) Each auxiliary verb requires that the immediately following verb (whether auxiliary or main) be in a particular morphological form. **Modal** auxiliary verbs such as *may, must, will,* and *should* require that the following verb be in the bare infinitive form (2a), *have* and passive *be* that it be in the past participle form (2b, c), and progressive *be* that it be in the present participle (*-ing*) form (2d):

(2) a. Ann may spend/*spending/*spends/*spent her vacation in Italy.

207

   b. It has rained/*raining/*rains/*rain every day for the last week.
      Oscar has been/*being/*is/*was/*be drinking again.
   c. Gilyak is spoken/*speaking/*speak/*speaks/*spoke in Sakhalin.
   d. The roof is leaking/*leaked/*leaks/*leak.

(ii) If there are two or more auxiliary verbs, they must come in the order (Modal)(*have*)(*be*$_{\text{Prog}}$)(*be*$_{\text{Passive}}$), and no more than one modal,[2] one auxiliary *have*, one progressive *be*, and one passive *be* may occur in each clause:[3]

(3) a. *Americans have musted pay income tax ever since 1913. (cf. . . .
        have had to . . .)
      *Moisei Avramovich is maying emigrate to Israel. (cf. . . . is being
        allowed to . . .)
  b. *George is having lived in Toledo for thirty years.
      *The students are had notified of the increase in tuition fees.
  c. *The house is been remodeling.
  d. *George may must quit his job. (cf. . . . may have to . . .)
      *Margaret has had already left.
      *The birds are being singing.
      *A medal was been given by the mayor by the sewer commissioner.
      (as passive of *The sewer commissioner was given a medal by the mayor*).

(iii) Inflection for tense is borne by the first verb, whether that is a main or an auxiliary verb.[4]

    The most celebrated and influential account of these restrictions on the occurrence of auxiliary verbs is that of Chomsky 1957. Chomsky sets up deep structures conforming to his rule (4), which directly stipulates that in deep structure auxiliary verbs may occur in the orders noted in (ii) and in no others:[5]

(4) Aux→Tense (Modal)(*have -en*)(*be -ing*)

In (4), parentheses indicate "optional" material. The parentheses are employed in such a way that if either *have* or progressive *be* is present, *-en* or *-ing* (respectively) will accompany it. In the deep structures conforming to (4), the "affixes" (Tense, *-en,* and *-ing*) precede the words that they are affixed to[6] in surface structure, and transformations must thus be posited that move the affixes from their underlying to their surface positions:[7]

(5) a. Deep structure according to Chomsky 1957 analysis

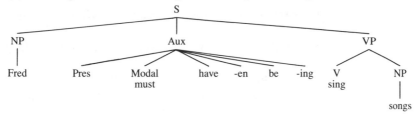

b. Surface structure according to Chomsky 1957 analysis

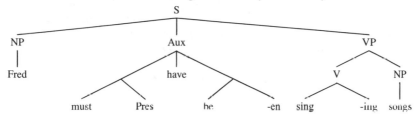

Since Chomsky accounted for the order of auxiliary verbs simply by giving a rule that said what their order was to be and since the descriptive machinery of early transformational grammar allowed an order to be imposed on constituents only through a rule (such as (4)) that specified what could be the daughters of a node of a given category and what the order of those daughters was, he was forced to accept a constituent structure in which the auxiliary verbs were sisters of one another. There is considerable evidence, however, that the surface constituent structure of sentences with multiple auxiliaries is not as in (5b) but rather as in (6), while there is to my knowledge no evidence at all that it is as in (5b):

(6)

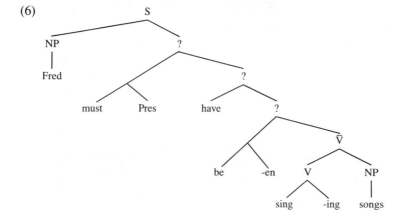

The various constituents posited in (6) are possible loci of conjoining:

(7) a. Fred both [must have been singing songs] and [probably was drink-
          ing beer].
     b. Fred must both [have been singing songs] and [have been drinking
          beer].
     c. Fred must have both [been singing songs] and [been drinking beer].
     d. Fred must have been both [singing songs] and [drinking beer].

The possibilities for $\bar{V}$-deletion (as we have renamed VP-deletion in accordance with the revised category nomenclature adopted in chap. 7) argue
that *been singing songs* and *have been singing songs* are not only constituents but indeed $\bar{V}$s, as well as that *singing songs* remains a $\bar{V}$ when combined with auxiliary verbs:

(8) a. Fred must <u>have been singing songs</u>, and Nancy must ∅ too.
     b. Fred must have <u>been singing songs</u>, and Nancy must have ∅ too.
     c. Fred must have been <u>singing songs</u>, and Nancy must have been ∅
          too.

Since $\bar{V}$-deletion never deletes a tense-bearing auxiliary verb, it is not possible to use it to determine whether *must have been singing songs* is also a
constituent. Note that while (9a) involves deletion of a repetition of *must
have been singing songs,* it cannot be $\bar{V}$-deletion that is involved but must
be the quite different process of ellipsis (sometimes called **Stripping**) that
deletes all but one constituent of a second conjunct, as in (9b–c):

(9) a. Fred must have been singing songs, and George too.
     b. Tom gives candy to his girlfriend, and flowers too.
     c. Alice talks about baseball with Fred, but not about politics.

Stripping but not $\bar{V}$-deletion is restricted to coordinate structures, and
where the clause with the ellipsis is not coordinated with the antecedent
clause (and thus only $\bar{V}$-deletion would be applicable), the reduced form
found in (9a) is not possible:

(10) a.   That Fred was singing songs suggests that George was ∅ too.
      a'. *That Fred was singing songs suggests that George too.
      b.   Since Tom gave candy to his girlfriend, George did ∅ too.
      b'. *Since Tom gave candy to his girlfriend, not flowers.

I accordingly tentatively accept (6) rather than (5b) (not to suggest that
those are the only imaginable possibilities) as the surface constituent struc-

ture of sentences in which the subject NP is followed by one or more auxiliary verbs. There is less than complete agreement that the words that I have been referring to here as auxiliary **verbs** are in fact verbs. Indeed, due to some quirks in the way that the notion of syntactic category has been treated in all of Chomsky's work, the Chomsky 1957 analysis forced Chomsky to treat them as not being verbs, indeed as belonging to no category at all (other than that of "Modal" in the case of modal auxiliaries). In the conception of syntactic category adopted here, however, there is nothing to prevent auxiliary verbs from being classed as verbs, and I indeed wish to make an assumption that will **require** that they be classed as verbs, namely, that words that allow inflections appropriate to a particular lexical category are automatically themselves members of that category, e.g., a word that is inflected for tense is ipso facto a verb irrespective of anything else that can be said about it.[8] *Have, be* and at least some of the modals (*can, will*) have distinct present and past forms and thus pass this test for being verbs. The other modals have only a single form, which I claim is a present tense form, though demonstrating that it is present tense rather than tenseless is not easy. For the moment I will simply declare such forms as *must* and *may* to be present tense forms and thus to be verbs.

If the various units in (6) consisting of an auxiliary verb and another constituent are appropriately described as having a head (which is about as unclear a question as that of whether a prepositional phrase has a head), it is presumably the auxiliary verb that is the head, in which case the various constituents marked with "?" in (6) are V̄s. We can thus fill in the missing details in (6) and obtain:

(11)

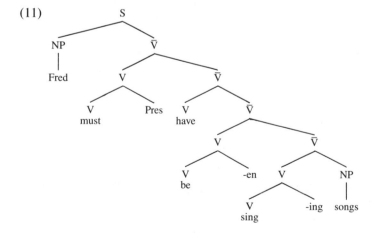

This structure contains three occurrences of the by now familiar [$_{\bar{V}}$V $\bar{V}$] configuration. Since that configuration appears in the output of Raising-to-subject (e.g., in *Fred seems to sing songs*), a possibility for the deep structure of sentences with auxiliary verbs now emerges. Suppose all auxiliary verbs are given the treatment that we have adopted for *seem:* that each auxiliary verb is taken to have a sentential subject in deep structure and to trigger an application of Raising. To see what derivations this would allow for, let us look at that for *Fred must have been singing songs,* ignoring for the moment the tense, *-en,* and *-ing.* The deep structure is as in (12):

(12)

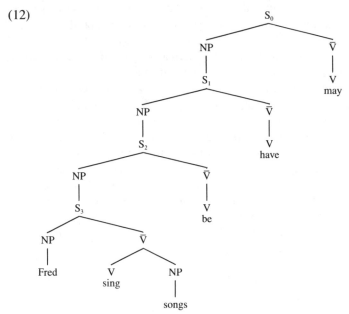

The derivation proceeds as follows, with applications of Raising on S_2, S_1, and S_0:

(13)

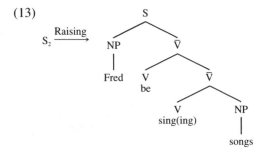

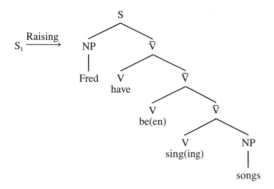

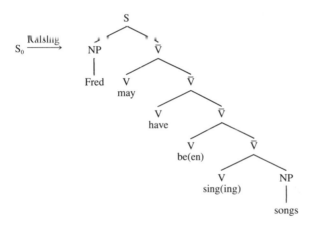

Note that the last tree in (13) is identical to the desired (11) except for being noncommittal as to how the affixes fit in.

What we need in order to develop the proposal of (12)–(13) into a full-fledged analysis of English auxiliary verbs is (i) an account of the syntax of the verbal affixes (Pres, Past, *-en, -ing*) and (ii) an account of the order in which auxiliary verbs can occur. Note that the proposal as developed so far says nothing about the order of auxiliary verbs. All that it says about each is that it takes a deep sentential subject and triggers Raising; that does not exclude deep structures such as (14a) and corresponding surface structures such as (14b):

(14) a.

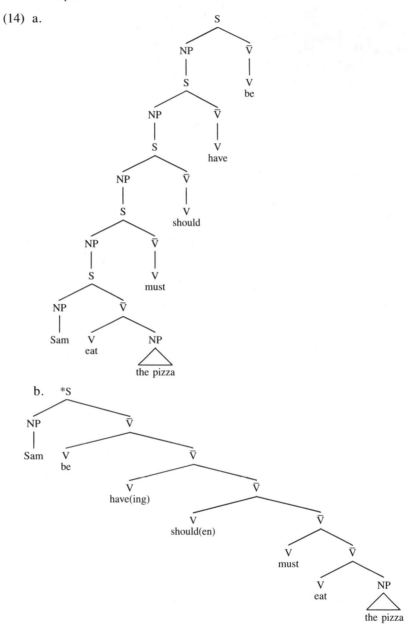

Before jumping to the conclusion that the treatment of auxiliary verbs as main verbs with underlying sentential subjects implies that surface structures such as (14b) should be possible, let us examine the ways in which we could exclude such surface structures other than by simply retreating to an analysis like Chomsky's. Note first that over and above any purely syntactic considerations, there is a morphological reason for the ill-formedness of (14b), namely that that structure requires a past participle form of *should* and an infinitive form of *must,* and those verbs lack such forms. English modal auxiliaries have only finite forms, a present tense form (e.g., *can*) and a past tense form (*could*), and for most speakers *should* and *must* do not even have a past tense form, let alone infinitive and participle forms.[9] There is thus no need to exclude the deep structure (14a) in order to exclude the surface structure (14b): the defective morphology of modal auxiliaries is sufficient to exclude (14b). It is in fact necessary to invoke the defective morphology of modals even under the Chomsky 1957 analysis of auxiliaries (though this has not been acknowledged by adherents of that analysis), because of those modal auxiliaries that have no past tense forms: Chomsky's formula (4) provides for all combinations of a present or past tense and any modal auxiliary, and defective morphology is the only plausible grounds for excluding combinations such as *must* + Past and *should* + Past.

The defective morphology of modal auxiliaries thus provides an explanation of why modal auxiliaries precede all other auxiliary verbs: a modal that followed another auxiliary verb would have to be in a form that its morphology does not allow.[10] Let us now see whether there are any details of the behavior of perfect *have* that can provide an explanation of why it occurs where it does in sequences of auxiliary verbs. Consider the possibilities for combining tenses and/or *have* with various kinds of time adverbs:[11]

(15) a.   My brother is in Uruguay right now.
       *My brother was in Uruguay right now.
       *My brother has been in Uruguay right now.
       *My brother had been in Uruguay right now.
   b.   Fred arrived at 2:00 yesterday afternoon.
       *Fred arrives at 2:00 yesterday afternoon.
       *Fred has arrived at 2:00 yesterday afternoon.
       ?Fred had arrived at 2:00 yesterday afternoon.
   c.   George has drunk a gallon of beer by now.
       *George drinks/drank a gallon of beer by now.
       *George had drunk a gallon of beer by now.
   d.   Nancy had already mailed the letter when I spoke to her.
       *Nancy already mails the letter when I spoke to her.
       *Nancy already mailed the letter when I spoke to her.
       *Nancy has already mailed the letter when I spoke to her.

Adverbs referring to the present time (like *right now*) require the present tense, those specifying a past time (like *two hours ago* or *at noon yester-day*) require a simple past tense, those specifying a range of times extending from the past through the present (like *by now* or *since the last election*) require a present perfect, and combinations of an adverb that indicate a past time and one that places the event or state of affairs prior to that time (like *already* + *when I spoke to her*) require a past perfect.[12]

In infinitives, however, the four-way distinction among present, past, present perfect, and past perfect is reduced to a two-way distinction between infinitive without *have* and infinitive with *have:*[13]

(16) a.   My brother is believed to be in Uruguay right now.
              *My brother is believed to have been in Uruguay right now.
        b.   Fred is believed to have arrived at 2:00 yesterday.
              *Fred is believed to arrive at 2:00 yesterday.
        c.   George is believed to have drunk a gallon of beer by now.
              *George is believed to drink a gallon of beer by now.
        d.   Nancy is believed to have already mailed the letter when I talked to her.
        d'.   *Nancy is believed to already mail the letter when I talked to her.
        d".   *Nancy is believed to have already had mailed the letter when I talked to her.

Note that not only the adverbs that in finite clauses require present perfect or past perfect but also those that require simple past tense require *have* in infinitives.

I assume that the rules governing co-occurrence between tenses, auxiliary verbs, and time adverbs are basically the same for nonfinite as for finite Ss. Let us provisionally implement that assumption by taking infinitive complements to have underlying structures in which the same four-way distinction is drawn as in finite clauses, with *right now* requiring a present tense, *at 2:00 yesterday* a past tense, etc., in infinitival Ss as well as in finite Ss. There then must be transformations having the following overall effect:[14]

(17) $\left.\begin{array}{l} \text{Pres}\rightarrow\emptyset \\ \text{Past}\rightarrow have_{en} \\ \text{Pres } have_{en}\rightarrow have_{en} \\ \text{Past } have_{en}\rightarrow have_{en} \end{array}\right\}$ in infinitives

This correspondence between underlying and more superficial structure can be broken up into unitary processes as follows. Suppose that the first two lines of (17) are separated out as a transformation of **Tense-replacement** and that that transformation applies to **all** occurrences of Pres or Past in infinitives, even those that are followed by $have_{en}$. This will give exactly the desired result when it applies to Pres $have_{en}$. In the case of Past $have_{en}$, however, it will result in $*have_{en}\,have_{en}$, thus yielding ill-formed sentences such as (16d″) unless the grammar is altered in some way. Since the difference between (16d″) and the sentence that expresses what (16d″) ought to express, namely, (16d), is that (16d″) has one extra occurrence of $have_{en}$, we need to supplement Tense-replacement by an additional rule that deletes one of two consecutive occurrences of $have_{en}$. Thus, the rules in (18) will have the overall effect summarized in (17):[15]

(18) a. Tense-replacement   Pres→∅   ⎫ in infinitival Ss (to be revised
                             Past→ $have_{en}$ ⎭   in (21))

    b. *Have*-deletion

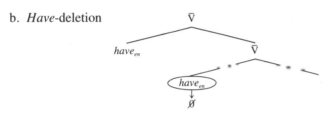

Let us now look at some other nonfinite complements. The formulation of Tense-replacement in (18a) is insufficiently general, since Tense-replacement (with concomitant *Have*-deletion in the past perfect cases) evidently applies in *-ing* complements:

(19) a. Fred's being in Uruguay right now wouldn't surprise me at all.
    a′. *Fred's having been in Uruguay right now wouldn't surprise me at all.
    b. *Fred's arriving at 2:00 yesterday wouldn't surprise me at all.
    b′. Fred's having arrived at 2:00 yesterday wouldn't surprise me at all.
    c. *George's drinking a gallon of beer by now wouldn't surprise me at all.
    c′. George's having drunk a gallon of beer by now wouldn't surprise me at all.
    d. *Nancy's already mailing the letter when I talked to her wouldn't surprise me at all.
    d′. Nancy's already having mailed the letter when I talked to her wouldn't surprise me at all.

It also evidently applies in the bare infinitives that follow modal auxiliaries:

(20) a. Fred may be in Uruguay right now.
    a′. *Fred may have been in Uruguay right now.

    b.   *Fred may arrive at 2:00 yesterday.
    b'.   Fred may have arrived at 2:00 yesterday.
    c.   *George may drink a gallon of beer by now.
    c'.   George may have drunk a gallon of beer by now.
    d.   *Nancy may already mail the letter when I talked to her.
    d'.   Nancy may have already mailed the letter when I talked to her.

Under the assumptions that I am making in this chapter, the four grammatical sentences in (20) have respectively embedded present, past, present perfect, and past perfect structures which undergo Tense-replacement.[16]

    The above observations suggest that we should generalize the statement of Tense-replacement to something on the lines of (21):

(21) Tense-replacement   Pres→∅   ⎫ in a nonfinite S
                          Past→ $have_{en}$ ⎭

This statement presupposes that the various Ss in a syntactic structure can be identified as finite or nonfinite; we will return to this point later.

    It is now time for us to return to the question of how tense markers fit into syntactic structures. In the above discussion of Tense-replacement, I have been assuming that tense markers appear somewhere or other in the sort of syntactic structure proposed in (12)–(13) but have been noncommittal as to exactly where they appear. Tense-replacement opens up a new possibility for the syntax of tense markers. If Tense-replacement simply replaces Past by $have_{en}$ without changing the structure, Past will have to appear in the same position in the input to Tense-replacement that $have_{en}$ appears in in the output. This suggests that tense markers should be given the same treatment that we have been giving to $have_{en}$, i.e., a tense marker should be a deep structure predicate element with a sentential subject and should trigger Raising:

(22)

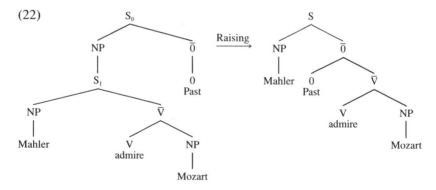

The "0" in (22) is a makeshift device to indicate that Past (likewise, Pres) has no lexical category: it is not a verb, or an adjective, or a noun, etc. Then $\bar{0}$ will mean "phrasal unit whose head does not belong to any lexical category."

If tenses are predicate elements with deep sentential subjects, then they pose the same problem as auxiliary verbs did: that of reconciling the infinite number of possibilities that the deep structure seems to allow for with the quite small number of combinations in surface structure. The objection against Chomsky's formula (4) that I raised in footnote 16, namely, that it allows too few combinations of tenses in deep structure, must thus be balanced against the objection that the alternative approach advanced here allows too many.

Note, however, that what multiple underlying tenses should correspond to depends on how exactly the condition on Tense-replacement in (21) is interpreted. Consider a deep structure such as (23), which is not excluded by anything that I have said so far:

(23)

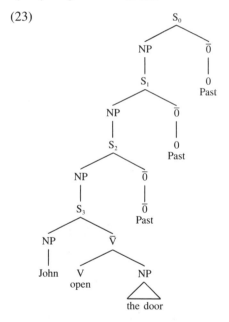

Whether Tense-replacement is applicable on S_2 and S_1 depends on whether those Ss count as "finite" or not. Suppose that we in fact take the complements of tenses to be **nonfinite**. This is not as counterintuitive as it might at first sound—it would follow, for example, from a policy that indicative main clauses and indicative *that*-clauses are finite and that all other Ss are nonfinite,[17] i.e., a policy in which "nonfinite" is taken to be the unmarked member of the finite/nonfinite opposition. Tense-replacement would then convert the Pasts of S_2 and S_1 into *have$_{en}$*, and *Have*-deletion would delete one of those two *have$_{en}$*s, so that what results would be simply the past perfect *John had opened the door.* Indeed, the way that Tense-replacement works guarantees that tenses will appear only on the first verb (main or auxiliary) of a finite S: a tense in any other position would undergo Tense-replacement and thus either be deleted or appear in surface structure as *have$_{en}$*.

With this interpretation of "finite," the formulation of Tense-replacement in (21) in fact allows one to take **all** instances of *have$_{en}$* to be underlying Pasts: all instances of *have$_{en}$* occur in what by the above stipulation are nonfinite Ss, and thus if a Past underlay them the condition for converting it into *have$_{en}$* would be met. Under this proposal, the present perfect always corresponds to underlying Pres + Past and past perfect to Past + Past.

Actually, it would be more accurate here to write Pres . . . + Past and Past . . . + Past, since additional Pres's and Pasts would have no effect on the surface form. The multiple underlying structures for present and past perfects that this proposal makes available are in fact no embarrassment, since they provide a natural account of some ambiguities in the perfect tenses that have largely been overlooked. On the basis of the time adverbs with which they co-occur, different instances of the past perfect can be identified as pasts of pasts, pasts of present perfects, and pasts of past perfects:

(24) a.   When John arrived, Mary had left an hour before.
     a′. Mary left an hour ago.
     b.   When John arrived, Mary had already left.
     b′. Mary has already left.
     c.   When John arrived, two days earlier Mary had already finished the manuscript.
     c′. Two days ago Mary had already finished the manuscript.

In (24a, b, c), *when John arrived* specifies the time that is used as **reference point** for the main clause, and the content of the main clause, if expressed at that time, would have called respectively for the past (24a′), the present perfect (24b′), or the past perfect (24c′). Suppose that each occurrence of a tense refers to a point or interval of time, that it is normally accompanied by a time adverb specifying that point or interval unless the time reference can be supplied from the context, and that a tense is past if its time reference is prior to that of the structure in which it is embedded (or, if it is not embedded, to the time at which it is uttered), and present if the time reference coincides with or is contained in that of the structure in which it is embedded. Our analysis then provides an account of the co-occurrence restrictions between tenses and time adverbs; in particular, it shows why past perfects usually require two time adverbs: there is one time adverb for the main past tense and one for the embedded past tense, realized as *have*$_{en}$.

For this approach to be generally valid, present perfects must be analyzed as involving a Past in the complement of a Pres, and multiple sources of present perfects, with more tenses than just the minimal Pres + Past must be admitted. While multiple sources of the present perfect are much harder to find examples of than multiple sources of the past perfect, the contrast between (25a) and (25b) is between a present perfect with an embedded past and one with an embedded present perfect:

(25) a. Ever since I started practicing surgery, most of my patients have had a stiff drink an hour before I start operating.
   b. As long as I've been conducting radio talk shows, the people who call in have all lived in Chicago since they were children.

The possibilities for co-occurrence with time adverbs, while not as neat as in the case of the past perfect, still fit this analysis reasonably well. The time adverbs that co-occur with the present perfect denote intervals that extend from the past through the present (*by now, already, since 1950, for the last ten years*), and the present tense can be taken as having that interval as its time reference. The embedded past tense that this analysis posits normally has no corresponding time adverb, as a result of the role that the interval plays in the meaning of the present perfect: the present perfect expresses "at some time(s) in that interval" or "at all time(s) in that interval," and the understood "at some/all times" fills the semantic role that could otherwise be filled by a time adverb that expressed a specific time.[18]

Let us thus assume that *have*$_{en}$ never occurs as such in deep structure, *i.e.*, that all surface occurrences of it are derived from underlying Past by Tense-replacement. We then have an explanation of the surface distribution of tenses and *have*$_{en}$. As observed above, a tense marker can appear in surface structure only on the first verb of a finite S because in any other position it would undergo Tense-replacement. A tenseless *have*$_{en}$ cannot be the first verb in a finite S, because the underlying Past that it corresponds to would then not be in the environment for Tense-replacement. And there cannot be more than one *have*$_{en}$ in a row in surface structure, because if there were more than one (each derived from a Past), *Have*-deletion would delete all but one of them. Finally, the obligatoriness of a tense in a finite S amounts to a definition of "finite": in certain contexts (viz. as main indicative clause and as sister of a *that* or an interrogative complementizer), a S is required to have a tense as its topmost predicate: a S in such a context is (by definition) finite.

We have by now accounted for most of the distributional restrictions on auxiliary verbs that are built into Chomsky's formula (4), but without the need to adopt such a formula or the incorrect constituent structure that it commits one to. What remains to be accounted for is the fact that progressive *be* cannot precede modals or auxiliary *have,* the fact that passive *be* cannot precede any other auxiliary verbs, and the fact that the complements of *have,* progressive *be,* and passive *be* must be respectively in the *-en, -ing,* and *-en* forms.

I will argue that the restriction on progressive *be* is semantic rather than syntactic in nature and is the same restriction that applies to combinations of progressive *be* with main verbs. Progressive *be* is subject to the constraint that its complement refer to an **activity** or a **process** rather than a **state**:

(26) a.   Alice is solving the problem.
  a′. *Alice is understanding the problem.
  a″.   I'm understanding this problem less and less the more I think
        about it.
  b.   Ted is acting like his father.
  b′. *Ted is resembling his father.
  b″.   Ted is resembling his father more and more every day.
  c.   When I ran into Janet, she was cursing her boss.
  c′. *When I ran into Janet, she was disliking her boss.

Solving a problem is an activity, understanding it is a state, and gradually understanding it less is a process; acting like one's father is an activity, resembling him is a state, and day-by-day increase in the extent to which one resembles him is a process. An additional restriction on progressive *be* is that the time to which it refers must be included in the interval in which the activity or process is said to be going on, e.g., in (26c), the cursing takes place on an interval of time containing the time at which I ran into Janet.

Let us see whether these observations imply anything about the oddity of such sentences as

(27) a.   *Fred is having arrived at 2:00 yesterday.
  b.   *George is having drunk a lot of beer by now.
  c.   *Irene is having played the bassoon nonstop for six hours.

If auxiliary *have* in (27a) is an underlying past tense corresponding to the time adverb *at 2:00 yesterday,* then the oddity of (27a) simply reflects the restriction that the complement of *be* denote an activity or process going on in an interval containing the time in question: arriving at 2:00 yesterday isn't something that Fred can be in the middle of right now. The oddity of (27b) is a little trickier to account for, since George's drinking can very well be going on at the moment when (27b) is uttered, and if he has already drunk a lot of beer, he is in the middle of a larger act which will to an even greater extent constitute drinking a lot of beer. To say why (27b) is odd, we must be careful to distinguish what is actually the case from what a sentence says is the case. The sentence *George has drunk a lot of beer by now* is noncommital as to whether George has finished drinking or will continue drinking. It refers to the result of an activity carried on up to the present, not to the possible continuation of that activity into the future. If the restriction that the complement of *be* refer to an activity or process is regarded as not being fulfilled by sentences that refer to "results" (like the embedded *George has drunk a lot of beer by now* in (27b), which by this stipulation will count as denoting a state), then that restriction will exclude (27b). The same stipulation will then cover the oddity of (27c): while playing the bassoon is an activity, the complement of *be* in (27c) refers not to the (possibly ongoing) activity of playing the bassoon but to the state consisting in six nonstop hours of the activity having taken place.

The conditions on the use of progressive *be* are in fact somewhat more complicated than this. Even state predications allow (often, indeed, require) the progressive when they refer to temporary rather than permanent states:

(28) a. The bottle is lying on its side.
    a'. *Libya is lying between Egypt and Tunisia.
    b. After the bombing, only three buildings were still standing.
    c. Several books were sitting on the shelf.

The requirement for a progressive in examples like (28a, b, c) is to some extent an idiosyncracy of "gestalt" verbs such as *lie, stand,* and *sit.* However, virtually any stative verb can appear in a progressive when the sentence refers to repeated temporary states:

(29) a. You amaze me—you're always knowing things that I would expect only an expert to know.
    b. It's uncanny—whenever I run into you, you're always looking like some other person I know.
    c. Whenever I see you, you're always just having returned from a vacation.

Of particular interest is (29c), discovered by Schachter (1983:161), in which progressive *be* precedes auxiliary *have*, a possibility that Chomsky's formula does not allow for. Schachter concludes that the *be having* combination is actually not systematically excluded, though it is rare because in most cases it would violate the semantic restrictions on progressive *be*.[19]

I turn now to passive *be*. According to the analysis adopted in chapter 4, the passive transformation adjoins passive *be* to the $\bar{V}$, creating a $[_{\bar{V}}V\ \bar{V}]$ configuration, as it moves the two NPs. With the deep structure (30b), in the derivation of (30a) Passive must apply to S_4 rather than to any of the higher Ss if passive *be* is to follow all the other auxiliary verbs:

(30) a. Sam may have been being interrogated by the FBI.

b.

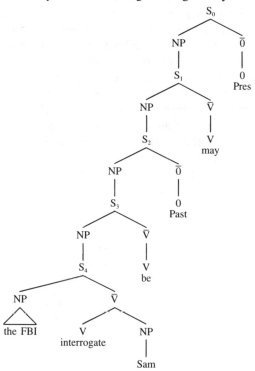

That is, if Passive applies to S_4, it will form the derived $\bar{V}$ *be interrogated by the FBI*, and subsequent applications of Raising will yield structures in which the other auxiliary verbs precede that $\bar{V}$, but if Passive were to apply to one of the higher Ss (after Raising had applied to that S, since otherwise there would be no NP in the $\bar{V}$ to be turned into a derived subject), passive *be* would be adjoined to a $\bar{V}$ that began with *be interrogating, have been interrogating*, etc., and one of the sentences in (31) would result:

(31) a. *Sam may have been interrogating by the FBI.
     b. *Sam may be had been interrogating by the FBI.
     c. *Sam is may-en have been interrogating by the FBI.

However, we have already seen a condition on the application of Passive that will exclude its application to any of the higher Ss in (30b). For Passive to apply to, say, S_3, Raising would have to have already applied to S_3, and thus the input to Passive would be (32):

(32)

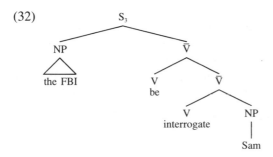

However, application of Passive to a structure like (32) would violate the constraint noted in chapter 4 that the NP that is to become the derived subject must be a $\bar{V}$-mate of the verb, e.g., (33a–b) do not have the passive counterparts (33a′–b′):

(33) a.   Small businessmen [$_{\bar{V}}$ seem to [$_{\bar{V}}$ fear the IRS]].
     a′. *The IRS is seemed to fear by small businessmen.
     b.   Alice [$_{\bar{V}}$ happens to [$_{\bar{V}}$ dislike Marvin]].
     b′. *Marvin is happened to dislike by Alice.

Note that in (32) *Sam* and *be* are not $\bar{V}$-mates. Thus, the same condition on Passive that excludes (33a′, b′) will also exclude (31a) (and similarly, (31b–c)): under an analysis in which each auxiliary verb is the predicate element of its own deep structure S, a derivation of (31a–c) would have to involve an application of Passive that extracted the NP from a structure of the form [$_{\bar{V}}$V [$_{\bar{V}}$ . . . NP . . .]], and Passive is subject to a condition that rules out such a step.

    Now let us take up *-en* and *-ing*. In the deep structures proposed in Chomsky 1957, *-en* and *-ing* are immediate right sisters of *have* and *be* (see (5a) above); they are attached to the following verb by the same transformation ("Affix-hopping") that purportedly attaches a tense to a following verb. The only reason that I have ever seen adduced for having *-en* and *-ing* present at all in deep structures is that by having them in the particular deep structure positions where Chomsky posits them, one can "catch a free ride on" the independently necessary "Affix-hopping" transformation, which will then suffice to put *-en* and *-ing* into the right surface positions. However, that argument loses what little force it had when one notes that the conditions for attachment of an affix to a verb are different for different combinations of verb and affix, and thus it is impossible to have a single rule that is responsible for the attachment of all affixes to all verbs.

Chomsky's Affix-hopping transformation conflates three different processes of attachment of affixes to verbs: (i) **Attraction-to-tense,** which combines a tense with an auxiliary verb and is in the cycle, (ii) **Tense-hopping,** which combines a tense with a main verb and is postcyclic, and (iii) insertion of *-en* and *-ing* into the complements of verbs that demand them. That (i) differs from (ii) in being in the cycle can be shown by contrasting the evidence that Tense-hopping was postcyclic given in §6c with analogous examples where there is an underlying auxiliary verb:

(34) a. Alice bought a computer, and Fred did ∅ too.
     b. Alice has bought a computer, and Fred has/*does ∅ too.
     c. Alice is writing a novel, and Fred is/*does ∅ too.

The "Affix-hopping"of (34a) has to be postcyclic in order for the input to $\bar{\text{V}}$-deletion to contain two copies of tenseless *buy a computer:* if it were in the cycle, Tense-hopping on the two conjuncts would have replaced *buy a computer* by *bought a computer* before $\bar{\text{V}}$-deletion had a chance to apply to the whole S, and there would thus be no derivation for (34a). But if the step that combines the tense with the auxiliary verb of *have bought a computer* or *be writing a novel* in (34b–c) were also postcyclic, it should be possible to delete those $\bar{\text{V}}$s and obtain the asterisked versions of (34b–c). By contrast, if that step is cyclic, *bought a computer* and *writing a novel* will be the only tenseless $\bar{\text{V}}$s in the input to $\bar{\text{V}}$-deletion, and thus only the acceptable versions of (34b–c) will have derivations.

In cxamples like (34b–c), attachment of *-en* and *-ing* behaves like the cyclic Attraction-to-tense and unlike the postcyclic Tense-hopping:[20]

(35) a.   Alice has bought a computer, and Fred has (*done) ∅ too.
     a′. Alice has been working overtime, and Fred has (been (*doing)) ∅
         too.
     b.   Alice is writing a novel, and Fred is (*doing) ∅ too.

Attachment of *-en* and *-ing* within each conjunct cannot be postponed until $\bar{\text{V}}$-deletion gets its chance to apply to the whole sentence, since if it could, it should be possible to delete the $\bar{\text{V}}$ leaving the *-en* and *-ing* behind, thus obtaining the unacceptable versions of (35). By contrast, if attachment of *-en* and *-ing* is in the cycle, there will be no well-formed derivations for those sentences, while derivations for the acceptable sentences will still be available. A further difference among the three rules (a concomitant of the fact that one of them is postcyclic and the other two cyclic, if Pullum's conjecture that postcyclic transformations must be "local" is correct) is that while an intervening adverb or *not* inhibits the application of Tense-hopping (and thus results in a sentence with *do*), it does not inhibit the other two cases of "Affix-hopping":

(36) a. Fred didn't buy a computer.
  b. Fred has [not given me any money] many times.
  b'. *Fred has done not give me any money many times.
  c. Fred has been [not giving anyone any money] recently.
  c'. *Fred has been doing not give anyone any money recently.

Since Attraction-to-tense is restricted to auxiliary verbs, while attachment of *-en* and *-ing* affects main and auxiliary verbs alike, no two of the three cases of "Affix-hopping" have the same conditions of application.

Since there is no possibility of taking attachment of *-en* and *-ing* in under either of the other two "Affix-hopping" transformations, there is no particular reason why it must be regarded as a **movement** transformation, like the other two rules, as in (37a), rather than as an **insertion** transformation that simply attaches *-en* and *-ing* to the verb of the complement of a verb that demands them (37b):

(37) a.

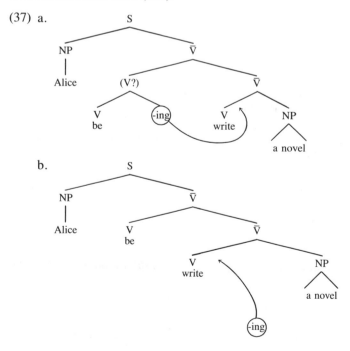

  b.

Either version of attachment of *-en* and *-ing* is consistent with the approach to auxiliary verbs adopted in this chapter. If one wants the movement transformation version, one simply has to have *be -ing* and *have -en* where structures such as (12) have just *be* and *have* (in which case Tense-replacement must replace Past not with *have* but with *have -en*). If one wants the insertion transformation version, one posits a transformation adding *-en* or *-ing* to the topmost predicate element of the complement of *have* or passive *be* (*-en*), or progressive *be* (*-ing*).

To recapitulate, auxiliary elements come in the order in which they do because (i) tenses other than on the first verb undergo Tense-replacement, so only the first verb can bear a tense; (ii) modal auxiliaries have only finite forms and a modal that was preceded by another auxiliary would have to be in a nonfinite form, so the morphology of modal auxiliaries prevents them from following any other auxiliary verb;[21] (iii) *Have*-deletion deletes all but the first of two or more consecutive auxiliary *have*'s, so no more than one can occur; (iv) complements headed by auxiliary verbs other than passive *be* usually (though not always—cf. (29c)) violate the restriction that the complement of progressive *be* denote an activity or a process, so progressive *be* normally cannot be followed by any other auxiliary verb besides passive *be;* (v) passive *be* could precede an auxiliary verb only as a result of passivization of a clause headed by that auxiliary, which would violate the constraint that the V and the NP that become the derived subject be $\bar{\text{V}}$-mates, so passive *be* must follow any other auxiliary verbs; and (vi) Ss in certain contexts are required to have a tense as the topmost predicate, and being in such a context is what it is to be a finite S, so every finite S must have a tense.

This last remark calls for some comment. The use of the term "finite" in this chapter presupposes that the different contexts in which Ss occur impose on the S either a requirement that there be a surface tense or a requirement that there not be any surface tense. This distinction between finite and nonfinite Ss is independent of the distinction between semantically tensed and semantically tenseless Ss. There have in fact been numerous examples in this chapter in which a nonfinite S has an underlying tense (which must then undergo Tense-replacement), and indeed, all four combinations of deep and surface tensed and tenseless are attested:

	deep tensed	deep tenseless
surface tensed	John said <u>that he was tired</u>.	Jap. *John wa <u>piano o hiku koto ga dekiru</u>*. 'John can play the piano.'
surface tenseless	We believe John <u>to have stolen the money</u>.	John can <u>play the piano</u>.

The combination "surface tensed, deep tenseless" does not occur in English but is common in such languages as Japanese, in which certain constructions demand a tensed verb (e.g., the present tense form *hiku* in the given example) even though the construction does not admit a tense opposition (the past tense form *hiita* is not possible in the given construction) and the complement is semantically tenseless. The transformation of Tense-replacement makes it possible for complementizers that demand a surface tenseless complement to be used nonetheless with semantically tensed complements.

b. Some Phenomena Involving Auxiliary Verbs

Yes-no questions are one of a number of syntactic constructions in English in which the tense-bearing auxiliary verb of a clause plays a special role. In a yes-no question, the subject must be preceded by a tense auxiliary verb:

(1) a. Has Ann read the report?
    b. Were you being followed?
    c. Will John have been drinking?
    d. Does Roger play tennis?

With the exception of cases in which the tensed auxiliary verb is a form of **do**, as in (1d), to which I will return shortly, the tensed auxiliary verb is one that could follow the given subject in a corresponding declarative sentence, and any auxiliary verbs (necessarily, nonfinite ones) that follow the subject in the yes-no question are ones that could follow the tensed auxiliary verb in a corresponding declarative sentence:

(2) a. Ann has read the report.
    b. You were being followed.
    c. John will have been drinking.

(3) a. *Is George having lived in Toledo for thirty years?
    a'. *George is having lived in Toledo for thirty years.
    b. *Is the house been remodeling?
    b'. *The house is been remodeling.
    c. *Has Margaret had already left?
    c'. *Margaret has had already left.
    d. *Are the birds being singing?
    d'. *The birds are being singing.

This state of affairs lends itself to a description in which a yes-no question differs in underlying structure from a corresponding declarative only to the extent of having some marker of interrogative status (which we will write "Q" and, in accordance with the remarks of §6b, take to be outside of the S corresponding to a declarative) and the derivation of yes-no questions involves a step in which the tensed auxiliary verb is moved to the beginning of the sentence. Ignoring tenses, for the moment, the derivations would then be as in (4):

(4)

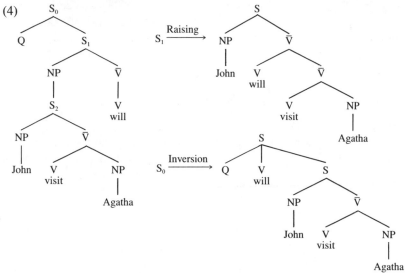

Now let us bring tenses into the picture. According to what we have said so far (including the analysis of tenses and auxiliary verbs developed in the last section), the deep structure of (1a) should be (5a), and prior to Inversion there should be steps as in (5b):

(5) a.

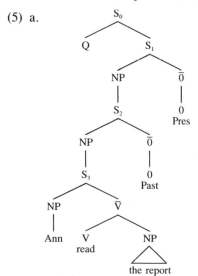

b.

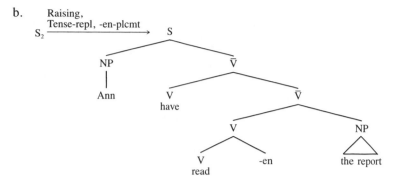

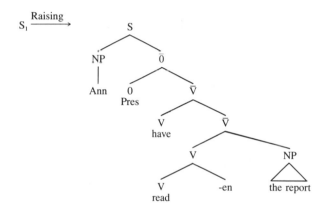

Note that what undergoes Inversion in (1) is not a bare auxiliary verb but the combination of an auxiliary verb and a tense, in this case, *have* combined with Pres. It would be highly desirable if we could limit movement transformations to moving a single constituent, since what the constituent structure is supposed to represent is the status of the various constituents as syntactic units, and being moved by a transformation is a clear case of behaving as a syntactic unit. In the last tree in (5b), *have* and Pres do not make up a constituent. Since they do make up a constituent in surface structure, however, a transformation will have to combine them somewhere in the derivation. If we assume that that transformation (dubbed **Attraction-to-tense** in the last section, henceforth abbreviated **AT**) applies according to the cyclic principle, the remainder of the derivation will be as in (6):

(6)

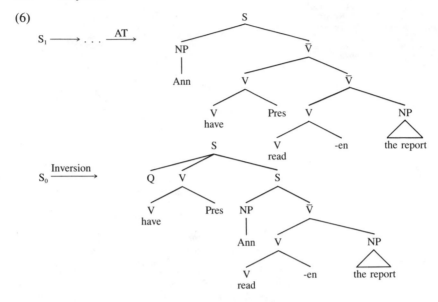

I emphasize that AT must not be confused with Tense-hopping, from which it differs in applying to auxiliary rather than to main verbs and in being cyclic rather than postcyclic.

Let us now take up yes-no questions that begin with a form of *do*. These questions correspond to declaratives that have no auxiliary verb:

(7) a.   Birds eat worms.
    a′. Do birds eat worms?
    b.   Schubert died in poverty.
    b′. Did Schubert die in poverty?

The assumptions made so far imply that such questions have deep structures like (8):

(8)

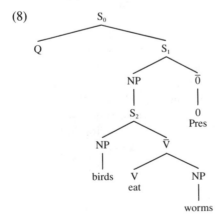

Since AT is not applicable to S_1 (because it affects only auxiliary verbs), S_1 will undergo only Raising, and the input to Inversion$_0$ will be (9):

(9)

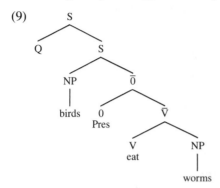

Since the tense in such questions shows up (attached to *do*) in the position to which Inversion moves tensed auxiliary verbs, we can get almost the right surface structure by taking Inversion as applying not only to a V but also to a tense that is not attached to a V. All that remains to get the right surface structure is to posit a transformation (**Do-support,** necessarily postcyclic), that attaches *do* to an unattached tense:

(10)

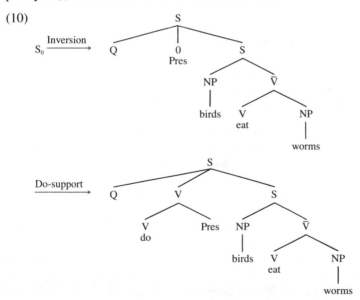

The statement above that AT affects only auxiliary verbs is actually not completely correct. Consider questions corresponding to declarative sentences whose topmost verb is either *have* or *be:*[22]

(11) a.   Tom has a lot of money.
　　　　　%?Has Tom a lot of money?
　　　　　Does Tom have a lot of money?
　　　b.   Joe has to wash the dishes.
　　　　　??Has Joe to wash the dishes?
　　　　　Does Joe have to wash the dishes?
　　　c.   Jane has the problem solved.
　　　　　*Has Jane the problem solved?
　　　　　Does Jane have the problem solved?
　　　d.   God had mercy on them.
　　　　　*Had God mercy on them?
　　　　　Did God have mercy on them?
　　　e.   Bill had the tailor make him a new suit.
　　　　　*Had Bill the tailor make him a new suit?
　　　　　Did Bill have the tailor make him a new suit?
　　　f.   They had a good time.
　　　　　*Had they a good time?
　　　　　Did they have a good time?
(12) a.   The broom is in the closet.
　　　　　Is the broom in the closet?
　　　　　*Does the broom be in the closet?
　　　b.   You are to leave right away.
　　　　　Am I to leave right away?
　　　　　*Do I be to leave right away?
　　　c.   There is an error in the proof.
　　　　　Is there an error in the proof?
　　　　　*Does there be an error in the proof?

While *have* and *be* as they are used in (11)–(12) are main rather than auxiliary verbs, nonetheless all the uses of *be*, and for at least many speakers one of the uses of *have*, behave like auxiliary verbs in Inversion. Note that for British speakers, the "possession" *have* in (11a) behaves both like a main verb and like an auxiliary verb: it may either invert or be left behind by Inversion.

There is a fairly straightforward way in which we can reconcile these observations with our approach to the syntax of yes-no questions. Suppose that AT is simply taken as applying to the verbs that participate in Inversion in the given variety of English, which includes all uses of *be*, regardless of whether main or auxiliary, and some uses of *have*, which ones being subject to dialect variation. Since we would then be making AT responsible for which verbs undergo Inversion, our analysis would imply that exactly the same verbs would "behave like auxiliary verbs" with regard to **all** transformations that are fed by AT. If this prediction is verified, then we will have reason to accept the version of AT in which it is the locus of irregularity with regard to what verbs behave like auxiliary verbs.

Consider the placement of *not* or *-n't* in negations of simple sentences:

(13) a. Ann hasn't read the report.
   b. You weren't being followed.
   c. John won't have been drinking.
   d. Roger doesn't play tennis.

In each case the negative marker is suffixed to a tensed auxiliary verb: the tensed auxiliary verb of the corresponding affirmative sentence if that sentence has an auxiliary verb, and an appropriately tensed form of *do* if it does not. But as in the case of yes-no questions, this statement is not exactly right. The negative marker is suffixed to *be* regardless of whether it is a main or an auxiliary verb, and for some (chiefly British) speakers to a tensed possessive *have* though not to other main verb uses of *have:*

(14) a. %?Tom hasn't a lot of money.
        Tom doesn't have a lot of money.
   b. ??Joe hasn't to wash the dishes.
        Joe doesn't have to wash the dishes.
   c. *Jane hasn't the problem solved.
        Jane doesn't have the problem solved.
   d. *God hadn't mercy on them.
        God didn't have mercy on them.
   e. *Bill hadn't the tailor make him a new suit.
        Bill didn't have the tailor make him a new suit.
   f. *They hadn't a good time.
        They didn't have a good time.
(15) a. The broom isn't in the closet.
        *The broom doesn't be in the closet.
   b. You aren't to leave right away.
        *You don't be to leave right away.
   c. There aren't any errors in the proof.
        *There don't be any errors in the proof.

It appears as if exactly the same verbs "count as auxiliary verbs" for the placement of negation as for Inversion, a class of verbs that fails to coincide with "auxiliary verbs" by taking in main verb uses of *be* and (with dialect variation) the "possession" sense of *have*.

To give derivations for (13), we will have to adopt some policy regarding how negation fits into deep structure. I will anticipate here the conclusions that will be argued for in chapter 17 and assume that *not* appears in deep structure as a sister of the S that it negates and that it triggers the application of a transformation (possibly to be identified with Raising to Subject) that makes it a sister of the $\overline{V}$ of the negated S, the latter structure being the input to **Negative-placement,** which adjoins it to the tensed auxiliary verb:[23]

(16)

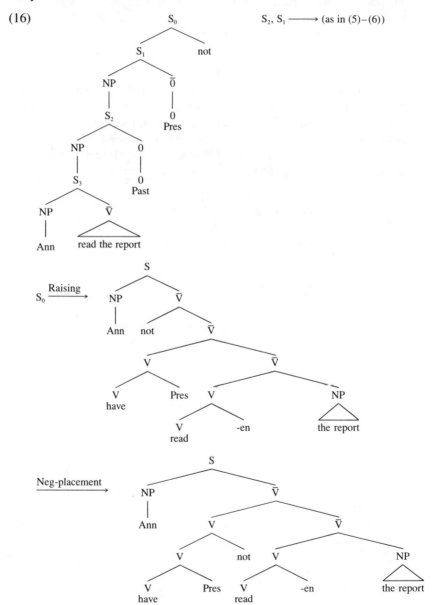

The analysis proposed here implies that the same verbs will behave like auxiliaries with regard to $\bar{V}$-deletion (that is, they will be retained in the output of $\bar{V}$-deletion) as behave like auxiliaries in Inversion. This prediction is verified:

(17) a. Ann has read the report, and Otto has/*does too.
    b. You were being followed, and I was/*did too.
    c. John will have been drinking, and Sam will/*does too.
    d. Roger plays tennis, and Nina does too.
(18) a. Tom has a lot of money, and Alice does/%?has too.
    b. Joe has to work hard, and Fred does/*has too.
    c. Jane has the problem solved, and Nancy does/??has too.
    d. God had mercy on sinners, and Mencken did/*had too.
    e. Smith has students shine his shoes, and Brown does/*has too.
    f. George had a good time, and I did/*had too.
(19) a. The broom is in the closet, and the fly-swatter is/*does too.
    b. George is to leave right away, and Susan is/*does too.
    c. He said there was an error in the proof, and there was/*did.

In these examples, we have two Ss, S_1 and S_2, contained in a larger sentence S_0. AT gets its chance to apply on the S_1 and S_2 cycles, and thus when $\bar{V}$-deletion applies to S_0, deleting a $\bar{V}$ in S_2 under identity with its counterpart in S_1, only those tenseless $\bar{V}$s that remain after the application of AT are available to delete. Since, e.g., the main verb uses of *be* in (19) are combined with the tense on the S_2 cycle, only *in the closet* and not *be in the closet* can be deleted in (19a), etc.[24]

As a final example of a type of sentence in which the same verbs, not all of them strictly speaking auxiliary verbs, behave like auxiliary verbs, consider what I will refer to as **retorts:**[25]

(20) a. John HAS mailed the letter.
    b. Margaret IS practising the piano.
    c. The meeting WILL start at 2:30.
    d. Hindemith DID write a horn concerto.

In these examples, capitalization indicates contrastive stress. Such sentences must be distinguished from those with contrastive stress on a main verb (e.g., *The meeting will START at 2:30*), which only contrast that verb with an alternative (e.g., contrastive stress on *start* is used in denying the suggestion that the meeting will end at 2:30, whereas (20c) is a rejection of the suggestion that it won't start at 2:30). The stress on retorts must be on a tensed auxiliary verb, once again with the qualification that all uses of *be* and some of *have* (subject to the same dialect variation as before) behave like auxiliary verbs:

(21) a. %?Tom HAS a lot of money.
          Tom DOES have a lot of money.
      b. ??Joe HAS to wash the dishes.
          Joe DOES have to wash the dishes.
      c. *Jane HAS the problem solved.
          Jane DOES have the problem solved.
      d. *God HAD mercy on them.
          God DID have mercy on them.
      e. *Bill HAD the tailor make him a new suit.
          Bill DID have the tailor make him a new suit.
      f. *They HAD a good time.
          They DID have a good time.
(22) a. The broom IS in the closet.
          *The broom DOES be in the closet.
      b. You ARE to leave right away.
          *You DO be to leave right away.
      c. There ARE some errors in the proof.
          *There DO be some errors in the proof.

c. Evidence for the Extra Ss Posited in This Analysis

If tenses, auxiliary verbs, and *not* are the predicate elements of their own
Ss, then the cyclic principle predicts that applications of cyclic transformations to the complements of those elements will precede applications of
cyclic transformations that involve those elements. Thus, under this approach many details of rule interaction that in treatments based on the
"Aux" analysis had required the imposition of an ordering on the rules are
predictable from the cyclic principle. For example, since (as shown in §8a)
Passive cannot apply to Ss headed by auxiliary verbs, any application of
Passive must precede any derivational steps involving auxiliary verbs or
tenses. The data reflect precisely that interaction of rules:

(1) a.   Is Reagan admired by all Americans? [Inversion]
     a'. *Does Reagan be admired by all Americans?
     b.   Reagan isn't admired by all Americans. [Negative-placement]
     b'. *Reagan doesn't be admired by all Americans.
     c.   I am feared by everyone present.
     c'. *I is feared by everyone present. [Agreement]

For example, the derivation of (1a) is (2):

(2)

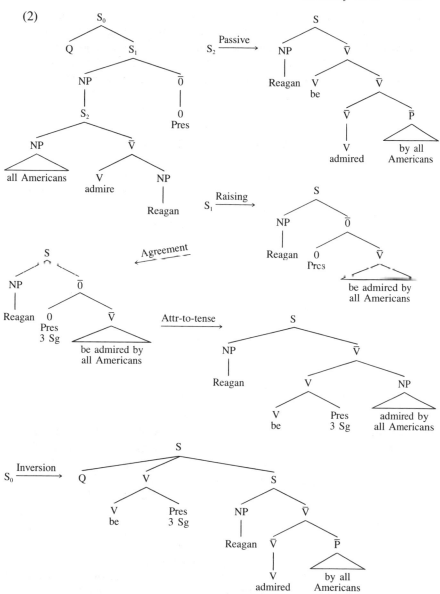

Since Passive can apply only to S_2, AT only to S_1, and Inversion only to S_0, the input to Inversion will have *be* + Pres in the position from which Inversion does its extraction. A derivation of (1a') would have to have Inversion applying to S_0 before AT applies to S_1 or before Passive applies to S_2, and would thus violate the cyclic principle. Moreover, note that if (as is assumed here) the Agreement transformation copies features of the subject NP **onto the tense,** its conditions for application are met in S_1 (which has a tense) and not in S_2 (which does not), which means that the derived subject of the passive and not its underlying subject will be in subject position at the point of the derivation at which Agreement applies, and thus the agreement is 3rd person singular (not plural) in (1a), and 1st person singular (not 3rd person) in (1c). Similarly, the deep structure of (1b) will have *not* outside of the S to which Passive applies and thus Negative placement will apply to a structure that contains passive *be.*

The cyclic principle also predicts that any application of *There*-insertion will precede Inversion, Negative-placement, and Agreement.[26] The situation is somewhat different from that with Passive, since *There*-insertion can apply to a S headed by passive *be* or progressive *be:*

(3) a. There was someone killed. (passive *be*)
    b. There were several dogs barking. (progressive *be*)

It has often been noted that when two *be*s co-occur (of necessity, a progressive *be* followed by some other kind of *be*), if there is *There*-insertion the underlying subject can follow only the first (progressive) *be:*

(4) a.   There was a man being tortured.
    a′. *There was being a man tortured.
    b.   There was someone being obnoxious.
    b′. *There was being someone obnoxious.

The analysis of auxiliary verbs adopted here places such examples in a quite different light than they are usually seen in. Under the analysis adopted here, the acceptable sentences in (4) differ from the unacceptable ones with regard to what domain *There*-insertion applies to: in (4a, b), *There*-insertion is applied to the S headed by progressive *be,* while in (4a′, b′) it is applied to the complement of progressive *be.* In §18b, in the context of a discussion of the relationship between syntax and the scope of quantifiers and negations, I will suggest a possible semantic explanation of the unacceptability of (4a′, b′), namely that (i) the S to which *There*-insertion applies is the scope of an existential quantifier on the subject NP and (ii) if the complement of progressive *be* is the scope of an existential quantifier, there is a violation of the semantic restriction that the complement of progressive *be* denote an activity or process. The deviance of (4a′, b′) is then caused not by any violation on the conditions for the application of *There*-insertion but by an anomaly in the semantic structures that would correspond to the derivations of those sentences.

The various Ss posited in the analysis of §8a are not only domains for the application of cyclic transformations but also possible loci for negation and conjoining. The additional loci for negation provide derivations for examples that have more than one negation[27] in a clause and for sentences in which less than the whole sentence is negated, e.g.,

(5) a. You can't not say anything—we insist on hearing your opinion!
   b. Tom has been not watching television for quite a while now.
   b'. Tom hasn't been watching television recently.
   c. Has she ever not said hello to you?
   c'. Hasn't she ever said hello to you? ($\neq$ (5c))

The anlysis proposed above, in which *not* is a deep structure sister of the S that it negates, provides derivations for all of these examples and, moreover, allows them to be assigned deep structures that indicate correctly what the **scope** of each negation is. For example, the deep structures of (5b) and (5b'), aside from the adverbs, which are omitted here, will be:

(6) a.

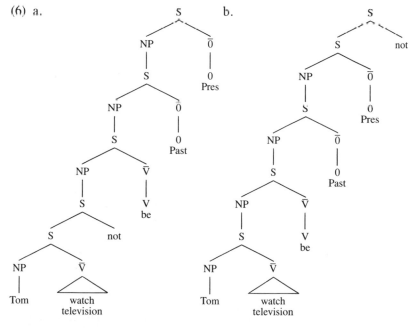

Note that these structures conform to the fact that (5b') is the negation of *Tom has been watching television*, whereas (5b) is not the negation of anything but is rather the present perfect of the progressive of the negation of something.

The treatment of negation adopted here requires that Negative-placement be restricted to **finite** Ss, i.e., while the *not* of (6b) will be adjoined to the *have* + Pres, the *not* of (6a) will remain a sister of the lower $\bar{\text{V}}$, i.e., the surface structures are:

(7) a.

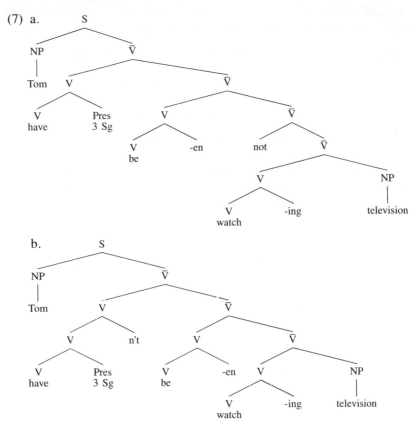

b.

This observation will be of some importance in the account of negation to be developed in chapter 17.

There is one obvious problem for this treatment of negation, namely, that it appears to have the blatantly false consequence that negatives can be iterated without limit. Nothing in the analysis as it stands excludes deep structures in which *not* is combined with a S of the form [S *not*] whose S is in turn of the form [S *not*]. Depending on how exactly the multiple negatives would interact with relevant rules such as Negative-placement, this seems to imply that there are derivations for one or other of the monstrosities in (8):

(8) a. *Tom not not not isn't watching television.
     b. *Tom isn't-n't-n't-n't watching television.

I will postpone until chapter 10 the question of how such sentences can be excluded while retaining the central features of the above analysis of negation. It will be argued there that there is nothing ill-formed about deep structures involving multiple negations (even the deep structure that corresponds to (8)) but that the occurrence of multiple negations is subject both to a surface restriction on the co-occurrence of negative words and to restrictions imposed by the morphology (i.e., the morphology of contracted negatives as in (8b) provides for only one negation).

Conjoining of the extra Ss posited in the above analysis of auxiliary verbs is illustrated by sentences such as those in (9):

(9) a. Have you ever eaten pizza and drunk champagne at the same meal?
  b. Larry has been stealing cars and reselling them for years.
  c. You should either eat less or do more exercise.

In none of these examples can the most natural interpretation be paraphrased in terms of conjoined main clauses, e.g., (9c) does not mean that either you should eat less or you should do more exercise—it is consistent with the proposition that it doesn't matter whether you eat less as long as you do more exercise and it doesn't matter whether you do more exercise as long as you eat less. The analysis of auxiliary verbs adopted here allows the following deep structures, which accurately represent the meanings of (9):

(10) a.

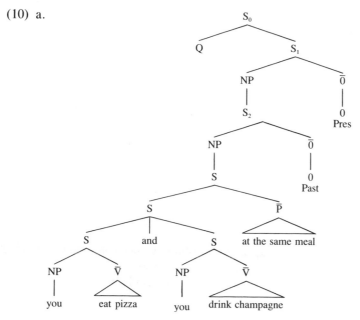

b.

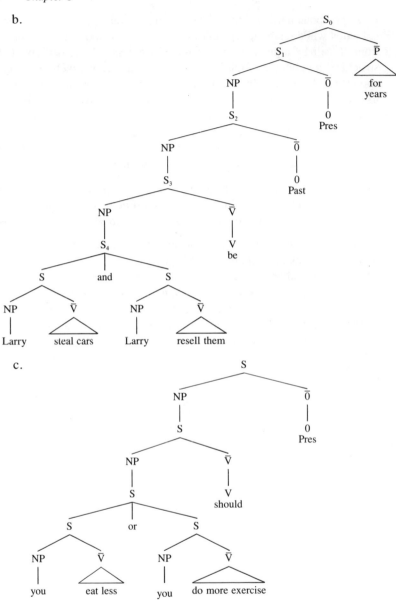

c.

The derivations will involve an application of Conjunction-reduction to the conjoined S, e.g., in the derivation with the deep structure (10b), CR_4 will replace the conjoined S by a simple S with a conjoined $\overline{V}$; the derivation then continues as follows:

(11)

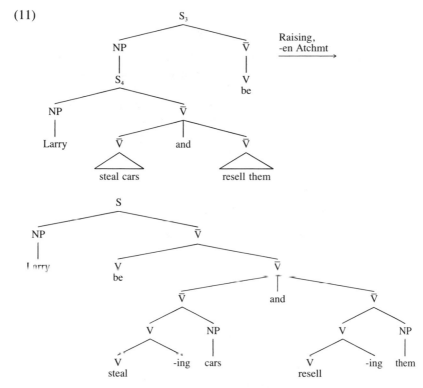

Raising,
-en Atchmt

Note, by the way, that placement of *-en/-ing* here attaches *-ing* to the Vs of both conjuncts of the conjoined V̄. This illustrates the Coordinate Structure Constraint (to be discussed in §9a), according to which a transformation can do something to a coordinate structure only by doing it to all the conjuncts of the structure.

Finally, I will point out that by contrast with the "Aux" analysis of Chomsky 1957, which required that the formulations of such transformations as Passive explicitly allow for an "Aux" between the elements that actually played a role in the transformation, the approach developed here allows those transformations to be stated in a pristine form in which extraneous elements such as auxiliary verbs and negation play no role. Under the approach of this chapter, passive constructions allow auxiliary verbs over and above passive *be* not because the passive transformation is formulated so as to allow for "Aux" but because there is nothing to prevent Passive from applying in the complement of any verb, auxiliary or not. This approach implies that a language in which Passive was allowed only in Ss that have no auxiliary verbs would not be a possible language.

d. Which Verbs Are Auxiliary Verbs?

So far, I have sidestepped the question of how one identifies particular words as auxiliary verbs. In some cases one can justify a decision as to whether something is an auxiliary verb in a trivial way, i.e., if a nonelliptical S contains only one verb, one can identify that verb as a main rather than an auxiliary verb by invoking the assumption that every nonelliptical S in English must have a main verb. Thus, since (1a) has no verb other than "possessive" *have* and (1b) has no verb other than existential *be,* those verbs must be main verbs:

(1) a. John has a lot of money.
    b. There is a unicorn in the garden.

This, however, leaves a large body of cases in which there is more than one verb, and in many of those cases there is a serious question as to whether the tense-bearing verb is an auxiliary verb. For example, all of the underlined items in (2) have been called auxiliary verbs by some linguist or other, but in no case has that judgment achieved unanimous acceptance:

(2) a. We had to go home.
    b. Bill had the tailor make him a suit.
    c. You are to leave at once.
    d. They began singing songs.
    e. I dare not leave them alone.
    f. We used to play cards every Thursday.
    g. The landlord is going to cancel our lease.
    h. I would rather have coffee after the meal.

Before taking up some syntactic phenomena that can serve as criteria for auxiliaryhood, I must bring up a fact of life that we have to contend with, namely that there are syntactic phenomena typical of auxiliary verbs that main verb uses of *be* and sometimes of *have* also participate in. I will take the position here that the auxiliary-like behavior of those uses of *be* and *have* are parasitic on similar behavior by auxiliary *be* and *have*. That is, I conjecture that verbs that can be used only as main verbs never exhibit behavior that is typical of auxiliary verbs, and that those main verb uses of a given verb that are in some sense "closest" to its auxiliary verb uses can most readily take on auxiliary-like behavior. The tests to be given below, then, can be interpreted as showing that a given verb is at least sometimes an auxiliary verb, though they do not necessarily show that it is one in the particular examples tested.

Let us start by showing how the possibilities for Inversion, Negative-placement, and V̄-deletion distinguish between a clear-cut auxiliary verb such as progressive *be* and a verb generally agreed not to be an auxiliary, such as *begin:*

(3) a. They were singing songs.
    a′. They began singing songs.
    b. Were they singing songs?
    b′. *Began they singing songs?
    b″. Did they begin singing songs?
    c. They weren't singing songs.
    c′. *They begann't singing songs.
    c″. They began not singing songs.
    c‴. They didn't begin singing songs.
    d. The children were singing songs, and the adults were too.
    d′. The children began singing songs, and the adults began too.
    d″. The children began singing songs, and the adults did too.

Be undergoes Inversion (3b) but *begin* does not (3b′); *begin* remains in its place and only the tense undergoes Inversion (3b″). Sentences like (3a) can be negated by attaching *n't* to *be* (3c), while those like (3a′) cannot be negated by attaching it to *begin*. In sentences like (3c″), although *not* does immediately follow *began*, it expresses negation not of the whole sentence but of the embedded V̄: (3c″) has the meaning not of (3c‴), the negation of (3a′), but roughly that of *They ceased singing songs*—it refers to not sing-ing rather than to not beginning. In (3d), a repetition of *singing songs* is deleted, leaving Past + *be* behind. Since *begin* has so far shown the be-havior of main verbs, we would expect (3d″) to be normal and (3d′) not to be, but in fact both are quite normal. I would argue that (3d′) involves not V̄-deletion as we so far know it but rather a special process of ellipsis that is peculiar to *begin* and a number of other verbs, though justifying that claim would not be practical this early in this book. I raise this possibility here simply to point out a difficulty that sometimes arises in interpreting linguistic data: there is no reason why two distinct syntactic rules cannot have similar effects, and it is thus difficult to justify claims as to **what** syn-tactic rule has applied in the derivation of a given example. At any rate, the acceptability of (3d″) shows that *begin* in sentences like (3a′) **can** be treated as a main verb, since it is deleted and only the tense left behind.

The following are some further syntactic phenomena in which auxiliary verbs behave differently. In **Tag-questions,** a declarative sentence is fol-lowed by an expression consisting of the tensed auxiliary verb, possibly with an attached -*n't,* and a pronoun corresponding to its subject:[28]

(4) a.   John has bought a new car, hasn't he? (**reversal** tag)
 a'. John has bought a new car, has he? (**reduplicative** tag)
 b.   There's a gas station ahead, isn't there?
 c.   Ann will be at the party tonight, won't she?

One factor that complicates the use of tag questions as a criterion for main or auxiliary verb status is that a reversal tag with an affirmative host S requires a contracted form of the auxiliary verb, and only a rather restricted set of verbs have a contracted negative form. Indeed, for most speakers of English, one verb that by all other criteria is an auxiliary verb, namely *may,* has no contracted negative form (*mayn't* occurs only sporadically). This difficulty can be circumvented by basing one's test for auxiliary status on reduplicative tags:

(5) a.   So they were singing songs, were they?
 a'. So they began singing songs, did/*began they?

Retorts, in which contrastive stress is placed on the tense-bearing auxiliary verb (expressing a contrast with the negation of the given proposition) can also be used as a test of auxiliary status, e.g., the *be* of (3a) but not the *begin* of (3a') can bear the contrastive stress in a retort:

(6) a.   You doubt that they were singing songs? Well, I saw them with my
    own eyes, and they WERE singing songs.
 a'. You doubt that they began singing songs? Well, I was with them,
    and I can assure you that they ⎰DID begin⎱ singing songs.
             ⎱*BEGAN⎰

The following examples illustrate how these phenomena can be used in deciding the status of an item whose status as an auxiliary verb has in fact been in some dispute:

(7) a.   Ought we to help him?
    *Do we ought to help him?
 b.   We oughtn't to help him.
    *We don't ought to help him.
 c.   You ought to help us, and your brother ⎧*ought also.⎫
               ⎨ ought to   ⎬
               ⎩*does   ⎭
 d.   We ought to help him, ⎰oughtn't we?⎱
          ⎱*don't we? ⎰
 e.   We OUGHT to help him.
    *We DO ought to help him.

In each of these five cases, *ought* does not act like a main verb, and with a qualification about (7c), it does act like an auxiliary verb. The one respect in which (7c) involves a deviation from clear-cut auxiliary behavior is that the *to* must be retained, like that of *have to* (which involves a main verb *have*) and unlike that of *is to* (our one instance so far of an auxiliary verb with *to*):

(8) a. Bill has to leave at once, and Alice has to/*∅ also.
    b. Bill is to leave at once, and Alice is (to) also.

Since deletion of a $\bar{\text{V}}$ that follows *to* appears always to be possible regardless of the category of what precedes *to*, the version of (7c) with *ought to* probably is irrelevant to whether *ought* is an auxiliary verb. In the other two examples in (7c) *ought* acts like neither an auxiliary verb nor a main verb.

In one important class of cases, the above tests for auxiliary status yield no information, namely, combinations of two or more words that could perhaps be regarded as forming a complex auxiliary, e.g., *be going to*, *would rather*, and *had better*. The tests provide evidence that the first word of these combinations is an auxiliary verb but say nothing about the remainder. Also, hortative *let's* and imperative *do*, as in (9), are too restricted in their syntactic possibilities for these tests to yield a clear decision as to their auxiliaryhood:

(9) a. Let's take a break.
    b. Don't be late![29]

Besides critera of auxiliaryhood, something should be said here about criteria of modalhood. There is only partial agreement among linguists as to which words are modal auxiliaries. The following are among the properties that have been held by at least some linguists to be necessary conditions for something to be a modal: (i) that it behave like an auxiliary verb in all the respects just discussed, (ii) that it precede any other auxiliary verbs with which it is combined, (iii) that it not manifest agreement with its subject (or at least, that it not take the ending -*s* with a third person singular subject), (iv) that the expression with which it is combined be in the bare infinitive form (thus, that it not take a *to* after it), (v) that it have only finite forms, and (vi) that it express a "modal" meaning, i.e., that it express a notion such as possibility, necessity, or desirability which refers to "alternative possible worlds" (cf. the analysis of *necessarily* by modal logicians as "in all possible worlds").

The trouble with these criteria is that, first, aside from (vi) they have no hope of standing up as universal criteria of modals, and second, no combination of them seems to delineate a class of items whose behavior differs systematically from that of items not in the class. Note the following respects in which particular items that behave quite similarly to hard-core modals such as *may* and *must* violate one or more of these conditions. In dialects that allow double modals such as *might could*, the second modal violates (ii). In German, (ii) (or an appropriately revised version of (ii) that allows for German word order) and (v) are systematically violated, since modal auxiliaries have infinitive and participle forms and can be combined with other modal auxiliaries or with perfect *haben*. The *is* of *is to*, which satisfies criteria (i)–(ii) and (v)–(vi), shows the same agreement with its surface subject as does any other use of *be* (*I am to leave, you are to leave, . . .*), violating (iii). German and Old English modals agree with their subjects (*Ich kann, du kannst, wir können, ihr könnt*), though they lack an agreement marker in the third person singular, whence the apparent lack of agreement in English modals, since for verbs other than *be* in modern English, only the third person singular shows an agreement marker.[30] *Ought to* and *is to*, which share most of the characteristics of the hard-core modals, have a *to* rather than a bare infinitive, thus violating (iv). Finally, while future *will* meets criteria (i)–(v), I have argued (McCawley 1981a: 342–44) that it does not have a modal meaning in the sense of (vi).

It is really not necessary, however, to delimit precisely a class of modal auxiliaries. The various verbs that we have been calling modals can be treated as verbs taking infinitive complements (some with, some without *to*) and in general having defective morphology and thus restricted to appearing in environments whose morphological demands can be satisfied within their defective morphology. The morphological peculiarity noted in (iii), which is exhibited mainly by verbs meeting condition (vi), can be regarded as a historical accident without synchronic significance.

Indeed, with the analysis of auxiliary verbs that is developed in this chapter, there is no real need to recognize even a category of "auxiliary verbs." The special behavior of auxiliary verbs is localized in the various rules (e.g., Inversion) that affect a V that is combined with a tense in the cycle, and the verbs that fit that description are those that undergo Attraction-to-tense. Since that set of verbs is not exactly the same as what have traditionally been called "auxiliary verbs," it is the feature "allows Attraction-to-tense" and not the traditional category "auxiliary verb" that draws the distinction that plays a role in the analysis given here.

e. Introduction to the Syntax of Adverbs

In view of the existence of co-occurrence restrictions among tenses, auxiliary verbs, and time adverbs, and the concomitant necessity of including time adverbs in examples illustrating tenses and auxiliary verbs, it is worth-while to include in this chapter a sketch of some details of the syntax of adverbs. It has already been pointed out (§3b) that "adverbs" differ with respect to what category of constituents they modify, e.g., *mildly* in (1a) modifies the V and *intentionally* in (1b) the V̄:

(1) a. John mildly reprimanded Mary.
    b. John intentionally insulted Mary.

The point will be elaborated in chapter 19, where it will be argued that there are also S-modifying adverbs, e.g., *probably* in (2) modifies the S:

(2) Probably there has been a riot.

It will also be argued in chapter 19 that S-modifiers are optionally con-vertible into modifiers of the V̄, i.e., there is an optional transformation with the effect in (3):

(3)

This is the same transformation that was posited in the treatment of nega-tion in §8b, with *not* in the role of the Adv, subject to two qualifications: (i) with most adverbs this transformation is optional, whereas with *not* it is obligatory, and (ii) while many adverbs are allowed to appear both before and after the constituent that they modify, *not* is allowed only to precede the modified V̄. (I intend the trees in (3) to be interpreted as **unspecified** with regard to whether the Adv precedes or follows the modified constitu-ent, with both orders allowed except where a specific restriction, e.g., the requirement that *not* precede what it modifies, excludes one of the orders). As was remarked in §8b, the transformation in (3) may be identifiable with Raising-to-Subject.

I wish to take all of the time adverbials that have figured in this chapter to be S-modifiers, thus to allow the option of appearing as V̄-modifiers in derived structures. It is not completely obvious how a time adverbial should be combined with a tense—should it be higher than the tense (4a)? or lower than it (4b)? or on the same level as it (4c)? or should the tense be treated as predictable from the time adverbial and not present as such at all in deep structure (4d)?[31]

(4) a.

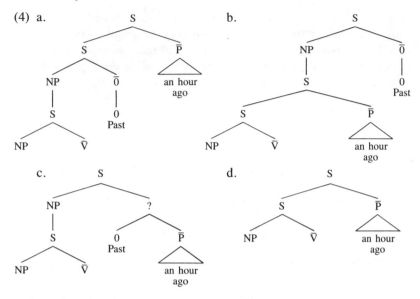

I will arbitrarily adopt the (4a) structure and thus implicitly adopt a restriction that in deep structure every time adverb have an appropriate tense as its niece. A sentence like *When I saw John, he had finished the report an hour before* will then have a derivation as in (5):[32]

(5)

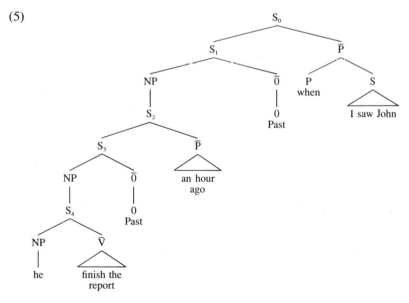

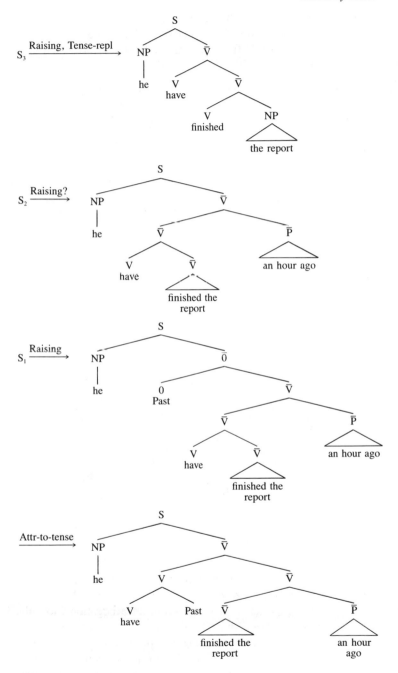

I will conclude this section with an illustration of a fairly complex derivation that exploits the above treatment of adverbs (including *not*), namely the derivation of (6a) (example from Linebarger 1981 : 17), to which I assign the deep structure (6b):

(6) a. I haven't gone to church because I wanted to in years.

b.

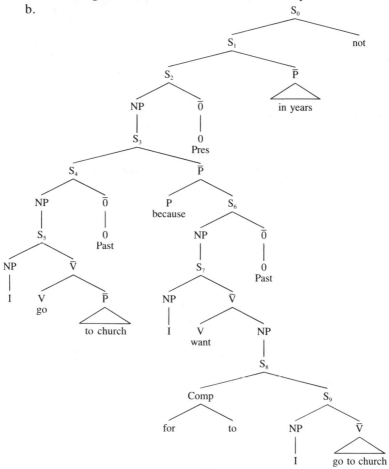

A couple of comments on this deep structure are called for. *In years* is lower than *not* in (6b) because it is a **Negative polarity item** (cf. chap. 17), i.e., an item that is normal only when it is in the scope of a negation (note the deviance of *I've been there in years*). The Pasts in S_4 and S_6 are instances of a single time variable, i.e., the meaning of a present perfect is roughly "there is a past time t at which . . . ," the Past of the structure that underlies a present perfect corresponds to that time variable, and multiple Pasts as in (6b) will correspond to multiple instances of that variable; this fits the meaning of (6b), which has to do with going to church at some time or other because one wanted at that time to go to church.

Omitting the obvious steps of Comp-placement$_8$, Equi$_7$, and Raising$_{4,6,}$ we come to S$_3$, on which $\bar{\text{V}}$-deletion, Tense-replacement, and the rule turning S-adverbs into $\bar{\text{V}}$-adverbs apply, yielding:

(7)

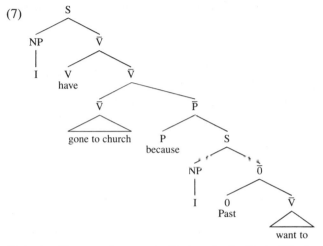

Note that Tense-replacement affects only the Past of S$_4$, because while S$_4$ is nonfinite, S$_6$ is finite. The *because* expression has to be converted into a $\bar{\text{V}}$-modifier since it will otherwise be impossible to do so with *in years,* which has to be a surface $\bar{\text{V}}$-modifier so that it can be lower than *not* in surface structure. That step, plus Raising, Attraction-to-tense, Negative-placement, and postcyclic Tense-hopping on S$_7$ yield the surface structure (8):

(8)

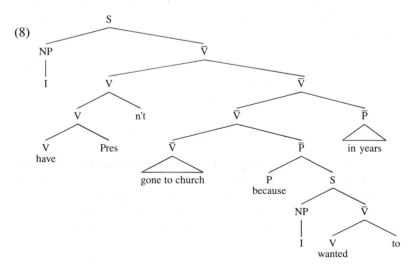

Or at least, that will be the case on one interpretation of Negative placement. I have not really made clear whether Negative placement moves the
not down to the auxiliary verb or raises the auxiliary verb up to the *not;* it is
in fact the latter version that I will argue for in chapter 17, and (8) corresponds to that version of Negative placement. Note how the rules proposed
here make it possible for a deep structure S-modifier such as *because I
wanted to* to occur lower than the auxiliary verb *haven't* in surface structure.

EXERCISES

1. Give full derivations (including everything relating to tenses and
auxiliary verbs) for:
   a. John is believed to have left an hour ago.
   b. There may have occurred a disaster. (Make clear which S *There-*
      insertion applies to.)
   c. Has there been an accident?
   d. Don't your brothers all play tennis?
   e. Has John sold his car and bought a bicycle?
   f. John may have gone on vacation and not been getting his mail.

2. Each of the following sentences contains something that one might
want to call an auxiliary. In each case, construct relevant examples that
will clarify whether it actually is one.
   a. John got sent to prison.
   b. We used to play tennis.
   c. You had better go home.
   d. Lester went and spilled the soup.
   e. You should go help your mother.
In each case, say what conclusion, if any, the examples lead you to; don't
assume that a clear conclusion will always emerge: different tests may give
conflicting results, and in some cases it may not be possible to construct
relevant examples.

3. Show why it is impossible to form a passive of a passive S, e.g.,
why there are no derivations like:

John give Mary the money $\xrightarrow{\text{Passive}}$
*Mary be given the money by John $\xrightarrow{\text{Passive}}$
*The money be given by John by Mary.

4. Given the analyses adopted in this chapter, what horrible consequence would result if Attraction-to-tense were not restricted to finite Ss?

5. In this chapter, I have not assumed any Comp in the complements
of auxiliary verbs. Presumably the *-ing* that accompanies progressive *be*
could be treated as an underlying complementizer, as with such verbs as

start in *He started drinking the beer.* Say why, with the analyses adopted in this book, the *-en* that accompanies *have* and passive *be* could not be treated the way that *-ing* is treated in that proposal.

6. Using the phenomena discussed in this chapter in which finite and nonfinite Ss diverged in their behavior, test whether it can be maintained, as suggested in §5e, that subjunctive *that*-clauses (e.g., *The king ordered that the prisoner be beheaded*) are nonfinite.

7. For any language other than English, find three words that have at some time been called auxiliary verbs (not necessarily by anyone whose word you trust: terms like "auxiliary verb" are often applied uncritically to unfamiliar languages), and for each of them determine whether it can be used in sentences like those given in §8c as evidence that auxiliary verbs have underlying complement Ss.

8. In the analysis adopted in this chapter, the various auxiliary verbs have been treated as having underlying sentential subjects and Raising to Subject (like *seem*). However, some or all of them might instead have sentential objects and Equi-NP-deletion (like *want* or *try*). For any two auxiliary verbs, apply the full battery of tests for distinguishing Raising structures from Equi structures and decide whether those verbs behave like *seem* or like *try* and *want*. Do not overlook the possibility that a verb might behave both ways.

9. Some of the derivations given in this chapter conflict with the extra strict cyclic principle that was proposed in chapter 6, according to which all constituents (thus, even $\bar{V}$s and other phrasal constituents) are cyclic domains. Identify at least two such derivations and suggest how the analysis might be altered so as to make it consistent with that version of the cyclic principle.

10. Show why $\bar{V}$-deletion is inapplicable in such sentences as:
   i. *John is in the next room and Bill may ($\emptyset$ = be in the next room) too. (Steele et al. 1981:240)
   ii. *Alice has invested in IBM, and Julia may ($\emptyset$ = have invested in IBM) too.

Formulate a conjecture as to why (ii) is far more acceptable if $\emptyset$ = *invest in IBM*.

NOTES

1. For the moment, I will assume that we know what words are auxiliary verbs. In §8d, some syntactic properties characteristic of auxiliary verbs will be discussed that can be used as criteria for deciding whether certain unclear cases are auxiliary verbs. I note in passing that there are a fair number of speakers who reject sentences like the last two examples in (1). As far as I can determine, such speakers differ

from speakers of the variety of English discussed here only in having a constraint that excludes the combination *be(en) being,* irrespective of whether the second *be* is an auxiliary verb.

2. This statement is false of those dialects (spoken mainly in the south of the United States) in which multiple modals, e.g., *He might could help you,* occur. See Boertien (1986) for detailed discussion of such dialects.

3. In accordance with (i), only examples that satisfy the morphological demands of each verb are given.

4. Boertien (1986) notes that in dialects with multiple modals, it is sometimes the first modal and sometimes the second in such a combination that is the bearer of the tense. These dialects have some syntactic phenomena that affect the tense-bearing auxiliary verb and others that affect the first auxiliary verb. The distinction between the two types of phenomena is lost in standard varieties of English, in which the first verb is always the tensed verb.

5. Actually, (4) says nothing about how passive *be* combines with other auxiliary verbs. In the analysis of Chomsky 1957, as in that presented above in chap. 4, passive *be* does not appear in deep structure. I will ignore passive *be* for the moment, returning later to the question of why it cannot precede an auxiliary verb.

"Aux" is pronounced [ɔ̄ks]. It shares with *Ms.* the peculiarity of looking like an abbreviation but not really being an abbreviation **of** anything. Note that it does not mean "auxiliary": a sequence of auxiliaries (*may have been*) is no more an auxiliary than a sequence of adverbs (*inadvertently in Boston last week*) is an adverb.

6. In surface syntactic structures, I will treat markers of past tense and of past participle (here written *-en*) as suffixed regardless of whether the verb in question undergoes internal modification rather than suffixation, e.g., I will represent *sang* and *sung* respectively as *sing* + Past and *sing* + *-en*.

7. In accordance with the conception of syntactic constituents adopted in this book, I have altered Chomsky's structures in the following two respects: (i) I have treated each lexical item and its syntactic category as corresponding to a single node, rather than as divided between two nodes as in Chomsky 1957 and the bulk of the transformational literature, where, e.g., there would be a node labeled V connected by a line to a separate node labeled *sing,* and (ii) I have represented the various words in (5b) as surface constituents, e.g., *-ing* is represented as combining with *sing* into a syntactic unit and not (as in most early transformational grammar) as simply placed between *sing* and the following NP. In addition, in (5a) I have placed the Aux in a position that deviates from Chomsky 1957 but accords with the analytic tradition that stems from that book. Chomsky 1957 had the Aux and the V making up a constituent labeled "Verb" (sic) that was a daughter of the VP.

8. I emphasize that this is a sufficient condition for membership in a category but not a necessary condition. For example, not all adjectives have meanings that are compatible with the characteristically adjectival inflections (comparative and superlative) that English allows.

9. *Should* and *must* are historically the past tenses of *shall* and the obsolete *mot,* but they function in current English as present tense forms. For some speakers, *must* can be used both as a present and as a past tense form. Such speakers accept sentences like (i), which most speakers of English can express only as (ii):

    i. %When I received the news, I must leave.

    ii. When I received the news, I had to leave.

10. Later in this chapter, two cases will be brought up that make this an overstatement, i.e., cases in which failure of modal auxiliary verbs to occur in nonfinite forms cannot plausibly be attributed to defective morphology.

11. The significance of these facts for the syntax of auxiliary *have* was first noted in Hofmann 1966.

12. The reason that *Fred had arrived at 2:00 yesterday afternoon* sounds more normal than the two examples preceding it in (15b) is that it can be embedded in contexts that provide a time between 2:00 yesterday and the present to serve as a "reference point."

13. There is some individual variation in the acceptability of nonfinite counterparts of past perfect clauses. For example, Schachter (1983) accepts a sentence analogous to (16d″) and rejects one analogous to (16d). This suggests that in Schachter's dialect rule (18b) is inapplicable in at least some contexts in which it is obligatory in my dialect.

14. I use $have_{en}$ as a makeshift to distinguish auxiliary *have* from main verb *have*. The latter does not participate in the alternation summarized in (17):

    Popov had a heart attack last week.

    Popov is believed to have had a heart attack last week.

    *Popov is believed to have a heart attack last week.

15. The rules in (18) are adapted from Hofmann 1966. In (18b) the lower $have_{en}$ is the one indicated as deleted, because syntactic influence normally is exerted downwards: a higher verb will cause deletion of a lower one and not vice versa.

16. Since the embedded tenses are in the underlying structure over and above the present tense of *may*, I conclude that Chomsky's formula (4) allows too few underlying combinations of tenses and auxiliary verbs: in the structures underlying these sentences, **two** tenses are required, e.g., in (20b′) the present tense on *may* and the past tense that is realized as $have_{en}$.

17. In addition, modifiers and coordination must be treated as "transparent" to finiteness, in the sense that if a sentence of the form [S Modifier] or [S₁ . . . Conj Sₙ] is finite, the component Ss will be finite, and if it is nonfinite, the component Ss will be nonfinite.

18. An analysis of English tenses and auxiliary verbs in terms of "reference points" was first developed in Reichenbach 1947. A very similar approach to Spanish terms, apparently developed independently, is found in Bull 1963. For further details of the meaning of the present perfect, see McCawley 1971, 1981c. While the present perfect does not allow time adverbs that pick out a particular time, as in (i), it does allow adverbs that pick out an open-ended set of times, as in (ii).

    i. *In the last month, I have received an obscene phone call last Monday.

    ii. In the last year, I have often received obscene phone calls on Mondays.

19. Akmajian, Steele, and Wasow (1979:19) give an example in which *be having* is deviant notwithstanding its apparent semantic well-formedness:

    ??Every time I see George, he's having gotten up later.

Perhaps part of the reason why (29c) is more normal-sounding than this example is that the adverbs that intervene between *is* and *having* in (29c) make it less obvious that a normally impermissible combination of auxiliary verbs is present.

20. The asterisked version of (35a) is in fact normal in British English, though the asterisked versions of (35a', b) are not. I make no attempt here to account for this difference between British and American English; for further discussion of that difference, see Baker (1984) and Trudgill and Hannah (1985:53–54).

21. Boertien (1979:88–90) discusses a case where this statement is inaccurate. By all reasonable criteria of modalhood, the *is to* of *Fred is to leave at 5:00* is a modal auxiliary. In particular, it never appears in nonfinite forms:

> *Fred is believed to be to leave at 5:00.
> *Fred's being to leave soon is scandalous.
> *Fred may be to leave at 5:00.

However, it cannot be defective morphology that rules these sentences out, since *is to* shows the same spectacularly suppletive paradigm that *be* has elsewhere (*I am to leave, You are to leave, I was to leave, . . .*) and thus must be held to involve the same morpheme *be* that occurs in other constructions and that in its other uses has a full set of non-finite forms. Akmajian, Steele, and Wasow (1979:18) make a similar point about the modal and nonmodal uses of *need:* the absence of nonfinite forms of modal *need* cannot be because of defective morphology, since nonmodal *need* has the missing forms:

> Sam doesn't need to go home.
> Sam need not go home.
> Sam is believed to not need to go home.
> *Sam is believed to $\left\{\begin{array}{l}\text{need not}\\\text{not need}\end{array}\right\}$ go home.
> Sam's not needing to go home is remarkable.
> *Sam's $\left\{\begin{array}{l}\text{needing not}\\\text{not needing}\end{array}\right\}$ go home is remarkable.

22. The % indicates dialect variation in the acceptability of the example. This sentence is normal in British English but slightly odd in American English. The '?' after the % indicates that the variation is between being completely normal and having the slight oddity that is indicated by ?.

23. In attaching the label V to *have + not* and V̄ to *not + have read the report* in the last two trees, I am anticipating the claim of chap. 17 that *not* is a modifier, i.e., that it combines with items of certain categories into a larger unit of the same category.

24. As these examples illustrate, "V̄-deletion" sometimes deletes a P̄, Ā, or NP rather than a V̄. See the brief discussion in §7c of the (very limited) conditions under which it may delete an item of those categories.

25. There is no standard name for such sentences. They are often referred to as "emphatic," which is a poor term since it applies equally well to several quite different types of sentences. In calling these sentences retorts, I do not mean to imply that they can only be used as responses to sentences that overtly assert the contrary;

indeed, they are often used in anticipation of what another person **might** say.

26. It might be thought that because of the agreement observed in (i–ii), in which the verb appears to agree with its underlying subject rather than with *there*, Agreement must be ordered before *There*-insertion:

  i. There is a <u>unicorn</u> in the garden.
  ii. There are some <u>unicorns</u> in the garden.

However, that suggestion is untenable in view of sentences like (iii–iv):

  iii. There seems to be a unicorn in the garden.
  iv. There seem to be some unicorns in the garden.

Here the NP that appears to control agreement is not the subject of *seem* at any stage of the derivation. The only known viable account of agreement in sentences with *there* as surface subject is that *there* takes on the number of the NP that it replaces and that it is actually *there* that controls agreement. Under that account, if *there* is inserted in a lower S and moved by Raising into a higher S, it will bear the number of the NP that it replaced in the **lower** S, thus giving rise to a situation like that of (iii–iv), in which the verb of the main clause appears to agree with a NP that is inside a subordinate $\bar{\text{V}}$.

27. What is at issue here is multiple negations and not multiple negative words. In many dialects of English, a single negation may be expressed by multiple negative words, e.g., the meaning of standard English (i) is expressed by (ii):

  i. Nobody said anything.
  ii. Nobody didn't say nothing.

The discussion that follows deals exclusively with the "standard" varieties of English in which the negation of *Somebody said something* can be expressed by (i) but not by (ii), i.e., in the following examples each negative word is to be interpreted as expressing a separate negation.

28. See Bolinger (1957) and Cattell (1973) for a more complete account of tag questions than is provided by this grossly oversimplified sketch, and §§14c, 21c of this book for discussion of differences between reversal and reduplicative tags.

29. Note that a *do* is used here even though the main verb is *be*. This deviation from the usual auxiliary-like behavior of all uses of *be* cannot be attributed just to the absence of any such contracted form as **ben't*, since negative imperative *don't* also occurs with auxiliary *have:*

$\left\{ \begin{array}{l} \text{Don't have} \\ \text{*Haven't} \end{array} \right\}$ eaten yet when you arrive.

30. Actually, the second person singular ending *-st*, though obsolete, is familiar to most speakers of modern English and is readily added to modals (*canst, mayst*) when one affects an archaic style.

31. In labeling *an hour ago* as a $\bar{\text{P}}$, I do not mean to suggest that *ago* is a P. I rather regard these examples as involving a zero P whose object (a NP) is *an hour ago*.

32. Note that the assumptions in force here require us to allow Attraction-to-tense to apply even over an intervening adverb.

||||||| 9. *Coordination*

a. What Is Special about Coordinate Structures

In both (1a) and (1b) a complex sentence has the same two simpler sentences as constituents, and indeed both complex sentences express propositions that are true under roughly the same circumstances:

(1) a. Tom left before Jane arrived.
   b. Tom left and then Jane arrived.

However, the ways in which the simpler sentences are combined give rise to major differences in the syntactic structures of (1a) and (1b).

In (1a), *Jane arrived* is a subordinate clause and the expression *before Jane arrived* functions as a time adverb; i.e., the overall structure of (1a) is like that of *Tom left before 2:00* except that *before* has a sentential object. We can tentatively ascribe to (1a) a deep structure as in (2a) and a surface structure as in (2b), a decision that will be supported by considerations to be taken up shortly:

(2) a.

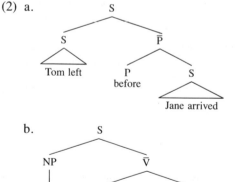

   b.

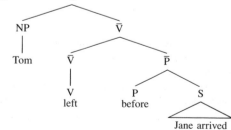

In (1b), on the other hand, *Jane arrived* is not "subordinate": *Tom left* and *then Jane arrived* are equally much main clauses. I will argue below that **coordinate** sentences like (1b) have an overall structure of the form (3a), or better, since the number of **conjuncts** need not be just two, (3b):[1]

(3) a.

That is, a coordinate S consists of two or more Ss and a conjunction, with the Ss being sisters of one another. The possibility of coordinate Ss with three or more conjuncts is illustrated by such examples as (4a), which contrast with examples like (4b) that illustrate the impossibility of combining more than two Ss at a time by a single use of a subordinating element like *before:*[2]

(4) a.   Tom went to Boston, Alice went to Toledo, and Jane went to Seattle.
    b. *Tom went to Boston, Alice went to Toledo, before Jane went to Seattle.

The bulk of this section will be devoted to syntactic phenomena that confirm the claimed difference in syntactic structure between (1a) and (1b).

Examples (5)–(7) show that while an adverbial clause is simply ignored when transformations that affect something in the main clause apply, a transformation cannot apply to a conjoined sentence unless it affects all the conjuncts in the same way:

(5) a.   Did Tom leave before Jane arrived/*arrive?
    b.   Did Tom leave and then Jane arrive/*arrived?
    c. *Did Tom once live in Detroit and he now lives in Toledo?
(6) a.   Who did you talk to before Jane arrived?
    b. *Who did you talk to and then Jane arrive/arrived?
    c.   Which theory did Tom attack and then Jane defend?
    d. ?Which theory did Tom attack before Jane defended/*defend?
(7) a.   Tom left before Jane arrived, didn't he?
    b.   Tom left and then Jane arrived, didn't *he/*she/??they?[3]
    c.   Tom grew up in Toledo, and he went to college at Oberlin, didn't he?
    d. ?Tom plays the violin and Jane plays the cello, don't they?

In (5a), Inversion moves the Past of the main clause to the front while leaving the Past of the subordinate clause unaffected; in (5b), by contrast, the Past on *did* applies to both conjuncts jointly (note the ungrammaticality of the version of (5b) in which a Past remains in the second conjunct), which is to say that the Pasts of both conjuncts must be extracted together by Inversion and conflated in a single Past preceding the conjoined S:[4]

(8)

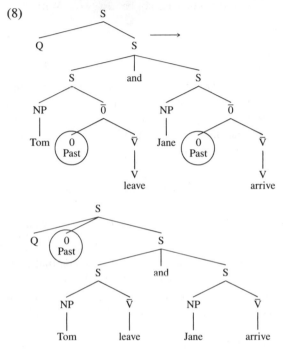

If the conjuncts differ in tense (5c), there is no way in which a single tense marker can be extracted from both conjuncts together, and the result of moving the tense marker out of only one conjunct is (as in the case of (5b)) ungrammatical.

Similarly, in a WH-question the interrogative expression can be extracted from the main clause of a noncoordinate sentence (6a) but not from only one conjunct of a coordinate sentence (6b). However, it can be extracted from all the conjuncts of a coordinate sentence simultaneously, as in (6c) (which can be paraphrased as "Identify the theory such that Tom attacked it and then Jane defended it"). An interrogative expression cannot in general represent material of a main clause and a subordinate clause together (6d).[5]

A similar pattern appears in sentences involving tag-questions. The tag of a tag-question is formed from the tensed auxiliary verb of its host S and a pronominalized form of the subject of the host S. *Tom* is the subject of (1a), and there is correspondingly a tag question containing a pronoun corresponding to *Tom* (7a). However, (1b) strictly speaking does not have a subject (each of the two conjuncts has a subject, but neither qualifies as the subject of the whole conjoined S), and accordingly a tag question cannot be formed from (1b) except marginally in the form with *didn't they,* in which a pronoun is used that represents the subjects of both conjuncts jointly (7b). The latter form is more normal in cases like (7d), in which the conjunct clauses have not only the same tense but also the same time reference; still better are sentences like (7c) in which the conjuncts have coreferential subjects and thus a single pronoun can refer to all the subjects jointly.

The facts presented in (5)–(7) illustrate a principle known as the **Coordinate structure constraint** (**CSC** [Ross 1967]), namely, that a transformation can apply to a coordinate structure if and only if it has the same effect on all the conjuncts. This principle has both a negative aspect and a positive aspect. The negative aspect is illustrated in (6b): the impossibility of derivations in which a transformation applying to a coordinate structure affects only one (or more generally, fewer than all) of the conjuncts, as here, where only one conjunct of the underlying structure contained an interrogative expression and thus WH-movement could affect only that one conjunct. In cases that come under the negative aspect of the CSC, a well-formed deep structure may correspond to no well-formed surface structure, in consequence of conflicts between demands imposed by the CSC and by the syntactic rules of the particular language, as here, where the obligatory nature of English WH-movement requires that *who* be moved to the beginning of the question, whereas the CSC excludes that step since it would affect only one conjunct. The positive aspect of the CSC was illustrated in chapter 8 by sentences such as *Have you ever eaten pizza and drunk champagne at the same meal?* in which a single *have* imposes the past participle form on both conjuncts of the conjoined $\bar{V}$ with which it is combined.

It should be emphasized here that the CSC constrains only the application of transformations to a domain that contains a coordinate structure, not their application to domains that happen to be within coordinate structures. It is of course possible to form conjoined Ss in which one conjunct is active and the other passive, or in which one conjunct but not the other undergoes *There*-insertion:

(9) a. Mary works for IBM and her sister has just been hired by Xerox.
   b. There are many rich people in Palm Springs, and most of them own swimming pools.

According to the cyclic principle, transformations get their chance to apply to the conjunct Ss of a structure [$_S$ S *and* S] before they get their chance to apply to the whole conjoined structure. Thus, in the derivation of (9a), Passive gets a chance to apply to *Xerox has just hired her sister* regardless of the fact that that happens to be a conjunct of a coordinate structure; the domain to which Passive applies here is not the whole coordinate structure but a (noncoordinate) S contained in that structure. What the CSC excludes is derivational steps in which something outside of a coordinate structure influences only one conjunct of the structure, as in (6b), where the step excluded by the CSC would be one in which WH-movement applies to a structure of the form [Q [S *and* S]]. In (9), by contrast, the applications of Passive and *There*-insertion are completely internal to one conjunct and do not involve any application of a transformation **to** a coordinate structure.

Further illustration of the CSC is provided by examples (10)–(12), which show that, while adverbial clauses neither inhibit nor are affected by placement of the *to* complementizer or by Raising, those two transformations cannot affect just one conjunct of a conjoined complement S:

(10) a.   I want you to leave before Jane arrives.
      b.   *I want you to leave and then Jane arrives.
      b'. *I want you to leave and then Jane will arrive.
(11) a.   For Tom to have left and Jane then to have come back is ironic.
      a'. *For Tom to have left and then Jane came back is ironic.
      b.   *For Tom to have left before Jane to have come back is ironic.
      b'.   For Tom to have left before Jane came back is ironic.
(12) a.   We believe Tom to have left before Jane came back.
      b.   *We believe Tom to have left and then Jane came back.
      c.   Tom seems to have left before Jane came back.
      d.   *Tom seems to have left and then Jane came back.

Note, by the way, that (11a) involves one *for* and two *to*'s, in accordance with the CSC plus the claim of chapter 5 that *for* is a sister of the S and *to* a sister of the V̄; here *for* is combined with a single conjoined S and remains outside the coordinate structure, but *to* is inserted into the conjoined S and must thus be adjoined to the V̄ of each conjunct according to the positive aspect of the CSC. By contrast, in *for Tom to leave and then come back would be ridiculous,* the surface structure involves a conjoined V̄ rather than a conjoined S, and the *to* is a sister of the whole conjoined V̄.

The possibility of preposing adverbial clauses, as in (13a), illustrates a further difference between adverbial clauses and conjoined clauses, in that the combination of coordinating conjunction and S cannot be preposed (13b):

(13) a.   Before Jane arrived, Tom left.
      b.   *And Jane arrived, Tom left.

This observation should not be taken as implying that *and S* is not a surface constituent; indeed it will be argued in chapter 16 that it **is** one, contrary to the claim embodied in the makeshift structures in (3). However, *and S* is not a constituent of a type that allows the mobility that time adverbs be such as *before S* have. Further confirmation that *before S* functions as an adverbial adjunct to the other clause but *and S* does not is provided by the possibilities for cleft sentences shown in (14):

(14) a.   It was before Jane arrived that Tom left.
       b. *It was and Jane arrived that Tom left.

Examples (15)–(16) illustrate the phenomenon of **Conjunction Reduction (CR),** in which a coordinate structure whose conjuncts are identical except for one constituent can be simplified by factoring out the shared parts and creating a conjoined constituent in place of the nonshared parts, as indicated in (17):

(15) a.   Tom called Ed and then wrote to Martha.
       b. *Tom called Ed before wrote to Martha. (Cf. . . . before writing to Martha.)
(16) a.   Tom rinsed and then dried the dishes.
       b. *Tom rinsed before dried the dishes.

(17)

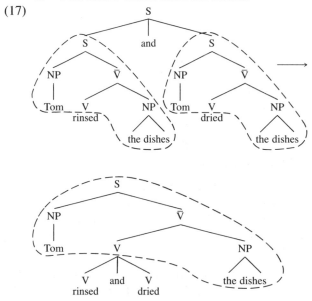

In the underlying structure of (16a), for example, there are conjoined Ss that are identical except that each has a different verb; the surface structure consists of the shared part of those conjuncts, with a conjoined verb in the place where they differed in the underlying structure. This factoring out of shared parts is not possible in structures in which a main clause and an adverbial clause differ in only one constituent, as in (15b, 16b).

Conjunction Reduction is one of several mechanisms by which conjoined Ss can be given a shortened form, and it is important to be careful not to confuse these different mechanisms. A second such mechanism, illustrated in (18), is **Gapping,** in which repeated verbs in conjoined Ss are deleted:[6]

(18) a.   Tom ordered lasagna and (*then) Jane manicotti
      b. *Tom ordered lasagna before Jane manicotti.

This phenomenon is restricted to coordinate structures, as (18b) illustrates. The same is also true of another device for shortening coordinate structures, namely, **Right-node-raising (RNR),** in which a final constituent shared by all the conjuncts (but not necessarily having the same syntactic role in all of them) is factored out:

(19) a.   Tom is a fan of, and I hear that Jane is writing a book about, Ringo Starr.
      b. ??Tom became a fan of, after Jane wrote a book about, Ringo Starr.

And and *or* share the property of allowing not just two but any number of conjuncts from two on up:

(20) a.   Tom went to Boston, Alice went to Toledo, and Jane went to Seattle. (= (3a))
      b. Boston, Toledo, and Seattle are my favorite cities.
      c. Either I've put the letter in my briefcase, or I've put it in my coat pocket, or I've already mailed it.
      d. Do not fold, spindle, or mutilate.

By contrast, other coordinating conjunctions allow only two conjuncts:[7]

(21) a.   Ned has very little money, but he's happy.
      a'. *Ned has very little money, he's unpopular, but he's happy.
      b. Mary asked John as well as Lucy embarrassing questions.
      b'. *Mary asked John, Nancy, as well as Lucy embarrassing questions.

Most logicians and some linguists treat *and* and *or* as also basically conjoining only two terms at a time and hold (explicitly in the case of the linguists, implicitly in the case of the logicians) that examples like those in (20) are derived by deletion of a repeated conjunction from a structure in which that conjunction conjoins things two at a time. That analysis is implicit in logic textbooks in which the rules of inference and truth conditions

for *and* and *or* are given only for the case where there are two conjuncts
and the student is directed to analyze examples like (20a) as having a logical form as in (22a) or (22b) rather than as in (22c):[8]

(22) a. (p and q) and r
     b. p and (q and r)
     c. and(p,q,r)

There is considerable linguistic evidence, however, that sentences like
those in (20) involve a single multiterm coordinate structure rather than the
nested two-term structure that logicians usually assume. Consider, for example, the fact that Gapping can only apply "across the boards," that is,
that in the sorts of sentences that are claimed here to involve multiterm
conjoining, Gapping is possible only when the conjuncts are all parallel in
form and the same deletions are carried out in all conjuncts after the first:[9]

(23) a.   Tom ordered a daiquiri, Alice a manhattan, and Jane a screw-
           driver.
     b.   ??Tom ate a hamburger, Alice a Polish sausage, and Jane drank
           a beer.
     b'.   *Tom ate a hamburger, Alice drank a martini, and Jane a beer.

If Gapping in sentences like (23a) had as its input an iterated two-term conjoined structure, as in (24), it would have to be divided into two transformations, one applying to sister conjuncts (S_3 and S_4, with S_1 as the domain
of application), and one applying to an aunt-niece combination (S_2 and S_3)
in a structure to which the former deletion has applied:

(24)

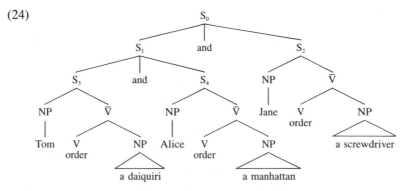

Moreover, the latter transformation would have to apply obligatorily if the
putative deletion of repeated *and* applies (so as to avoid sentences like
(23b)). This intricate division of labor between two separate and very different Gapping transformations is avoided if Gapping applies as suggested

above, i.e., its input would be a structure like (25) having any number of conjuncts, all participating in the requisite parallelism, and it would affect all conjuncts after the first if it applies at all:

(25)

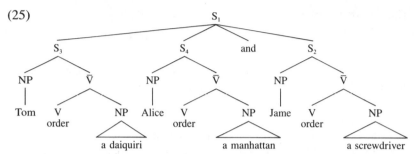

It should be emphasized that the position adopted here does not **exclude** underlying structures in which a two-term coordinate structure appears as one of the conjuncts of a two-term coordinate structure. Indeed, I assume throughout this book that conjoined Ss can occur in any position in which simple Ss can, which implies that structures **are** possible. According to the position taken here, a structure like (26a) is not ill-formed but simply must be distinguished from structures like (26b,c):

(26) a.   b.   c.

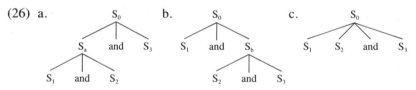

In view of the cyclic principle, that distinction affects how transformations apply. For example, different ways of grouping the same three conjuncts give rise to different possibilities for CR:

(27) a. Tom and Lucy are overweight, and Lucy is knock-kneed.
     b. Tom is overweight, and Lucy is overweight and knock-kneed.
     c. Tom is overweight, Lucy is overweight, and Lucy is knock-kneed.

The three sentences in (27) have as their respective deep structures combinations as in (26). In the derivations of (27a) and (27b), CR is applicable to S_a of (26a) and S_b of (26b), respectively, yielding a conjoined subject in the one case and a conjoined $\bar{V}$ in the other case: CR is not applicable when the deep structure is as in (26c) and the conjuncts are as in (27), because then the three conjuncts are not all parallel.[10]

Before concluding this section, I should say a little about one further phenomenon in which a transformation affects multiterm coordinate structures as wholes, rather than merely affecting pairs of adjacent conjuncts, namely, the possibilities for multiple realization of an underlying conjunction. I will assume in the following discussion that *both* and *either,* when they introduce a conjoined constituent, are simple variants of *and* and *or,* respectively. English is in fact unusual in having a different word to introduce the first conjunct than is used to introduce subsequent conjuncts; far more common is the situation in Spanish, where the same word is used in both positions: *o esta noche o mañana* 'either tonight or tomorrow'. Consider the possibilities for multiple realization of *or* in an analog to (20a) in which there are four conjuncts:

(28) a.   Tom went to Boston, Alice went to Seattle, Mike went to Omaha, or Jane went to Denver.

 b.   Tom went to Boston, or Alice went to Seattle, or Mike went to Omaha, or Jane went to Denver.

 c.   Either Tom went to Boston, or Alice went to Seattle, or Mike went to Omaha, or Jane went to Denver.

 d.   *Either Tom went to Boston, Alice went to Seattle, or Mike went to Omaha, or Jane went to Denver.

 e.   *Either Tom went to Boston, or Alice went to Seattle, Mike went to Omaha, or Jane went to Denver.

 f.   *Either Tom went to Boston, or Alice went to Seattle, or Mike went to Omaha, Jane went to Denver.

 g.   Either Tom went to Boston, Alice went to Seattle, Mike went to Omaha, or Jane went to Denver.

Multiple realization of the conjunction seems to conform to the following generalizations: (i) the conjunction must appear before the last conjunct; (ii) it may optionally also introduce the first conjunct (taking a special form: *either* instead of *or*); (iii) irrespective of whether it introduces the first conjunct, it may also introduce all of the other conjuncts before the last one, though if it introduces any of them it must introduce all of them. *Both . . . and* works the same way, with the qualification that for most speakers of English *both* is acceptable only when there are only two conjuncts. (Some further restrictions on *both* are given in note 11.) These generalizations can be expressed in terms of transformations that optionally copy a coordinating conjunction onto the conjuncts, as in (29), which is given here not in terms of the makeshift structures of (3) but in terms of the surface constituent structure that is argued for in §16a:

(29)

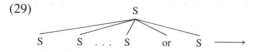

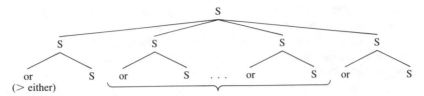

b. Conjoined Constituents of Ss

The examples of coordination given so far have mainly been of conjoined Ss. Only in a couple of examples were there conjoined non-Ss, e.g., the conjoined $\bar{V}$ of (15a) and the conjoined V of (16a) of §9a, which I maintained were derived through a transformation of **Conjunction Reduction** from conjoined Ss that were identical except for one item in each. In this section I will provide some justification of the claim that such a transformation exists and will also take up the question of whether **all** conjoined constituents can be derived from underlying conjoined Ss.

The claim that there is a transformation of CR embodies two separate claims: that the structures underlying the examples in which it supposedly applies involve conjoined Ss, and that the surface structures of those examples involve conjoined constituents such as the conjoined V that §9a(9a) was claimed to involve. It is conceivable that one of these claims could be true and the other false. For example, many authors who assign to such examples deep structures with conjoined Ss speak of them as undergoing deletion of repeated matter rather than the factoring out of shared structure that I take to characterize CR. If deletion is responsible for the reduced form of these sentences, their surface structures will not be as in (1a, b) but rather as in (1a′, b′):

(1) a.

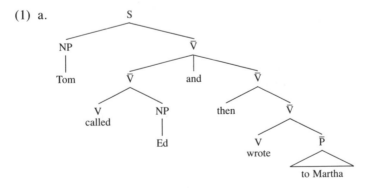

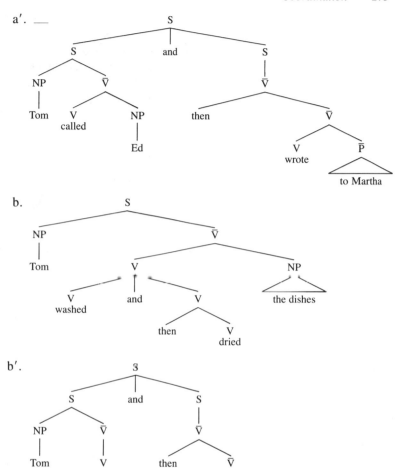

It is fairly easy to demonstrate that the derived constituent structure of these Ss is along the lines of (1a, b) and not (1a′, b′). First, only with the former structure does the whole S have a [NP V̄] gross shape, and all transformations that are contingent upon a S having that form treat the sentences in question as if that in fact is their gross form:

(2) a. Tom seems to have called Ed and written to Martha, does't he?
     b. This floor is easy for us to sand and then varnish.
     c. Alice went downtown and bought a radio, and Ted did too.

In (2a), Raising has broken up the complement of *seem* into its subject *Tom* and its $\overline{V}$ *to have called Ed and written to Martha;* the possibility of the tag *doesn't he?* confirms that *Tom* is the subject of *seems to have called Ed and written to Martha.* In (2b), *Tough*-movement has extracted the object NP from *we sand and then varnish the floor,* which ought not to be possible if the structure were as in (1b'), since *Tough*-movement cannot extract a NP from just one conjunct of a coordinate structure:

(3)   [We polish the floors and vacuum the rugs] is easy
  *The rugs are easy for us to polish the floors and vacuum.

In (2c), $\overline{V}$-deletion has deleted a repetition of *go downtown and buy a radio,* which confirms that the latter combination is in fact a $\overline{V}$. More generally, in the cases where I am claiming that Ss contain conjoined constituents, the S behaves exactly the way it would if there were a single constituent in that position and not the way that a maimed conjoined S like (1a', b') would be expected to behave, e.g., transformations apply to *washed and dried the dishes* exactly the same way that they would apply to *wash the dishes.*

  A second reason why factoring out of shared matter and not deletion of repeated matter is involved in the derivations in question is that a deletion account does not suffice to get *both* and *either* in the right place. *Both* and *either* occur at the beginnings of the coordinate structures that are claimed here to occur in the output of CR:

(4) a.   Tom either called Ed or wrote to Martha.
  a'. *Either Tom called Ed or wrote to Martha.
  b.   Tom both washed and dried the dishes.
  b'. *Both Tom washed and dried the dishes.

With the deletion analysis, only the Ss are conjoined constituents in surface structures, and simply placing *both* and *either* before the first conjunct would yield the deviant word order of (4a', b') and would not yield the normal word order of (4a, b).[11] This means that under a deletion analysis there would have to be a special rule for placement of *both* and *either,* either moving it from a S-initial position, as in (4a', b'), or inserting it into a structure like (1a', b'), in either case putting it into a position that would have to be determined from a structure like (1a', b') by in effect reconstructing the conjoined Ss from which it is derived and inserting *both* or *either* before the "nonshared" constituent. By contrast, with the CR analysis, the position of *both* and *either* is determined exactly the same way for conjoined constituents as for conjoined whole Ss: it goes immediately before the first conjunct.

A third and, for present purposes, final reason for assigning to sentences like those in (1) a surface constituent structure like (1a, b) rather than (1a', b') relates to the possibilities for dividing the sentence into phonological phrases. The question of the relationship between phnonological phrase boundaries and syntactic constituent structure is in fact a rather complicated one, and no attempt will be made here to answer it beyond suggesting that the preferred phonological phrase boundaries are boundaries around major syntactic constituents, subject to the qualification that unstressed items (e.g., *and, the*) cannot make up separate phonological phrases but must be put into the same phonological phrase as some adjacent material. If that hypothesis is correct, then if the surface constituent structure of *Tom washed and dried the dishes* were as in (1b'), it should be possible to make a phonological phrase out of *and dried the dishes,* which is in fact not possible:[12]

(5) *Tom washed % and dried the dishes.

It is possible to put a phrase boundary after *washed* only if there is also one after *dried:*

(6) Tom washed % and dried % the dishes.

The latter pronunciation fits (1b') better than (1b'): according to (1b') and the hypothesis stated above, if *washed* is a sufficiently "major" constituent to allow a phrase boundary after it, then so is *dried,* since both are equally "major."

I turn now to the second claim embodied in the CR analysis, namely, that in at least some sentences with conjoined pieces of Ss the deep structure has conjoined Ss. The necessity of deriving a conjoined constituent from conjoined Ss is clearest in cases where one of the conjuncts is derived by a transformation that moves material into or out of it:

(7) a. Bert robbed a bank and was caught by the police.
    b. Lucy is both intelligent and easy for us to get along with.
    c. George owns an apartment building and appears to have a lot of other property.

For the passive $\bar{V}$ in (8a) to be derived by the usual Passive transformation, there must be a S *the police catch Bert* for it to apply to, and *rob a bank* must be outside that S. Thus the derivation must be as in (8), with Passive applying to S_2 and creating the conditions for CR to apply to S_0:

(8)

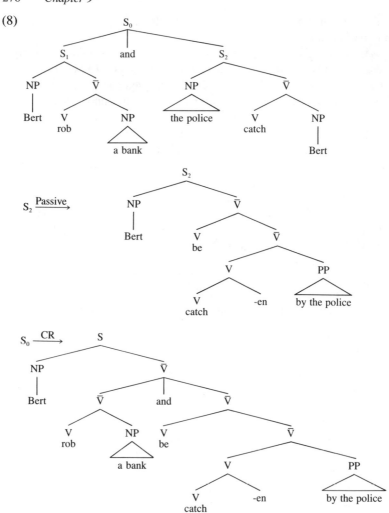

Similarly, (7b) requires an underlying structure containing [*We get along with Lucy*] *be easy* for *Tough*-movement to apply to, and (7c) requires one containing [*George has a lot of other property*] *seem* for Raising to apply to. In each case, the assumption that the conjoined V̄ is derived by CR from a conjoined S provides the required conjoined S.

There are, however, conjoined constituents that cannot be derived through CR from conjoined Ss, for example,

(9) a. The king and the queen are an amiable couple.
     b. Tom, Dick, and Harry are similar.

   c. Mix the soy sauce, the vinegar, and the sesame oil.

   d. Mississippi, Alabama, and Georgia are contiguous.

In each of these cases, a corresponding conjoined S in which each conjunct of the conjoined NP was in a separate S would be semantically anomalous:

(10) a. *The king is an amiable couple and the queen is an amiable couple.

     b. *Tom is similar, Dick is similar, and Harry is similar (too).

     c. *Mix the soy sauce, mix the vinegar, and mix the sesame oil.

     d. *Mississippi is contiguous, Alabama is contiguous, and Georgia is contiguous.

Moreover, it is not even possible to derive (9) from analogs to (10) in which the sources of their anomaly have been eliminated, e.g. (9a) cannot be derived from a structure underlying *The king is amiable and the queen is amiable,* since that would misrepresent the meaning of (9a): two persons can be individually amiable without making up an amiable couple (they might be an unpleasant couple even if each is amiable by himself) or without even making up a couple. Likewise, (9b) cannot be derived from a conjunction of Ss of the form *X is similar to Y* (six such Ss in this case), since similarity of all pairs does not imply that all three individuals are similar: as Goodman (1951) has pointed out, three or more individuals can be such that any two of them share important properties (taking that as our analysis of what it is for them to be "similar") without any important properties being shared by all of them. For example, suppose that Tom and Dick are linguists and music lovers (while Harry is a geologist and nonmusical), Dick and Harry are anarchists and Catholics (while Tom is a socialist and a Presbyterian), and Tom and Harry are gourmets and sports enthusiasts (while Dick doesn't care much about either food or sports). And while (9d) is true, it is false that Mississippi is contiguous to Georgia.

   The clearest cases of conjoined constituents that cannot be derived by CR from conjoined Ss are those like (9), in which NPs conjoined with *and* are used to describe a set or a group by listing its members and the conjoined NP is combined with a $\bar{\text{V}}$ that expresses a property of that set or group as a whole. Another class of items that clearly are not derived by CR, though some doubt can be raised about whether they are strictly speaking coordinate structures, is the iterative and intensive constructions that involve repeated conjuncts:[13]

(11) a. The city grew bigger and bigger and bigger.

     b. He pushed and pushed and pushed on the door.

I will exclude the constructions of (11) from further consideration here.

   When a conjoined non-S cannot be derived by CR from a conjoined S, the conjunction is usually *and;* however, there is one clear case in which *or* conjoins constituents that cannot be derived from conjoined Ss, namely, that in which *or* is used in giving a list of alternatives:

(12) Nixon or Humphrey was a horrible choice to have to make.

There is thus good reason both for having a CR transformation and for admitting in deep structure not only conjoined Ss but also at least some kinds of conjoined non-Ss—NPs conjoined with *and* (and under restricted circumstances, *or*) at the very least. As a consequence of this, there are many cases in which it does not particularly matter whether a conjoined structure is derived by CR from conjoined Ss. For example, I know of no respect in which it matters whether (13) is taken to have a deep structure conjoined NP or to be derived from a deep structure involving conjoined Ss:

(13) I enjoy London and Copenhagen.

It might be thought that the latter analysis is favored by the fact that (13) implies both that I enjoy London and that I enjoy Copenhagen. However, that fact is an instance of a more general fact, namely, that there are NPs—not only conjoined NPs such as *London and Copenhagen* but also plural NPs such as *those cities*—that denote sets and can be used with expressions that predicate properties of the individual members of the set. For example, *I enjoy those cities* implies that I enjoy London, if London belongs to the set denoted by *those cities.* Since London is a member of the set denoted by *London and Copenhagen,* there is thus nothing to prevent an account of (13) that takes *London and Copenhagen* as a deep structure constituent from giving a correct account of what it implies. As far as I can see, there is nothing to rule out either of the possible derivations of (13), notwithstanding the fact that (13) does not appear to be ambiguous and thus require multiple deep structures. I do not, however, see anything wrong with nonetheless admitting both derivations for (13) and many similar examples: I see no reason for excluding the possibility that distinct syntactic means should in some cases pair the same surface syntactic form with equivalent semantic interpretations.

Whether a particular conjoined constituent can be derived from conjoined Ss by CR depends on how the syntactic constructions that it involves are analyzed, since different analyses of a given construction can differ as to what underlying Ss are posited and thus (since in principle any structure in which a S can occur allows a conjoined S to appear in that position) can differ as to what underlying conjoined Ss could occur. Thus, whether one can treat the conjoined $\overline{A}$ in (14) (example from Partee 1970: 153) as derived by CR depends on how one analyzes quantified NPs.

(14) Few rules are both correct and easy to read.

Note that (14) cannot be paraphrased as *Few rules are correct and few rules are easy to read,* since (14) can be true and the supposed paraphrase false simultaneously (as would be the case if many rules are correct but most of them are hard to read, and many rules are easy to read but most of them are wrong). It is in fact possible to derive *both correct and easy to read* in (14) by CR, with a deep structure that correctly represents the meaning of (14), but only if quantified NPs are analyzed as derived from something outside the clauses in which they appear in surface structure. If such an analysis is accepted (see chap. 18 and McCawley 1981a: 125–36 for arguments in favor of a particular version of that proposal), then (14) can be derived from a structure in which *few rules* is combined with *x is correct and* [*for one to read x*] *is easy,* with *Tough*-movement and CR converting the latter into *x is both correct and easy to read.*[14]

Similarly it is only by virtue of the Raising analysis that it is possible to treat the two possible interpretations of (15a) as differing with regard to what clause is underlyingly conjoined and undergoes CR:

(15) a. Either Schwartz or Knudsen is likely to get the Stanford job.

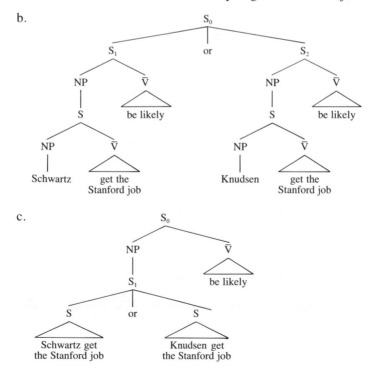

The derivation with (15b) involves Raising on S_1 and S_2 and CR on S_0. The derivation with (15c) involves CR on S_1 and Raising on S_0. The same surface structure results from both derivations. The more likely interpretation of (15a) is the one corresponding to (15c): that it is likely that one or other of Schwartz and Knudsen will get the job (though the choice between them may be so hard that neither of them can be described as likely to get it); (15b) corresponds to a less likely though still possible interpretation: that either Schwartz is likely to get the job or Knudsen is likely to get it (you aren't sure which one of them the chairman was referring to when he spoke of one of the applicants as being far and away the best prospect). The conjoined NP in the more likely interpretation of (15a) can thus be derived by CR from a conjoined S even though only the other interpretation can be paraphrased as *Either Schwartz is likely to get the Stanford job or Knudsen is likely to get it;* the Raising analysis makes available a subordinate S that can serve as the locus of the conjoining.

c. *Less Central Instances of Coordination*

There are several words and expressions that share some but not all syntactic characteristics of *and* and *or* and whose status as coordinating conjunctions is thus unclear. For example, *as well as, in addition to,* and *rather than* appear in what look like conjoined constituents of a variety of syntactic categories:

(1) a.   John put <u>records as well as books</u> in the closet.
    a'.   John put books <u>on the piano as well as in the closet.</u>
    a".   John ate pizza <u>yesterday as well as today.</u>
    b.   Alice is taking <u>psycholinguistics in addition to archeology.</u>
    b'.   Alice has written <u>books in addition to articles</u> on Burushaski intonation.
    b".   ?Alice put books <u>on the piano in addition to in the closet.</u>
    c.   Nancy sent <u>a telegram rather than a letter</u> to Oscar.
    c'.   Nancy went <u>to Detroit rather than to Toledo</u>
    c".   Nancy left <u>at 6:00 rather than at 7:00.</u>

Examples like (1a), in which *records as well as books* appears in the middle of a $\overline{V}$, are particularly clear evidence that *X as well as Y* is a syntactic constituent, and that *as well as Y* is not (to take the most obvious possibility) simply an adverb. In this respect, *as well as* and the like differ sharply from such words as *before* and *after,* which form $\overline{P}$s with reduced forms of Ss as objects but which can occur only in adverbial positions:

(2) a.   Tom sent Dick money before he sent Lucy money.
    b.   Tom sent Dick money before Lucy.
    c.   *Tom sent Dick before Lucy money.
    c'.   Tom sent Dick as well as Lucy money.

While sentences in which *as well as* and the like conjoin Ss or V̄s the way that *and* and *or* do (with the verbs of all conjuncts inflected alike) are generally quite odd, many of them allow alternative forms in which the putative second conjunct is in the *-ing* form:

(3) a.   *The president is incompetent as well as the governor is crooked.
          The president is incompetent as well as the governor being crooked.
          John looks like Robert Redford as well as having/??has a lot of money.
    b.   The president is incompetent in addition to the governor being/*is crooked.
          It rained in addition to snowing/??snowed.
    c.   The president resigned instead of Congress impeaching/*impeached/??impeach him.
          It rained instead of snowing/%snowed.

The sentences with *-ing* forms in (3) can be treated as involving conjoined Ss and V̄s, but only if the CSC is weakened somewhat: inflections that are imposed on the whole putative coordinate structure are realized on just the first conjunct, with the second conjunct taking an *-ing* form irrespective of what inflection the first conjunct has. This state of affairs is reminiscent of that in Japanese, Tamil, and many other languages, in which there are coordinate Ss and V̄s in which one conjunct (the last conjunct in those two languages) takes the inflection that the whole coordinate structure is to bear, with the other conjuncts taking a participial form. I propose distinguishing two separate dimensions of coordinateness, namely, syntactic and morphological coordinateness, and allowing for the possibility of structures in which one constituent is syntactically coordinate with but morphologically subordinate to another. I suggest that that is an accurate description of the situation in Japanese and Tamil coordinate Ss and V̄s, and in English sentences in which *as well as* and the like introduce an *-ing* form S or V̄.

A third possibility, that of a morphologically coordinate structure that is not syntactically coordinate, is exemplified by the English *go and* construction, in which the conjuncts must bear the same inflection but extraction from the second conjunct occurs freely:[15]

(4) a.   He went and told the police about us.
    a'. *He went and will tell the police about us.
    b.   Which secret did she go and reveal Ø to them?

A particularly striking case of a morphologically coordinate but syntactically subordinate structure is a Swedish construction roughly analogous to that of (4) (but with the meaning of *go V-ing*), in which both conjuncts must bear the same inflection but the verb of the first conjunct behaves like the main verb of the whole sentence even with regard to Inversion and Negative placement:

(5) a. Han gick och badade.
       he   went and swam
       'He went swimming'
    b. Gick han och badade?
       went he   and swam
       'Did he go swimming?' (lit. 'Went he and swam?')
    c. Han gick inte och badade.
       he   went not and swam
       'He didn't go swimming'. (lit. 'He didn't go and swam')

As evidence that *X as well as Y* and the like are syntactically coordinate structures even when the structure is morphologically noncoordinate (e.g., when X is a finite $\overline{V}$ and Y is a $\overline{V}$ in the *-ing* form), I note that they allow RNR:

(6) a.   John admires, in addition to having a lot of affection for, his uncle
         Oscar.
    b.   Ann has written several books about, as well as many articles on,
         the diet of polar bears.
    b'.   Ann is the author of several books about, as well as having written
         many articles on, the diet of polar bears.

Another respect in which they behave like coordinating conjunctions, even though it is a respect in which they differ from *and*, is with regard to agreement when they occur in subject position:

(7) a.   Susan and I are/*am/*is happy.
    a'.   Susan as well as I ??are/??am/??is happy.
    a''. Susan as well as I will be happy.
    a'''. Either Susan or I *are/??am/??is happy.
    a''''. Susan but not I *are/*am/*is happy.
    b.   Susan and you are/*is happy.
    b'.   Susan in addition to you ?is/*are happy.

    c.   Susan and Tom are/*is happy.

    c'.   Susan as well as Tom is/*are happy.

When the subject is a coordinate NP with *or* or *but* as the conjunction, the individual conjuncts make their demands for verb agreement separately, and all the demands must be satisfied; for example, the reason that no version of (7a''') is acceptable is that *you* demands that *be* take the form *are* and *I* demands that it take the form *is,* and those two demands cannot be met simultaneously. When the coordinating conjunction is *and,* the demands of the conjuncts are pooled, i.e., *NP and NP* is treated as having the union of the referents of its conjuncts as its referent, and the agreement form is chosen accordingly.[16] This description given for *or* and *but* holds also for *as well as* and *in addition to,* except that with *or* the most acceptable of the (unacceptable) agreement forms is that in which the verb agrees with the last conjunct, whereas with *as well as,* etc. there is a preference for agreement with the first conjunct, reflecting presumably the fact that the first conjunct is at least morphologically superordinate to the second.

    Expressions of the form *as well as X, in addition to X,* etc. are mobile in ways in which *and X* and *or X* are not. Specifically, they may appear not only immediately following the other conjunct (as in (3) and (7)) but also at the beginning or end of the sentence:

(8) a. As well as books, John put records in the closet.

     b. In addition to archeology, Alice is taking psycholinguistics.

     c. Rather than at 7:00, Nancy left at 6:00.

     d. As well as the governor being crooked, the president is incompetent.

     e. Instead of snowing, it rained.

(9) a. John put records in the closet as well as books.

     b. Nancy took the bus yesterday rather than the train.

     c. Tom put rum in the punch in addition to vodka.

When there are only two conjuncts, *or, but,* and (to a limited extent) *and* allow the sentence-final position of (9) but never the sentence-initial position of (8):

(10) a. *Or his books, John put (either) his records in the closet.

      b. *But not money, Alice gives old clothes to the Salvation Army.

      c. *And vodka too, Tom put rum in the punch.

(11) a. John put either his records in the closet or his books.

      b. Alice gives old clothes to the Salvation Army, but not money.

      c. Tom put rum in the punch, and vodka too.

    When *as well as X,* etc. is put at the beginning or end of the sentence, *X* loses its status as a conjunct, in that (i) it ceases to influence agreement:

(12) a.   John was invited to dinner as well as you.
      a′.   As well as you, John was invited to dinner.
      a″.   John as well as you ?was/??were invited to dinner.

(ii) As pointed out by Thompson (1972), it cannot be a finite $\bar{V}$, i.e., the structure does not behave as morphologically coordinate if the conjuncts are separated:

(13) a.   It rained instead of snowing/%snowed.
      a′.   Instead of snowing/*snowed, it rained.
      b.   Sam recites poems as well as playing/plays the piano.
      b′.   As well as playing/*plays the piano, Sam recites poems.

And (iii) RNR is quite deviant when the second conjunct is preposed:

(14) a.   *As well as having a lot of affection for, John greatly admires his uncle Oscar.
      b.   *As well as many articles on, Ann has written several books about the diet of polar bears.

There are in addition a number of putative coordinating conjunctions that are in reality only adverbs occurring in a clause that is strictly speaking not conjoined with the preceding clause but rather is linked to it by **parataxis,** that is, the mere juxtaposition of Ss that may well unite into a phonological unit or some unit of discourse but not into a S:

(15) a.   Ned is poor; <u>nevertheless</u> he is happy.
      b.   Rodney is English; <u>therefore</u> he is brave.

That (15a) and (15b) are not Ss is shown by the fact that they cannot be embedded as sentential constituents of larger Ss:

(16) a.   *Everyone realizes that [Ned is poor, nevertheless he is happy].
      b.   *Although [Rodney is English, therefore he is brave], I think you should hire someone else as your bodyguard.

Words like *nevertheless* can be combined with true coordinating conjunctions like *and* and *but,* and in such sentences it is the *and* or *but* and not the *nevertheless* or *therefore* that conjoins the two component Ss:

(17) a.   Ned is poor, but nevertheless he is happy.
      b.   Rodney is English, and therefore he is brave.

The addition of *and* or *but* to the embedded material in (16) renders the sentence normal and thus presumably makes the difference between whether the embedded material is a single S or merely the juxtaposition of two separate Ss. *Nevertheless,* etc. can occur in the same positions as S-modifying adverbs:

(18) a. Ned is poor; he nevertheless is happy.
    a'. Ned is poor; he is happy, nevertheless.
    b. Rodney is English; he therefore is brave.

It is accordingly plausible to treat them as simply being S-modifying adverbs in examples like (16), having a grammatical relation (that of modifier) only to the second of the component Ss and having only an anaphoric relation (the relation of a pronoun to its antecedent, as in the paraphrases 'despite that' and 'because of that') to the first of the component Ss.

EXERCISES

1. To simplify exposition, tenses have been omitted from the structures given in this chapter. Redo derivation §9b(9) with a tense or tenses placed appropriately in the structure, in conformity with the treatment of tense in chapter 8. There are in fact two ways that tense could be accommodated in those structures in conformity with chapter 8; if you feel like it, give both versions of the derivation (the deep structures will differ but the surface structures will be the same).

2. Give derivations for the following sentences. Make the maximum use of CR, i.e., whenever it is possible to treat a conjoined constituent as derived by CR from a conjoined S, do so.
    a. John either denounced Reagan and Mondale or ridiculed Bush.
    b. John has been either drinking too much liquor or not eating enough food.
    c. John either forgot our appointment or remembered it but couldn't come.
    d. Aren't the candidates expected to run dirty campaigns and all be elected?
    e. John isn't believed to have either left the country or been arrested by the police.
    f. I prevented John from folding, spindling, or mutilating the card.
    g. There was a defendant convicted of murder but not sent to prison.

3. What do the following examples tell us about the surface constituent structure of WH-questions?
    a. What did John buy and Mary borrow?
    b. *What has John bought and will Mary borrow?
    c. I asked Jerry what John has bought and Mary will borrow.

(An item of trivia to be noted here: this shows that there are questions that can't be asked but still can be reported in indirect discourse.)

4. Determine whether each of the following items is a coordinating conjunction:

    a. besides

    b. along with

    c. plus

    d. not to mention

    e. because

    f. likewise

    g. so (as in *felt sick, so I went home*)

5. Go through the full range of examples with *as well as* presented in §9c and determine whether extraction from one of the two putative conjuncts (check both of them) is in fact excluded, as the CSC says it should be.

6. Show that sentences like the following are not counterexamples to the claim (made in connection with §9a(16)) that sentences of the form S_1 *before* S_2 do not allow Conjunction Reduction:

    John denounced Mary before Alice.

(Conside only the temporal interpretation of *before*, i.e., ignore the meaning "in the presence of"). Show that *before Alice* in that sentence is an adverbial modifier of the $\overline{V}$ or the S.

7. The treatment of coordination presented here strongly suggests that all sentences of the form NP $\overline{V}_1$ $Conj$ $\overline{V}_2$ have a conjoined $\overline{V}$ derived by CR and do not result from deletion of a repeated subject in a conjoined S. There nonetheless are some cases where deletion of a repeated subject must be posited. Show that the following example is such a case:

    Lou is Italian and yet hates pizza.

Specifically, show that *yet* is subject to a restriction that rules out an analysis of that example as having a conjoined $\overline{V}$ but is consistent with an analysis of it in which the subject of the second conjunct of a conjoined S is deleted under control of the subject of the first conjunct.

8. For any language other than English, find a type of sentence that might involve a coordinate structure and test whether it behaves like a coordinate structure with regard to a selection of the properties of coordinate structures discussed in this chapter.

NOTES

1. The structures in (3) are a makeshift with regard to the specific way in which the Conj is fitted into the structure. In §16a arguments will be given for a slightly different structure, in which a Conj is not simply placed between two conjuncts but is adjoined to one of them (in English, to the following conjunct), so that instead of (3a) we will have

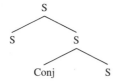

2. One must not confuse (4b) with sentences in which a conjoined S serves as one of the component clauses in a structure involving subordination, for example:

[Tom went to Boston and Alice went to Toledo] before Jane went to Seattle. Hitler committed suicide before [the Allies occupied Berlin and Germany surrendered].

3. The asterisk on (7b: *she*) applies to the interpretation in which *didn't she* is attached to the whole coordinate S. There is another, perfectly normal sentence in which there is an intonation break after *Tom left* and the tag applies only to *(then) Jane arrived* rather than to *Tom left and then Jane arrived:*

Tom left; and then Jane arrived, didn't she?

In that case we have a declarative sentence conjoined with a tag question, not a tag question formed from a conjoined declarative sentence.

4. Here and at several places below, the *then* of examples like (1b) will be ignored.

5. To a large extent it in fact is possible for a single WH-expression to represent jointly a constituent of a main clause and one of a subordinate clause, as in (6d), which many persons in fact find perfectly normal, and such examples as Ross's (1967a: §4.2.4.4) *The curtain which Fred tore Ø in rolling up Ø was a gift from my Aunt Priscilla.* For discussion of **parasitic gaps,** as the second Ø of these examples has come to be known, see Chomsky 1982, Engdahl 1983, and Sag 1983. Note that while WH-movement can create parasitic gaps, Inversion cannot, as witness the sharp unacceptability of the version of (6d) in which the verb of the subordinate clause is tenseless (as it would be if the inverted Past corresponded to the tense of the subordinate clause as well as to that of the main clause).

6. This formulation is a stopgap that will be improved in chapter 16. A more accurate statement is that Gapping deletes all but two constituents in each conjunct after the first, where one of the retained constituents is a nonpredicate element of the $\bar{V}$ and the other one is outside the $\bar{V}$. The words "outside the $\bar{V}$" are an allusion

to the fact that while one of the retained constituents is usually the subject, it can also be a S-modifier:

On Thursdays Tom plays bridge with his neighbors, and on Fridays poker.

This improved version of Gapping indicates why (18a, *then*) is not normal: in that case three constituents are retained.

7. The status of *as well as* as a coordinating conjunction is not completely clear. In §9c there is some discussion of ways in which its behavior parallels and deviates from that of *and, or,* and *but.*

8. Considerations internal to logic do not provide reasons of any substance for analyzing multiterm conjoining as if it were iterated two-term conjoining. In McCawley 1981a, which is to my knowledge the only logic textbook in which *and* and *or* are treated explicitly as combining with arbitrarily many conjuncts at a time (i.e., logical forms like (22c) are admitted), a trivial reformulation of the standard rules of inference and truth conditions is given, allowing them to apply without regard to the number of propositions with which each *and* or *or* is combined.

9. I have no explanation for the fact that (23b′) is odder than (23b).

10. A further difference among sentences as in (27) relates to a characteristic of conjoining that is not taken up here: Wierzbicka (1972) argues that different groupings of the same conjuncts can differ with regard to what general proposition the conjoined sentence is taken to instantiate, e.g., (27a) would be a better answer than (27b) to the question "Which of your friends might need the services of a plastic surgeon?" and (27b) would be a better answer than (27a) to the question "How will I recognize your friends?"

11. A further complication is presented by the fact that *both* never introduces main clauses, though it may introduce conjoined subordinate clauses (examples from Terazu 1981):

*Both John sang and Mary danced.

I'm absolutely certain that both Tom will sing and Mary will dance.

I returned to the house where both I was born and my parents died.

A coordinate structure introduced by *both* must be, or be derived by CR from, a coordinate S, i.e., it is not normal in a conjoined NP that simply enumerates the members of a set:

*Both the king and the queen are an amiable couple.

There are many speakers for whom *either* can in fact appear as an adjunct not to the first conjunct but to a constituent containing the first conjunct, e.g., *Either Mary is looking for a maid or a cook.* Larson (1985) gives a detailed discussion of the placement of *either* in that variety of English and concludes that *either* can be higher in the structure than the corresponding *or* only if it precedes the **underlying** first conjunct, i.e., the speakers in question can use *either* to indicate overtly the **scope** of *or.*

12. Phrase boundary is indicated here by %. There is an alternative understanding of (6) on which it is acceptable, namely, that in which *washed* makes up a

whole $\bar{V}$ and *the dishes* is the object only of *dried,* not also of *washed.* Attention is restricted here to reduced versions of *Tom washed the dishes and Tom dried the dishes.*

13. These constructions are discussed in detail in Knowles 1979.

14. A problem remains, however: why doesn't (14) have a second interpretation, paraphraseable as *Few rules are correct and few rules are easy to read,* corresponding to a derivation in which CR applies to conjoined main clauses? See McCawley 1981a:400–401 for a solution to this problem that exploits a treatment by Ivan Sag of the conditions under which two items count as identical.

15. Apparent violations of the coordinate structure constraint are in fact not confined to structures that can be claimed to be syntactically noncoordinate, as illustrated by Lakoff's (1986) example (i), in which there is extraction from the first, third, and fifth of seven conjuncts:

> i. This is the kind of brandy that you can sip after dinner, watch tv for a while, sip some more of, work a bit, finish off, go to bed, and still feel fine in the morning.

Lakoff argues that there is no general constraint against extraction from some but not all conjuncts but rather a constraint that the S be conceptualizable as expressing a property of an entity corresponding to the extracted element (e.g., a brandy may have the property that you can drink it, watch tv, sip some more of it, . . .).

16. This generalization applies even to cases in which the conjuncts of a conjoined NP provide alternative descriptions of the same individual, as in Quirk et al.'s (1972:362) example:

> His aged servant and the subsequent editor of his papers <u>was</u> with him at his death bed.

Here the conjuncts have the same referent, and the union of the referents of the conjuncts is the same entity that is the referent of each conjunct individually.

||||||| 10. Surface Combinatoric Rules

a. "Structure Preserving" Transformations; Surface Gross Combinatorics

The picture of syntax that was universally accepted in early transformational grammar took deep structure to be the only level of syntactic structure to which any syntactic combinatoric rules applied. Thus, the celebrated rule S → NP VP said (charitably misinterpreting it a little) that in deep structure a S could consist of a NP followed by a VP, but no rules specified directly or indirectly what a S in **surface** structure could consist of. In that picture of syntax, combinatoric regularity was expected to be found in deep structure and nowhere else: if any combinatoric regularities were exhibited by surface structures (e.g., if all surface $\bar{\text{P}}$s consisted of a P followed by a NP), that was supposed to reflect a regularity of deep structure that, by accident, was left undisturbed by the transformations that the language happened to have.

Emonds (1970, 1976) has made the important point that there is far more regularity in surface structure than the above picture of syntax would lead one to expect. For example, the formulas that were commonly used in stating a passive transformation made it look as if it wreaked wanton destruction on the structure to which it applied:

(1) NP AUX   V (P) NP X
    1   2   3 4   5   6   →
    5 2 be -en 3 4   0   6 by + 1

However, as Emonds notes, each of the component operations of this transformation puts something in a position where items of the category in question are allowed anyway in the language. Specifically, term 5, a NP, is moved into a position ("subject position") where NPs normally can occur; term 1, a NP, is combined with *by*, a P, into an expression having the [P NP] shape that $\bar{\text{P}}$s can take in English, and that expression is put in a position (at the end of the $\bar{\text{V}}$) where English allows $\bar{\text{P}}$s to occur; and *be*, a V, is inserted in a position (before a $\bar{\text{V}}$) where verbs can occur anyway in English in such [$_{\bar{\text{V}}}$ V $\bar{\text{V}}$] combinations as *stop paying taxes*.

290

Emonds suggests that it is not accidental that English does not have instead a passive transformation that would be expressible for the formula (2):

(2) NP   AUX   V (P) NP X
      1   2   3 4 5   6   →
    3 + by 2   1 Ø 4 5   6 be + -en

The outputs from (2) would be made up of syntactic configurations (e.g., an item consisting of a verb and a preposition) that the language systematically excludes. Emonds argues that, subject to two systematic classes of exceptions ("root" transformations, taken up in §6d, and "local" transformations, about which a little was said in §6c), movement and insertion transformations behave the way that Passive was just described as behaving: constituents are inserted only into positions where the language otherwise allows an item of the category in question to occur.

How exactly one might incorporate Emonds's conclusion into a scheme of syntax depends on how one conceives of the rules that specify what syntactic configurations "the language allows anyway." Emonds took them to be rules of deep structure combinatorics (i.e., rules saying how items may combine with one another in deep structure) and hence took movement transformations (other than the two systematic classes of exceptions) to be "structure preserving," i.e., to yield outputs that were subject to the same rules of gross combinatorics as were their inputs. Alternatively, one might conjecture that the situation discovered by Emonds has nothing to do with deep structure: that there is simply a set of surface combinatoric rules and that surface structures, regardless of what deep structures they correspond to, are required to conform to those rules. In this book I will adopt the second alternative in view of the existence of a fair number of well-motivated analyses involving deep structures and/or intermediate structures that do not conform to combinatoric regularities that surface structure displays. For example, there will be reason to treat such nominalizations as *the destruction of the city* or *the death of the archbishop* as having an underlying structure that lacks the preposition, i.e., an underlying structure involving an $[_{\bar{N}}$ N NP] combination. But such combinations are systematically excluded in surface structures of English: only $\bar{P}$s are allowed as adjuncts to the N.

Among the surface configurations that English exploits are $[_S$ NP $\bar{V}]$, $[_{\bar{V}}$ V NP], $[_{\bar{V}}$ V $\bar{V}]$, and configurations in which an adverb precedes or follows a S or V that it modifies, e.g., $[_{\bar{V}}$ Adv $\bar{V}]$. The derived constituent structure that passive clauses are claimed in §4a to have is made up of such configurations:

(3)

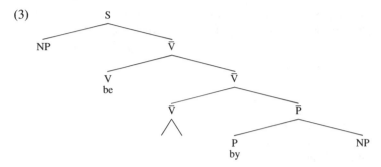

Let us look at some other examples of transformations that move or insert items in such a way as to yield outputs made up of these familiar configurations. In Raising-to-subject, the subject of the embedded S is moved into the NP position of the [$_S$ NP $\bar{\text{V}}$] configuration, and in Raising-to-object it is moved into the NP position of the [$_{\bar{\text{V}}}$ V NP S] configuration; in Raising-to-subject, the remainder of the embedded S (for the moment, let us assume that there is no "tree pruning," i.e., that it retains the category S) is moved into the S position of the [$_{\bar{\text{V}}}$ V (P) S] configuration (e.g., *seem (to me) to be lying*) or of the [$_{\bar{\text{A}}}$ A S] configuration (e.g., *likely to succeed*). In *there*-insertion, the underlying subject NP is moved into the NP position of the [$_{\bar{\text{V}}}$ V NP X] configuration (e.g., *There was a man being tortured; There was a sign on the door*). *There*-insertion is excluded in cases where putting the subject after the V would result in a V with a configuration of elements that is in general excluded in English:

(4) a.   A man vowed to God that he would stop drinking.
           *There vowed a man to God that he would stop drinking.
           (*[$_{\bar{\text{V}}}$ V NP $\bar{\text{P}}$ S])

There are also cases in which Passive is inapplicable because its application would give rise to violation of a surface combinatoric constraint. Specifically, when the underlying subject is a *that* or *for-to* complement, Passive is excluded because it would yield a surface structure in which such a complement was the object of a preposition:[1]

(5) a.   [That the butler had blood on his hands] proves nothing.
     a′.   *Nothing is proved by that the butler had blood on his hands.
     b.   [For the president to suggest devaluation] would anger the bankers.
     b′.   *The bankers would be angered by for the president to suggest devaluation.
     b″.   [Our suggesting devaluation] would anger the bankers.
     b‴.   The bankers would be angered by our suggesting devaluation.

Note also that while the preposition of a [V $\bar{P}$] or [A $\bar{P}$] combination is deleted when it has a *that* or *for-to* complement (as in *I'm afraid (of → Ø) that he'll catch me* and *He insisted (on → Ø) that we help him*), deletion of *by* does not improve (5a′, 5b′). The preposition deletion transformation would in fact be inapplicable in examples like (5a′, b′), since the *by NP* combination is not within the innermost V (this claim, which has been repeated several times already, will be justified in chapter 19 on the basis of facts about the placement and interpretation of adverbs) and preposition deletion applies only within the innermost V or A of the given clause.

Movement of a "*for*-dative" NP into the $\bar{V}$ is also contingent on the resulting $\bar{V}$ being a configuration that the language otherwise allows. A *for*-dative expression[2] in underlying structure is external to the V with which it is combined, in view of the fact that the latter behaves as a unit with regard to all relevant syntactic phenomena:

(6) a. John has *endured great indignities* for Mary, and Bill has Ø for Nancy.

   b. What John did for Mary was sell his stamp collection. (Cf. **What John did to Mary was send $100*, based on the *to*-dative *send $100 to Mary*)

The object of the *for* can often be moved into the $\bar{V}$ when the results in a $\bar{V}$ of the form [V NP NP], but never when it results in such inadmissable configurations as [$_{\bar{V}}$ V NP NP $\bar{P}$]:[3]

(7) a. John roasted a chicken for Mary.
      John roasted Mary a chicken.

   b. John put olives in the martinis for Mary.
      *John put Mary olives in the martinis.

A similar explanation can be given for why only verbs and not adjectives allow Raising to Object (while both allow Raising to Subject) (8a–a‴), namely, that while verb phrases in English can have the surface shape [V NP S] or [V NP $\bar{V}$], adjective phrases never take the shape [A NP S] or [A NP $\bar{V}$] or even [A $\bar{P}$ $\bar{V}$] (8b–b′):

(8) a.   We believe that Harry is the culprit.
    a′.   We believe Harry to be the culprit.
    a″.   We are certain that Harry is the culprit.
    a‴.   *We are certain (of) Harry to be the culprit.
    b.   We told Mary that Harry was the culprit.
    b′.   *This report is informative (to) us that Harry is the culprit.

The system of rules to which I have been alluding in the last few pages is simply a list of the gross syntactic configurations that the language allows in surface structure. Only surface structures that are made up of those configurations are allowed, i.e., an otherwise well-formed derivation is inadmissible if the surface structure does not conform to these rules of **surface gross combinatorics.** The following is a selection of the surface gross combinatoric rules of English:

(9)

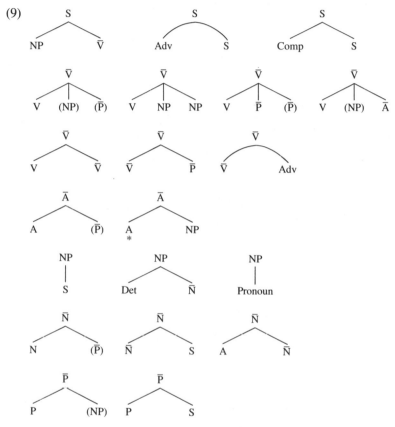

In (9) I have sprung the following new notation on the reader: (i) parentheses are used to combine two rules, one with the parenthesized item and one without it, e.g., the first item in the fourth line of (9) says that an $\bar{A}$ may consist of an A followed by a $\bar{P}$ or of just an A; (ii) curved lines indicate unspecified order, e.g., in the second item in the first line, the Adv is allowed to precede or follow the S; and (iii) an asterisk under a category symbol indicates that the configuration is allowed only for certain members of that category, e.g., an $\bar{A}$ is allowed to consist of A plus NP only if the A is *near, like, worth,* or two or three other adjectives.

The requirement that surface structures conform to the rules of surface gross combinatorics renders many of the details of the application of transformations predictable. Surface structures are more restricted than deep structures, e.g., such combinations as [$_S$ NP $\overline{\text{A}}$] and [$_{\overline{\text{N}}}$ N NP] are permitted in deep structure but excluded in surface structure in English. The raison d'être of many (perhaps, most) transformations is to provide acceptable ways of saying things: to associate to semantically well-formed deep structures surface structures that conform to the surface combinatoric rules (and the morphology) of the given language. It is an idiosyncrasy of English that the verb *be* is part of the passive constructions (many other languages mark their passive constructions with a special inflection on the main verb or with an auxiliary verb meaning "become," "go," or "get"). However, **where** the *be* goes is not an idiosyncrasy of the English passive construction but rather a consequence of the limited possibilities for where verbs can occur in English surface structures. Suppose that the insertion of items by transformations is required to (i) maximize the extent to which the derived structure conforms to the surface combinatoric rules, (ii) have a uniform effect on the class of structures to which the transformation applies, and (iii) disrupt the input structure as little as possible. Since *be* is a verb, it will have to be inserted in a position where the surface combinatoric rules allow a verb. Aside from inversion constructions, which I will ignore here, the only configurations in which English admits a verb are those in which it is the head and leftmost constituent of a $\overline{\text{V}}$, listed in the second and third lines of (9). *Be* could not be made a daughter of the $\overline{\text{V}}$ node of the input, since the surface syntactic rules provide for only one V per $\overline{\text{V}}$, and assumption (iii) disallows the replacement of the V of the input by the *b*. Adjoining *be* as a left sister of the input $\overline{\text{V}}$ yields an instance of the admissible [$_{\overline{\text{V}}}$ V $\overline{\text{V}}$] configuration, and it is in fact in that position that I want to claim that *be* is inserted. In certain particular cases, insertion of *be* in some other position within the $\overline{\text{V}}$ would yield a structure that conforms to (9), e.g., if the input $\overline{\text{V}}$ were, say, *put the money in the safe*, adjunction of *be* to the $\overline{\text{P}}$ would (in conjunction with movement of the object NP into subject position) yield a $\overline{\text{V}}$ of the admissible [V $\overline{\text{V}}$] form (**put [be in the safe]*); however, since that possibility would not be available for all structures to which Passive can apply, condition (ii) would exclude that position for insertion of *be*. This makes adjunction to the left of the $\overline{\text{V}}$ the only possibility that conforms to assumptions (i)–(iii).

The combination of *by* and the underlying subject is a $\overline{\text{P}}$ and thus must be put in a position that allows a $\overline{\text{P}}$.[4] There are in fact three ways that [$_{\overline{\text{P}}}$ *by* NP] could be fitted into the derived structure in conformity with (9). It could be made an extra daughter of the main $\overline{\text{V}}$ node, it would be made a sister of the main $\bar{\text{V}}$ (thus a niece of the inserted *be*), or it could be made a sister of the $\bar{\text{V}}$ headed by the inserted *be* (thus an aunt of the *be*):

(10) a.

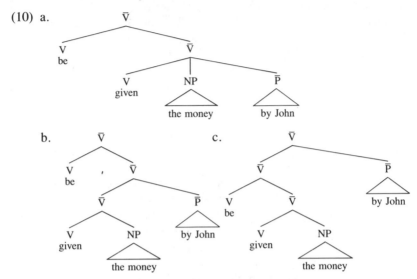

In chapter 19, some facts about the distribution of adverbs will be taken up that argue that the *by*-phrase must be outside the main $\bar{\text{V}}$, i.e., that the derived structure can be as in (10b) or (10c) but not as in (10a). Specifically, such a constituent structure will be required in order to account for the possibility of putting $\bar{\text{V}}$-modifying adverbs before the *by*-phrase, as in *Mary was ignored intentionally by John.* Assumption (i) above can in fact be interpreted in such a way as to prefer (10b–c) over (10a), i.e., we can take the adding of extra daughters to a node to be a greater "disruption of structure" than the addition of a modifier as a sister to a node. While I have in fact consistently given structures as in (10b) rather than (10c) in chapters 4–9 and in fact cited some positive evidence that the (10b) structure exists (namely, the possibility of conjoining the putative $\bar{\text{V}}$ *given the money by John* with other such expressions), nothing that I have touched on really excludes the possibility of the (10c) structure being available **in addition to** the (10b) structure. It is probably impossible to use facts about conjoining as an argument for a (10c) structure, since any putative instance of conjoining of **be given the money** could alternatively be taken to reflect Right-node-raising applied to a (10b) structure. Since I see nothing objectionable in having both structures available as outputs of Passive and since the available facts seem not to exclude either of them, I will tentatively take both to be possible outputs of Passive, in which case the *by*-phrase can go precisely where the surface combinatoric rules and the assumptions (i)– (iii) allow it to go.

b. Filler Filters

The surface combinatoric rules considered so far have been "phrase structure rules," i.e., rules specifying the gross configurations that can make up constituents of particular categories, without regard to what exactly fills each position in the configuration. In this section we will take up a number of restrictions that relate to specific items or features in particular positions of a construction.

I will begin by sketching a classic example of a restriction of this sort, namely the restriction on combinations of Spanish clitic pronouns argued for in Perlmutter 1970. In Spanish, unstressed object pronouns, as well as unstressed pronouns with a number of other functions, appear immediately before a finite verb or immediately following a nonfinite verb:

(1) a.   Juan rompió el vaso.   'Juan broke the glass'.
　　 b.   Juan lo rompió.   'Juan broke it'.
　　 b'. *Juan rompió lo/él.
　　 c.   No quiero romperlo.   'I don't want to break it'.
　　 c'. *No quiero lo romper.

Clauses with more than one clitic pronoun are common:

(2) a.   Juan dio el dinero al gobernador.
　　　　 'Juan gave the money to the governor'.
　　 a'. Juan me lo dio.   'Juan gave it to me'.
　　 b.   Maria enseña música a los niños.
　　　　 'Maria teaches music to the children'.
　　 b'. Maria nos la enseña.   'Maria teaches it to us'.

When more than one clitic pronoun occurs, they must occur in the order (3a) (*se* is the 3rd person reflexive clitic pronoun):

(3) a.   (*se*) (2nd person) (1st person) (3rd person nonreflexive)
　　 b.   Juan te me presentó. (2nd + 1st)
　　　　 'Juan introduced me to you'.
　　 b'. *Juan me te presentó. (* 1st + 2nd)
　　　　 'Juan introduced you to me'.
　　 c.   Juan me la presentó. (1st + 3rd)   'Juan introduced her to me'.
　　 d.   Juan se te/me presentó. (*se* + 2nd/1st)
　　　　 'Juan introduced himself to you/me'.

e.   Me lo echaron. (1st + 3rd)
     'They threw him out on me (= to my disadvantage)'.[5]

No more than one *se,* one 2nd person clitic, one 1st person clitic, or one 3rd person nonreflexive clitic may appear:

(4) a. *Juan le lo dio. (3rd dative + 3rd accusative)
         'Juan gave it to her/him'.
    b. *Me nos echaron. (1st + 1st)
         'They threw us out to my disadvantage'.
    c. *Nos me echaron. (1st + 1st)
         'They threw me out to our disadvantage'.

It is not generally possible to improve the unacceptable examples by deletion or rearrangement of the clitic pronouns. If there is a definite object, it must normally be expressed by either a full NP or a clitic pronoun and not omitted, and the order of the clitic pronouns is to a large extent determined by their syntactic function and not by the person of the pronoun:

(5) a.   Te recomendaron a nosotros.   'They recommended you to us'.
    a'. Te nos recomendaron.
    b.   Nos recomendaron a ti.   'They recommended us to you'.
    b'. *Nos te recomendaron.
    b". *Te nos recomendaron. (*if meaning is to be that of (5b) rather than (5a))

Many Spanish verbs have obligatory reflexive objects, e.g., *escapar-se* 'escape', *desmayar-se* 'faint', *enfrentar-se* 'face'. These verbs exhibit defective syntactic paradigms because of cases in which clitic pronouns contributed by constructions in which they are used cannot combine with the obligatory reflexive clitic in a way that conforms to (3a):

(6) a.   Te escapaste.   'You escaped'
    a'. Te le/me/nos escapaste.   'You escaped, to his/my/our detriment'.
    b.   Me escapé.   'I escaped'.
    b'. Me le/*te escapé.   'I escaped, to his/your detriment'.
    c.   Juan se escapó.   'Juan escaped'.
    c'. Juan se me/te/nos escapó.   'Juan escaped, to my/your/our detriment'.

The ethical dative clitic is required to follow the reflexive object clitic, with the result that when there is a 1st person subject and a 2nd person ethical dative, a combination of clitics is required in which a 1st person clitic precedes a 2nd person clitic, in violation of the template (3a), and consequently there is no acceptable form of the "your" version of (6b').

Spanish does possess one device that enables one to say many of the things that would otherwise involve clitic combinations that deviated from (3a). In cases where one would expect a 3rd person dative clitic plus a 3rd person accusative clitic, *se* replaces the dative clitic:

(7) a. *Juan le lo dio.   'Juan gave it to him'. (cf. (2a'))
     b. Juan se lo dio.   'Juan gave it to him'.

Perlmutter (1970) refers to this use of *se* as "spurious *se*." Besides its uses as a true reflexive and as a substitute for a 3rd person dative clitic as in (7b), *se* is also used in an "impersonal" construction:

(8) En Vietnam se sufre mucho.   'In Vietnam they suffer a lot'.

Perlmutter points out that while replacement of a 3rd person dative clitic by "spurious *se*" often enables one to avoid impermissible sequences of 3rd person clitics, it does not always yield a well-formed result, since when it is combined with the impersonal *se* of (8), it merely exchanges the impermissible *le lo* for an equally impermissible *se se*. For example, a repeated $\bar{V}$ can be replaced by a pronoun, which appears as a clitic:[6]

(9) a. Juan me permitió <u>tomar cerveza,</u> pero a tí no te <u>lo</u> permitió.
         'Juan permitted me to drink beer, but he didn't permit you to'.
     b. Se me permitió <u>tomar cerveza,</u> pero a tí no se te <u>lo</u> permitió.
         'They permitted me to drink beer, but they didn't permit you to'.

In (9b) there is a permissible sequence of three clitics: *se* (from the impersonal construction) *te* (the indirect object of *permitir*) *lo* (from pronominalization of the repeated $\bar{V}$). However, Perlmutter notes that if the NPs in the acceptable (9b) are replaced by NPs that differ from them in person, sentences that violate (3a) can result:

(10)   A mi se me permitió tomar cerveza, pero a Sarita
          'Me they let drink beer, but Sarita . . .'
     a.   no se le permitió tomar cerveza.   '. . . they didn't let drink
          beer'
     b.   *no se le lo permitió.
          '. . . they didn't allow it'
     b'. *no se se lo permitió.
     b". *no se lo permitió.

The result of pronominalizing the $\bar{V}$ is the impermissible *se le lo* sequence of (10b). Replacing *le* by "spurious *se*" eliminates the source of the unacceptability of that sequence but creates a different unacceptable combination, namely *se se* (10b′); and deletion of any of the pronouns (10b″) is not permitted either (in particular, clauses with a preposed dative phrase such as *a Sarita* are required to have a matching dative clitic pronoun). Were the two conjuncts in (10) reversed, though, pronominalization of the $\bar{V}$ would yield an acceptable combination of clitics (*se me lo*) which indeed conforms to (3a):

(11)   A Sarita se le permitió tomar cerveza, pero a mí no se me lo permitió.
       'They let Sarita drink beer, but they didn't let me'.

Perlmutter's extensive survey of the diverse ways of combining syntactic constructions and lexical items that give rise to clitic pronouns yielded the result that the impermissible combinations were precisely those having a surface structure in which the clitic pronouns appeared in a combination that did not conform to the template (3a), irrespective of the source of the clitic pronouns. He concluded that it was misguided to attempt to account for the unacceptability of the various impermissible combinations by restricting the application of particular transformations (e.g., by imposing a condition on $\bar{V}$-pronominalization that makes it inapplicable in cases like (10)), since the oddity of the unacceptable examples cannot be attributed to any specific transformation but only to the particular combination of clitics that the derivation results in. Moreover, the offending combination yields unacceptability only if it appears in surface structure, i.e., it is allowed in intermediate stages of derivations so long as it is deleted in the subsequent course of the derivation, as in (12a; b):

(12)   a.   *A Juan me le escapé, pero a tí no me te escapé.
            'From Juan I escaped, but from you I didn't escape'.
       a′.   A Juan me le escapé, pero a tí no.
            '. . . but from you I didn't'.
       b.   A mí se me permitió tomar cerveza, pero a Sarita no.
            'They let me drink beer, but not Sarita'.

The difference between (12a) and (12a′) is in whether the Spanish analog to Stripping (§9a) applies, reducing the second conjunct to one constituent plus a limited number of items such as *no*.[7] The impermissible *me te* of (12a) thus presumably occurs in an intermediate stage of the derivation of (12a′) but is deleted and does not render (12a) unacceptable. A restriction on combinations of reflexive verbs and preposed datives such as one might propose as a means of excluding (12a) would have the undesirable consequence of also excluding (12a′). Likewise, (12b) differs from (10b) in having undergone Stripping, which eliminates the disallowed *se le lo* or *se se lo* sequence. In both cases, the deviance of the unacceptable version of the sentence is thus due not to what its deep structure is or to what rules apply in its derivation but to what its surface structure is. Perlmutter concludes that the template (3a) is part of a grammar of Spanish, serving as a constraint on the well-formedness of surface structures that is independent of any constraints on the well-formedness of deep structures.

I have gone at such length into this Spanish example because it allows a stronger and more detailed case to be made for a surface structure constraint than does any phenomenon in English that I know of. There are, however, a fair number of phenomena in English that likewise require analyses in terms of such a constraint (what I will henceforth call a **filler filter**). I will now take up a few such cases.

Consider the restriction on the occurrence of personal pronouns illustrated in (13)–(15):

(13) a.   We threw the garbage out.
     a'.   We threw out the garbage.
     b.   We threw it out.
     b'. *We threw out it.
(14) a.   I gave the books to John.
     a'.   I gave John the books.
     b.   I gave them to John.
     b'. *I gave John them.
(15) a.   John built the house for Mary.
     a'.   John built Mary the house.
     b.   John built it for Mary.
     b'. *John built Mary it.

The alternative word orders illustrated by (13a, a'), (14a, a'), and (15a, a') can be described in various ways in terms of movement transformations, and conceivably one could take in all three cases under one single movement transformation, though I find that prospect implausible in view of the differences in the structures of the sentences, e.g., *build a house* in (15a) is a $\bar{V}$ but *give the books* in (14a) is not even a constituent. If there were one single transformation that covered all three cases, then perhaps one could formulate a single restriction on that transformation (e.g., a condition making it obligatory if the object NP is a personal pronoun) that would exclude (13b', 14b', 15b').

There are reasons, however, for believing that the restriction here is not on the application of a transformation but on where personal pronouns can occur in surface structure, irrespective of where they appear in underlying structures. For example, NPs consisting of a personal pronoun conjoined with something else are fairly acceptable in the positions where a personal pronoun by itself is excluded:

(16) a. We threw out it and some other things.
     b. I gave John them and the books you had given me.
     c. John built Mary it or something just like it.

If these sentences are derived by CR, they will have underlying structures in which the first conjunct has the pronoun as direct object. But if the deviance of (13b′) etc. is accounted for by a restriction on a particular transformation, the transformation would apply to the first conjunct so as to yield *We threw it out,* etc., with the pronoun immediately after the verb. But then CR, applying to the conjoined S, cannot yield the sentences in (16), for which it requires an input with *We threw out it,* etc. However, if we have instead a surface restriction that, say, an object NP that is a personal pronoun must immediately follow its verb, the problem vanishes: *it and some other things* is the surface object of *threw* in (16a) but is not a personal pronoun and thus would not violate the constraint, irrespective of what underlies (16a). In addition, extraction transformations can remove the anomaly of (14b′), etc., if they remove the pronoun from the combination in which it is separated from the verb:[8]

(17) a. It was them that I gave John.
     b. Them I gave John.
     c. They were difficult to give John.

There is actually more than this to the constraint on personal pronoun objects. Jacobson (1982) notes that while extraction of the pronoun removes violation of the constraint, extraction of the NP that separates it from the verb does not:

(18) a. *It was John that I gave them.
     b. *John I gave them.
     c. *John was difficult to give them.

Jacobson argues that personal pronoun direct objects are acceptable only when they are cliticized, e.g., that (13b) has a surface structure in which the personal pronoun is an adjunct to the verb,[9] whereas the unacceptable (13b′) corresponds to a surface structure in which the personal pronoun, in view of the intervening particle, is not an adjunct to the verb:

(19) a.

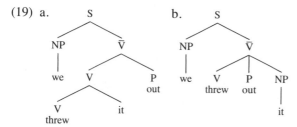

b.

She suggests that the relevant surface structure constraint is one excluding structures in which a personal pronoun is a daughter of a $\bar{V}$ node, as in (19b). This proposal allows one to distinguish between (17) and (18) by invoking the principle of the cycle with regard to the **Cliticization** transformation that must be posited if we continue to assume that all direct objects are underlying daughters of $\bar{V}$ nodes. In the examples in (17)–(18), *I gave John them* is embedded in a larger structure. If Cliticization is to apply, the domain to which it applies would be either [$_\bar{V}$ *give John them*] (according to the policy tentatively adopted in §6c, that all constituents are cyclic domains) or [$_S$ *I give John them*] (according to more conventional assumptions as to what is a cyclic domain). Either way, Cliticization is blocked by the intervening indirect object *John*. Extraction of *John* by Topicalization or *Tough*-movement does not make Cliticization of the pronoun possible, since Cliticization subsequent to one of these steps would violate the cyclic principle (the domain to which those transformations might apply is a S that properly contains the domain to which Cliticization would need to apply). Thus the pronoun in the surface structures of (18) cannot be an adjunct of the V and consequently Jacobson's constraint against nonclitic surface pronoun objects is violated. However, if the pronoun is extracted, as in (17), it is not a surface daughter of the $\bar{V}$ and thus does not violate Jacobson's constraint.[10]

In §8b, I tentatively adopted an analysis of *not* as being a deep structure sister of the S that it negates. As I pointed out there, there is nothing in principle to rule out deep structures in which that [$_S$ *not* S] configuration is iterated, which should thus correspond to surface structures with more than one *not*. Precisely what surface structures, if any, such deep structures should correspond to will depend on what the possibilities for surface realization of *not* are, and one relevant complication that should be pointed out here is the possibility of "incorporating" *not* into such negative words as *nothing, no one, never*, and *nowhere*. I will in fact assume an analysis whose details are worked out in §17a, in which e.g., (20a) and (20b) share a deep structure of roughly the form (20c):[11]

(20) a. I talked to no one.
      b. I didn't talk to anyone.
      c. [I talked to someone] not

Multiple *not*'s to which "Negative Incorporation" does not apply ought to correspond to surface forms as in (21), while multiple *not*'s for which Negative Incorporation is applicable (to at least some of the *not*'s) ought to correspond to surface forms as in (22): [12]

(21) a.   *John hasn't-n't-n't-n't bought a car.
      a'. *John not not not hasn't bought a car.
      b.   *I'm surprised at John not not not not having bought a car.
(22) a.   Nobody didn't congratulate Fred.
      a'. ??Fred wasn't congratulated by nobody.
      b.   Nobody didn't give any beggars handouts.
      b'. *Handouts weren't given to no beggars by anybody.
      b". ??Handouts were given to no beggars by nobody.

Whether a deep structure with *not*'s piled four deep above the deep structure of *John has bought a car* should correspond to (21a) or to (21a') depends on fine details of the conditions for the application of Negative Placement—it isn't clear whether it would apply to just one of the *not*'s or to all four of them. If it applies to all finite Ss of the form [S *not*] and if *not* does not affect finiteness (i.e., [S *not*] is finite if the S within it is finite, and nonfinite if the S within it is nonfinite), then it would be applicable to all four *not*'s, and thus the surface form ought to be something like (21a). Contracted negatives are morphologically quite idiosyncratic: *will* + *not* = *won't* is phonologically irregular, as are *mustn't* and *don't*, even if the spelling suggests otherwise; and there is no form for *may* + *not* in most varieties of English. Accordingly, they may be restricted to those forms that the morphology explicitly provides for (as argued in Zwicky and Pullum 1983), and we could then claim that it was for morphological rather than syntactic reasons that (21a) was excluded, since English morphology does not explicitly provide for contracted multiple negatives. However, such an account wouldn't suffice to exclude nonfinite analogs of (21a) such as (20b): it will be argued in §17a that Negative Placement applies only to finite Ss and that *not* in nonfinite Ss remains a sister of a $\bar{V}$ unless it is incorporated into a *some*-word by Negative Incorporation. Since the [$_{\bar{V}}$ *not* $\bar{V}$] configuration imposes no morphological demand on the *not*, whatever is wrong with (21b) cannot be morphological in nature.

Keeping the unresolved problem of (21b) in mind, let us turn to (22). The examples in (22) are in fact subject to considerable dialect and idiolect variation, and the judgments reported in (22) are for my own idiolect. The differences in acceptability of the various examples in (22) correspond not to how many negative words there are but to **where** the negative words are. Two negatives are fine if one is on the subject and the other is in the $\bar{V}$, while sentences with two negative words in the same $\bar{V}$ are to at least some extent deviant. I will not make the substantial digression that it would take to describe in detail the different degrees of unacceptability corresponding to different structural relations between negative words in the same $\bar{V}$. For the present, it will suffice to note that since the possible places for the realization of negation depend on the application of optional transformations such as Passive, it is implausible to suppose that any constraint on deep structures could distinguish the acceptable from the unacceptable combinations. Moreover, the surface constraint that is suggested by (22), namely that two negative words in the same $\bar{V}$ are not allowed, will also exclude (21b), at least if "in the same $\bar{V}$" is understood appropriately.

A particularly common sort of filler filter is a constraint excluding a second occurrence of some element in close proximity to its first occurrence. For example, the almost complete syntactic parallelism between the *more . . . than* comparative construction and the *as . . . as* construction fails in cases where *as* would introduce a phrase that itself begins with *as:*

(23) a.   You can earn more money as a lawyer than you can earn as an accountant.

   a′.   You can earn more money as a lawyer than as an accountant.

   b.   You can earn as much money as a lawyer as you can earn as an accountant.

   b′.   *You can earn as much money as a lawyer as as an accountant.

It will be argued in chapter 20 that reduced comparatives such as (23a′) have the same deep structures as corresponding full comparatives such as (23a). The transformation that deletes all of the *than*-clause except for one constituent that contrasts with its counterpart in the host S ("Comparative Stripping") applies in exactly the same way in the *as . . . as* comparative construction as it does in the *more . . . than* construction, so that (23b′) ought to be a possible reduced version of (23b). However, the output of Comparative Stripping is deviant precisely when it contains a constituent of the form [*as* [*as* X]].

Suppose that we take this as establishing that (23b′) is unacceptable because of violation of a surface constraint rather than because of anything wrong with any of the steps in its derivation. We then have to decide what exactly the constraint is that it violates. In the last paragraph I suggested that the relevant constraint is against constituents of the form [*as* [*as* X]]. Before we can accept that constraint, however, we have to ask an obvious question, namely, whether the constraint really needs to refer to the way in which the two *as*'s fit into the constituent structure. Might it do instead to have a constraint simply excluding sentences in which the word following *as* is itself *as?* To answer that question, we must find ways in which two *as*'s might be adjacent without being in the indicated configuration. The one obvious way in which such a sequence of *as*'s might arise is through the extraction of the object of *as* from an *as*-phrase that is itself followed by an *as*-phrase, e.g.,

(24) I pay as much attention to [people that I'm as tall *as* Ø] *as* to people that I'm taller than.

Since such examples do not share the deviance of (23b′), I conclude that an invocation of syntactic structure in the constraint is necessary: an *as as* sequence does not always result in syntactic anomaly but does so only when it is in particular syntactic structures, and so far [*as* [*as* X]] is the only combination that we have in which the deviance is observed.

Another restriction on repetition of an item in surface structure relates to multiple occurrences of -*ing*. Ross (1972b) noted that certain constructions involving -*ing* became unacceptable when embedded in a construction that required its main verb itself to be in the -*ing* form:

(25) a.   It began to rain.
      a′.   It began raining.
      b.   It was beginning to rain.
      b′. *It was beginning raining.
      c.   I can't imagine it beginning to rain.
      c′. *I can't imagine it beginning raining.
      d.   With it beginning to rain, everyone was running for shelter.
      d′. *With it beginning raining, everyone was running for shelter.

The deviance of examples like (25a′, b′, c′, d′) is not confined to one particular syntactic construction but appears to extend to all constructions in which a verb is put in the -*ing* form. Moreover, not all sentences with an -*ing* complement yield deviant results when embedded in one of those constructions. Rather, only those in which the -*ing* complement immediately follows the verb give rise to this deviance:

(26) a.   We kept working hard.
      a′.   We kept the employees working hard.
      b.   *We were keeping working hard.

    b'.   We were keeping the employees working hard.
    c.   *I can't imagine you keeping working hard.
    c'.   I can't imagine you keeping the employees working hard.
    d.   *With the employees keeping working hard, production was high.
    d'.   With the managers keeping the employees working hard, production was high.

This might suggest that the source of the deviance is a V-*ing* V-*ing* sequence with nothing intervening between the two words. However, as in the case of the restrictions on *as as*, mere adjacency of two verbs in the -*ing* form is not sufficient to create the deviance (examples (27b–c) from Ross):

(27) a. I'm surprised at the applicants [we were considering] turning out to be unqualified.
      b. Waldo keeps molesting sleeping gorillas.
      c. His having [getting into college] to consider was a drag.

In (27a), the first V-*ing* is at the end of a relative clause. In (27b), it is a modifier. And in (27c), it is at the beginning of a complement but the second V-*ing* is the main verb not of the complement but of a still more deeply embedded complement. The deviance that we are discussing appears to be confined to configurations of the form (28):

(28)

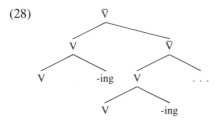

However, merely having a V̄ in the -*ing* form as a right sister of a V in the -*ing* form is not enough to create a deviant V-*ing* V-*ing* combination, as (27c) shows. The deviance appears to arise only when the dependent V̄ is the complement of the higher V, not when it is the complement of some other V (as *getting into college* is the complement of *consider* in (27c)) and serves as a derived direct object of the higher V (i.d., *getting into college* is the surface direct object of *have* in (27c)).

As evidence that the constraint on V-*ing* V-*ing* combinations must be a constraint on surface structure, Ross notes that violations of it can be created in the course of a derivation through extractions that cause a verb and its complement to become adjacent:

(28) a.   I watched Mary writing a letter.
    a'.   I was watching Mary writing a letter.
    b.   Which person did you watch writing a letter?
    b'.   ??Which person were you watching writing a letter?

Here the two -*ing*'s are acceptable unless the derivation takes a course that leaves them adjacent. Ross also notes examples of the opposite sort, in which a normally unacceptable combination of -*ing*'s becomes acceptable if the offending combination is broken up by a derivational step:

(29) a.   I don't want to try wrestling a bear.
    b.   *I'm not keen on trying wrestling a bear.
    c.   Wrestling a bear, I'm not keen on trying.
    c'.   What I'm not keen on trying is wrestling a bear.

The acceptable (29c, c') are topicalized and pseudo-cleft versions of the unacceptable (29b). Their presumable underlying structures contain a S that would underlie the unacceptable (29c), but the derivation includes a step that removes the second-*ing* form from the complement of the first. The generalization about what combinations of -*ing* forms are acceptable thus appears to operate in terms of surface structures rather than in terms of underlying structures.[13]

c. Internal Structure Constraints

In this section I will take up certain phenomena that lend themselves to a description in terms of a restriction on the internal structure of certain surface constituents. Ross (1967a) and Kuno (1973) have dealt with examples such as the following, in which a complement S is unacceptable in contexts in which by all rights it ought to be able to occur:

(1) a.   That John showed up pleased me.
    b.   *Did that John showed up please you?
    b'.   Did the fact that John showed up please you?
    c.   Did it please you that John showed up?
(2) a.   That Reagan won baffled Sam.
    b.   *I was talking to the man who that Reagan won baffled.
    b'.   ?I was talking to the man who the fact that Reagan won baffled.
    c.   I was talking to the man who was baffled that Reagan won.

Ross's description of the oddity of (1b, 2b) attributed it to their having a S that was "in the middle." The problem dealt with by Ross and Kuno is that of making this rough observation precise, which means at least (i) specifying what kinds of embedded S yield the sort of oddity found in (1b, 2b) and (ii) specifying what it has to be in the middle **of.**

In view of the acceptability of sentences with *the fact that S* in place of just *that S,* it takes more than just "being in the middle of" a larger S to make *that S* unacceptable—it is just as much in the middles of (1b', 2b') as in the middles of (1b, 2b). Likewise, *that S* in each of the following is "in the middle of" the whole sentence and no oddity such as that of (1b, 2b) occurs:

(3) a. That John said <u>that he was quitting</u> surprised me.
    b. The accountant who told the boss <u>that he was quitting</u> has found a better job.

Note that in these examples, while the underlined *that S* constituent is in the middle of the whole S, it is not in the middle of the S that it is **immediately** a constituent of, e.g., in (3a), *that he was quitting* is not in the middle but at the end of *John said that he was quitting.* This suggests that if the constraint at issue is really an exclusion of some sort of "S in the middle," what is important is not where it is in the whole sentence that it is a part of but rather in some specific superordinate constituent, e.g., the immediately higher S. Examples like (1b', 2b') show that the last suggestion is not correct: in those examples the *that S* constituent is in the middle of (i.e., preceded and followed by nonzero parts of) the next higher S. Ross exempted examples like (1b', 2b') from his **Internal S Constraint** by stating it as excluding not just any internal S but only an internal [$_{NP}$ S] constituent, i.e., a S that makes up a whole subject, direct object, etc., rather than just making up part of one.

There are, however, many cases in which a sentential direct object can be followed by material such as adverbial expressions:

(4) a. Archimedes proved <u>that the earth is round</u> at the age of fifteen.
    b. John said <u>that he was angry</u> in a high-pitched voice.

In view of examples such as these, Kuno (1973) proposed a revision of Ross's constraint, to the effect that what a [$_{NP}$ S] constituent cannot be in the middle of is not the next higher S (as Ross had proposed) but rather the next higher "major constituent." In these examples, the next higher constituent is the $\bar{V}$ *proved that the earth is round* or *said that he was angry,* and the sentential object is not in the middle but at the end of that constituent. Kuno's suggestion is confirmed by the observation that V-modifying adverbs and the "particles" of Verb-particle combinations behave differently from the $\bar{V}$-modifiers that figure in (4):

(5) a.   Archimedes proved that proposition conclusively.

   a.   ?? Archimedes proved that the earth is round conclusively.

   b.   Bill shouted several obscenities loudly.

   b′.   *Bill shouted that he was fed up loudly.

   c.   Sam pointed several things out.

   c′.   *Sam pointed that we were running out of money out.

According to the analysis of adverbs developed in chapter 19, the adverbial expressions in (4) modify V̄s, so that the *that*-clause is in a configuration as in (6a), whereas the adverbs in (5a,b) (likewise, particles as in (5c)) are V-modifiers and thus appear in the configuration (6b), and thus in the latter case but not the former the *that*-clause is followed by material of the minimal V̄ in which it is contained:

(6) a.

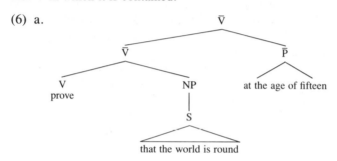

   b.

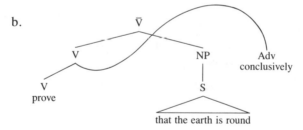

Ross's statement of the Internal S Constraint allowed him to treat examples like (7a) as being odd for the same reason that (1b, 2b) are:

(7) a.   *[That [that John showed up] pleased Mary] was obvious.

   b.   That the fact that John showed up pleased Mary was obvious.

   c.   That it pleased Mary that John showed up was obvious.

Note, however, that with the constituent structure that was argued for in chapter 5, (7a) doesn't violate Kuno's version of the Internal S constraint, since *that John showed up* is at the beginning, not in the middle, of S_2:

(8)

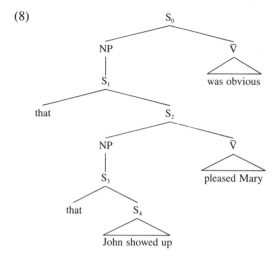

Two possibilities suggest themselves here. Maybe (7a) and (1b, 2b) are odd for the same reason, but we have just misidentified what it is bad for *that*-clauses to be in the middle of, e.g., perhaps we should interpret "major constituent" in such a way that only S_1 and not S_2 counts as being one, in which case S_3 would indeed be in the middle of the next higher major constituent, i.e., S_1. Or maybe (7a) is odd for a different reason than are (1b, 2b), say, because of the juxtaposition of the two *that*'s.

Kuno argues for the latter conclusion, noting that the oddity of examples like (6a) is greatly reduced if the word order is changed so that the two *that*'s do not abut:

(9) a.   *John said that [[that the world was round] was obvious to him].
     a'. ?John said that [to him [that the world was round] was obvious].
     b.   *John said that [[that the world was round] had been clear to him for years].
     b'. ?John said that [for years [that the world was round] had been clear to him].

Since the *that*-clauses of (9a', b') are just as much in the middle of any superordinate major constituent as are those of (9a, b), Kuno concludes that a different constraint is responsible for their oddity than for that of (1b, 2b). Kuno's constraint, the details of which we will not go into here, excludes not only *that*-clauses that begin with a *that*-clause but also, e.g., *because*-clauses that begin with a *because*-clause and *if*-clauses that begin with an *if*-clause. Further confirmation of Kuno's conclusion is provided by the fact that *for-to* complements exhibit the same sorts of oddities noted above with *that*-clauses:

(10) a.　　For Bush to be elected would be horrible.
　　　a'.　??Would for Bush to be elected be horrible?
　　　a".　　Would it be horrible for Bush to be elected?
　　　b.　　*For [for Americans to visit Cuba] to be illegal is unthinkable.
　　　b'.　　For it to be illegal for Americans to visit Cuba is unthinkable.

To see that the oddity of (10b) is due to the juxtaposition of *for*'s rather than to the occurrence of *for Americans to visit Cuba* in the middle of a larger constituent, note that changing the higher *for-to* complement into a *that*-complement, which does not affect the status of the lower *for-to* complement as "internal," greatly increases acceptability: [14]

(11) [That [for Americans to visit Cuba] is illegal] is unthinkable.

　　Some serious problems for the proposed restriction on internal Ss should be noted here. First, Higgins (1973) has pointed out that the sort of oddity that Ross and Kuno attribute to the presence of an "internal S" in surface structure is also found in sentences in which, due to WH-movement and Inversion, a subject clause comes to be in final position and is thus not "internal" to any surface constituent:

(12) a.　*How likely is that John will show up?
　　　b.　*How frightening is to be held a hostage?

If there were an auxiliary verb, *be* would not participate in the inversion and the complement would then be "internal":

(13) a.　*How likely can [that John will show up] be?
　　　b.　*How frightening has [to be held a hostage] been?

Kuno accordingly proposed reconciling the unacceptability of (12) with his version of the constraint by taking it to apply not to surface structure but to a stage prior to the application of Inversion. Kuno does not work this suggestion out in enough detail to make clear that it can indeed be made to work. Grosu and Thompson (1977:114) point out that if the oddity of (12) is to be accounted for by "ordering" the Internal S constraint before Inversion, one would also have to order it before some other transformations that can remove material that follows an internal S, notably the preposing of Ā before *though* (as in *tired though he was*) and some of the rules for reduction of comparative clauses:

(14) a.　*I won't say another word about John, scandalous though I may consider [that he jilted Mary].
　　　b.　*Mary rated your having gone into linguistics as more irresponsible than she rated [that you spied for Libya].

Even if that suggestion can be made precise in a way that conforms to the facts, it still will not provide any explanation of why (13–14) are bad, i.e., of why the internal S constraint would apply to the input rather than to the output of the above transformations.

Second, Grosu and Thompson (1977: 129) point out that there are pairs of sentences that arguably have completely parallel surface constituent structures but only one member of which exhibits the oddity in question:

(15) a.   *I called [that Bill was in danger] to the attention of the people responsible for his safety.

   a′.   I explained [that my license had expired] to the brother of the judge presiding over my case.

   b.   *Bill took [that Mary got angry at him] as a sign that she loved him.

   b′.   Bill heard [that Mary was angry at him] from the boy that she was tutoring.

Since the *that*-clause in each of these examples is in the NP position of a [$_{\bar V}$ V NP $\bar P$] combination, any definition of "internal" in terms of just constituent structure and categories that makes the *that*-clause in (15a, b) internal will also make the one in (15a′, b′) internal.

Grosu and Thompson argue that the relevant difference between (15a) and (15a′) is not one of constituent structure but rather of whether the constituent that follows the sentential NP is an obligatory or an optional constituent of the $\bar V$. Note that it is followed by an obligatory constituent of the $\bar V$ in (15a, b), which are odd-sounding, but by an optional constituent in (15a′, b′), which sound normal. This generalization would allow one to place a different interpretation on the acceptability of (4a–b), in which a *that*-clause was followed by a $\bar V$-modifier. According to Kuno, they did not violate the Internal S constraint because the *that*-clause was final in the minimal $\bar V$. Under Grosu and Thompson's identification of the source of the oddity of (15a, b), what matters is not whether the *that*-clause is final in the next higher constituent but whether the material following it is optional or obligatory, and the optionality of the $\bar V$-modifiers is enough to exempt (4a–b) from (Grosu and Thompson's version of) the Internal S constraint irrespective of whether the relevant larger constituent is a S or a constituent of any major category.

Why would the optionality or obligatoriness of a constituent make any difference to the acceptability of a sentence in which that constituent is present? Grosu and Thompson take up a hypothesis about mechanisms for understanding language that suggests an answer to this question. Specifically, they propose that material held in short-term memory is transferred to a longer-term memory when it adds up to something semantically coherent, and that the obligatory parts of a constituent are enough to achieve semantic coherence. According to this hypothesis, the *that*-clause in (15a, b) must remain in short-term memory while the following $\overline{P}$ is being understood, since until that $\overline{P}$ has been understood, a semantically coherent constituent containing the *that*-clause has not been recovered, while in (15a′, b′) the *that*-clause combines with the preceding material into a semantically coherent constituent and thus can be transferred immediately to the longer-term memory. Thus, optionality of the final constituent determines whether the direct object must remain in short-term memory while the following constituent is being understood and accordingly can affect whether an overload of the short-term memory occurs. Grosu and Thompson are then able to use this hypothesis to account for the oddity of examples like (12). Although the *that*-clause in (12) is final in surface structure, it is part of a construction in which it is followed by an obligatory constituent. The obligatory constituent can of course be supplied by identifying the constituent that has been extracted or deleted from that position. But that means that in those cases the *that*-clause would not be transferred immediately into the longer-term memory but would be retained until it was combined with the moved or deleted constituent; again, a sentential constituent would have to be retained in short-term memory while steps of understanding the constituent that it is part of continued.[15]

There are two ways that one might interpret the account of (12–15) that has just been sketched. One is to say that there is no such thing as an Internal S Constraint but only a sentence-understanding mechanism that sometimes encounters an overload of the short-term memory, with the result that the sentence causing the overload is perceived as deviant. The second is to say that the oddity of (12–14, 15a, b) need not correspond to an overload of the short-term memory whenever one attempts to understand them; rather, the sentence-understanding mechanism provides motivation for a constraint (a revised version of the Internal S constraint) that excludes a class of sentences that place language users in serious danger of overloading their short-term memories (or the short-term memories of their hearers). Grosu and Thompson suggest the latter approach to the above phenomena when they contrast the relative sharpness of contrasts such as (15a)/(15a′) with the gradience of degrees of acceptability of sentences that can be held to place different degrees of strain on the short-term memory. For example, they point out that "the presence of a relatively light clause-mate following a non-NP-clausal heavy constituent lowers acceptability, **regardless of the optionality of the former,** and the removal of such a light constituent raises acceptability—again, **regardless of its optionality**" (1977:146, with original emphasis), citing the examples in (16):

(16) a. ?*I gave <u>the book which you put on my table yesterday</u> to her.
    a'.   To whom did you give the book that I put on your table yesterday Ø?
    b.   ?*I consider <u>the book that you put on my table yesterday</u> silly.
    b'.   How silly do you consider the book which I put on your table yesterday Ø?

Before concluding this section, I will sketch a further constraint on the internal structure of surface constituents that Kuno (1973) proposed. Consider the contrasts in (17):

(17) a.   ??Which actor were pictures of Ø on display?
    a'.   Which actor did they display pictures of Ø?
    b.   *Alex, I suggested to Ø that we leave.
    b'.   To Alex, I suggested Ø that we leave.
    c.   *It was Marcia who he admitted to Ø that he was under age.
    c'.   It was to Marcia that he admitted Ø that he was under age.

Kuno argues that these examples illustrate a constraint on nonfinal "incomplete constituents," i.e., that constituents of which a piece has been removed (e.g., *pictures of Ø* in (17a–a'), where the object of the preposition is missing) are acceptable only in final position. Note that the difference between (17b, c) and (17', c') is in whether the preposition is moved along with the extracted NP or is left behind in its underlying position: only in the latter case is an incomplete constituent (as opposed to no constituent at all) left in the middle of the $\bar{V}$. We again have the problem of determining the appropriate notion of "final," and Kuno again argues that what is relevant is where the potentially offending constituent is in the next higher major constituent, e.g., the $\bar{V}$ in (17b–c). Testing whether that is the right interpretation of the constraint is left to the reader as an exercise.

EXERCISES

1. Give derivations for the following sentences, in accordance with the analyses developed so far in this book (NB, including Jacobson's proposed cliticization of object pronouns), and in those cases where the surface structure violates one of the constraints discussed in this chapter, identify the violation:
    a.   We believe him to have left.
    b.   *I believe that the world is round to be obvious.
    c.   The team finally won their coach a game.
    d.   *At no time did that we were short of money worry us.
    e.   *I'm amused at their being drinking beer when we walked in on their meeting.

2. a. In §10c, the Ross-Kuno "internal S constraint" was illustrated with examples of internal *that* and *for-to* complements. Construct examples for at east two other complement types that will show whether they too are subject to the internal S constraint.

   b. For those complement types that are subject to the internal S constraint, give examples that will show whether reduced forms of such complements are also subject to it.

3. a. Give examples that will test whether the appropriate notion of "final position" for Kuno's "incomplete constituent constraint" is "final in the next higher major constituent," as suggested at the end of §10c.

   b. Give examples that will test whether it makes a difference with respect to that constraint whether the material following the incomplete constituent is optional or obligatory.

4. Give as complete a list as you can of syntactic structures in which two verbs in -*ing* are adjacent but do not violate Ross's "double -*ing*" constraint, as stated in §10b.

5. Determine whether the possibilities for using *take NP for granted* with a sentential object are those that conform to the internal S constraint.

6. Give examples that will clarify what exactly the constraint against "full NP before pronoun" must exclude. Specifically,

   a. Check how broadly or narrowly "full NP" and "pronoun" must be taken (e.g., do *this* and *that* count as "pronouns"?)

   b. Check whether the constraint is restricted to NPs in some specific syntactic relation (e.g., sisters) by constructing examples illustrating a variety of ways in which one NP might immediately follow another.

7. Use the internal S constraint and the following sentences to argue that *believe X to Y* involves Raising (i.e., that X is the surface direct object of *believe*):

   *I believe [that John left] to have upset you.
   *I believe [for John to kill Mary] to be unlikely. (Examples from Grosu and Thompson 1977 : 117).

8. For any language other than English, construct examples that will test whether that language is subject to Kuno's version of the Internal S Constraint.

NOTES

1. Examples (5b–b') are modeled after Emonds (1976:66).

2. I will restrict my attention here to benefactive *for*-datives. See Green 1974 for a detailed treatment of the syntactic and semantic differences among the various dative constructions.

3. "*For*-dative movement" is excluded even in many cases where the resulting $\bar{V}$ does not violate the surface combinatoric rules, e.g.,

> *John endured Mary great indignities.
> *John looked Mary for a job.

These examples illustrate that *for*-dative movement is subject to additional restrictions and in this case suggest a restriction to the effect that the object of the verb is required to denote something that is "received" by the beneficiary (e.g., in (7a) Mary receives the chicken, but in (6a) she does not receive the indignities).

4. Actually, to a limited extent $\bar{P}$s can appear as subjects (*Under the bed is a good place to hide the money*), so that, strictly speaking, the [$_{\bar{P}}$ *by* NP] combination would not have to be moved anywhere to conform to the surface combinatorics of English. I assume, however, that Passive requires that a NP be moved from the $\bar{V}$ into subject position and that the underlying subject must thus vacate that position. $\bar{P}$ subjects are discussed in detail in Jaworska (1986).

5. The construction in which a dative NP denoting "person affected" is combined with a full sentence is known as the **ethical dative** construction. The ethical dative construction can sometimes be translated into English with *on NP*, e.g., *Sam drank all the beer on me,* but I will gloss it below as *to the detriment of NP* to avoid ambiguities that *on* sometimes creates.

6. This pronominalization is more directly analogous to English *do so* than to $\bar{V}$-deletion.

7. This deletion does not require that the deleted and retained material be identical in form, e.g., the *me te escapé* of the second conjunct counts as identical to the *me le escapé* of the first. On the relevant notion of "sloppy identity" that is illustrated here, see Sag 1976.

8. These sentences in fact sound somewhat odd, because of the strong pressure to use instead the form with *to* (e.g., *It was them that I gave to John*) so as to avoid ambiguity as to which NP is the direct object of *give* and which one the indirect object.

9. I would in fact claim that Spanish clitic pronouns are also adjuncts to the verb, though that point plays no real role in the matters discussed earlier in this section.

10. Jacobson contrasts extraction of the intervening NP by *Tough*-movement (18c) with extraction of it by Passive (*John was given them by Mary*), which does not share in the deviance of **Mary gave John them*. According to the assumptions in force here, the passive should be equally bad, since the domain to which Cliticization would have a chance to apply would be the $\bar{V}$ *give John them,* on which Cliticization is blocked. This observation can be used as an argument that $\bar{V}$s are

not cyclic domains, though I have not yet come to any firm conclusion as to whether that is the right conclusion to draw. (It is not Jacobson's conclusion, for which the reader is referred to her paper.)

11. This analysis takes *anyone, anything,* etc., as the forms that *someone, something,* etc., have when they are in the scope of a negation.

12. I emphasize I am describing an idiolect in which each negative word expresses a separate negation (e.g., (22a) is the negation of *Somebody didn't congratulate Fred* and thus implies that everyone congratulated him), not a variety in which a single negation is "spread" over all words that have a negative form, i.e., I am not talking about those varieties of English in which (22a) has the meaning of *Nobody congratulated Fred.* For discussion of dialects with "Negative Spreading," see Labov 1972.

13. For further discussion of the details of this constraint, see Milsark 1972, Pullum 1974, Berman 1973b, and Bolinger 1979.

14. Replacing the lower *for-to* complement by a *that*-complement does not significantly increase acceptability:

??For [that the world is flat] to be widely believed is unthinkable.

However, this follows from the observation (Grosu and Thompson 1977:131–32) that the subject of a *for-to* complement can never be a *that*-clause.

15. Yet another account of the unacceptability of (12), proposed in Iwakura (1976), is taken up briefly in §15b.

||||||| *11. Anaphora*

a. Introduction

English possesses a fair number of words and expressions that take their interpretation from some other part of the sentence or discourse, as in the following examples, in which the **anaphoric device (AD)** is in boldface and the *antecedent* from which it takes it interpretation is italicized:

(1) a. *Mary* said that **she** was angry.
 b. *John* pities **himself.**
 c. *Your brother* is always insulting **other** people.
 c'. *Your brother* is always insulting everyone **else.**
 d. If *your brother* insults me again, I'll punch **the bastard** in the nose.
 e. Fred says that there are politicians *who don't accept bribes,* but I strongly doubt that there are any **such** politicians.
 f. Mary said *that Roger was an idiot,* but I'm sure she doesn't really think **so.**
 g. Janet drives a small *car* and Alice drives a big **one.**

Besides overt ADs, as in (1), there are also phonologically zero ADs, as in (2):

(2) a. Many people *like pizza,* but Sam doesn't Ø.
 b. Mary is younger *than Tom,* and Alice is older Ø.
 c. Alice's *car* is bigger than Janet's Ø.
 d. Sam kept arguing *that Lenin was Jewish,* but he couldn't convince us Ø.

In this chapter, we will take up a number of questions relating to the syntax of ADs, including (a) What underlies each of the various ADs? (b) Under what conditions may a given AD have a given item as antecedent? (E.g., where may it occur in the syntactic structure in relation to a potential antecedent?) And (c) what determines the choice among the various ADs? Before taking up any of those questions, however, I wish to emphasize that we have no reason to assume that the answer to any of those questions must be the same for all ADs. It will develop that there are major

319

syntactic differences among the various ADs. For example, I will argue in §11c that some ADs are derived from copies of their antecedents (e.g., the zero $\overline{V}$ of (2a) is derived by a transformation that deletes one of two identical $\overline{V}$s, and thus a $\overline{V}$ identical to the antecedent $\overline{V}$ underlies the zero $\overline{V}$), but I will also argue that some ADs (for example, most instances of personal pronouns) cannot be derived from copies of their antecedents.[1] In addition, we are not justified in assuming that because two ADs differ with regard to one of these questions they will necessarily differ with regard to the others. I will indeed argue that irrespective of whether a copy of the antecedent underlies a given AD, the AD will be subject to general constraints on where it can appear in relation to the antecedent, e.g., if an AD is in one conjunct of a coordinate structure, the antecedent may be in an earlier but not in a later conjunct:

(3) a.   John got drunk on Tuesday and Mary did Ø on Wednesday.
    a'.   *John did Ø on Tuesday and Mary got drunk on Wednesday.
    b.   John praised *Mary* on Tuesday and Bill denounced **her** on Wednesday.
    b'.   *John praised **her** on Tuesday and Bill denounced *Mary* on Wednesday.

The goal of this chapter will be to develop an analysis that accommodates the differences among the various ADs while accounting for those characteristics that the different kinds of AD share.

b. The Classical Account of Anaphoric Devices

In the earliest studies of ADs by transformational grammarians, all ADs were treated as derived by transformations from copies of their antecedents. Thus, for each type of AD that was studied, a transformation was posited that applied to structures containing two identical constituents, replacing one of them by an AD of the type in question. Where the given type of AD could take more than one form (e.g., *he, she, it,* and *they* are different forms of the personal pronoun), the choice among the forms was taken to be determined by features of the constituent that underlay the AD. Thus, (1) was derived from a deep structure containing two occurrences of *John* and the derivation contained a step in which one of those two occurrences was replaced by a personal pronoun, with the choice of *he* (rather than *she, it,* etc.) determined by the person, number, and gender of the occurrence of *John* that underlay it:

(1) John said that he was tired.

The possibility or the necessity of using ADs depends on the purported reference of NPs.[2] For example, (2) is a normal thing to say only if the two occurrences of *John* purport to refer to two different individuals both called John:

(2) John said that John was tired.

In (1), either *John* and *he* purport to refer to the same individual and *he* has *John* as its antecedent, or *he* refers to some other individual and it either has an antecedent in an earlier sentence of the discourse or has no overt antecedent at all.

In virtue of the assumption generally made by transformational grammarians in the mid-1960s that sentences differing in meaning must have a corresponding difference in their deep structures, the account of ADs was developed in such a way that deep structures contained an indication of the purported reference of NPs. Specifically, each NP was taken as bearing a **referential index,** and the pronominalization transformations were taken as requiring full identity of the constituents in question, including identity of referential indices. Thus, (1) and (2) were taken as having deep structures like (3a) and (3b), respectively, where the referential indices are represented as numerical subscripts on the NP nodes:

(3) a.   b.

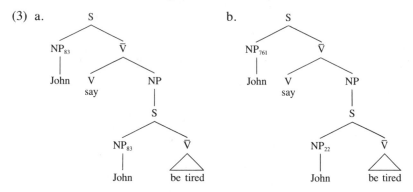

The two NPs in (3a) meet the identity condition on the pronominalization transformation, but the NPs in (3b) do not, in view of the discrepancy in their indices.

Note that since it is NPs and not Ns or $\bar{\text{N}}$s that bear referential indices,[3] a difference in the referential indices of two NPs does not affect the identity of the $\bar{\text{N}}$s contained in those NPs. Thus, one can posit a transformation that replaces a repeated $\bar{\text{N}}$ by *one* and have it apply without regard to the indices on the NPs in which the $\bar{\text{N}}$s are contained, e.g.:

(4)

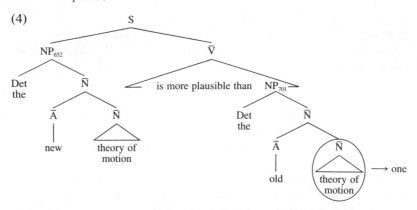

While the referential indices on *the new theory of motion* and *the old theory of notion* are distinct, it is not identity of the NPs that is relevant to the transformation but rather identity of the N̄s, and those are in fact identical. Referential indices do indeed play a role in the applicability of the transformation that replaces a repeated N̄ by *one,* but only when they are inside the N̄s in question. Thus, while the indices on the whole NPs *the old picture of George* and *the new picture of George* are irrelevant to whether the N̄ → *one* transformation can apply in (5a), the indices on the two occurrences of *George* must be identical for the two occurrences of *picture of George* to count as identical, i.e., both NPs must refer to pictures of the same George:

(5) a. The old picture of George is more attractive than the new one.

   b.

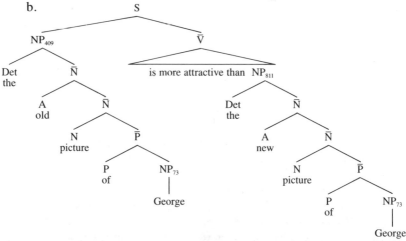

In this approach to ADs, which I will henceforth refer to as the **classical approach,** restrictions on where an AD could occur in relation to its antecedent were stated as conditions on the application of the transformation that derived that particular kind of AD. For example, since reflexive pronouns in English generally have to follow and be in the same clause as their antecedents, the "Reflexive transformation" was formulated as converting into a reflexive pronoun the second of two coreferential NPs in the same clause:[4]

(6) a. John$_i$ asked Bill$_j$ about himself$_{i/j}$.
  b. Susan$_i$ thinks that we like her$_i$/*herself$_i$.
  c. Francine$_i$ forbade Tom to talk to her$_i$/*herself$_i$.

Similarly, a transformation converting one of the two identical NPs into a personal pronoun was formulated in such a way as to embody restrictions on when one of the two NPs could be the antecedent of a personal pronoun in the position of the other NP. One important restriction on the relative positions of a personal pronoun and its antecedent, discovered independently by Ross (1967b) and Langacker (1969), is that, roughly speaking, a personal pronoun may precede its antecedent only if it is in a subordinate clause in relation to the antecedent:

(7) a.   I talked to John$_i$ before he$_i$ went home.
  a'. *I talked to him$_i$ before John$_i$ went home.
  b.   Before John$_i$ went home, I talked to him$_i$.
  b'. Before he$_i$ went home, I talked to John$_i$.
(8) a.   It disturbs John$_i$ that he$_i$ wasn't invited.
  a'. *It disturbs him$_i$ that John$_i$ wasn't invited.
  b.   That John$_i$ wasn't invited disturbs him$_i$.
  b'. That he$_i$ wasn't invited disturbs John$_i$.
(9) a.   John$_i$ is in Pittsburgh today, and he'll be in Toledo tomorrow.
  b.   *He$_i$ is in Pittsburgh today, and John$_i$ will be in Toledo tomorrow.

For Ross and Langacker, these sentences had deep structures containing two identical NPs, and a condition on the application of the pronominalization transformation determined which of the two NPs could be converted into a pronoun: **forwards pronominalization,** in which the second NP was turned into a pronoun, was always possible, while **backwards pronominalization,** in which the first of two identical NPs was replaced by a pronoun, was possible only when that NP was subordinate in relation to the second NP.

One of the most notable achievements within the classical approach was Ross's (1967b) explanation of why in sentences like (10) forwards pronominalization appears to be excluded:

(10) a.   Realizing that he$_i$ was unpopular didn't bother John$_i$.
  b.   *Realizing that John$_i$ was unpopular didn't bother him$_i$.

The deep structure for (10), according to Ross, was as in (11), and the derivation involved an application of Equi-NP-deletion, deleting the subject of the subject complement under control of the the object of *bother:*

(11)

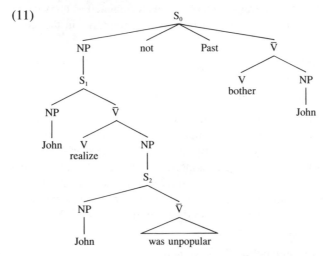

Ross assumed that a pronominalization transformation (allowing either forwards or backwards application, subject to the Ross-Langacker constraint as a restriction on its backwards application) both was obligatory and applied in accordance with the cyclic principle. Since in S_1 only the conditions for forwards pronominalization are met, on the S_1 cycle the *John* of S_2 is obligatorily pronominalized and thus the input to the S_0 cycle is (12):

(12)

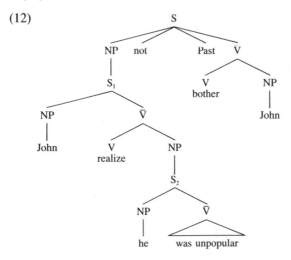

There is thus no derivation for (10b): the *John* of S_2 cannot escape pronominalization on the S_1 cycle. On the S_0 cycle, both forwards and backwards pronominalization between the remaining instances of *John* are possible, as in Equi-NP-deletion. Thus, besides (10a), (13a–b) are also sentences that correspond to the deep structure (11):

(13) a. John's realizing that he was unpopular didn't bother him.
  b. His realizing that he was unpopular didn't bother John.

What in (10) appears at first to be obligatory backwards pronominalization is, according to Ross, actually obligatory forwards pronominalization, but with a NP that does not appear in the surface form of the sentence as the antecedent of the pronoun. Both forwards and backwards pronominalization between the two NPs in (10) is possible if an overt subject of *realize* other than *John* appears (14a–a') or if something (here, *widespread*) forces the understood subject of *realize* to be interpreted as "unspecified" rather than as referring to John (14b):[5]

(14) a. Mary's realizing that he$_i$ was unpopular didn't bother John$_i$.
  a'. Mary's realizing that John$_i$ was unpopular didn't bother him$_i$.
  b. The widespread realization that he$_i$ was stupid annoyed John$_i$.
  b'. The widespread realization that John$_i$ was stupid annoyed him$_i$.

The classical approach to anaphora involves several important assumptions that are open to challenge, including the assumption that **all** ADs work essentially the same way (that each is derived by a transformation from a copy of its antecedent, with different ADs differing from one another at most in the conditions under which the corresponding transformation applies), and the assumption that the conditions under which a given constituent can be realized as a given AD relate only to the stage of the derivation at which the corresponding transformation applies, rather than, say, to where the AD and its putative antecedent appear in surface structure. The latter assumption makes accounting for interactions between pronominalization and movement transformations a significant problem, e.g., to exclude (8a'), one must insure that Extraposition cannot apply to the output of (forwards) pronominalization. In view of the general acceptance of a fixed ordering of transformations by transformational grammarians in the 1960s, such an ordering was the mechanism most commonly invoked by adherents of the classical approach in order to exclude undesirable derivations; e.g., (8a') was excluded by positing an ordering of transformations in which Extraposition preceded Pronominalization.

Ordering of transformations was also sometimes invoked to account for cases like the following, in which forward pronominalization appears to be excluded:

(15) a.   Near him$_i$, John$_i$ saw a snake.
   a'.   *Near John$_i$, he$_i$ saw a snake.
   b.   John$_i$ saw a snake near him$_i$.
   b'.   *He$_i$ saw a snake near John$_i$.

Under that proposal, the unacceptability of (15a') was accounted for by ordering Pronominalization before a transformation that preposed a certain class of $\bar{P}$s: at the point in the derivation where Pronominalization applies, the word order is then as in (15b–b'), only forwards pronominalization is thus possible, and obligatory forwards pronominalization followed by preposing of the $\bar{P}$ results in an illusion of obligatory backwards pronominalization.

   Lakoff (1968) demonstrated the inadequacy of such an account of the unacceptability of (15a') by nothing that it has false implications for sentences in which the object of the P contains a relative clause:

(16) a.   Near the car that he$_i$ was repairing, John$_i$ saw a snake.
   a'.   Near the car that John$_i$ was repairing, he$_i$ saw a snake.
   b.   John$_i$ saw a snake near the car that he$_i$ was repairing.
   b'.   *He$_i$ saw a snake near the car that John$_i$ was repairing.

Under the account of the unacceptability of (15a') in terms of the ordering of a $\bar{P}$-preposing transformation after a (single, obligatory) pronominalization transformation, (16a') should also be unacceptable, since in the structure to which $\bar{P}$-preposing has not applied (as in (16b–b')), only the conditions for forwards pronominalization are met. Moreover, one could not even maintain that a different rule, ordered before Pronominalization, preposed the $\bar{P}$ in (16a–a'), since no matter which of the two putative $\bar{P}$-preposing rules was taken as applying in a sentence like (17a), in which the $\bar{P}$ contains two NPs, one inside and one outside a relative clause, a false prediction would be made about Pronominalization:

(17) a.   Near the manuscript of his$_i$ that Mary$_j$ was editing, she$_j$ saw John$_i$.
   b.   *Near the manuscript of John$_i$'s that Mary$_j$ was editing, she$_j$ saw him$_i$.
   b'.   *Near John$_i$'s manuscript, she saw him$_i$.
   c.   *She$_j$ saw John$_i$ near the manuscript of his$_i$ that Mary$_j$ was editing.

To account for the acceptability of *his . . . John* in (17a), the preposing would have to apply after the stage to which the anaphora constraint applies, since (17b) is anomalous in the way that (15a') or (17b') is. But then *Mary . . . she* in (17a) should be unacceptable because the anaphora constraint would apply to a structure in which the word order was as in the unacceptable (17c).[6]

In addition, serious doubt as to the validity of Ross's account of (10) was raised by Postal (1971:84–85) and Lakoff (1968). Postal observed that under Ross's account there should be no derivation for (18):

(18)   Which of Mary$_i$'s friends did John say that she$_i$ had invited?

In the deep structure that (18) would require, the lowest S would be *Mary$_i$ had invited which of Mary$_i$'s friends*. But application of obligatory Pronominalization to that S could only be forwards, since it is only when WH-movement applies to the topmost S that *Mary's friends* would assume a position that was not subordinate to the other *Mary*. But then only a derivation of *Which of her friends did John say that Mary had invited?* would be possible.

Lakoff observed that there are examples similar to (10) that exhibit the same apparent blockage of forwards Pronominalization as in (10), but for which Ross's account is unavailable because the NP that must be posited as the underlying subject of the embedded S is the wrong one for an account like Ross's:

(19)   a.   Realizing that he$_i$ was incompetent seemed to John$_i$ to be bothering Mary.
      b.   *Realizing that John$_i$ was incompetent seemed to him$_i$ to be bothering Mary.

Here the understood subject of *realize* must be *Mary*, not *John*, and thus Pronominalization cannot apply on the *realize* S. Only in the topmost S are there two occurrences of *John*, and by Ross's account Pronominalization should be able to apply in either direction.

c. Derived and Essential Anaphora

In the late 1960s, a disturbing discovery was made, namely, that sentences exist in which two pronouns are each contained in the other's antecedent:

(1)   **The boy who wanted <u>it</u>** got <u>the prize that **he** deserved</u>.

According to the classical approach, such sentences (generally called **Bach-Peters sentences** and first discussed in Bach 1970) would require infinite deep structures. Underlying the *it* there would be a copy of whatever underlies *the prize that he deserved*, but underlying the *he* of the latter there would be a copy of whatever underlies *the boy who wanted it*, etc., without end, and thus the deep structure would be something like (2):

(2)   The boy [who wanted the prize that the boy [who wanted the prize that
    . . . deserved] deserved] got the prize that the boy [who wanted the
    prize that the boy [who wanted . . . deserved] deserved].

Many linguists (e.g., Jackendoff 1972) reacted to this fact by adopting an approach diametrically opposite to the classical approach, i.e., by maintaining that **no** ADs are derived from copies of their antecedents and treating referential indices as not playing any role in the application of syntactic rules. Both the classical approach and Jackendoff's "interpretive" approach are what Hankamer and Sag (1976) refer to as "monolithic" approaches to anaphora: they treat all ADs as having essentially the same nature. An important exception to the general tendency of transformational grammarians to adopt "monolithic" accounts of anaphora is Lakoff 1968, in which it is observed that the phenomenon that prompted many linguists to reject the classical account, namely Bach-Peters sentences, is found only with certain types of AD. For example, Lakoff (1968:333) notes that anaphoric *one* and zero $\bar{V}$ do not give rise to Bach-Peters sentences:

(3) a. ****That Bill wants to $\underline{\emptyset}$** suggests that Mary <u>expects to $\emptyset$</u>.
    b. **Inexperienced **writers of lurid <u>ones</u>** often enjoy elegant <u>novels about successful **ones**</u>.

To account for such differences along ADs, Lakoff accordingly proposed a "mixed" account of anaphora, in which some types of AD are derived from copies of their antecedents and others are not, and offered the acceptability of Bach-Peters sentences as a criterion for whether a particular type of AD is or is not derived from a copy of its antecedent. He conjectured that precisely those ADs that never give rise to Bach-Peters sentences are derived by a transformation that is sensitive to the identity of two constituents. According to this conjecture, *one* and zero $\bar{V}$ would be derived by "pronominalization transformations," while personal pronouns would not be.[7]

Hankamer and Sag (1976) likewise distinguish between ADs that are derived from copies of their antecedents and ADs that are not, though they differ with Lakoff regarding how certain ADs should be classified and what criteria can be used for classifying ADs. In the remainder of this section, I will discuss the various criteria that have been offered either by Lakoff or by Hankamer and Sag for identifying a given AD as a **derived AD** (that is, derived by a transformation that replaces one of two identical items by an AD) or as an **essential AD** (that is, as not so derived; the deep structure counterpart of the AD is something that 'normally' is expressed by an AD rather than something that allows a "full" expression).[8]

(i) Since the identical constituents that figure in the derivation of a derived AD could perfectly well have undergone insertion or removal of material in the course of the derivation, derived ADs should allow transformationally derived constituents as antecedents. Whether we can also claim

the converse will depend on what we can say about what can be an antecedent of an essential AD. However, if we adopt the hypothesis (as Hankamer
and Sag do) that essential ADs take their antecedents from the meanings of
sentences, without regard to their surface forms, we obtain not only the
prediction that essential ADs do not allow transformationally derived antecedents but also the following prediction:

(ii) Essential but not derived ADs can take as antecedent a deep structure constituent that is "broken up" in the course of the derivation, e.g., if
there is such a thing as an essential AD whose antecedent can be a $\overline{V}$, its
antecedent can be an underlying active $\overline{V}$ that does not appear as such in
surface structure because its object has been extracted by Passive.

(iii) As Lakoff observed, if we make the assumption that deep structures cannot be infinite,[9] we can conclude that derived ADs cannot give rise
to Bach-Peters sentences. (We would have to make some positive claims
about Bach-Peters sentences, however, before we could also conclude that
essential ADs **always** allow them).

(iv) Lakoff also suggested, in line with the assumption (made here,
though rejected by such authors as Chomsky and Jackendoff) that deep
structures are approximate semantic structures, that derived ADs should
contribute to the meanings of sentences not just the **reference** but also the
sense of the antecedent.[10] Essential ADs, on the other hand, could perfectly
well just represent identity of reference, though at the moment we do not
have any grounds for assuming that essential ADs can **only** represent identity of reference, i.e., nothing that we have said so far really excludes the
possibility of essential "identity of sense anaphora."

(v) Hankamer and Sag argue that derived anaphora allow, while essential anaphora do not, the **missing antecedent** phenomenon (Grinder and
Postal 1971), in which the constituent underlying the AD (or more neu-
trally, the copy of the antecedent that one might regard as implied by the
AD) contains a constituent that serves as antecedent for another AD, as in
examples like (4a), in which the antecedent of *he* is the understood occurrence of *an astronaut* in the second clause, or (4b), in which the antecedent
of *they* is the occurrence of *girls* in the second clause:

(4) a. Studs Terkel has never interviewed an astronaut, but Barbara Walters has Ø, and he didn't have much to say.
    b. Fred doesn't pick up girls, but Mark does Ø, and they're generally
stunningly beautiful.

In both cases, the intended interpretation of the first clause is with *an astronaut* or *girls* in the scope of the negation, e.g., the first clause of (4a) is to
be taken as implying that there is no astronaut that Terkel has ever inter-

viewed. With such an interpretation, the indefinite NP of the first clause does not provide a possible antecedent for the pronoun, as is shown by the incoherence of the sentence if the second conjunct is omitted:

(5) a. *Studs Terkel has never interviewed <u>an astronaut</u>, and <u>he</u> didn't have much to say.[11]

   b. *Fred doesn't pick up <u>girls</u>, and <u>they</u>'re generally stunningly beautiful.

The *he* of third clause of (4a) refers to the astronaut that the second clause says Barbara Walters has interviewed, and the *they* of the third clause of (4b) refers to the girls that the second clause says Mark picks up, but it is only in the structure prior to $\overline{V}$-deletion that the second clause contains a constituent that can be the antecedent of the pronoun in the third clause. Note in this connection that it is not sufficient for the understood expression merely to have an appropriate meaning (that is, to imply the existence of an entity such as the pronoun could plausibly refer to)—it must also have an appropriate form, that is, it must contain a linguistic expression that can serve as the antecedent of the pronoun (examples provided by Guy Carden):

(6) a.   John hasn't lost his wife, but Bill has; she died last month.

   a'.   Bill has lost his wife; she died last month.

   b.   ??John isn't a widower, but Bill is; she died last month.

   b'. ??Bill is a widower; she died last month.

By contrast, while *do it* is often interchangeable with a zero $\overline{V}$ (*Sam has climbed Mt. Fuji, and I have (done it) too),* it does not give rise to the missing antecedent phenomenon and is, by Hankamer and Sag's criteria, an essential rather than a derived AD:

(7) a. Studs Terkel has never interviewed an astronaut, but I've done it (??and he didn't have much to say).

   b. Fred doesn't pick up girls, but Mark does it (??and they're generally stunningly beautiful).

On Hankamer and Sag's analysis, the $\overline{V}$ of the second clause of (7a–b) has the form *do it* throughout its derivation and thus does not contain any antecedent for the pronoun in the third clause.

(vi) Since the possibility of using a derived AD is supposed to be contingent on the identity of two syntactic constituents at the stage of the derivation where a pronominalization transformation applies, a derived AD should require a linguistic antecedent. An essential AD, on the other hand, might allow a "pragmatic" or "situational" antecedent: a notion or entity that is present in the speech situation and thus available to be referred to with an AD even if the given sentence and the preceding discourse contain no constituent corresponding to that entity, as when a person asks *Who's he?* upon seeing a stranger enter the room, even though no party to the conversation has so far mentioned the person in question.

To see whether these criteria for derived/essential anaphora in fact agree with each other, let us examine a couple of ADs in relation to the criteria. Let us start with the zero $\bar{V}$. A zero $\bar{V}$ can have a transformationally derived constituent as antecedent, as it should (by criterion (i)) if it is a derived AD:

(8) a. *Hamlet* is <u>easy to remember lines from</u>, and *Macbeth* is ∅ too.
    b. Someone said there were <u>prisoners being tortured</u>, and in fact there were ∅.

The antecedent of a zero $\bar{V}$ cannot be provided by a deep constituent that is broken up by transformations, which is the behavior for derived ADs predicted by criterion (ii):

(9) a. John is hated by his relatives, but his friends don't hate him.
    a′. *John is hated by his relatives, but his friends don't ∅.
    b. *Lear* is easy for me to remember lines from, but I bet you can't remember lines from it.
    b′. **Lear* is easy for me to remember lines from, but I bet you can't ∅.

It was pointed out above (3a) that zero $\bar{V}$ cannot be the AD in a Bach-Peters sentence, which is the way that a derived AD ought to behave according to criterion (iii). A zero $\bar{V}$ is also a prima facie case of identity of sense anaphora, and according to criterion (iv) derived anaphora should be identity of sense anaphora. The examples in (4) show that zero $\bar{V}$s can provide missing antecedents, which is the behavior for derived anaphora predicted by criterion (v). Finally, Hankamer and Sag show that zero $\bar{V}$ contrasts with *do it* with regard to pragmatic antecedents, only the latter allowing them: if two persons are watching someone juggle three tennis balls, one of them can say to the other *I can do it too*, but not **I can ∅ too*. This is what is predicted by criterion (vi) if zero $\bar{V}$ is a derived AD and *do it* an essential AD.

Let us now apply these criteria to personal pronouns. The most obvious potential examples of pronominalization of a transformationally derived constituent (e.g., a constituent from which something has been removed by interrogative movement or topicalization) are highly deviant:

(10) a. He said that Lincoln he'd never buy <u>Sandburg's</u>
<u>biography of Ø</u>, and I'm pretty sure that
Lincoln he'll never buy $\begin{cases} \text{Sandburg's biography of.} \\ *\text{it.} \end{cases}$

b. I asked Mary which persons she admired Holbein's
portraits of, but he refused to tell me which
persons she admired $\begin{cases} \text{Holbein's portraits of.} \\ *\text{them.} \end{cases}$

While this is in fact the behavior that is predicted if personal pronouns are
essential ADs, we should keep in mind that there may be alternative expla-
nations of the deviance of such examples. There in fact appears to be a
restriction against deleting or replacing a constituent containing the "gap"
lefy by extraction of interrogative and relative elements or by topicalization, e.g., analogs to (10) involving a zero $\bar{V}$ (a derived AD according to
all of our criteria) are equally bad:

(11) a. *He said that Lincoln he'd never <u>buy Sandburg's biography of</u>,
and I'm pretty sure that Lincoln he never will <u>Ø</u>.

b. *I asked Mary which persons she <u>admired Holbein's portraits of</u>,
but she refused to tell me which persons she did <u>Ø</u>.

At present, I know of no instances where criterion (i) has any clear implications about the acceptability of personal pronouns that are not accounted
for by other principles.

According to criterion (ii), if personal pronouns are essential ADs, sentences such as (12) should be possible, whereas if they are derived ADs,
they should be impossible:

(12) a. Lincoln I would never buy <u>Sandburg's biography of</u>, though I
imagine you would buy <u>it</u> if you could find a copy.

b. Which persons do you admire <u>Holbein's portraits of</u>, and which
museums are <u>they</u> owned by?

The behavior of personal pronouns thus appears to be that of essential ADs
according to criterion (ii).

We have already noted that personal pronouns allow the formation of
Bach-Peters sentences, which is the way that essential ADs should behave
according to criterion (iii). Personal pronouns normally contribute only the
reference of the antecedent and not its sense to the semantic interpretation
of the sentence. For example, in (13a) the meaning of *my five-foot-tall
cousin* is not part of the belief that the sentence attributes to the cousin, and
in (13b) the proposition that a homicidal maniac is said not to realize is the
proposition that he is insane, not the proposition that a homicidal maniac
is insane:

(13) a. My five-foot-tall cousin thinks he's seven feet tall.
    b. A homicidal maniac never realizes that he's insane.

There are, however, cases in which personal pronouns are used as what Geach (1962) calls "pronouns of laziness," making the same contribution to the interpretation of the sentence as would a full repetition of the antecedent:

(14) a. The man who gave <u>his paycheck</u> to his wife was wiser than the man who gave <u>it</u> to his girl friend. (Karttunen 1969:114).
    b. Books that bring <u>their author</u> fame and fortune are usually better written than books that bring <u>him</u> nothing.

Let us refer to such uses of a personal pronoun as **identity of sense (IS)** personal pronouns, as contrasted with the more common **identity of reference (IR)** personal pronouns. IS pronouns ought to be derived ADs and IR pronouns essential ADs according to criterion (iv). The difficulty in verifying whether this is the case is in finding cases in which the phenomena to which the criteria for derived versus essential AD might arise with IS pronouns. The use of IS pronouns is in fact heavily restricted (e.g., they require contexts as in (14) that set up a correspondence between two "scenes," where the referent of the pronoun is the counterpart in the one scene of the referent of the antecedent in the other scene),[12] and, for example, the conditions for getting an IS interpretation of the pronouns appears always to be violated when they are in the configuration that defines the notion "Bach-Peters sentence." In view of the fragmentariness of my knowledge of IS pronouns, I will simply assume henceforth that IS pronouns and IR pronouns are two distinct types of AD (an assumption that it is actually hard to find solid justification for) and will concentrate on the clear case, that of IR pronouns.

According to criterion (v), if IR pronouns are essential ADs (which they are on all the criteria considered so far, except for (i), which yielded inconclusive results), they should not support the missing antecedent phenomenon. This prediction is hard to test, because any example where the possibility arises demands that the pronouns be interpreted as IS rather than IR:

(15) John didn't admit his infatuation with a Hollywood starlet, but Fred did admit <u>it</u>, though she still paid no attention to him.

For this to be an instance of the missing antecedent phenomenon, the starlet mentioned in the first clause and the one mentioned in the last clause have to be distinct, but then the *it* of the second clause, since it alludes to Fred's infatuation with the latter starlet, must be an IS pronoun. Thus, criterion (v) provides additional evidence that IS pronouns are derived ADs but provides no information about IR pronouns.

Finally on criterion (vi), IR pronouns are essential ADs, since a situational antecedent is possible:

(16) [with attention of speaker and addressee focused on a stranger who has just entered and has not yet been mentioned]
   a. What do you think <u>he</u> wants?
   b. Have you ever seen <u>him</u> before?

Zero $\bar{\text{V}}$ is as clear a case as there is of derived anaphora, and IR personal pronouns are as clear a case as there is of essential anaphora. Let us now take up an AD that is not so clear a case of either (it has been claimed by some linguists to be one and by some to be the other), namely, pronominal *one*. Criterion (i) yields inconclusive results, since the potentially relevant examples are deviant for reasons extraneous to the derived-essential anaphora distinction (cf. the discussion of (10) above):

(17) Which authors does Mark collect old <u>portraits of</u>, and which authors does Lucy collect new $\begin{cases} \text{portraits of?} \\ \text{*ones?} \end{cases}$

However, the deep constituents from which material is extracted do appear to be possible antecedents, which means that by criterion (ii) *one* should be an essential AD:

(18) a. Lincoln my brother wants to write a new <u>biography of</u>, though I personally think that the old <u>ones</u> are quite satisfactory.
   b. Which authors does Mark collect old <u>portraits of</u>, and why doesn't he also collect new <u>ones</u> [= portraits of them]?

We have already maintained (see (3b)) that *one* does not support Bach-Peters sentences, which means that by criterion (iii) it should be a derived AD. (We thus have a conflict between criteria (ii) and (iii)).

Pronominal *one* is a prima facie case of IS anaphora. Note, e.g., that the clause in which *one* occurs can be contradictory in virtue of the sense of the antecedent; e.g., (19) attributes to twenty-year-old midgets the belief that "thirty-year-old midgets are all over 6 feet fall":

(19) Twenty-year old <u>midgets</u> believe that thirty-year old <u>ones</u> are all over 6 feet tall.

Thus by criterion (iv) *one* should be a derived AD. However, *one* does not support the missing antecedent phenomenon and thus by criterion (v) should be an essential AD:

(20) ??I've never read a long <u>biography of a lieutenant governor</u>, but I once read a short <u>one</u>, and he sounded like a complete nonentity.

Finally, as Hankamer and Sag note, *one* does allow situational antecedents and thus by criterion (vi) should be an essential AD:

(21) [with speaker's and addressee's attention focused on an apple that the addressee has just removed from his bag]
    You should have seen the <u>one</u> that Agnes brought.

By criteria (iii)–(iv), *one* is a derived AD, while by criteria (ii), (v), and (vi), it is an essential AD. Since the notions of derived and essential AD, as we have characterized them, seem to be absolute notions, rather than notions that admit degrees and dimensions, we should reexamine the criteria to see whether we are making too strong assumptions regarding what properties should be correlated. Recall that we provided justification only for half of a correlation between status as a derived or an essential AD and the possibility of Bach-Peters sentences: we argued that derived ADs cannot support Bach-Peters sentences, and while we gave an example of one type of essential AD that does support them, we had no argument that **all** types of essential AD must. Similarly, while the assumption that deep structures are approximate semantic structures provides an argument that all derived ADs are IS, that assumption merely made it plausible that all essential ADs are IR—it did not really rule out the possibility of essential IS anaphora.

I accordingly suggest the following as the best that we can get out of criteria (i)–(vi), in view of the behavior of *one;* there are both essential and derived IS ADs (though only an essential AD can be IR), and Bach-Peters sentences are possible not for essential ADs in general but only for IR anaphora. This weakens criteria (iii) and (iv) to one-way implications but retains the correlation between Bach-Peters sentences and IR anaphora that the original versions of criteria (iii)–(iv) took to be a reflection of the derived-essential distinction. We can then say that criteria (iii)–(iv) no longer provide evidence that *one* is a derived AD, and we can conclude that it is unequivocally an essential IS AD.

d. Notions of Command

I have already alluded several times to the claim that an AD may precede its antecedent if it is "subordinate" to it. In this section I wish to consider ways in which one might explicate the notion of "subordinate" and thereby make that claim more precise. Let us start by listing some of the possible structural relations between two positions in a syntactic structure and seeing whether an AD in the one position may have an antecedent in the other position.

(1) a. 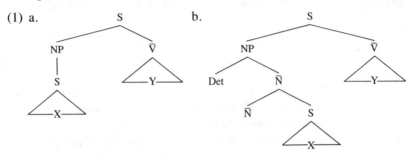 b.

c.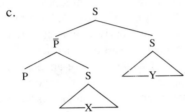

(2) a. 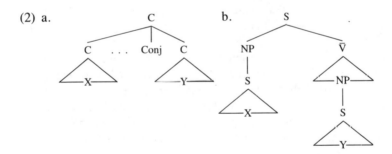 b.

c.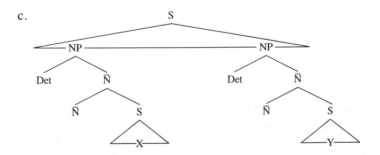

In the trees in (1), X is in a clause subordinate to the one of which Y is an immediate constituent, and one might wish to say in such cases that X is (derivatively) subordinate to Y. In (2a), where X and Y are in separate conjuncts of the same coordinate structure, and in (2b–c), where X and Y are in different clauses that are subordinate to the same clause, one would probably want to say that neither was subordinate to the other. The following are some instances of the various structures, with an AD in the position of the X and a putative antecedent in the position of the Y; some related examples are also included for purposes of comparison:

(3) a.   ?That <u>John</u> would lose was obvious to <u>him</u>.
    a′.   That <u>he</u> would lose was obvious to <u>John</u>.
    b.   It was obvious to <u>John</u> that <u>he</u> would lose.
    b′.   *It was obvious to <u>him</u> that <u>John</u> would lose.

(4) a.   The policeman who arrested <u>John</u> beat <u>him</u>.
    a′.   The policeman who arrested <u>him</u> beat <u>John</u>.
    b   <u>John</u> denounced the policeman who had arrested <u>him</u>.
    b′.   *<u>He</u> denounced the policeman who had arrested <u>John</u>.

(5) a.   After <u>Mary</u> finished the report, <u>she</u> went home.
    a′.   After <u>she</u> finished the report, <u>Mary</u> went home.
    b.   <u>Mary</u> went home after <u>she</u> finished the report.
    b′.   *<u>She</u> went home after <u>Mary</u> finished the report.

(6) a.   I saw <u>John</u> yesterday, and I asked <u>him</u> about the meeting.
    a′.   *I saw <u>him</u> yesterday, and I asked <u>John</u> about the meeting.
    b.   Mary kicked <u>John</u> and then slapped <u>him</u>.
    b′.   *Mary kicked <u>him</u> and then slapped <u>John</u>.
    c.   <u>John</u>'s mother and the woman <u>he</u> is living with have never met.
    c′.   ?<u>His</u> mother and the woman <u>John</u> is living with have never met.

(7) a.   The woman who loves <u>John</u> denounced the policeman who arrested <u>him</u>.
    a′.   The woman who loves <u>him</u> denounced the policeman who arrested <u>John</u>.
    b.   That <u>John</u> couldn't finish the job suggests that <u>he</u> is incompetent.
    b′.   That <u>he</u> couldn't finish the job suggests that <u>John</u> is incompetent.
    c.   The policeman who arrested <u>John</u> said that <u>he</u> had been stealing hubcaps.
    c′.   The policeman who arrested <u>him</u> said that <u>John</u> had been stealing hubcaps.

In (3a′, 4a′, 5a′) we see acceptable backwards pronominalization corresponding to each of the configurations in (1). In the related sentences (3b′,

4b′, 5b′), which involve mirror images of the configurations in (1), we find backward pronominalization unacceptable.[13] In (6), where the AD is in one conjunct of a coordinate structure and the antecedent is in a different conjunct, backwards pronominalization is odd, though the degree of oddity is slight in such cases as (6c′), perhaps because of the subordinate status of *he* and/or *John* in relation to the conjunct in question. In (7), where both pronoun and antecedent are in separate subordinate clauses of a larger S, backwards pronominalization seems generally to be acceptable. We can thus hypothesize that backwards pronominalization is excluded only when either (i) the AD and its antecedent are in separate conjuncts of a coordinate structure or (ii) the antecedent is in a clause subordinate to the one of which the AD is an immediate constituent.

This last generalization can be made more precise in terms of the notion of **command.** A node X^1 is said to command a node X^2 in a given tree if one can get from X^2 to X^1 by tracing upwards along the branches of the tree until one hits a S node and then tracing downwards from there:

(8)

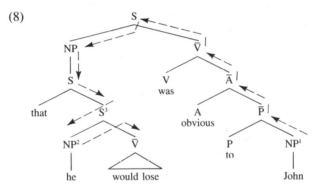

Here NP^1 commands all the nodes in the tree, since the first S node that one reaches in tracing upwards from NP^1 is the root of the tree, i.e., the node that dominates all the other nodes. While NP^1 thus commands NP^2, NP^2 does not command NP^1: the first S node that one reaches by tracing upwards from NP^2 is S^3, and NP^1 is not in the part of the tree dominated by (= reachable by tracing downwards from) S^3.

One correction will have to be made in this characterization of "command" if the constraint on backwards pronominalization is to be stated as allowing an AD to precede its antecedent only if it does not command the antecedent. The notion of command was originally introduced (Langacker 1969, Ross 1967b) within a framework in which a S-modifier was a daughter of the modified S-node (9a), rather than being a sister of it the way that it is in the analyses adopted here (9b):

(9) a.

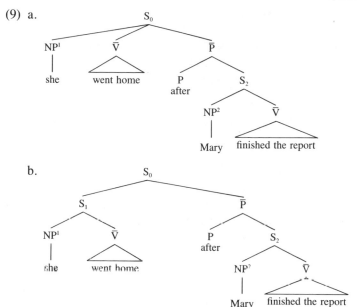

The first S-node that one hits in tracing upwards from NP[1] is S_0 in the case of (9a) but S_1 in the case of (9b), and only in the former case can one reach NP[2] by tracing downwards from that node. So that we can accept roughly the same generalization that Langacker and Ross proposed while retaining structures such as (9b), we need to alter the definition of command so that NP[1] will command NP[2] even in (9b). The most straightforward way of doing this is to allow the upward part of the path in the definition to go beyond the first S-node until a node is reached that dominates all the modifiers (if any) of the first S-node. We thus arrive at the following definition:[14]

(10) In any labeled tree, a node X[1] commands a node X[2] if and only if X[2] is dominated by the lowest S-node that dominates X[1] or by a modifier of that S.

We may then formulate our tentative generalization about the cases in which backwards pronominalization was unacceptable in (3)–(7) as the following condition, first proposed by Langacker and Ross:

(11) An AD X may not precede its antecedent Y if either (i) X is in one conjunct of a coordinate structure and Y in a later conjunct or (ii) X commands Y.

Clearly, (11) is only an approximation to the truth. For one thing, it says nothing about the degrees of acceptability that we noted above, e.g., it does not distinguish between the mild oddness of (6c′) and the gross deviance of (6b′). When we take up certain structures that we ignored in arriving at (11), we find discrepancies between prediction and observation. For example, according to (11), (12) should be unacceptable, but in fact many speakers find it fully acceptable and most others only mildly deviant:

(12)   %?His mother loves John.

While (11) imposes no restriction on forward anaphora, we have already encountered cases in which forward anaphora is excluded:

(13) a.   Near him, John saw a snake.
     b. *Near John, he saw a snake.

Reinhart (1976, 1983) argues that not command but another notion of subordination must be invoked in order to account adequately for examples like (12)–(13) and also suggests that the dichotomy that has been drawn between forwards and backwards anaphora is a mistake. Note that the *he* (of *his* = *he* + *'s*) in (12) is in a sense subordinate to the rest of the sentence, in virtue of being a proper part of the NP *his mother*. If the procedure for determining what commands what involved tracing upwards not necessarily to a S-node but to a node of a "major category," where NP as well as S counts as a major category, then *he* in (12) would not "command" *John* and thus would not violate a constraint against ADs commanding their antecedents. Reinhart accordingly invoked a revised notion of command that (following G. N. Clements) we will call **c-command:** [15]

(14) In any labeled tree, a node X^1 c-commands a node X^2 if and only if X^2 is dominated by the lowest node of a major category (i.e. S, NP, or $\overline{X}$) that dominates X^1, or by a modifier of that node.

That is, the nodes that a given node X^1 c-commands are those that can be reached from X^1 by tracing up the tree until one reaches a major category node, continuing upwards if there are any modifiers of that node until one reaches a node that dominates all of them, and then tracing downwards. Thus, e.g., in (8) the A node c-commands everything dominated by the $\overline{A}$ node, and nothing else; the *was* node c-commands everything dominated by the $\overline{V}$ node, and nothing else.

Reinhart proposes (15) as a constraint not only on backwards but also on forwards anaphora:

(15) An AD must not c-command its antecedent.   [revised in (32)]

Since *he* in (13b) c-commands *John,* (13b) violates (15). However, in (12), neither of *he* and *John* c-commands the other (*he* c-commands only the material of *his mother,* and *John* c-commands only the material of *loves John),* and thus there is no violation of (15). According to (15), there should be an asymmetry between subjects and nonsubjects, since the subject c-commands everything in its S, while a NP within a $\bar{V}$ c-commands nothing outside of the $\bar{V}$ (and the modifiers of the $\bar{V}$) and a NP that is properly contained in the subject c-commands nothing outside of the subject. Thus it should be possible for a subject to violate (15) even though an object, or even a NP that is a proper part of the subject, in an otherwise similar example does not violate it. Reinhart provides ample illustrations of such asymmetries, e.g.,

(16) a. *Near <u>John</u>, <u>he</u> saw a snake. (= (13b))
      b. Near <u>John</u>, <u>his</u> brother saw a snake.
      c. Near <u>John</u>, I saw <u>his</u> snake.

In (16a), *he* c-commands *John,* while in (16b–c) it does not, so that (16a) but not (16b–c) violates (15).

A particularly striking class of examples in which c-command correctly draws a distinction that is missed by command is that of sentences with backwards pronominalization in which the antecedent is inside an adverbial clause:

(17) a.   Mary hit <u>him</u> before <u>John</u> had a chance to get up.
      a'. *<u>He</u> ran into Mary before <u>John</u> had a chance to hide.
      b.   Mary gave <u>him</u> a dollar before <u>John</u> could refuse.
      b'. *<u>He</u> took a dollar from Mary before <u>John</u> realized that Ann was watching.

Here backwards pronominalization appears to be allowed (or at least to be reasonably acceptable) when the pronoun is within the $\bar{V}$ of the main clause but to be thoroughly unacceptable when the pronoun is the subject of the main clause.

How exactly the notion of c-command applies to the examples in (17) depends on a detail of constituent structure that was taken up briefly in §8e. Recall that it was claimed there that S-modifying adverbs are underlying adjuncts to the main S but can optionally be made adjuncts of the $\bar{V}$. The optionality of this step is shown by the fact that both the underlying host S (*Mary hit Bill,* in the case of (17a)) and the derived $\bar{V}$ (here, *hit Bill before John could stop her*) can serve as conjuncts in related sentences involving coordination:

(18) a. [Mary hit Bill and Nancy hit Tom] before John could stop them.
      b. Mary [[hit Bill before John could stop her] and [started screaming at John]].

According to this claim, (17a) could have either (19a) or (19b) as its surface structure:

(19) a.

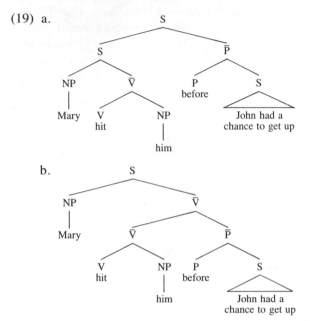

As long as (17a, b) have a surface structure as in (19a) with the adverbial clause a S-modifier, they do not violate (15), since *him* will in either case not c-command *John*. If they have a surface structure as in (19b), with the adverbial clause a S-modifier, there will be a violation of (15), in that *him* will then c-command everything in the adverbial clause, but since there is at least one analysis on which (15) is not violated (that with the (19a) surface structure), this does not conflict with the acceptability of (17a, b). By contrast, in (17a′, b′), the subject of the main clause c-commands everything in the adverbial clause irrespective of whether the surface structure is as in (19a) or (19b), and thus no structure is available for (17a′, b′) that avoids violation of (15).

The account of (17a, b) just given implies that if anything forces (17a, b) to be given the analysis in which the adverbial clause modifies the $\bar{\text{V}}$ rather than the S, analogs to (17a, b) should be unacceptable in virtue of violation of (15). This prediction is in fact borne out:

(20) a. *Mary both [[hit <u>him</u> before <u>John</u> had a chance to get up] and [screamed at the top of her lungs].

      b. *What Mary did was [hit <u>him</u> before <u>John</u> had a chance to get up].

Let us return to (13) and (16) and present their analysis in more detail than was given above. Our observations about (13) and (16) require only that the subject in such sentences as *Near Mary, John saw a snake* c-command the preposed $\bar{P}$, and that condition is guaranteed to be met no matter how the $\bar{P}$ fits into the derived constituent structure. If we can find examples of similar syntactic structures in which the **object** NP could stand in an anaphoric relation to something in the $\bar{P}$, however, it will make a difference where the $\bar{P}$ fits into the constituent structure, since different positions of the $\bar{P}$ in the structure differ with regard to whether the direct object c-commands the material in the $\bar{P}$. Consider, then, examples like the following:

(21) a. *In <u>Mary</u>'s apartment, John put <u>her</u>.
     a′. In Mary's apartment, John put Joan.
     b. *Next to <u>Mary</u>'s house, John found <u>her</u>.
     b′. Next to Mary's house, John found Lucy.

The oddity of (21a, b) provides evidence that the object NP in (21a′, b′) and (16a) c-commands the material of the preposed $\bar{P}$ and thus that the $\bar{P}$ of those examples is a surface constituent of the $\bar{V}$. This means that those examples have a discontinuous surface structure: the $\bar{P}$ is separated by the subject from the rest of the $\bar{V}$ that it is a part of. By contrast, examples in which a S-initial $\bar{P}$ is a S-modifier rather than an underlying constituent of the $\bar{V}$ are acceptable (22), which provides evidence for a difference in constituent structure as in (23):

(22) a. In <u>Mary</u>'s apartment, John attacked <u>her</u>.
     b. Next to <u>Mary</u>'s house, John kissed <u>her</u>.

(23) a.

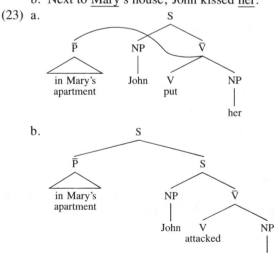

   b.

Those adverbial expressions that can only function as V̄-modifiers, as in (24a), also behave like surface V̄ constituents, though in that case the surface constituent structure will be as in (24b) if, as by now appears to be the case, S-initial position of adverbial expressions in all cases involves change of word order without any concomitant change in constituent structure:

(24) a.   *With <u>Rosa</u>'s peacock feather, <u>she</u> tickles people.
            (Reinhart 1983:60)
      a'.   *With <u>Rosa</u>'s peacock feather, I tickled <u>her</u>.
      b.

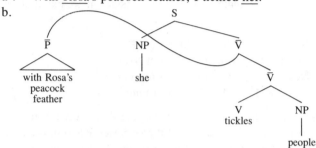

The c-command account of anaphoric relations also explains why analogs to (16a) involving *one* rather than a personal pronoun are acceptable:

(25) Near the little <u>robin</u>, the big <u>one</u> saw a worm. (Carden 1986a:269)

While personal pronouns are entire NPs, pronominal *one* makes up only the N̄ of a NP. Thus, while the subject pronoun in (16a) c-commands everything in the sentence, the *one* of (25), like the *he* of (16b), c-commands only material within the subject NP; thus, (25) does not violate (15). By contrast, in (26), where the N̄ c-commands everything in the relative clause that is adjoined to it,[16] the acceptability of the examples parallels that of the examples in (13):

(26) a.   The young <u>robin</u> that the old <u>one</u> had pecked was bleeding.
      b.   *The young <u>one</u> that the old <u>robin</u> had pecked was bleeding.

The c-command account of pronoun-antecedent relations has worked so well for the examples treated so far in this section, yielding among other things the totally unexpected prediction that examples like (20) are unacceptable, that it is disconcerting to note that, at least in its pristine form, it fails for some very simple and well-known examples, namely, those in which a subject pronoun has its antecedent in a preposed adverbial clause:

(27) After <u>Mary</u> had finished the report, <u>she</u> went home.

Since a subject NP c-commands everything that is contained in modifiers of its S, *she* in (27) c-commands *Mary* and thus violates (15). Reinhart was of course aware of examples like (27) and dealt with them by gerrymandering the constituent structure so as to make subjects c-command the material only of postposed and not of preposed S-modifiers. She took preposed S-modifiers to be outside the main S and postposed modifiers to be inside it, so that (under her definition of c-command, according to which material inside a constituent does not c-command the material of a modifier external to that constituent) the subject c-commands the material of the modifier only in the latter case. To my knowledge, all independent evidence supports structures in which modifiers are sisters of what they modify, and Reinhart is able to maintain her version of the c-command constraint only by assuming structures that have no independent justification and excluding structures that do have independent justification. For example, while the acceptability of sentences like (18a) provides evidence that the postposed modifier can be outside the main S, Reinhart must exclude that structure, since in combination with her definition of c-command it would falsely imply that (5b′) should be acceptable.

A second class of cases for which the c-command account leads to false predictions is that of analogs to (13b) in which the antecedent is in a relative clause contained in the object of the preposed P̄:

(28) a. Near the car that <u>John</u> was repairing, <u>he</u> saw a snake.
      b. Inside the vase that <u>Mary</u> had bought, <u>she</u> found a gold coin.

The main clause subject c-commands not only the object of the preposition but also everything contained in the latter NP, and thus (28) should violate (15) in the same way that (16a) does.

In both (27) and (28), the discrepancy between Reinhart's condition and the facts involves forwards pronominalization with an antecedent in a subordinate clause. Such examples led Carden (1986a) to conclude that anaphoric relations between clausemates are subject to different restrictions than are anaphoric relations between nonclausemates. In particular, it appears as if an appealing feature of Reinhart's condition, namely, its blindness to word order, cannot be maintained in general: while a pronoun c-commanding its antecedent seems to be enough to make the anaphoric relation unacceptable if the pronoun and antecedent are clausemates, it is not enough if they are not clausemates.

Carden also noted a class of cases that present a serious difficulty for another characteristic of Reinhart's analysis, namely, that her restriction on anaphoric relations (15) is supposed to apply only to surface structure:

(29) a. Near <u>him</u> is where <u>John</u> saw the snake.
    a′. *Near <u>John</u> is where <u>he</u> saw the snake.
    b. It was near <u>him</u> that <u>John</u> saw the snake.
    b′. *It was near <u>John</u> that <u>he</u> saw the snake.

Under the most commonly accepted surface structures for such sentences, neither of the two NPs c-commands the other and thus no violation of (15) is possible. Moreover, there are acceptable sentences whose surface structures appear to differ in no relevant detail from those of the unacceptable (29a′, b′):

(30) a. Near <u>John</u> was what <u>he</u> desperately wanted.
    b. It was obvious to <u>John</u> that <u>he</u> was in danger.

Carden took such examples to show that in at least some cases anaphoric relations are constrained by a condition that relates to an underlying level of structure. Specifically, he assigned to cleft sentences a deep structure containing the noncleft analog as a constituent and took the unacceptability of examples like (29a′, b′) to reflect the unacceptability of the anaphoric relation in an intermediate stage in the derivations of (29a′, b′). Specifically, he proposed that anaphoric relations are subject to constraints not only on the surface structure of the sentence but also on the **cyclic outputs,** i.e., the structures at the end of the application of the cyclic transformations to each domain. Since the cyclic output for the embedded S that he posits in (29a′, b′) corresponds to *He saw the snake near John,* he takes the whole sentence to inherit the unacceptability of the cyclic output even though the surface positions of the pronoun and antecedent violate no plausible constraint on surface structures. By contrast, the sentences in (30) would not involve any embedded S whose cyclic output had *John* and *he* in an inadmissible structural relationship. Carden's proposal likewise accounts for the unacceptability of pseudo-cleft sentences such as (31a, b, c), in which the antecedent of a pronoun is in an underlying complement that is moved into predicate position; here again, the pronoun c-commands its antecedent in a cyclic output but not in surface structure:

(31) a. *What <u>he</u> denied was that <u>Nixon</u> was a crook.
    a′. *<u>He</u> denied that <u>Nixon</u> was a crook.
    a″. What <u>Nixon</u> denied was that <u>he</u> was a crook.
    b. *What <u>he</u> was oblivious to was <u>John</u>'s being regarded as a fool.
    b′. *<u>He</u> was oblivious to <u>John</u>'s being regarded as a fool.
    b″. What <u>John</u> was oblivious to was <u>his</u> being regarded as a fool.
    c. *What I told <u>him</u> was that <u>John</u> should leave me alone.

    c'.   *I told <u>him</u> that <u>John</u> should leave me alone.
    c".   What I told <u>John</u> was that <u>he</u> should leave me alone.

In (32) I sketch a set of conditions on anaphoric relations that salvages what can be retained of Reinhart's approach while accommodating in a nondevious fashion (i.e., without ad hoc monkeying with the constituent structures) the problems for Reinhart's analysis that Carden and I have adduced. The account will of necessity be inhomogeneous—different restrictions evidently apply to different classes of cases:

(32) a. **Condition on cyclic outputs.** If a constituent X c-commands a coreferential constituent Y, Y must be an AD with X as antecedent.
      b. **Conditions on surface structure.** An AD may not c-command its antecedent if it (i) is a clausemate of the antecedent (i.e., is not separated from it by any S nodes) or (ii) precedes the antecedent.

There is a class of cases subject to a condition not on surface structures but on cyclic outputs (32a), illustrated in (29, 31). In view of the differences between the cases where AD and antecedent are clausemates and where they are not, I am forced to set up the two separate surface constraints given in (32b), (32bi) so as to exclude (33a) while not excluding (33a'), and (33bii) so as to exclude (33b) while not excluding (33b'):

(33) a.   *Near <u>John</u>'s mother, <u>he</u> saw a snake.
      a'.   Near the car that <u>John</u> was repairing, <u>he</u> saw a snake.
      b.   *<u>She</u> went home after <u>Mary</u> had finished the report.
      b'.   After <u>Mary</u> finished the report, <u>she</u> went home.

In the remainder of this section, I will take up two classes of sentences that appear at first to be counterexamples to (32) and ways in which they can be reconciled with (32). Consider first sentences such as (34a), whose derivation would presumably include a cyclic output corresponding to (34b), in which the pronoun c-commands its antecedent:

(34) a.   It was the diamonds that <u>John</u> had stolen that <u>he</u> was offering me.
      b. *<u>He</u> was offering me the diamonds that <u>John</u> had stolen.

There is a way of altering our conception of deep structures so as to make such examples conform to (32). In chapter 18 I argue that it is necessary to posit underlying structures in which each full nonsentential NP is external to its host S, more specifically, in which it is a sister of the S that is its "scope," e.g., the ambiguous (35a) would correspond to two deep structures ((35b, b'), given here with tenses and complementizers omitted), each indicating a determinate scope for the quantifier ((35b) corresponds to

the paraphrase "There is someone that John wants to kill," (35b′) to the
paraphrase "John wants to commit homicide (without necessarily having a
particular victim in mind)"):

(35) a. John wants to kill someone.

b.

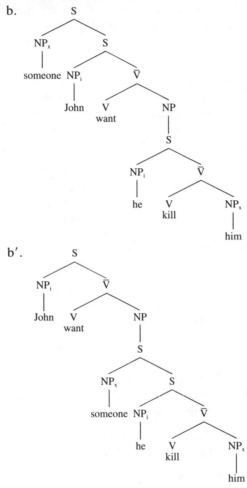

If such deep structures are accepted, along with a transformation (**Quantifier-lowering**) moving an "external NP" into the position occupied by
the corresponding variable, as is required if deep structures are as in (35),
(34a) can be given a deep structure as in (36) (where the pseudo-cleft construction, for which no specific deep structure has been proposed here, is
indicated schematically):

(36)

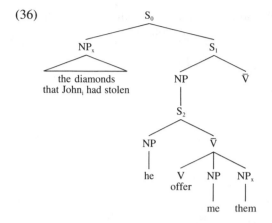

No cyclic output will violate (32a): the cyclic output of S_1 will be of the form *What he offered me was them$_x$*, which does not contain *John*, and in the cyclic output of S_0, derived by an application of Quantifier-lowering is essentially the surface form of (34a), in which *he* does not c-command *John*. However, setting up a deep structure with an external NP will not avoid any violation of (32) in the case of the noncleft (34b): there *he* c-commands *John* in surface structure, violating (32bii). If the principle of strict cyclicity is taken as applying not only to transformations but also to constraints such as (32), antecedents contained in a larger NP (with NP here taken in the narrow sense of a constituent of the form [Det $\bar{\text{N}}$], i.e., not a complement S) will never violate (32a) (that is, they can be excluded only in virtue of (32b)), because the application of Quantifier-lowering to a structure (37) will move the NP into S_{i+1}; since all of the material in the cyclic output of S_i will then be contained in S_{i+1}, the principle of strict cyclicity will prevent any cyclic transformations, or any cyclic constraints such as (32a), from applying on the S_i cycle to the output of Quantifier-lowering.

The "external NP" analysis makes it possible to reconcile (32) with another type of example that appears to conflict with it. In (37a–b), anaphoric relations in either direction are possible even though under the *Tough*-movement analysis, which I wish to maintain here, (37a) would have a derivation involving a cyclic output (37c) that violates (32a):

(37) a. <u>Bill</u>'s mother is easy for <u>him</u> to like.
    b. <u>His</u> mother is easy for <u>Bill</u> to like.
    c. *<u>He</u> likes <u>Bill</u>'s mother.

However, if NPs can appear external to their clauses, one can assign to

(37a) a deep structure roughly as in (38a), and the cyclic outputs of S_2 and S_1 would then be (38b–c), neither of which violates (32a):

(38) a.

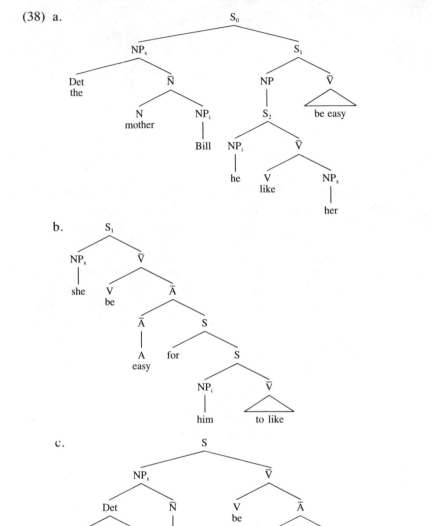

b.

c.

Thus, only the surface conditions (32b) constrain the anaphoric possibilities for the pair of NPs in (37a–b) on which our attention is focused. The same treatment will be appropriate for all cases in which either the pronoun or its antecedent is contained in a larger nonsentential NP, i.e., all such cases will be effectively exempt from the restriction in (32a), since an "external NP" analysis as in (38) will be available that will allow them to be absent from the relevant cyclic output.

The other class of examples that appear to conflict with (32) are familiar examples like (33b–b'), which were cited above as an embarrassment for Reinhart's treatment of anaphora, i.e., irrespective of whether a S-modifier precedes or follows the main S, the subject of the main S c-commands everything in the modifier both in surface structure and in the relevant cyclic output, and thus while (33b') escapes violation of (32b) in virtue of its word order, both it and (33b) should violate (32a). Here it may in fact be necessary to revise (32a) so as to build into its formulation a brute-force exclusion of S-modifiers. Conceivably such an exclusion could be made to follow from the principle of strict cyclicity if we take seriously the idea that a combination of constituent and modifier is "the same constituent as" the modified constituent, i.e., that in (39), with the $\overline{P}$ a modifier of S_{i+1}, S_i is the same S as S_{i+1}, but with a broader conception of what that S takes in:

(39) S_i

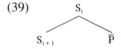

If the material of the $\overline{P}$ counts as being inside S_{i+1}, the principle of strict cyclicity would render (32a) inapplicable to S_i. It is tricky to keep this suggestion from having the undesirable consequence of making all cyclic transformations inapplicable to S_i, even the optional conversion of S-modifiers into $\overline{V}$-modifiers, which must not be prevented from applying. There is at least one way of avoiding that consequence, namely, to have the $\overline{P}$ acquire its status as a modifier in the course of the derivation, so that prior to its taking on the status of a modifier the principle of strict cyclicity would not prevent transformations from applying to S_i; it is not clear whether this alternative has any real advantage over simply excluding S-modifiers in the formulation of (32a).

e. Choice among Pronouns; Morphological Indeterminacy

In this section, we leave the problem of determining whether a particular position can be filled by a pronoun with an antecedent in such-and-such other position and turn to the quite different question of **what** pronoun can occupy a given position.

In the "classical" account of pronouns (see §11b), a pronoun was considered to be derived in all cases from a copy of its antecedent, and features of the antecedent, especially features of the head noun, in the case of pronouns with a NP antecedent, were taken to determine the choice of the pronoun. These policies led, e.g., Chomsky (1965) to posit deep structures in which a noun such as *neighbor* could bear a specification of either "masculine" or "feminine," so that the pronouns in such examples as (1) could be derived from constituents containing information such as was held to determine pronoun choice:

(1) a. My neighbor has injured himself.
    b. My neighbor has injured herself.

That particular analysis ascribes to the head noun of the antecedent a role which it often has, particularly in languages having grammatical gender:

(2) a. Me gustan ricos caldos, pero no sé como prepararlos/*las.
       'I like good-tasting soups, but I don't know how to make them'
       (*los* agrees with *caldos*, masculine plural)
    b. Me gustan ricas sopas, pero no sé como prepararlas/*los.
       (same translation; *las* agrees with *sopas*, feminine plural)

It is not obvious, however, that the noun in (1) plays any such role in determining the choice between *himself* and *herself,* and in fact the noun in such examples as (1) is clearly not **ambiguous** but only **unspecified** with regard to the masculine-feminine opposition, since different occurrences of *neighbor* count as identical irrespective of whether their purported referents are of the same or opposite sex:

(3) a. John can't stand his neighbor, and Fred can't ∅ either.
    b. I have a neighbor who once played third base for the White Sox, and I have one who was Miss Georgia of 1976.

Neither of these two sentences excludes the possibility that the neighbors are of opposite sex, as they would have to if the underlying occurrences of *neighbor* were determinately masculine or feminine, under the assumption that identity of the deleted or pronominalized constituent to its antecedent is necessary for the ADs in (3).

Alternatively, the choice of the pronoun in (1) could plausibly be held to reflect not features of the head noun of the antecedent but rather semantic information about the purported referent of the pronoun, i.e., whether it purports to refer to a man or to a woman. It is often difficult to say whether the choice of a particular pronoun is dictated by features of its antecedent (such as plural number or feminine gender) or by features of its referent (such as being a set of two or more entities or being a female person).

Often, especially in a language such as English, where nouns do not have grammatical gender, the relevant features of the antecedent and of the referent correspond to the same pronoun, e.g., if the pronoun in (4) is to have *those persons* as its antecedent, it will take the form *they* regardless of whether one takes the form as determined by the plural number of the NP *those persons* or by the fact that the referent of *they* is purportedly a set of persons:

(4) Those persons think that they are entitled to better treatment.

Sometimes, however, there is a conflict between the choice of pronoun that would be dictated by the form of the antecedent and that which would be dictated by the referent. For example, there are a few types of English nouns (*scissors, shears, tweezers; glasses, goggles; pants, trousers, shorts*) that are plural in grammatical number even when used to refer to one object of the sort in question (generally, an object that would be described as *a pair of X*). Here, the pronoun is normally plural, i.e., the choice of pronoun is determined by the singular or plural form of the head of the antecedent rather than by the number of objects in the denotation, or as I will henceforth say, the pronoun is chosen on the basis of **morphological number** rather than **semantic number:**

(5) a. The scissors that I bought are so dull that I'll have to sharpen them/*it.
 b. He kept taking his glasses off and putting them/*it back on again.
 c. Someone stole Sam's trousers and threw them/*it in the lake.

Part of the grammar of a language consists of a set of conventions for the resolution of conflicts between morphological number and semantic number (likewise, between morphological gender and semantic gender, etc.) whenever a linguistic form needs to be put in a particular number, gender, etc. (Besides choice of pronouns, this will also cover agreement of verbs with their subjects, of adjectives with the nouns that they modify, etc.; note, e.g., that the form *are* in (5a) [cf. . . . *is* . . .] is also chosen on the basis of morphological number.) The resolution of the conflict, however, is not always in favor of morphological number. Note the following cases in which semantic, not morphological, number determines what pronoun is used:

(6) a. A group of students left their/*its books here.
 b. John loves baked beans, but Mary hates it/%them.

The most obvious case in which the choice of a pronoun is sensitive to semantic rather than morphological number is that in which there is no linguistic antecedent and thus nothing, at least in the overt form of the sentence or discourse, for the pronoun to agree with in morphological features. For example, if a sentence of the form *Who be PRONOUN?* is used to inquire about the identity of whoever has just unexpectedly entered the room, it will take the form (7a) if used with reference to two or more persons, (7b) if used with reference to one male human being, and (7c) if used with reference to one female human being:

(7) a. Who are they?
  b. Who is he?
  c. Who is she?

Even in such cases, though, there is sometimes a morphological basis for the number and gender assigned to the pronoun. Tasmowski-de Ryck and Verluyten (1984) point out that the antecedentless pronoun in both French and English is normally the one whose number and gender are that of the noun by which one "standardly" refers to[17] an object of the sort of question, e.g.:

(8) a. Put them/?it on. (with reference to trousers)
  a′. Put it/*them on. (with reference to a shirt)
  b. Tu n'arriveras jamais à la/*le faire entrer dans la voiture.
    'You'll never manage to get it [a table] into the car.'
    (feminine pronoun, corresponding to feminine *la table*)
  b′. Tu n'arriveras jamais à le/*la faire entrer dans la voiture.
    (same translation, but with reference to a desk; masculine pronoun, corresponding to masculine *le bureau*)

Another case in which pronoun choice reflects semantic number rather than just morphological number is that of coordinate NPs. Whether a NP of the form *NP and NP* is treated as singular or plural depends on whether the conjuncts purport to refer to the same individual or not. Most often they refer to different individuals and the coordinate NP is treated as plural, but there are also cases as in (9b), where the conjuncts purport to be coreferential and the coordinate NP is treated as singular:

(9) a. Her husband and her lover said that they couldn't live without her.
  b. Her longtime companion and the future editor of her papers was happy to give his approval to her request. (Adapted from Quirk et al. 1972:362)

In the literature that has been alluded to so far in this section, pronouns are taken always to be **determinate** with regard to number and gender (and person and any other features that distinguish among pronouns). In the remainder of this section I will take up seriously the possibility that pronouns in at least some stages of derivations may be unspecified with regard to some or all of these features, i.e., the possibility of syntactic structures containing items that are pronouns but are not determinately singular or determinately plural, do not belong determinately to any one gender, etc. One consideration that makes an analysis in terms of indeterminate pronouns attractive is that such transformations as Quantifier-float may alter what the antecedent of a pronoun is and concomitantly alter what form it is appropriate for a given pronoun to have. For example, while a NP with the qualifier *each* is always singular, the NP that becomes subject through the application of Quantifier-Float to *each* is normally plural, and a pronoun with the subject as antecedent is accordingly respectively singular or plural.[18]

(10) a. Each of the boys admires his/*their teachers.
      b. The boys each admire their/*his teachers.

Earlier in this chapter we argued against the idea that a copy of the antecedent must underlie every pronoun. While we did not determine precisely which pronouns were "derived anaphora" and which were "essential anaphora," it is fairly clear that the pronouns in (10) must be essential anaphora—there is no plausible deep structure in which *his* or *their* is a repetition of the antecedent NP. We have spoken as if essential anaphora appear **as such** in deep structure, but we have not been clear about whether "as such" means simply a pronoun of the type in question or the specific form that the pronoun takes in the surface structure of the sentence. Examples like (10) provide a reason for adopting the former alternative, which would allow us to set up a single underlying structure shared by (10a) and (10b), containing a pronoun that is unspecified for number, gender, and person, with the form of the pronoun chosen on the basis of features of its surface antecedent, so that the pronoun would be singular in the case of (10a) and plural in the case of (10b).

Another possible case of an item that is unspecified for number in underlying structure emerges from a consideration of the relationship between the reciprocal pronoun *each other* and paraphrases in which it corresponds to *each . . . the other(s):*

(11) a.   The boys hate each other.
      a'. Each of the boys hates the other.
      a". Each of the boys hates the others.
      b.   The two/three boys helped each other.
      b'. Each of the two boys helped the other/*others.
      b". Each of the three boys helped the others/*other.

One can paraphrase (11a) with either (11a') or (11a"), but both paraphrases are more specific than (11a) with regard to how many boys are referred to:

(11a′) is appropriate only when exactly two boys are referred to, (11a″) only when more than two boys are referred to. This distinction is brought out more clearly in (11b–b″), where *each other* is appropriate regardless of whether *two boys* or *three boys* occurs, but *the other* combines only with *two boys* and *the others* with *three boys*. Suppose that we adopt the suggestion of Dougherty (1970–71) that *each other* is derived from a structure containing *each . . . the other(s)* by optional detachment of *each* from its NP and replacement of *the* in *the other(s)* by it. Since no distinction between singular and plural forms is allowed in *each other*, this would mean that unless an underlying structure in which *other* is unspecified for number is allowed, sentences like (11a) would be ambiguous with regard to whether *other* has underlying singular or plural number (thus, whether *the boys* refers to two or to more than two boys), rather than just unspecified. But the former alternative is untenable, since the supposedly singular *each other* and the supposedly plural one act as identical with regard to transformations calling for identity:

(12) Mary and Susan helped each other, and Tom, Dick, and Harry did ∅ too.

Thus, to accept the suggested derivation of *each other,* we must allow instances of *other* that underlie *each other* to be unspecified with regard to number.

f. Conditions on the Use of Some Other ADs

This section will be devoted to a brief discussion of the syntactic constraints on a number of ADs that have not been dealt with in detail so far in this book. Let us begin with **reflexive pronouns.** There is a common misconception that the antecedent of a reflexive pronoun must be the subject of its clause. While such a constraint in fact holds for many languages, it is not true of English, which allows not only a subject as an antecedent, as in (1a), but also a direct object, as in (1b), or in a very restricted class of cases, the object of a preposition, as in (1c):

(1) a. I told John about myself.
     b. John asked Mary about herself.
     c. I talked to John about himself.

The antecedent of a reflexive in English cannot be part of a larger NP:

(2) a. *[John's mother] admires himself.
     b. *I told [a story about Amy] to herself.

The reflexive usually must be a **clausemate** of its antecedent, though there is a limited class of cases in which a reflexive is (optionally) possible in a clause subordinate to the antecedent:

(3) a. *<u>Hilda</u> said [that <u>herself</u> was angry at us].
 b. *I told <u>Fred</u> [that we were angry at <u>himself</u>].
 c. [That pictures of <u>him(self)</u> are hanging in the post office] doesn't bother <u>Lou</u>.

The restrictions noted in connection with (2) and (3) are quite similar to one another: in both cases the reflexive and its antecedent are required to be within a certain domain, rather than one outside it and the other inside it, the domain being a NP in the case of (2) and a S in the case of (3). There are in fact acceptable examples in which a reflexive and its antecedent are both within the same NP, just as long as neither is within a smaller NP:

(4) a. [<u>Sergei</u>'s denunciation of <u>himself</u>] shocked everyone.
 b. [<u>John</u>'s affection for <u>himself</u>] has no limits.
 b'. *[[<u>John</u>'s wife]'s affection for <u>himself</u>] has no limits.

It has just been suggested that the reason for the unacceptability of (4b') is that the antecedent is contained in a NP subordinate to the one that contains the reflexive: that the domain of the rule allowing the reflexive is here the NP *John's wife's affection for himself,* and that that rule may not make reference to proper parts of a S or NP contained within that domain. What about the reverse kind of case, that in which it is not the antecedent but the reflexive that is contained in a subordinate NP? Some relevant examples are given in (5):

(5) a. [<u>John</u>'s fascination with [pictures of <u>him(self)</u>]] is embarrassing.
 b. [<u>John</u>'s quarrels with [friends of *<u>him</u>/*<u>himself</u>]] disgust me.
 c. [<u>John</u>'s responses to [denunciations of <u>him</u>/*<u>himself</u>]] are unconvincing.

The acceptability of the examples evidently depends not just on the gross syntactic structure but also on the particular choice of nouns. Recall now that in the one example given so far in which a reflexive had an antecedent that was not its clausemate, namely, (3c), the reflexive was an adjunct to the same noun that appears in (5a). Let us see whether the same dependence of acceptability on the choice of the noun is exhibited in sentences like (3c):

(6) a. [That picture of <u>himself/him</u> are hanging in the post office] doesn't bother <u>Lou</u>. (= (3c))

   b. [That friends of *himself/*him have been hanged] doesn't bother
      Lou.
   c. [That denunciations of him/*himself were published in Pravda]
      doesn't bother Sergei.

The unacceptability of both versions of (5b) and (6b) can be attributed to a
restriction on "kinship" nouns such as *friend,* requiring that a pronoun
"object" be in the genitive form: *a friend of his.* (The genitive form is
usually preferred, but is not obligatory, when the "object" is a full NP: *a
friend of that woman('s)).* Let us then turn to the difference between *picture* and *denunciation.*

   Picture belongs to a class of nouns (generally referred to as **picture
nouns,** following Warshawsky 1965) that allow their "objects" to take a
reflexive form under less stringent conditions on the location of the antecedent than those usually in force.[19]

(7) a.   John saw a description of himself/him.
    a'. John saw a letter to him/*himself.
    b.   Mary collects portraits of herself/??her.
    b'. Mary collects invitations to ?her/*herself.

A reflexive with an antecedent outside of the given NP is most natural
when the NP is indefinite and the picture noun has no "subject":

(8) a.   ?John saw the description of himself.
    a'.   ??John saw a description of himself by Ann.
    a''.   ???John saw a description by Ann of himself.
    a'''.   *John saw Ann's description of himself.

The unacceptability of examples in which a reflexive in a NP with a subject
has an antecedent outside that NP can be interpreted as a preference for the
reflexive to have its antecedent within as small a domain as possible: in this
case the subject of the NP (*Ann* in (8a'–a''')) takes priority over anything
outside the NP as a possible antecedent for the reflexive.

   The relationship of the reciprocal pronoun *each other* to its antecedent
is subject to constraints similar to those observed with reflexives.

(9) a.   The boys asked me about each other.
    b.   I asked the boys about each other.
    c. *[The mothers of the boys] insulted each other.
    d.   I showed the boys pictures of each other.
(10) a.   [The prisoners' denunciations of each other] shocked me.
     a'. *The prisoners were shocked at [the warden's denunciations of
          each other].

b.   [Matisse's and Derain's portraits of each other] are on display in
the Tate Gallery.

b′. *[Matisse's and Derain's wives] had affairs with each other.

b″. Matisse and Derain had affairs with each other's wives.

One difference between reciprocal and reflexive pronouns in English is that
only reciprocals have a distinct genitive form:

(11) a.   Max and Rita plagiarized each other's work.

a′. Max$_i$ sold his$_i$/*himself's car.

It is not clear, though, that this difference needs to be taken note of in the
syntax of English rather than being treated as just a morphological difference (like the difference between *I,* which has a distinct accusative form
me, and *you,* which takes the same form regardless of whether nominative
or accusative case is called for). Perhaps *his* (likewise *her, their*) should be
regarded as indeterminate with respect to the feature "reflexive" and treated
as reflexive when it is in a context that would call for a reflexive (as in
(11a)), the way that *you* is treated as accusative when it appears as the object of a verb or preposition.

A more substantial difference between reciprocal and reflexive pronouns is that reciprocals sometimes are ambiguous with regard to whether
the antecedent is a clausemate of or in a higher S than the pronoun. For
example, (12a) is ambiguous between (12b), where the antecedent is the
understood subject of the complement S, and (12b′), where the antecedent
is the main clause subject:[20]

(12) a.   Reagan and Mondale claimed to have caused each other trouble.

b.   Reagan and Mondale claimed ((each: x in {Reagan, Mondale}) (x
caused the other trouble)), i.e., both claimed that each caused
the other trouble. (Reagan: "Walter, you and I caused each
other trouble"; Mondale: "That's right, Ron, we caused each
other trouble")

b′. (Each: x in {Reagan, Mondale}) (x claimed (x caused the other
trouble)), i.e., each claimed that he caused the other trouble.
(Reagan: "I caused you trouble, Walter"; Mondale: "And I
caused you trouble, Ron")

Under the analysis suggested in §11e, in which the *each* of *each other* is
the ordinary quantifier *each,* this ambiguity is not surprising: it is basically
an ambiguity in the scope of *each* and reflects the fact that quantifiers in a
subordinate S often are ambiguous with regard to whether that S or a superordinate one is the scope. Since a reflexive pronoun does not include a

quantifier in its meaning, it does not in itself create possibilities for scope ambiguity.

A third type of AD that is subject to different constraints than in the case of personal pronouns is **anaphoric epithets** (AEs):

(13) a.　　John borrowed $100 from me, and the bastard never paid me back.

b.　　*Sam said that the son of a bitch was mad at me.

c.　　I won't talk to John until the bastard apologizes to me.

c′.　　?John won't talk to you until the bastard feels like it.

d.　　When John was here, I told the bastard what I thought of him.

d′.　　?When the bastard was here, I told John what I thought of him.

d″.　　When John was here, the bastard insulted me.

d‴.　　??When the bastard was here, John insulted me.

d⁗.　　Although I've never met the son of a bitch, I have a very low opinion of Schwartz.

e.　　*George III collected portraits of the bastard.

e′.　　George III's nephew collected portraits of the bastard.

e″.　　Every portrait of George III is a poor likeness of the bastard.

e‴.　　People who knew George III couldn't stand the bastard.

f.　　That John wasn't invited didn't bother the son of a bitch.

f′.　　??That the son of a bitch wasn't invited didn't bother John.

The least acceptable examples in (13) are in general those in which the antecedent c-commands the AE (13b, c′, d‴, e), though that generalization does not account for the fact that (13f′) is worse than (13c′).

One account of the restrictions on AEs that is of particular note is that of Lasnik (1976). Lasnik attempted to derive the restrictions on AEs from a general requirement that a NP other than a pronoun not be coreferential with any NP that c-commands it,[21] as illustrated by the following examples:

(14) a.　　People who know Tom_i think Tom_i is a nice guy.

a′.　　*Tom_i thinks Tom_i is a nice guy.

This generalization draws a distinction between cases in which pronominalization is optional (e.g. (14a), where either occurrence of *Tom* could be replaced by a pronoun but neither need be) from cases in which it is obligatory (in the sense that with the indicated purported reference, a pronoun is required in place of the second occurrence of *Tom* in (14a′)), and at the same time provides an account of restrictions on AEs, provided that AEs are taken as not counting as pronouns for the purposes of the constraint: an AE will then violate the constraint if it is c-commanded by its antecedent.

EXERCISES

1. a. In (38c) of §11d, give examples of:
        i.   a node that commands but does not c-command the Det node.
        ii. two nodes such that neither c-commands the other.
    b. State how the notion of clausemate can be defined in terms of command.

2. For each of the following ADs, construct examples that will test whether it conforms to the Ross-Langacker proposal that forwards anaphoric relations are unrestricted and backwards anaphoric relations are subject to the constraint that the AD not command its antecedent:
    a. one (as in *New cars cost more than old ones*)
    b. else
    c. zero $\bar{\text{V}}$

3. Determine which criteria of being a derived or an essential AD each of the following ADs passes:
    a. clse
    b. the bastard
    c. zero $\bar{\text{N}}$, as in *Alice's car is bigger than Janet's Ø.*

In any given case, it need not be possible to apply all of the criteria. Do not be overly alarmed if the criteria sometimes give conflicting results.

4. Say which, if any, of the conditions in (33) of §11d each of the following examples violates, and say enough about each to justify your conclusion (e.g., if you claim that the sentence violates a constraint on surface structure, give at least the relevant details of its surface structure):
    a. *To Mary's room, John sent her.
    b. *Mary hit him with the stick that John had given her.
    c. ?Mary hit his brother with the stick that John had given her.
    d. *What I promised her was to give Mary a string of pearls.
    e. *His denunciation of John's mother shocked me.

5. Pick any two ADs that were not discussed in detail in this chapter, and make up appropriate examples to test whether the conclusions of §11d account adequately for their behavior.

6. In the definition of c-command given in §11d, the notion of "major category" was invoked. While this notion takes in $\bar{\text{A}}$ and $\bar{\text{P}}$, in fact only examples where the relevant major category was S, NP, or $\bar{\text{V}}$ were taken up (e.g., examples where an AD inside a NP or $\bar{\text{V}}$ was acceptable if the antecedent was outside the NP or $\bar{\text{V}}$). Make up examples that will test whether $\bar{\text{A}}$'s and $\bar{\text{P}}$'s in fact behave like NPs and $\bar{\text{V}}$s in this respect. Since $\bar{\text{P}}$s can be used in quite a broad range of syntactic roles, it cannot be taken for granted

that they will all behave alike; accordingly, you should include a diverse range of $\bar{\text{P}}$s in your examples.

7. Lasnik actually formulated the constraint on coreference with nonpronouns (discussed in connection with §11f (14)) not in terms of c-command but in terms of a relation that he called "kommand" for which only S- and NP-nodes serve as "bounding nodes" (i.e., a node X kommands a node Y if and only if the lowest S- or NP-node that dominates X also dominates Y). Construct examples that will best whether kommand or c-command is the more appropriate choice of a structural relation in terms of which to formulate this constraint.

8. Select three words that were mentioned in chapter 9 (text or exercises) as possible but not clear cases of coordinating conjunctions. For each, make up examples involving pronouns that will serve to test whether the putative coordinating conjunction behaves like one with regard to pronoun-antecedent relations.

9. In §10b, data were given about the acceptability (in one dialect) of various sentences having two negative words in the same $\bar{\text{V}}$. Different degrees of acceptability (* versus ??) were noted. Use the notion of c-command to formulate a hypothesis on what degree of deviance different examples will have. Make up example sentences that will serve to test that hypothesis. If you are, or have access to, a speaker of such a dialect, give acceptability judgments for your examples and indicate whether they confirm or conflict with your hypothesis.

10. Make up examples that will test whether the behavior of pronouns and antecedents in extraposed complements that was noted in §11b(8) is shared by pronouns and antecedents in extraposed relative clauses. Give examples both of relative clauses extraposed from a subject NP and relative clauses extraposed from a direct object NP. If the acceptability judgments of your examples justify any conclusion about how extraposed relative clauses fit into surface constituent structure (even a negative conclusion, e.g., that they aren't adjuncts to the $\bar{\text{V}}$), show how that is the case.

11. In all of the examples in chapter 11 that illustrate personal pronouns, the antecedent is "definite" (*John, the boss*). Make up analogs to a selection of these examples, using quantified NPs as antecedents (*every lawyer, most linguists;* where necessary, change the pronoun so that it will agree in number and gender with the antecedent, or alter the tense or the lexical items to make the putative meaning plausible). If you can discern any systematic difference between the conditions under which pronouns with definite antecedents and pronouns with quantified antecedents are acceptable, indicate what you think that difference is. (This question will be taken up in §18d.)

12. For any language other than English, construct examples with personal pronouns parallel to the examples in §11d and determine to what extent §11d(32) accurately describes the restrictions on the use of personal pronouns in that language.

13. Two analyses of *one* as in (i) immediately suggest themselves:

    i. John bought a car, and Mary bought one too.

Perhaps it is the AD that stands for a repeated $\bar{N}$, in which case (i) goes through a stage with *a one* and the indefinite article of the latter is deleted. Alternatively, perhaps sentences like (i) involve deletion of a repeated $\bar{N}$ and *one* is a "strong form" that the indefinite article takes when it stands alone: *bought a car* → *bought a ∅* → *bought one ∅*. Make as good a case as you can for one or other of these alternatives. You may wish to bring in the following considerations:

    a. what happens if the $\bar{N}$ is plural.

    b. the possibility that *that/those* is a strong form of the definite article in such sentences as *My library is bigger than that/those of my predecessors.*

NOTES

1. For generality's sake, I should actually say "from constituents **containing** a copy of the antecedent," so as to allow, e.g., for an analysis in which *other than X* underlies *else,* where *X* is a copy of the antecedent.

2. I use the term "purported reference" to emphasize that what is relevant is whether the NPs **purport** to refer to the same individual, not whether the individuals that they refer to happen in fact to be identical.

3. Here I am considerably oversimplifying the history of transformational analyses of ADs. In the work where referential indices were introduced (Chomsky 1965:145–6), they were in fact treated (erroneously) as attached to Ns rather than to NPs.

4. There is in fact a limited class of cases where English allows reflexives to have antecedents in superordinate clauses, though the use of the reflexive in such cases in optional:

    [That pictures of himself$_i$/him$_i$ had been hung in the post office] shocked John$_i$.

See Jackendoff 1972 and Cantrall 1972 for discussion of such sentences.

English is unusual in allowing a nonsubject to be the antecedent of a reflexive (as in the interpretation of (6a) where *himself* refers to Bill). This is one of several respects in which reflexive pronouns differ from language to language. Some other such differences among languages are that Japanese and Korean allow reflexives in complement clauses to have an antecedent in the main clause, as in (6b: *herself*), and that Russian allows a reflexive in a nonfinite $\bar{V}$ to have the subject of the main clause as its antecedent, as in (6c: *herself*).

5. For Ross, sentences with nominalizations (see §12d) such as *the realization . . .* had similar derivations to those with *realizing . . . ;* the reader can verify that the acceptability of analogs to (10, 13, 14a–a′) parallels the judgments reported here. An example containing a nominalization rather than a complement is required here so that the structure can accommodate *widespread*.

6. Note that this argument depends on the assumption that the same Pronominalization transformation would be responsible for both pronouns in (17a). In §11d, we will in effect adopt an analysis in which the pronominalization affecting *John* and that affecting *Mary* in (17a) are two separate rules.

7. Or at least, they would not be **in general.** Lakoff's approach does not exclude the possibility that some personal pronouns are derived from copies of their antecedents and others not, and Lakoff himself gave examples like the following as evidence that *it* with a S antecedent **is** derived from a copy of its antecedent:

*That John maintains it suggests <u>that Mary believes **it.**</u>

8. This does not presuppose that "essential ADs" are necessarily present **as such** in deep structure, since it allows for the possibility of, e.g., a single type of deep structure element underlying two or more different types of AD and not being indentifiable with any specific one of them. In Hankamer and Sag's original terminology, essential ADs were called deep anaphora and derived ADs were called surface anaphora. I have replaced this terminology to avoid confusion of "surface AD" with the more obvious interpretation "AD in surface structure."

9. It is not an a priori certainty that linguistic structures must be finite, since a finite description is sometimes sufficient to fully characterize an infinite structure, and thus at least some infinite structures are in principle available to finite brains.

10. The notions of "sense" and "reference" were introduced into modern philosophy of language by Frege 1892, though the notions also figured in medieval logic. The sense of an expression is what the expression "says," the reference is what it purports to "refer to," e.g., in (i) the expressions *the President* and *the bastard* have the same reference (i.e., the individuals that they purport to refer to arc the same) but different sense (i.e., they say different things about that individual: the one says that he holds a certain office, the other says that the speaker has a certain negative attitude towards him).

    i. The President says a lot of stupid things, but the bastard usually gets away with it.

11. With an interpretation in which *an astronaut* is not in the scope of the negation (an interpretation paraphraseable as "Studs Terkel has never interviewed a certain astronaut"), (5a) is of course acceptable, as would be (4a). Such an interpretation is not possible for (5b) (you'd have to express it differently, say, "Fred doesn't pick up certain girls . . ."); an interpretation of the second clause in (5b), where it means "Girls (not: those girls) are generally stunningly beautiful" is pos-

sible, but (5b) would still be odd in virtue of the peculiarity of conjoining two sentences that do not really add up to a coherent whole.

12. See Fauconnier 1985 for a highly perceptive account of this phenomenon in these terms, and of its surprisingly broad ramifications.

13. The oddness of forwards pronominalization in (3a) is noteworthy. Kuno (1972) suggests that a pronoun rather than a full NP must be used when it denotes a person whose thoughts are represented by the clause in which it appears, i.e., that a pronoun must be used where a direct quote of the thought that the clause represents would involve *I* or *we*. Note that there is no oddity in parallel sentences in which the clause in question does not represent the person's thoughts:

> That <u>John</u> had lost was concealed from <u>him</u>.
> That <u>John</u> is so kind endears <u>him</u> to me.

Kuno's proposal also accounts for the oddity of §11b (19b):

> *Realizing that <u>John</u> was incompetent seemed to <u>him</u> to be bothering Mary.

Since the complement of *seem to him* expresses "his" thoughts, a pronoun is required any place in the complement that "he" is referred to. Note that this analysis defuses Ross's explanation of the oddity of:

> *Realizing that <u>John</u> was incompetent didn't bother <u>him</u>.

Under Kuno's approach it is immaterial what the underlying subject of *realize* is, as long as *realizing that John was incompetent* is in a context where it expresses John's thoughts.

14. For this definition to work, a node must be treated as dominating itself: if the lowest S-node dominating X^1 has no modifiers, the path must not go any higher than that S-node. I sidestep here the important question of how "S" must be interpreted in this definition, i.e., which constituents that are Ss on only some of the dimensions of S-hood discussed in chapter 7 are relevant to identifying "the lowest S-node such that. . . ."

15. The "c" of "c-command" stands for "constituent"; the notion of command defined in (10) might be renamed "S-command." "C-command" and "S-command" are two of a vast number of notions of "command" that can be defined by different choices of the condition that characterizes the "bounding node." An exhaustive taxonomy of such relations is given in Barker and Pullum (1987). The definition in (14) is not Reinhart's but incorporates a revision (like that in (10)) to make it accord with the conceptions of constituent structure and category adopted here, which differ considerably from Reinhart's.

16. I assume here the structures argued for in chapter 13, in which a restrictive relative clause is an adjunct of an $\bar{N}$.

17. The notion of "noun by which one standardly refers to X" has to be explicated in terms of the notion of "basic level of a taxonomy" (Berlin 1978). "Car" is a basic-level concept, whereas superordinate concepts such as "motor vehicle" and subordinate concepts such as "station wagon" and "Chevrolet" are not. Thus, in

the French examples, it should be immaterial whether there is a masculine noun referring to the specific type of table that is to be loaded into the car: with regard to pronoun choice, *la table* is the relevant way of referring to a table.

18. I ignore here the interpretation of (10a) in which *their teachers* refers to the teachers of any or all of the boys; the asterisks in both examples relate only to an interpretation involving the propositional function "x admires x's teachers."

19. Cantrall (1972) argues that the use of reflexives is favored by interpretations in which the judgment of identity between referents of pronoun and antecedent reflects the point of view of the person referred to. Such a distinction is fairly clear in such examples as:

A huge portrait of himself is hanging in Reagan's/*Lincoln's bedroom.

The identity of the subject of the portrait here can reflect Reagan's point of view but not Lincoln's. This hypothesis provides an explanation of why picture nouns provide a particularly congenial environment for reflexives: it is easy to impose on a depiction the viewpoint of a particular viewer.

20. This point is made in Lebeaux (1983). The existence of interpretations like (12b) appears to have been pointed out first by Sampson (1980: 186).

21. The structural relation in terms of which Lasnik stated the constraint was in fact not precisely c-command, though the difference is not relevant to the particular examples under discussion here. The relation that figured in Lasnik's account is taken up in exercise 7.

IIIIII *Selected Wrong Answers to Exercises*

Chapter 2

EXERCISE 1. This question asks what nodes are the sisters, etc., of a certain node. Don't misinterpret it as asking you where the sisterhood, motherhood, etc., relations hold within the structure dominated by that node. Note also that you are asked for nodes, not for categories, and you really aren't answering the question if you say, e.g., "NP and V are sisters of S." When there are two or more nodes with the same category, naming a category doesn't uniquely identify a node— you need to specify **which** S-node, NP-node, etc., you are referring to; here you can resort to ad hoc devices to your heart's content, e.g., put subscripts on all the nodes and identify the nodes in terms of the subscripts.

Chapter 3

EXERCISE 1. The examples that you construct should have a chance for survival, in the sense that only as much of the two parts should be identical as is going to be deleted from one of them. A sentence such as

   *John gave flowers to Mary, and Bill did Ø to Mary too.

does not really test whether *give flowers* is a constituent, since even if it is, there would be no point in retaining the repeated *to Mary* when you could delete it along with *give flowers*. To test whether *give flowers* is a constituent, you should choose examples in which the retained constituents contrast with their counterparts in the antecedent clause.

EXERCISE 2. Sentences like the following are irrelevant to this exercise, since coordination is irrelevant to their acceptability:

   John gave Mary a book, and Bill did Ø too.

VP-deletion applies without regard to whether the clauses containing the two identical VPs are conjoined with one another, which means that the acceptability of this example is not a fact about conjoining but only a fact about VP-deletion and is thus relevant to exercise 1 but not exercise 2.

Chapter 5

EXERCISE 2. Be sure that what you consider is a complement and not one of the various adverbial expressions that takes the form of an infinitive or participial VP. For example, the infinitive in (i) is a "purpose adverbial" rather than a complement, as evidenced by such facts as that it can be preposed (ii) and that it combines not just with specific verbs but with what on other grounds are entire VPs, even VPs that themselves contain an infinitive complement (iii):

    i.   John works to earn money.
    ii.   To earn money, John works.
         *To earn money, John tries/intends/seems.
    iii.   John put flowers in the vase to brighten the room.
         John [tried to finish the job] to please his boss.

Chapter 6

EXERCISE 6C. Don't make the error of confusing the direct quotation (which, by what was said in the text, is a "main clause") with the "frame" (*John said . . .*) in which it is quoted. The "frame" is not itself a direct quotation and can be made subordinate simply by embedding it as, e.g., a complement.

Chapter 7

EXERCISE 1. Strictly speaking, in 1f and 1g "pass the exam" is predicated of a variable ("Only for x = your brother, x passed the exam"). Avoid the error of saying that it is *your brother* rather than *only your brother* that takes the place of the argument of the predicate and thus is a NP "by succession."

EXERCISE 3. Your answer to this is relevant only if the question posed here arises, i.e., the constructions that you cite must provide at least the logical possibility of the occurrence of a complementizer.

Chapter 8

EXERCISE 1. Keep in mind that any of the Ss in the deep structures considered here can in principle serve as a locus for conjoining, and you are not justified in assuming that, e.g., it is necessarily the topmost S that is conjoined in deep structure. Sometimes conjoining of one of the embedded

Ss will yield a semantically more plausible structure than will conjoining of the topmost S.

Chapter 9

EXERCISE 2. The direction to make the maximum use of CR means only that if you can derive a conjoined constituent from conjoined Ss, you should do so. It does not mean that constituents as large as possible should be conjoined in deep structure. You have to decide **which** S is the locus of conjoining, and it could just as easily be a deeply embedded S as the top-most S. Indeed, in many cases there will be semantic reasons why the conjoining will have to be of an embedded S; for example, the deep structure of (1e) isn't something corresponding to *They don't believe John left the country or they don't believe the police have arrested John,* because that isn't what (1e) means.

||||||| *References*

Abbreviations

BLS	Berkeley Linguistics Society
CLS	Chicago Linguistic Society
FL	*Foundations of Language*
IJAL	*International Journal of American Linguistics*
IULC	Indiana University Linguistics Club
JL	*Journal of Linguistics*
LACUS	Linguistic Association of Canada and the United States
Lg.	*Language*
LI	*Linguistic Inquiry*
L&P	*Linguistics and Philosophy*
NELS	Northeastern Linguistic Society
NLLT	*Natural Language and Linguistic Theory*

Ajdukiewicz, Kazimierz. 1935. Über die syntaktische Konnexität. *Studia Philosophica* 1:1–27.

Akmajian, Adrian. 1977. The complement structure of perception verbs in an autonomous syntax framework. In Culicover, Wasow, and Akmajian 1977: 427–60.

———. 1984. Sentence types and the form-function fit. *NLLT* 2:1–23.

Akmajian, Adrian, and Tom Wasow. 1975. The constituent structure of VP and AUX and the position of the verb *be*. *Linguistic Analysis* 1:205–45.

Akmajian, Adrian, Susan Steele, and Tom Wasow. 1979. The category AUX in universal grammar. *LI* 10:1–64.

Anderson, Stephen R. 1969. West Scandinavian vowel systems and the ordering of phonological rules. Ph.D. thesis, M.I.T.

———. 1974. *The Organization of Phonology*. New York: Academic Press.

———. 1976. Concerning the notion "base component of a transformational grammar." In McCawley 1976b:113–28.

Anderson, Stephen R., and Paul Kiparsky, eds. 1973. *A Festschrift for Morris Halle*. New York: Holt, Rinehart & Winston.

Ashton, E. O. 1947. *Swahili Grammar.* London: Longmans.

Austin, J. L. 1962. *How to Do Things with Words*. Oxford: Clarendon.

Back, Emmon. 1970. Problominalization. *LI* 1:121–2.

———. 1977. Review of Postal 1974. *Lg.* 53:621–53.

———. 1979. Control in Montague grammar. *LI* 10:515–31.

Baker, C.L. 1970a. Notes on the description of English questions: The role of an abstract question morpheme. *FL* 6:197–219. Also in Seuren 1974a:123–42.

———. 1970b. Double negatives. *LI* 1:169–86.

———. 1984. Two observations on British English *do*. *LI* 15:155–56.

Banfield, Ann. 1982. *Unspeakable Sentences*. London: Routledge & Kegan Paul.

Barker, Chris, and Geoffrey K. Pullum. 1987. The smallest command relation. Paper read at annual meeting, Linguistic Society of America.

Berlin, Brent. 1978. Ethnobiological classification. In Rosch and Lloyd 1978: 11–26.

Berman, Arlene. 1973a. A constraint on tough-movement. CLS 9:34–43.

———. 1973b. Triple *-ing*. *LI* 4:401–3.

———. 1974. Infinitival relative constructions. CLS 10:37–46.

Bever, Thomas. 1970. The cognitive basis for linguistic structures. In J. Hayes, ed., *Cognition and the Development of Language*, 279–352. New York: Wiley.

Bing, Janet. 1979. Aspects of English prosody. Ph.D. thesis, Univ. of Massachusetts, Amherst.

Binnick, Robert I. 1968. On the nature of the "lexical item." CLS 4:1–13.

Boertien, Harmon. 1979. Ordering auxiliaries as main verbs. *Glossa* 13:81–114.

———. 1986. Constituent structure of double modals. In Michael B. Montgomery and Guy Bailey, eds., *Language Variety in the South*, 294–318. University, AL: University of Alabama Press.

Bolinger, Dwight. 1957. *Interrogative Structures in American English*. Publication 28 of American Dialect Society. University, AL: Univ. of Alabama Press.

———. 1961. Syntactic blends and other matters. *Lg.* 37:366–81.

———. 1967a. Adjectives in English: Attribution and predication. *Lingua* 18: 1–34.

———. 1967b. The imperative in English. In *To Honor Roman Jakobson*, 336–62. The Hague: Mouton. Revised version in Bolinger 1977:152–99.

———. 1967c. Apparent constituents in surface structure. *Word* 23:47–56.

———. 1971. *The Phrasal Verb in English*. Cambridge, MA: Harvard Univ. Press.

———. 1974. On the passive in English. *LACUS Forum* 1:57–80.

———. 1977. *Form and meaning*. London: Longmans.

———. 1978. Yes-no questions are not alternative questions. In Hiz 1978:87–105.

———. 1979. The jingle theory of double *-ing*. In D. J. Allerton et al., eds., *Function and Context in Linguistic Analysis*, 41–56. Cambridge: Cambridge Univ. Press.

Borkin, Ann. 1972. Coreference and beheaded NP's. *Papers in Linguistics* 5: 28–45. Reprinted in Borkin 1984.

———. 1975. Raising to object position. Ph.D. thesis, Univ. of Michigan. In Borkin 1984.

———. 1984. *Problems in Form and Function*. Norwood: Ablex.

Branden, Frank, and Lucy Seki. 1981. A note on COMP as a universal. *LI* 12: 659–65.

Bresnan, Joan W. 1970. On complementizers: Towards a syntactic theory of sentence types. *FL* 6:297–321.

———. 1972. Theory of complementation in English syntax. Ph.D. thesis, M.I.T.

———. 1973. Syntax of the comparative clause construction in English. *LI* 4: 275–343.

———. 1974. The position of certain clause particles in phrase structure. *LI* 5:614–19.

———. 1975. Comparative deletion and constraints on transformations. *Linguistic Analysis* 1:25–74.

Bresnan, Joan W., and Jane Grimshaw. 1978. The syntax of free relatives in English. *LI* 9:331–91.

Bull, George. 1963. *Tense, Time, and the Verb*. Berkeley and Los Angeles: Univ. of California Press.

Burt, Marina K. 1971. *From Deep Structure to Surface Structure*. New York: Harper & Row.

Cantrall, William. 1972. *Viewpoint, Reflexives, and the Nature of Noun Phrases*. The Hague: Mouton.

Carden, Guy. 1973. *English Quantifiers: Logical Structure and Linguistic Variation*. Tokyo: Taishukan.

———. 1982. Backwards anaphora in discourse context. *JL* 18:361–88.

———. 1986a. Blocked forwards coreference; unblocked forwards anaphora: Evidence for an abstract model of coreference. *CLS* 22:262–76.

———. 1986b. Blocked forward coreference: implications of the acquisition data. In B. Lust, ed., *Studies in the Acquisition of Anaphora*, 1:319–57. Dordrecht: Reidel.

Carlson, Greg. 1981. Distribution of free choice *any*. *CLS* 17:8–23.

———. 1983. Marking constituents. Heny and Richards 1983, 1:49–68.

Cattell, Ray. 1973. Negative transportation and tag questions. *Lg.* 49:612–39.

Chomsky, Noam A. 1957. *Syntactic Structures*. The Hague: Mouton.

———. 1964. Current issues in linguistic theory. In Fodor and Katz 1964: 479–518.

———. 1965. *Aspects of the Theory of Syntax*. Cambridge, MA: MIT Press.

———. 1968. *Language and Mind*. New York: Harcourt Brace Jovanovich.

———. 1970a. Remarks on nominalization. In Jacobs and Rosenbaum 1970: 184–221. Reprinted in Chomsky 1972:11–61.

———. 1970b. Deep structure, surface structure, and semantic interpretation. In Jakobson and Kawamoto 1970:52–91. Reprinted in Steinberg and Jakobovits 1971:183–216, and in Chomsky 1972:62–119.

———. 1972. *Studies on Semantics in Generative Grammar*. The Hague: Mouton.

———. 1973. Conditions on transformations. In Anderson and Kiparsky 1973: 232–86. Reprinted in Chomsky 1977a:81–160.

———. 1974. *Reflections on Language*. New York: Pantheon.

———. 1977a. *Essays on Form and Interpretation*. Amsterdam: North-Holland.

———. 1977b. On WH-movement. Culicover, Wasow, and Akmajian 1977: 71–132.

———. 1981. *Lectures on Government and Binding*. Dordrecht: Foris.

———. 1982. *Some Concepts and Consequences of the Theory of Government and Binding*. Cambridge, MA: MIT Press.

———. 1986. *Barriers*. Cambridge, MA: MIT Press.

Chomsky, Noam A., and Howard Lasnik. 1977. Filters and Control. *LI* 8:425–504.

Chung, Sandra. 1982. Unbounded dependencies in Chamorro grammar. *LI* 13: 39–77.

Clark, Herbert H., and Thomas Carlson. 1982. Hearers and speech acts. *Lg.* 58: 332–73.

Cole, Peter, ed. 1979. *Pragmatics.* Syntax and Semantics 9. New York: Academic Press.

Culicover, Peter, Thomas Wasow, and Adrian Akmajian. 1977. *Formal Syntax.* New York: Academic Press.

Cruttenden, Alan. 1981. Falls and rises: Meanings and universals. *JL* 17:77–91.

———. 1986. *Intonation.* Cambridge: Cambridge Univ. Press.

Davidson, Donald, and Gilbert Harman, eds. 1972. *The Semantics of Natural Language.* Dordrecht: Reidel.

Davison, Alice. 1980. Peculiar passives. *Lg.* 56:42–66.

de Rijk, Rudolf. 1987. *Euskara Batua.* University of Leiden, duplicated.

Dijk, Teun A. van. 1977. *Text and Context.* London: Longmans.

Dougherty, Ray C. 1970–71. A grammar of coordinate conjunction. *Lg.* 46: 850–98 and 47:298–339.

———. 1974. The syntax and semantics of "each other" constructions. *FL* 12: 1–47.

Dowty, David. 1979. Dative movement and Thomason's extensions of Montague Grammar. In S. Davis and M. Mithun, eds., *Linguistics Philosophy, and Montague Grammar,* 153–222. Austin: Univ. of Texas Press.

Dowty, David, Robert Wall, and Stanley Peters. 1981. *Introduction to Montague Semantics.* Dordrecht: Reidel.

Elliott, Dale. 1971. The grammar of emotive and exclamatory sentences in English. Ph.D. thesis, Ohio State Univ.

———. 1974. Toward a grammar of exclamations. *FL* 11:231–46.

Elliott, Dale, Stanley Legum, and Sandra A. Thompson. 1969. Syntactic variation in linguistic data. CLS 5:52–59.

Emonds, Joseph. 1970. Root and structure-preserving transformations. Ph.D. thesis, MIT.

———. 1976. *A Transformational Approach to English Syntax.* New York: Academic Press.

———. 1979. Appositive clauses have no properties. *LI* 10:211–43.

Engdahl, Elisabet. 1983. Parasitic gaps. *L&P* 6:5–24.

Ernst, Thomas. 1984. Towards an integrated theory of adverb position in English. Ph.D. thesis, Indiana Univ., distributed by IULC.

Fauconnier, Gilles. 1985. *Mental Spaces.* Cambridge, MA: MIT Press.

Fiengo, Robert, and Howard Lasnik. 1973. The logical structure of reciprocal sentences in English. *FL* 9:447–68.

Fillmore, Charles J. 1963. The position of embedding transformations in a grammar. *Word* 19:208–31.

———. 1966. A proposal concerning English prepositions. *Georgetown University Round Table* 17:19–33.

————. 1968. The case for case. In E. Bach and R. Harms, eds., *Universals in Linguistic Theory,* 1–88. New York: Holt, Rinehart & Winston.

Fillmore, Charles J., and D. T. Langendoen, eds. 1971. *Studies in Linguistic Semantics.* New York: Holt, Rinehart & Winston.

Fodor, Jerry A., and Herrold Katz, eds. 1964. *The Structure of Language.* Englewood Cliffs, N.J.: Prentice Hall.

Fraser, Bruce. 1970. Some remarks on the action nominalization in English. In Jacobs and Rosenbaum 1970:83–98.

————. 1976. *The Verb-Particle Construction in English.* Tokyo: Taishukan.

Frege, Gottlob. 1892. Über Sinn und Bedeutung. *Zeitschrift für Philosophie und philosophische Kritik* 100:25–50. English translation in P. T. Geach and M. Black, *Translations from the Philosophical Writings of Gottlob Frege* (Oxford: Blackwell, 1952), 56–78.

Fujimura, Osamu. 1973. *Three Dimensions of Linguistic Research.* Tokyo: TEC.

Geach, Peter T. 1962. *Reference and Generality.* Ithaca: Cornell Univ. Press.

————. 1968. Quine's syntactical insights. *Synthese* 19:118–29.

Gee, James Paul, 1977. Comments on Akmajian 1977. Culicover, Wasow, and Akmajian 1977:461–84.

Goffman, Erving. 1974. *Frame Analysis.* New York: Harper.

————. 1978. Response cries. *Lg.* 54:787–815. Reprinted in Goffman 1981: 78–123.

————. 1979. Footing. *Semiotica* 25:1–29. Reprinted in Goffman 1981:124–59.

————. 1981. *Forms of talk.* Philadelphia: Univ. of Pennsylvania Press.

Goldsmith, John. 1981. Complementizers and root sentences. *LI* 12:541–74.

Goodman, Nelson. 1951. *The Structure of Appearance.* Cambridge, MA: Harvard Univ. Press.

Green, Georgia. 1973. The logical expression of emphatic conjunction: Theoretical implications. *FL* 10:197–248.

————. 1974. *Semantics and Syntactic Regularity.* Bloomington: Indiana Univ. Press.

————. 1976. Main clause phenomena in subordinate clauses. *Lg.* 52:382–97.

Grice, H. Paul. 1973. Logic and conversation. In P. Cole and J. L. Morgan, eds., *Speech Acts,* 41–58. Syntax and Semantics 3. New York: Academic Press.

Grimshaw, Jane. 1979. Complement selection and the lexicon. *LI* 10:279–326.

Grinder, John. 1976. *On Deletion Phenomena in English.* The Hague: Mouton.

Grinder, John, and Paul M. Postal. 1971. Missing antecedents. *LI* 2:269–312.

Grosu, Alexander. 1976. A note on subject raising to object and Right Node Raising. *LI* 7:642–45.

Grosu, Alexander, and Sandra A. Thompson. 1977. Constraints on the distribution of NP clauses. *Lg.* 53:104–51.

Hall, Robert A., Jr. 1973. The transferred epithet in P. G. Wodehouse. *LI* 4: 92–94.

Hankamer, Jorge. 1974. On pruning NP and VP. *Papiere zur Linguistik* 7:26–49.

Hankamer, Jorge, and Ivan Sag. 1976. Deep and surface anaphora. *LI* 7:391–428.

Harris, Zellig S. 1957. Cooccurrence and transformation in linguistic structure. *Lg.* 33:263–340. Page references to reprint in Fodor and Katz 1964:153–210.

Hasegawa, Kinsuke. 1968. The passive construction in English. *Lg.* 44:230–43.

Heinämäki, Orvokki. 1974. Semantics of English temporal connectives. Ph.D. thesis, Univ. of Texas, Austin.

Heny, Frank. 1973. Sentence and predicate modifiers in English. In J. Kimball, ed., Syntax and Semantics 2:217–45. New York: Academic Press.

Heny, Frank, and Barry Richards, eds. 1983. *Linguistic Categories.* Dordrecht: Reidel.

Hetzron, Robert. 1975. Where the grammar fails. *Lg.* 51:859–72.

Higginbotham, James. 1980. Pronouns and bound variables. *LI* 11:679–708.

Higgins, F. Roger. 1973. On J. Emonds's analysis of Extraposition. In J. Kimball, ed., Syntax and Semantics 2:149–95. New York: Academic Press.

Hinds, John. 1977. Paragraph structure and pronominalization. *Papers in Linguistics* 10:77–99.

Hinds, Marilyn. 1974. Doubleplusgood polarity items. CLS 10:259–68.

Hiz, Henry. 1978. *Questions.* Dordrecht: Reidel.

Hofmann, T. R. 1966. Past tense replacement and the modal system. Harvard University report NSF-20. Reprinted in McCawley 1976b:85–100.

Holisky, Dee. 1974. Negative polarity. M.A. thesis, Univ. of Chicago.

Hooper, Joan, and Sandra A. Thompson. 1973. On the applicability of root transformations. *LI* 4:465–98.

Hopper, Paul J., and Sandra A. Thompson. 1980. Transitivity in grammar and discourse. *Lg.* 56:251–99.

Horn, George. 1974. The noun phrase constraint. Ph.D. thesis, Univ. of Massachusetts, Amherst.

———. 1985. Raising and complementation. *Linguistics* 23:813–50.

Horn, Larry. 1979. Remarks on Neg-raising. In Cole 1979:129–220.

———. 1985. Metalinguistic negation and pragmatic ambiguity. *Lg.* 61:121–74.

Hornstein, Norbert. 1984. *Logic as Grammar.* Cambridge, MA: MIT Press.

Huang, James. 1984. On the distribution and reference of empty pronouns. *LI* 15:531–74.

———. 1987. Existential sentences in Chinese and (in)definiteness. In Reuland and ter Meulen 1987:226–53.

Huddleston, Rodney. 1984. *Introduction to the Grammar of English.* Cambridge: Cambridge Univ. Press.

Hudson, Richard A. 1976a. *Arguments for a Non-Transformational Grammar.* Chicago: Univ. of Chicago Press.

———. 1976b. Conjunction reduction, Gapping, and Right node raising. *Lg.* 52:535–62.

———. 1982. Incomplete conjuncts. *LI* 13:547–50.

———. 1984. *Word Grammar.* Oxford: Blackwell.

Ikeuchi, Masayuki. 1972. Adverbial clauses in noun phrases. *Studies in English Linguistics* 1:96–101.

Ishihara, Roberta. 1982. A study of absolute phrases in English within the

Government-Binding framework. Ph.D. thesis, University of California at San Diego.

Ioup, Georgette. 1975. Some universals of quantifier scope. In John Kimball, ed., Syntax and Semantics 4:37–58. New York: Academic Press.

Iwakura, Kunihiro. 1976. Another constraint on sentential subjects. *LI* 7:646–52.

———. 1979. On surface filters and deletion rules. *Linguistic Analysis* 5:93–124.

Jackendoff, Ray S. 1971. Gapping and related rules. *LI* 2:21–35.

———. 1972. *Semantic Interpretation in Generative Grammar.* Cambridge, MA: MIT Press.

———. 1977. *X-Bar Syntax.* Cambridge, MA: MIT Press.

Jacobs, Roderick, and Peter S. Rosenbaum, eds. 1970. *Readings in English Transformational Grammar.* Boston: Ginn.

Jacobson, Pauline. 1982. Evidence for gaps. In Jacobson and Pullum 1982: 187–228.

Jacobson, Pauline, and Paul Neubauer. 1976. Rule cyclicity: Evidence from the intervention constraint. *LI* 7:429–61.

Jacobson, Pauline, and G. K. Pullum, eds. 1982. *The Nature of Syntactic Representation.* Dordrecht: Reidel.

Jakobson, Roman, and Shigeo Kawamoto, eds. 1970. *Studies in General and Oriental Linguistics.* Tokyo: TEC.

James, Deborah. 1972. Some aspects of the syntax and semantics of interjections. CLS 8:162–72.

———. 1973. Another look at, say, some grammatical constraints on, oh, interjections and hesitations. CLS 9:242–51.

Janda, Richard D. 1985. Echo questions are evidence for *what?* CLS 21:171–88.

Jaworska, Ewa. 1986. Prepositional phrases as subjects and objects. *JL* 22: 355–74.

Jespersen, Otto. 1885. Kortfattet engelsk grammatik for tale- og skriftsproget. Copenhagen: Carl Larsen.

———. 1913. *Om sprogets logik.* Copenhagen.

———. 1924. *The Philosophy of Grammar.* London: Allen & Unwin.

———. 1927. *Modern English Grammar.* Vol. 3. London: Allen & Unwin.

———. 1937. *Analytic Syntax.* London: Allen & Unwin. Reprinted in 1984 by the Univ. of Chicago Press.

———. 1940. *Modern English Grammar.* Vol. 5. London: Allen & Unwin.

Kachru, Braj, et al. 1973. (eds.) *Issues in Linguistics: Papers in Honor of Henry and Renée Kahane.* Urbana and Chicago: Univ. of Illinois Press.

Kajita, Masaru. 1977. Towards a dynamic model of syntax. *Studies in English Linguistics* 5:44–66.

Karttunen, Lauri. 1969. Pronouns and variables. CLS 5:108–16.

Katz, Jerrold J., and Paul M. Postal. 1964. *A Unified Theory of Linguistic Descriptions.* Cambridge, MA: MIT Press.

Kaufman, Ellen. 1974. Navajo spatial enclitics: A case for unbounded rightward movement. *LI* 5:507–33.

Keenan, Edward L., and Bernard Comrie. 1977. Noun Phrase accessibility and universal grammar. *LI* 8:63–99.

———. 1979. Data on the noun phrase accessibility hierarchy. *Lg.* 55:333–51.

Keenan, Edward L., and Alan Timberlake. 1985. Predicate formation rules in universal grammar. *Proceedings of West Coast Conference on Formal Linguistics* 4.

Kimball, John. 1971. Super-equi-NP-deletion as dative deletion. CLS 7:142–8.

Kiparsky, Paul. 1965. Phonological change. Ph.D. thesis, MIT.

———. 1973. "Elsewhere" in phonology. In Anderson and Kiparsky 1973: 93–106.

Klavans, Judith. 1982. Some problems in a theory of clitics. Ph.D. thesis, Univ. of London. Distributed by IULC.

Klima, Edward S. 1964. Negation in English. In Fodor and Katz 1964:246–323.

Knowles, John. 1979. Lexemic iteration. *Linguistics* 17:641–57.

Koutsoudas, Andreas, Gerald Sanders, and Craig Noll. 1974. The application of phonological rules. *Lg.* 50:1–28.

Krashen, Stephen. 1980. The input hypothesis. *Georgetown University Roundtable* 1980.

Kroch, Anthony. 1981. On the role of resumptive pronouns in amnestying island constraint violations. CLS 17:125–35.

Kuhn, Thomas. 1970. *The Structure of Scientific Revolutions*. 2nd ed. Chicago: Univ. of Chicago Press.

Kuno, Susumu. 1971. The position of locatives in existential sentences. *LI* 2: 333–78.

———. 1972. Pronominalization, reflexivization, and direct discourse. *LI* 3: 161–95.

———. 1973. Constraints on internal clauses and sentential subjects. *LI* 4: 363–85.

———. 1975. Super Equi-NP deletion is a pseudo-transformation. NELS 5: 29–44.

———. 1981. The syntax of comparative clauses. CLS 17:136–55.

———. 1982. The focus of the question and the focus of the answer. In R. Schneider, K. Tuite, and R. Chametzky, eds., *Nondeclaratives*, 134–57. Chicago: CLS.

Kuroda, S.-Y. 1968. English relativization and certain related problems. *Lg.* 44:244–66. Also in Reibel and Schane 1969:264–87.

———. 1970. Some remarks on English manner adverbials. In Jakobson and Kawamoto 1970:378–96.

Labov, William. 1972. Negative attraction and negative concord in English grammar. *Lg.* 48:773–818.

Ladd, Robert. 1980. *The Structure of Intonational Meaning: Evidence from English*. Bloomington: Indiana Univ. Press.

———. 1983. Phonological features of intonational peaks. *Lg.* 59:721–59.

Lakoff, George. 1965. Irregularity in Syntax. Ph.D. thesis, Indiana Univ. Published in 1970 by Holt, Rinehart, & Winston.

————. 1968. Pronouns and reference. Distributed by IULC. Appears in Mc-Cawley 1976b:273–335.

————. 1971. On generative semantics. In Steinberg and Jakobovits 1971:232–96.

————. 1972. Linguistics and natural logic. In Davidson and Harman 1972: 545–665.

————. 1973. Thoughts on transderivational rules. In Kachru et al. 1973:442–52.

————. 1974. Syntactic amalgams. CLS 10:321–44.

————. 1984. Performative subordinate clauses. BLS 10:472–80.

————. 1986. Frame semantic control of the coordinate structure constraint. CLS 2:152–67.

————. 1987. *Women, Fire, and Dangerous Things*. Chicago: Univ. of Chicago Press.

Lakoff, George, and Henry Thompson. 1975a. Introducing cognitive grammar. BLS 1:295–313.

————. 1975b. Dative questions in cognitive grammar. In R. Grossman, L. J. San, and T. Vance, eds., *Functionalism*, 337–50. Chicago: CLS.

Lakoff, Robin. 1969. A syntactic argument for negative transportation. CLS 5:140–49. Reprinted in Napoli and Rando 1979:93–101.

————. 1971. Passive resistance. CLS 7:149–62.

————. 1973. Questionable answers and answerable questions. In Kachru et al. 1973:453–67.

Langacker, Ronald W. 1969. Pronominalization and the chain of command. In Reibel and Schane 1969:160–86.

————. 1974a. The question of Q. *FL* 11:1–37.

————. 1974b. Movement rules in functional perspective. *Lg.* 50:639–64.

Langendoen, D. T. 1970. The *can't seem to* construction. *LI* 1:25–35.

Larson, Richard K. 1985. On the syntax of disjunction scope. *NLLT* 3:217–64.

Lasnik, Howard. 1976. Remarks on coreference. *Linguistic Analysis* 2:1–22.

Lebeaux, David. 1983. A distributional difference between reciprocals and reflexives. *LI* 14:730–35.

Lees, Robert B. 1960. The grammar of English nominalizations. Supplement to *IJAL* 26.

Lees, Robert B., and Edward S. Klima. 1963. Rules for English pronominalization. *Lg.* 39:17–28. Also in Reibel and Schane 1969:145–59.

Levi, Judith N. 1973. Where do all those other adjectives come from? CLS 9: 332–45.

————. 1975. The syntax and semantics of nonpredicate adjectives. Ph.D. thesis, Univ. of Chicago.

————. 1978. *The syntax and semantics of complex nominals*. New York: Academic Press.

Levine, Robert. 1984. Against "reanalysis transformations." *Linguistic Analysis* 14:3–30.

Lightfoot, David. 1977. On traces and conditions on rules. Culicover, Wasow, and Akmajian 1977:297–337.

Lindholm, James. 1969. Negative-raising and sentence pronominalization. CLS 5:148–58.

Linebarger, Marcia. 1981. The grammar of negative polarity. Ph.D. thesis, MIT. Distributed by IULC.

Longacre, Robert. 1981. The paragraph as a grammatical unit. In T. Givon, ed., *Discourse and Syntax*, 115–34. Syntax and Semantics 12. New York: Academic Press.

Maling, Joan. 1976. Notes on quantifier postposing. *LI* 7:708–18.

Maling, Joan, and Annie Zaenen. 1978. The nonuniversality of a surface filter. *LI* 9:475–97.

———. 1982. A phrase structure account of Scandinavian extraction phenomena. In Jacobson and Pullum 1982:229–82.

Matthews, Peter. 1981. *Syntax*. Cambridge: Cambridge Univ. Press.

May, Robert. 1985. *Logical Form*. Cambridge, MA: MIT Press.

McCawley, James D. 1964. Qualitative and quantitative comparison. Paper read at annual meeting, Linguistic Society of America. Appears in McCawley 1973a: 1–14.

———. 1970. English as a VSO language. *Lg.* 46:286–99. Also in McCawley 1973a:211–28.

———. 1971. Tense and time reference in English. In Fillmore and Langendoen 1971:96–113. Reprinted in McCawley 1973a:257–72.

———. 1972. A program for logic. In Davidson and Harman 1972:498–544. Also in McCawley 1973a:285–319.

———. 1973a. *Grammar and Meaning*. Tokyo: Taishukan and New York: Academic Press.

———. 1973b. Syntactic and logical arguments for semantic structures. In Fujimura 1973:259–376.

———. 1973c. The role of notation in generative phonology. In M. Gross, M. Halle, and M.-P. Schutzenberger, eds., *The Formal Analysis of Natural Languages*, 51–62. The Hague: Mouton. Reprinted in McCawley 1979: 204–16.

———. 1974. On identifying the remains of deceased clauses. *Language Research* 9:73–85. Reprinted in McCawley 1979:84–95.

———. 1975. Verbs of bitching. In D. Hockney, W. Harper, and B. Freed, eds., *Contemporary Research in Philosophical Logic and Linguistic Semantics*, 313–32. Dordrecht: Reidel. Reprinted in McCawley 1979:135–50.

———. 1976a. Morphological indeterminacy in underlying structures. *Papers from the 1975 Mid-America Linguistics Conference*, 317–26. Reprinted in McCawley 1979:113–21.

———, ed. 1976b. *Notes from the Linguistic Underground*. Syntax and Semantics 7. New York: Academic Press.

———. 1977. Evolutionary parallels between Montague grammar and transformational grammar. NELS 7:219–32. Reprinted in McCawley 1979:122–32.

———. 1978. Review of A. Akmajian and F. Heny, *Introduction to the Principles of Transformational Grammar*. *Studies in Language* 2:385–95.

————. 1979. *Adverbs, Vowels, and Other Objects of Wonder.* Chicago: Univ. of Chicago Press.

————. 1981a. *Everything That Linguists Have Always Wanted to Know about Logic—But Were Ashamed to Ask.* Chicago: Univ. of Chicago Press.

————. 1981b. The syntax and semantics of English relative clauses. *Lingua* 53:99–149.

————. 1981c. An un-syntax. In E. Moravcsik and J. Wirth, eds., *Current Approaches to Syntax,* 167–93. Syntax and Semantics 13. New York: Academic Press.

————. 1981d. Notes on the English present perfect. *Australian Journal of Linguistics* 1:81–90.

————. 1982a. Parentheticals and discontinuous constituent structure. *LI* 13: 91–106.

————. 1982b. The nonexistence of syntactic categories. *Thirty Million Theories of Grammar,* 176–203. Chicago: Univ. of Chicago Press.

————. 1983. Towards plausibility in theories of language acquisition. *Communication and Cognition* 16:169–83.

————. 1984. Exploitation of the cyclic principle as a research strategy in syntax. In W. de Geest and Y. Putseys, eds., *Sentential Complementation,* 165–83. Dordrecht: Foris.

————. 1985. Kuhnian paradigms as systems of markedness principles. In A. Makkai and A. Melby, eds., *Linguistics and Philosophy: Essays in Honor of Rulon S. Wells,* 23–43. Amsterdam: Benjamins.

————. 1986. Actions and events despite Bertrand Russell. In E. LePore and B. McLaughlin, eds., *Actions and Events,* 177–92. Oxford: Blackwell.

McCawley, Noriko Akatsuka. 1973. Boy, is syntax easy. CLS 9:369–77.

McConnell-Ginet, Sally. 1982. Adverbs and logical form. *Lg.* 58:144–84.

Milsark, Gary. 1972. Re: double *-ing. LI* 3:542–49.

————. 1974. Existential sentences in English. Ph.D. thesis, MIT. Distributed by IULC.

Morgan, J. L. 1972. Verb agreement as a rule of English. CLS 8:278–86.

————. 1973. Sentence fragments and the notion "sentence." In Kachru et al. 1973:719–51.

Napoli, Donna Jo, and Emily Rando. 1979. *Syntactic Argumentation.* Washington: Georgetown Univ. Press.

Narita, Hajime. 1986. The nature of the double genitive. *Descriptive and Applied Linguistics,* 19:193–206. Tokyo: International Christian Univ.

Newmeyer, Frederick J. 1971. The source of derived nominals in English. *Lg.* 47:786–96.

Oehrle, Richard. 1983. An adequate rule for English tag questions. Paper read at annual meeting, Linguistic Society of America.

Ogle, Richard. 1981. Redefining the scope of root transformations. *Linguistics* 19:119–46.

Partee, Barbara Hall. 1970. Negation, conjunction, and quantifiers: Syntax vs. semantics. *FL* 6:153–65.

————. 1971. On the requirement that transformations preserve meaning. In Fillmore and Langendoen 1971:1–21. Reprinted in Napoli and Rando 1979: 265–88.

————. 1974. Opacity and scope. In M. Munitz and P. Unger eds., *Semantics and Philosophy*, 81–101. New York: NYU Press.

Pentheroudakis, Joseph. 1977. Reference and indefinite descriptions in modern Greek. Ph.D. thesis, Univ. of Chicago.

Percival, W. Keith. 1976. On the historical sources of immediate constituent structure. In McCawley 1976b:229–42.

Perlmutter, David M. 1970. Surface structure constraints in syntax. *LI* 1:187–256.

————. 1983. *Studies in Relational Grammar*. Vol. 1. Chicago: Univ. of Chicago Press.

Perlmutter, David M., and Scott Soames. 1979. *Syntactic Argumentation and the Structure of English*. Berkeley and Los Angeles: Univ. of California Press.

Pesetsky, David. 1987. *Wh*-in-situ: movement and unselective binding. In Reuland and ter Meulen 1987:98–129.

Pinkham, Jessie. 1982. The formation of comparative clauses in French and English. Ph.D. thesis, Harvard Univ. Distributed by IULC.

Postal, Paul M. 1969. Anaphoric islands. CLS 5:205–39.

————. 1971. *Crossover Phenomena*. New York: Holt, Rinehart & Winston.

————. 1972. The derivation of English pseudo-adjectives. Unpublished.

————. 1974. *On Raising*. Cambridge, MA: MIT Press.

Prince, Ellen. 1981. Toward a taxonomy of given-new information. In P. Cole, ed., *Radical Pragmatics*, 223–55. New York: Academic Press.

Pullum, Geoffrey. 1974. Restating double -*ing*. *Glossa* 8:109–20.

————. 1979. Rule interaction and the organization of a grammar. Ph.D. thesis, University of London. Abridged version published in 1979 (New York: Garland).

Quang Phuc Dong. 1971. The applicability of transformations to idioms. CLS 7:198–205.

Quine, Willard van Orman. 1960. *Word and Object*. Cambridge, MA: MIT Press.

Quirk, Randolph, et al. 1972. *A Grammar of Contemporary English*. London: Longmans.

Reibel, David, and Sanford Schane. 1969. *Modern Studies in English*. Englewood Cliffs, NJ: Prentice-Hall.

Reichenbach, Hans. 1947. *Symbolic Logic*. New York: Macmillan.

Reinhart, Tanya. 1975. On certain ambiguities and uncertain scope. CLS 11: 451–66.

————. 1976. The syntactic domain of anaphora. Ph.D. thesis, MIT.

————. 1983. *Anaphora and Semantic Interpretation*. London: Croom Helm and Chicago: Univ. of Chicago Press.

Richardson, John F. 1986. Super-equi and anaphoric control. CLS 22:248–61.

Reuland, Eric, and Alice ter Meulen, eds. 1987. *The Representation of (In)definiteness*. Cambridge, MA: M.I.T. Press.

Rice, Sally. 1987. Towards a transitive prototype: evidence from some atypical English passives. BLS 13:422–34.

Rosch, Eleanor. 1978. Principles of categorization. In Rosch and Lloyd 1978: 28–48.

Rosch, Eleanor, and Barbara Lloyd, eds. 1978. *Cognition and Categorization.* Hillsdale, NJ: Erlbaum.

Rosenbaum, Peter. 1967. *The Grammar of English Predicate Complement Constructions.* Cambridge, MA: MIT Press.

Ross, John Robert. 1967a. Constraints on variables in syntax. Ph.D. thesis, MIT. Published in 1986 as *Infinite Syntax!* (Hillsdale, NJ: Erlbaum).

———. 1967b. On the cyclic nature of English pronominalization. In *To Honor Roman Jakobson,* 1669–82. Mouton: The Hague. Also in Reibel and Schane 1969: 187–200.

———. 1969. A proposed rule of tree pruning. In Reibel and Schane 1969: 286–99.

———. 1970. On declarative sentences. In Jacobs and Rosenbaum 1970: 222–72. Also in Napoli and Rando 1979: 30–82.

———. 1972a. The category squish: Endstation Hauptwort. CLS 8: 316–28.

———. 1972b. Double -*ing*. *LI* 3: 61–86.

———. 1973. Nouniness. In Fujimura 1973: 137–257.

———. 1976. To have have and not to have have. In M. Jazayery, E. Polomé, and W. Winter, eds. *Linguistic and Literary Studies in Honor of A. A. Hill,* 263–70. Lisse: de Ridder.

Ross, John Robert, and William Cooper. 1979. Like syntax. In W. Cooper and E. Walker, eds., *Sentence Processing,* 343–418. Norwood, NJ: Ablex.

Ross, John Robert, and David M. Perlmutter. 1970. Relative clauses with split antecedents. *LI* 1: 360.

Rudin, Catherine. 1981. "Who what to whom said?": An argument from Bulgarian against cyclic WH-movement. CLS 17: 353–60.

Russell, Bertrand. 1905. On denoting. *Mind* n.s. 14: 479–93.

Ruwet, Nicolas. 1979. On a verbless predicate construction in French. *Papers in Japanese Linguistics* 6: 255–85. French version in N. Ruwet, *Grammaire des insultes et autres études,* 147–71 (Paris: Éditions du Seuil, 1982).

Sadock, Jerrold J. 1971. Queclaratives. CLS 7: 223–31.

———. 1977. Modus brevis: The truncated argument. CLS 13: 545–54.

Sag, Ivan. 1976. Deletion and logical form. Ph.D. thesis, MIT.

———. 1983. On parasitic gaps. *L & P* 6: 35–45.

Sag, Ivan, and Jorge Hankamer. 1984. Toward a theory of anaphoric processing. *L & P* 7: 325–45.

Sampson, Geoffrey. 1980. *Making Sense.* Oxford: Oxford Univ. Press.

Schachter, Paul. 1983. Explaining auxiliary order. Heny and Richards 1983, 2: 145–204.

Schmerling, Susan. 1979. Synonymy judgements as syntactic evidence. In Cole 1979: 299–313.

———. 1982. How imperatives are special, and how they aren't. *Nondeclaratives,* 202–18. Chicago: CLS.

Selkirk, Elizabeth. 1977. Some remarks on noun phrase structure. In Culicover, Wasow, and Akmajian 1977:285–316.

Seuren, Pieter A. M. 1974a. *Semantic Syntax.* Oxford: Clarendon Press.

———. 1974b. Negative's travels. In Seuren 1974a:183–208.

Sjoblom, Todd. 1980. Coordination. Ph.D. thesis, MIT.

Sobin, Nicholas. 1981. On ADV/PP-first reductions. *LI* 12:488–91.

Steele, Susan, et al. 1981. *An Encyclopedia of AUX.* Cambridge, MA: M.I.T. Press.

Steinberg, Danny D., and Leon A. Jakobovits, eds. 1971. *Semantics.* Cambridge: Cambridge Univ. Press.

Stockwell, Robert P., Paul Schachter, and Barbara H. Partee. 1973. *The Major Syntactic Structures of English.* New York: Holt, Rinehart & Winston.

Tasmowski-de Ryck, Liliane, and Paul Verluyten. 1984. Linguistic control of pronouns. *Journal of Semantics* 2:323–46.

Terazu, Noriko. 1981. A note on correlative conjunctions. *Studies in English Linguistics* 9:102–19.

Thomason, Richmond, and Robert C. Stalnaker. 1973. A semantic theory of adverbs. *LI* 4:195–220.

Thompson, Sandra A. 1972. *Instead of* and *rather than* clauses in English. *JL* 8:237–49.

———. 1973. On subjectless gerunds. *FL* 9:374–83.

Timberlake, Alan. 1982. The impersonal passive in Lithuanian. BLS 8:508–24.

Tomlin, Russell, and Richard Rhodes. 1979. An introduction to information distribution in Ojibwa. CLS 15:307–20.

Todrys, Karol. 1979. On pruning: towards a disunified account. CLS 15:291–306.

Torrego, Esther. 1984. On inversion in Spanish and some of its effects. *LI* 15:103–29.

Trudgill, Peter, and Jean Hannah. 1985. *International English.* 2d ed. London: Edward Arnold.

Van der Auwera, Johan. 1985. Relative *that*—a centennial dispute. *JL* 21:149–79.

Vendler, Zeno. 1957. Verbs and times. *Philosophical Review* 66:143–60. Reprinted in Vendler, *Linguistics in Philosophy* (Ithaca: Cornell Univ. Press, 1967), 97–121.

Vergnaud, Jean-Roger. 1974. French relative clauses. Ph.D. thesis, MIT.

Wachowicz, Krystina. 1974. Against the universality of a single WH-question movement. *FL* 11:155–66.

Warshawsky, Florence. 1965. Reflexivization. McCawley 1976b:63–83.

Wasow, Thomas. 1979. *Anaphora in Generative Grammar.* Ghent: Story-Scientia.

Weisler, Steven. 1980. The syntax of *that*-less relatives. *LI* 11:624–31.

Wexler, Kenneth, and Peter Culicover. 1980. *Formal Principles of Language Acquisition.* Cambridge, MA: MIT Press.

Wierzbicka, Anna. 1972. "And" and plurality (Against "conjunction reduction"). *Semantic Primitives,* 166–90. Frankfurt: Athenaion.

Williams, Edwin. 1974. Rule ordering in syntax. Ph.D. thesis, MIT. Distributed by IULC.

————. 1978. Across-the-board rule application. *LI* 9:31–43.

Woisetschlaeger, Erich. 1983. On the question of definiteness in "An old man's book." *LI* 14:137–54.

Zaenen, Annie, and Jessie Pinkham. 1976. The discovery of another island. *LI* 7: 652–64.

Zwicky, Arnold M. 1985. Clitics and particles. *Lg* 61:283–305.

Zwicky, Arnold M., and Geoffrey K. Pullum. 1983. Cliticization vs. inflection: English *n't*. *Lg*. 59:502–13.

Zwicky, Arnold M., and Ann D. Zwicky. 1973. *How come* and *what for*. In Kachru et al. 1973:923–33.

|||||| *Index*

Note: The abbreviation SWA stands for Selected Wrong Answers to Exercises.